INTERNET AD PIONEERS

The Stories Of The Unsung People Behind
The Birth And Growth of The Internet Ad Industry

CORY R TREFFILETTI

ACKNOWLEDGEMENTS

This book has been over a year in the making. It took longer than i originally thought, and it could have taken significantly longer if i included all the amazing people that have driven this business to where it is today.

I need to thank first and foremost, my loving wife Gretchen. Without her support, her help and her love I could not have found the time or the motivation to drive this project to completion. I'd also like to thank my boys Mason and Dylan for always smiling when i need it. From a business perspective I need to thank John Durham and Rich LeFurgy, who originally mentioned the idea for a book like this and who planted the seed that people may want to hear and read these stories.

I also need to acknowledge and thank those of you who took the time with me to conduct an interview and be a part of this book, as well as all of those that I was unable to get to this time around. Without your ambition, your commitment and your passion, this business would not be where it is today. Finally, thank you for taking the time to read this book and engage with the stories of the people behind the most amazing business in the world.

TABLE OF CONTENTS

The Internet advertising business was created in 1994, as nothing more than a way to use a new and interesting medium to reach a very small sub-segment of the techie audience (many of whom were reading Wired Magazine at the time). It has since eclipsed all forms of advertising with the exception of television, and television is squarely in the crosshairs, with more than $40 billion projected in online advertising by 2014.

Have you ever wondered how things got started? How the companies today, like Yahoo, Google, Facebook and Amazon, began? What decisions were made regarding the monetization of their emerging platforms, and how did those decisions lead to the business we all work in today? What happened to those early companies that led the charge; brands such as CompuServe, Prodigy, Excite, WebCrawler, HotBot, InfoSeek and AltaVista? Each day tens and even hundreds of thousands are employed in making the Internet advertising business work, yet the vast majority of people don't know its history or the legacy of those early brands!

Most people see technology as the core of the Internet advertising business, though in truth it has always been about the people. From the beginning there was a core group of people with a passion. Ambitious people who saw a future where previously there was none. They had vision, foresight and a desire to help craft something that had never been done before. They understood the Internet was going to be a transformational medium unlike anything anyone had ever seen and they all wanted to be there and be involved. They were advertising agency people, publishers, marketers and technologists all working together to lay the groundwork for a large-scale publishing medium that would be supported by advertising revenue, providing no-cost content to millions upon millions of people across the globe.

They envisioned the potential for a social revolution led by technology, and never bought into the notion that the Internet could injure interpersonal relationships. Instead they foresaw the web as a tool to support and grow exponentially the number of interpersonal relationships that any one person could have. They developed the technology that would make this happen and then developed more technology that would make it interesting and intriguing. They brought creative vision to the field, under the best practices and highest industry standards. They did what had to be done so that today you would have the experience you see. Without them you wouldn't work where you work, spend time the way that you do, and you certainly wouldn't be reading this book.

Back in 1994, the whole business was created and managed by a small group of 100 to 150 people. It would quickly expand, but at the time it was all that was necessary. Ads were dropped into websites and the "rotation" depended on when the site owner felt like changing them out. There were no real ad-servers and very little actual measurement going on. From the mouths of those who ran the very first online ads, "For fifteen thousand dollars you got a month. And we don't think anyone came to the site, but we were there if they did."

"Targeting" meant you knew what time of day or day of week the ads would be on the site for the potentially hundreds (yes, hundreds) of people that would come. The audience was small because the penetration of the Internet was small, but that didn't stop anyone in the business from working sixty and seventy hour weeks to ensure it ran smoothly. Wired led the way with its HotWired brand, but not long after we saw companies like Time Warner launch Pathfinder. CompuServe and Prodigy came alive and amassed an audience, and then there was this little company called America Online that was launching and creating interest with chat rooms, email and those ubiquitous AOL CDs. The CDs were virtually everywhere; in your mailbox, on your coffee table as coasters, being erased and burned to create "mix tapes." It was the first brand built in the digital age and for better or worse, in some people's eyes, is still a marquee brand online.

Networks like DoubleClick and AdVenture popped up, and Starwave came along with such sites as the nascent ESPN. Netscape was becoming a name that everyone recognized as they took the first real web browser, Mosaic, and made it friendlier and more accessible. Softbank represented small and medium sized sites and you could buy ads across their platform, with reports that showed impressions and clicks each week. Then Search 1.0 with companies such as InfoSeek, WebCrawler, Excite and Yahoo (initially a directory with search capabilities). There were Yellow Page sites and search sites like BigBook and HotBot (also from Wired). All of these companies took the frameworks of print media and expanded upon them to set a precedent for what would come later.

Friendster launched the social networking craze, but failed to deliver on its promise at the time. Google saw what came before in the area of search and discovery and revolutionized the way we discovered information. Pointcast came and crashed your computer. Firefly flew in then out in what felt like a week. Flycast brought the self-serve network to your fingertips far before anyone ever uttered the term "DSP." Ad banners like the 468x60 static gif gave way to rich media and the 728x90, 300x250 and 160x600 that we see in wide adoption today. Whatever advertisers do tomorrow will be with a debt of gratitude to what was done back then and to what is being done today!

When I graduated from college in 1995, the world of advertising had few prospects. I had an advertising professor at Syracuse tell me I would never make more than $65,000 a year in advertising, and that was what I had to look forward to. That still sounded like a lot of money! My prospects were slim, but my passion was hot and I knew what I wanted to do.

I lucked out. When I got my first job in advertising after five months of "summer," they asked on the very first day, "Have you ever been online?" I said, "Yes, of course." That was how we wasted time in college. We went to computer clusters or into AOL chat rooms! Since I'd been online, suddenly I was planning online media campaigns, which no one had ever done before. It was 1995 and the first online ads had started running, but no one knew what to do with them. My first two campaigns were for Discovery CD-ROM and BMW, with the launch of the 318ti (a car targeted to a younger, affluent audience). I remember the campaign clearly; we spent $25,000 on five partners, one of which actually ran us on an adult website (that didn't go over well). I had to write a POV for our client on the definition of a browser versus a search engine. At the time Netscape was a confusing concoction of both. It was a crazy world, and it was just getting started!

After a year I left to follow my boss and mentor, Peter Meluso, to join a young agency called i-traffic. It was as much an experiment as it was an agency. It was a collection of motivated people and idealists who yearned to do something different; some with fifteen years experience, but most had just one or two. At i-traffic we worked on brands like CDNow and Hearst Publications, and one of our biggest clients at the time was Disney. I was twenty-three years old, and I took immense pride in the idea that one of the biggest brands in the world (Disney) was asking me and my team to drive the strategy for their entrance and growth in the fastest growing medium of all time, the Internet. We did everything from their travel and vacation campaigns to launching the Daily Blast, their first online subscription site for kids. We were successful for a number of years, and the business grew around us. When we sold i-traffic to Agency.com we were about 160 people and driving millions of dollars in billings where there had been none just four years prior.

I took a stab at the client side in Silicon Valley for a little while with a music site called The Internet Underground Music Archive (IUMA). IUMA had been around for a few years, and was previously bought by eMusic. The team there was stellar, and the property ahead of its time, laying the framework for what would eventually become MySpace Music before MySpace went south. The site was a home for thousands of unsigned bands, and in just seven months we more than doubled the size of the site, culminating in the national Battle of the Bands finals at the legendary Fillmore in San Francisco. As I stood on stage at the height of the bubble, introducing Primus to a packed house, it was the closest I ever came to having a rock star moment, and it was awesome!

When the bubble burst, I went back to what I knew – the agency world. I joined a small San Francisco agency called Freestyle Interactive to build a media practice in what had previously been a successful creative shop. The experience at Freestyle, which eventually was sold to Carat Interactive in the U.S., was amazing. The team we assembled at Freestyle and the rate of success we had there will likely never be equaled during the remainder of my career nor by another agency again. From senior management down to the most recent hires, we created a team that knew how to win. We worked with some of the best brands in the world and made measurable business growth for our clients while also having a lot of fun! The chemistry in that team was unmatched anywhere else in the business. When we rolled up into Carat, we added more parts, and more of the team to help us continue to grow, and in that time Carat became one of, if not the leading, digital agency in the U.S..

My next stop was where I partnered with a long time friend, colleague and mentor in John Durham and we launched Catalyst S+F to provide marketing acceleration for startups and brands in the digital marketplace. This company allowed us to be at the crossroads of innovation and execution. We saw the trends and the relationships that made the business work, and we applied that to our clients' businesses. Not many people get to work with friends and make it work, and I have been very lucky to do so throughout my career. My next stop is going to benefit significantly from that experience as I continue to build my career. That next stop is and was, a great company called BlueKai; the leading data activation system for intelligent marketing.

Through the years, through the agencies, conferences and networking I've met some of the brightest, most interesting people that anyone can ever meet. I know people who made millions in their twenties, and some who made it again in their thirties. I know men who gave it all up to risk their lives for their country and who wouldn't change a single decision they ever made. I know people who gave it all up to go run a coffee shop or become a gardener and none of them miss it, nor would they have done things differently. I remember the ups and the downs, and everything in between. I recall the euphoria that was the bubble as it grew, and the sense of loss and devastation that came when it burst, followed by September 11th. All of these experiences create character, and if I can say one thing about this business it sure as hell builds a lot of character.

The following are examples of the kinds of characters that are central to the story of this business. I couldn't interview everyone, but was able to take a sampling of some of the best I could get in front of. These are people from all walks of the business, who have left their mark on the business as it grew. These people bought and sold the first online ad, created the impression and defined it for future use. They developed the terms and conditions, and developed the IAB, an organization that continues to shape the business in every facet today. You'll hear in their own words how it happened, what worked and what didn't, and get a better overall understanding of the path that was laid, as well as a sense of the trajectory that lies before us as the business continues its exponential growth.

CHAPTER I

RICK BOYCE

Rick Boyce is currently VP of advertising sales for Monster MediaWorks, a division of Monster Worldwide, and lives in the Bay Area, operating out of San Francisco. Rick defines the term "industry veteran," having been involved in the first online ad deals back with *HotWired* in 1994. Rick has led a very successful career, taking him in, out and around the online media business. During his career he has held the positions of SVP, Business Development at Rooftop Media, president of IGN Entertainment Inc., VP of advertising sales for Lycos, and as the founding SVP of sales for *HotWired* (later renamed *Wired Digital*). Prior to his role on the sales side of the business, Rick spent ten years in the agency business and was VP, Associate Media Director at Hal Riney & Partners San Francisco before joining the digital revolution.

Rick Boyce, you were around from the very beginning, involved in the very first online ad transaction to take place. Can you think back and remember what it was like, who it was with, etc.?

The very first insertion order for a campaign to run on *HotWired* was signed on April 15, 1994 by AT&T Consumer Products Division. Jane Metcalfe, who was one of the founders of *Wired Magazine,* closed that first digital ad deal with Dana Lyon, the magazine's advertising director. The founders of *Wired,* Louis Rossetto and Jane Metcalfe, had this idea for an online magazine, for lack of a better word, called *HotWired.* Jane had been in the market selling the business plan for *Wired Magazine* for years and was very comfortable asking for money and being in the sales role. When I joined *HotWired* in early September 1994, Jane, Dana, Andrew Anker (founding CEO of *HotWired*) and the magazine sales team, including industry legends like Doug Weaver, Bill Peck and Mitchell Kreuch, had already sold four campaigns.

One of the big buyers, in addition to AT&T, was a gentleman named Steven Comfort. Steven was a media planner at Messner Vetere Berger McNamee Schmetterer, which is now Euro RSCG. He was a visionary and ended up bringing four campaigns onto *HotWired*, two for MCI. The Telecom category was big at the launch of *HotWired,* due in part to the role they had played, and would continue to play, in creating the backbone of the Internet. In addition to those two, Steven placed a Club Med campaign and also one for Volvo. So Steven was there early on the buy side. Within the year we hired him and he became an account executive. That's the beginning of the story.

At the same time I came aboard in the fall of 1994, many people joined the magazine sales force who you know: Mitchell Kreuch, currently a Senior VP with About.com in New York, Doug Weaver from the Upstream Group and Bill Peck who became the founding ad director at InfoSeek. Those guys were *Wired Magazine* sales people who also had the responsibility of selling the website. What worked well for us was our ability to leverage the magazine sales team to secure meetings, generate interest and close business for *HotWired*. It was that team, me and those three people, along with a few other AEs that took this site to fourteen advertisers when it launched October 27th, 1994. So basically we went from Labor Day to October 27th storming the country. We sold ten more sponsors. We basically sold everything we had so we could go live by October 27th with fourteen blue chip sponsors.

Do you remember how much revenue *HotWired* generated selling out back at that time?

We were selling twelve-week sponsorships, which were a series of static banners on the top of a content page. Those banners, to the best of my recollection, were 476x76 pixels. It wasn't until a couple years later when we standardized them to 468x60 to conform with the, at that time, new IAB standards. As for our revenue, we booked fourteen sponsorships at $30,000 each for twelve weeks. Somewhere in the neighborhood of $400,000 was booked at that time. I would guess the total industry revenue for the year of 1994 was less than $1 million. So if you want to talk about the very beginning, that was where it all began. I think that GNN, Global Network

3

Navigator, was also out there selling a few things. There were a few other sites that were selling but we had 40 percent to 50 percent of the market share for certain, in terms of total revenue. When you think about 2011 as we approach a $30 billion dollar U.S. industry, it's pretty amazing to think that it wasn't that long ago it was a couple hundred thousand, certainly less than a million dollars.

It's worth pointing out that it wasn't until the spring of 1995 that Excite, InfoSeek and Lycos started selling advertising, and not till the fall of 1995, I think November that Yahoo started doing so as well. We were a year ahead of Yahoo and seven to eight months in front of the other search engines. Many of those companies, at least Excite, had an original business model to power website search and be technology providers for websites like *HotWired.* Of course, what the search companies soon discovered was the power of search as an ad medium, and the search engines would go on to become the biggest ad platforms on the Internet.

Do you remember what the challenges were trying to get this thing, the Internet, sold through internally to advertisers and agencies? How difficult was that?

Well Jane and Louis, the founders of *Wired*, were visionaries and believed the Internet was going to connect everybody, and sure enough it has. Their vision was that the magazine would be the beginning of a digital media company that would follow. *HotWired* would be the beginning. A couple years later we followed up with products like HotBot, which for a while was recognized as the best search engine in the world. Then *Wired News* and a number of other products were launched to complete our offering.

On the flip side, you were talking to Steven Comfort and he was bringing the advertisers in. Do you remember how difficult it was for him to get these advertisers bought off on this idea?

I know that for us it was important to be selling to visionaries like Steven. Another guy who bought two sponsorships from us was GM O'Connell of Modem Media. Thom Campbell of J. Walter Thompson, here in San Francisco, bought a campaign for Sprint. Everybody who was buying at the time – you would recognize their names because they were people like yourself who got it early – they were visionaries, and really interested in helping their clients explore this new medium. It wasn't hard for us to generate interest on the buy-side, at least with our contacts at the agencies. They had some challenges selling to their clients but it was the most visionary of clients that came through.

For example, one of GM O'Connell's clients was Zima from Coors Brewing. Their whole positioning was around the future, being a futuristic beverage and it fit for them. When you talk to some of those agency people it'd be interesting to see what kind of struggles they might've had internally to sell these things through. I know with GM, when he reserved two of his sponsorships for *HotWired* with me over the phone, I asked him, "What clients should I reserve these placements for?" He said, "I don't know yet, but I want two. I'll get back to you!"

He was pretty convinced that he was going to be able to close with somebody, and in their case it ended up being Zima and AT&T. They had a portion of the AT&T account at the time, so this campaign was in addition to the Consumer Products campaign that Jane Metcalfe had closed earlier.

The campaigns that *HotWired* ran at that point in 1994 and 1995, were they considered successes by the advertisers? What were the metrics they used to evaluate success back then (in the dark ages)?

Success was measured on a number of levels. PR was extremely positive and pretty extensive, and was a primary metric initially. For the agencies, from a PR perspective, both internally and with their clients and new business pitches it was a coup. What a great way to be positioned, as a thought leader and an agency that is really pushing the envelope. Regardless of what the campaigns did, how well they performed, I think there was a lot of success in terms of the publicity, the buzz and the cool factor.

As for audience reach and impact, the truth is very few people were on the Internet in 1994. Our estimate at the time was that about 30 million people globally, were connected to the Internet. Today, we're at around 2 billion. It was a really small potential audience back then. The page views were very limited. For example, one of our channels in a week might have 3,000 views. That would be one of the lighter viewed channels. A heavily viewed channel on *HotWired* might have seen between 18,000 to 20,000 page views. To be honest I was surprised at how small the audiences were. In our favor though, one of the things that was most impressive was the click rate!

The click rates back then, were they between 16 percent and 20 percent, maybe even as high as 25 percent?

At the beginning they were even higher than that. It depended on the campaign, but 50 percent plus was not out of the realm of possibility back then. We did see a decline over time, those numbers were unsustainable. Initially what was happening was that VCs, entrepreneurs, the search engine companies who had an audience but hadn't quite figured out the revenue model yet, were coming, looking and clicking. They were artificially raising the click rates, plus these ads and the medium as a whole were a novelty. Most of the clicks were from various folks exploring the business model, not necessarily consumers wanting to know more about whatever was in the ads. The ads were a pretty cool phenomenon, though. Interestingly they were static GIFs (Graphical Image Files). No animation was available at that time. No Flash, no Java, there were simply no other technologies available to make the ads more interesting. They just kind of sat there! They looked, by today's standard, to be very primitive.

They were pretty much little print ads transported over to this new, exciting, yet very small world that loaded slowly and took forever to get anywhere!

Yes! Little print ads, some of them seemed a tad bit cartoony. They were very simple, illustrated ads that could have been created by anyone. What's funny is that most advertisers went through a world of effort just to get us one little gif image.

The other interesting thing about this stage was that some of the advertisers didn't have any logical place for the ads to click to; brands like IBM, out of Ogilvy NY at the time, which was placed by Sharon Katz. This new breed of media person was emerging and no one had any idea where to put them. In the case of Ogilvy, they found a home for these people in their non-traditional media group, which was mostly outdoor advertising at that time. In the case of IBM, they had a web presence at the time but it was really designed for B2B and internal communications. They were a tech company and companies like IBM were active on the web before anyone else, but their web presence wasn't necessarily consumer facing. So to create a consumer web presence they built an entire microsite called Digital Alchemy, which supported the banner and the banner supported the microsite thematically. That was probably a twelve-page website.

Club Med, which came out of Messner, was a pretty big microsite, maybe 100 pages in total. It was interesting that the simple banner buy, which was simple for these agencies to buy, became incredibly complex when the question arose; where are these things going to click to? It was kind of a scramble as *HotWired*'s launch approached and the advertisers got their microsites up and running.

This phenomenon helped launch a lot of website developers like Organic, who shared our building in San Francisco. We were friends with the folks from Organic. Some of our employees worked for Organic at night and vice-versa. And so Jonathan Nelson, who founded Organic, participated in a lot of our *HotWired* sales calls where we'd present to the agency media buyers together. He'd talk about building a microsite, we'd talk about the audience, and that's how it all began for us.

So the web development agencies sprung out of that desire to have microsites and somewhere for the ads to click through to. Because the traditional agencies didn't have the expertise, and in many cases the desire to be involved in this part of the business yet, they ended up out-sourcing all of this work. Those folks, when push came to shove, were ok at buying the media placements on *HotWired,* but weren't necessarily capable of handling what comes after, right?

Yeah, that's how it was in the 1994/95 timeframe anyway. Organic created many of the sites for the Messner clients that ran on *HotWired.* I think they created microsites for Volvo, Club Med and two for MCI. Jonathan, Steven and I became good friends and still are today. A lot of friendships were born out of that stage of the business. It was a small community of people getting together and creating something from nothing, virtually! In the case of IBM, they had some internal technical resources and were capable of creating both the microsite and banners, but most other companies seemed more limited in this regard.

What do you view as the big tipping point, when things had gone from something just launching to something that was taking off?

I can tell you exactly when that was! Bill Peck left *Wired Magazine* to become founding director of advertising at InfoSeek and probably a couple months after, he gave me a call. He wanted to share a couple things they were working on at InfoSeek on the advertising side of the business. What he brought to my attention not only convinced me that the medium was really going to take off, driven by the search engines, but that we also had to change and adapt our business model just to keep up, and it's only 1995.

He came to the office and told me about what kind of page views and traffic that InfoSeek saw, which dwarfed what we were doing at the time. The first epiphany I had was, wow, search trumps content big time! It was beyond what I could've even guessed. That was an interesting but scary revelation to me. The second thing he told me was their plan for their ad model, which was to offer run-of-site banners for a $20 CPM and keyword targeted banners for a $50 CPM.

At the time our CPM was in the hundreds of dollars, so the InfoSeek pricing would start to erode our rate card which was a huge concern of mine. The great thing about the medium early on was that despite the fact our page views were limited and CPMs were high, no one was really evaluating it that way. On the buy side they certainly did the math. On our side, we also did the math. We knew where the CPM was but in 1994/95 it wasn't part of the negotiation or the dialogue yet. We were selling flat rate sponsorships and advertisers were buying them without requiring delivery guarantees. What Bill was saying was they're going to enter the market in May of 1995 with an established rate card and go with CPM pricing. That was going to be their pricing model.

So the rise of the CPM was his fault? We should all blame Bill.

They did a lot of things right, and Bill was a big part of that! The rise of the CPM and search led me to believe we had to do something different and quickly. The very next day I met with our CEO and said, if we don't have a search strategy we're dead. I knew that if we didn't have a search engine we were never going to be able to compete with these guys and would simply be a niche player. That immediately started the ball rolling with companies like DEC, who owned AltaVista at the time. AltaVista came out of Digital Equipment Corporation and in a matter of months we were in conversation with the team within DEC that had built AltaVista.

Interestingly, and as the legend goes, they built AltaVista initially as a way to showcase their servers and not necessarily to be the killer search engine, although they did become that for a while. Those conversations didn't go that far, mainly because DEC was not interested in selling their platform, nor do I think they quite understood the amazing opportunity they had created within DEC.

We then discovered a startup search company out of Berkeley called Inktomi. With Inktomi's search technology we launched our first search engine within Wired Digital called HotBot, which was also the first search engine powered by Inktomi. Inktomi was later bought by Yahoo. By the spring of 1996 we were in the search business, one year after InfoSeek launched. That laid the landscape with Yahoo, InfoSeek, Excite, Lycos and WebCrawler becoming the primary players in that new search landscape, and HotBot coming on strong with what was, at the time, a superior technology powered by Inktomi.

In 1995, I recall I had to write a white paper for BMW on the differences between a search engine and a browser. At that time there was similarity with Netscape in the

market selling their browser and their search engine at the same time. It was confusing to the companies we worked with because none of this had been done before! People didn't know what the difference was.

You should republish that white paper! It would be fun to see what the differences were, then versus now. I just remember it was that conversation with Bill Peck that helped me realize that search was going to get real big and get real big fast. Clearly Internet advertising was going to be driven by the search engines.

So from your perspective, search was the epiphany? That was when you knew that business was going to be bigger than you had ever envisioned? What did you think when Google emerged?

I knew they were going to be big. We all knew pretty early. They came along at a good time, the economy was terrible and the opportunities were wide open in late 1999, particularly into the 2000s. Google's timing was good because the other search engines became portals and I think in a way ended up killing themselves off through products that just weren't effective at providing what the growing audience needed. The portals like Yahoo, Excite and Lycos, they were useful for a time and provided access to lots of sites and places to see, but they were not world-class search engines. When Google came along you got exactly what you were looking for. Some of the best companies emerged during down economic times and this was certainly one of them.

Internet advertising around and after the 2000 crash was pretty dismal. The kicker was that it was still early. In 2000 there were about 300 million people globally on the Internet, now we're at 2 billion, that's a pretty meteoric rise. It's hard to believe that it was only ten years ago that the Internet audience was so much smaller. It was still a small, quickly developing market and it was still really early. Even though Excite and those other guys had been around for a while, we all knew there were far bigger things to come.

So we come to about the year 2000. The Internet bubble is big, business is running hot, parties are everywhere and secretaries are making millions on IPOs. Then, BOOM! The bubble bursts, what did you think was going to happen at that point?

It was a very discouraging time. The bubble bursting was followed by 9/11, which further depressed everyone emotionally and most certainly economically. Those couple years were very tough for everyone in digital media. One of the positive things that came out of that period was the IAB (Internet Advertising Bureau) regrouped to basically reinvent the online ad standards. We made some important decisions during that period. We had standardized the banner in 1996 on the 468x60 pixel format, but the ad community felt things needed to change to reinvigorate the business.

In the spring of 2001 the IAB developed and launched new standards including the 300x250 rectangle, the skyscraper sizes, which were 160x600, and also the larger banners or leaderboards, which were 728x90. These were standardized as the three primary units that most of the business was going to follow. Commanding more real estate for advertisers was a big breakthrough, and it was the challenging economic times that allowed that to happen.

So it's pretty clear that from 1994 through 2002 is where the infrastructure of the whole business was being built up and standardized, laying the groundwork for the continued growth post-2003 or -2004. You mentioned the IAB and their regrouping the business and standards for a newer generation of advertisers in 2001 and 2002. Looking back and realizing where things were headed, what would you have done differently? Would there have been any difference in the trajectory or growth of the business if there'd been more standardization up front? Do you think there was even an opportunity to do that, or that things could've been done differently?

The IAB did a really good job standardizing pretty early back in 1996. Most of the business was standardized around the Yahoo specs and that made sense, they were the dominant player at the time. So I don't know that the IAB could've done anything differently.

What about the industry as a whole? What about the agencies or the marketers, could we have made a more concerted effort to bring the brands in earlier?

I don't know how we could've done things differently, but one of the things that frustrates me today is it seems the medium has become one which is viewed primarily as a direct-response tool. There are high expectations on actionable metrics, whether click-through or other back-end metrics, etc.. I have always believed the right message in front of the right person, whether they elect to click on it or not, is a positive brand experience. I feel the value the medium brings to the table is high because of the intense engagement with content and marketing messages. This is not a passive medium, it's a lean-forward medium. All of those things provide support for why brands should want to be here. But we focused very early on the click-through rate as a metric and that stuck.

Whether there's a click, an interaction or just an exposed user, advertising on the Internet can be highly effective and cost efficient. Branding metrics are not acknowledged widely enough by brands and agencies. Every medium can be used for direct-response campaigns, TV certainly is. But that doesn't mean the Internet is not effective for other types of campaigns, especially those intended to build brand metrics such as awareness, consideration and purchase intent.

For companies that are direct-response oriented, the Internet has proven its worth from the beginning. But for brand advertisers, there is an overemphasis on clicks and measuring the effectiveness from clicks rather than just ensuring people are aware of your brand and that they are influencing their perceptions in a positive manner. Brand perceptions are being changed by the ads and marketing messages displayed online. The fact that the Internet is undervalued as a tool for driving brand metrics has been a failure of those of us in digital media. I think we've tried. At *HotWired* we did the first ever brand effectiveness study in 1996 with Millward Brown. Rex Briggs was our research director and he has continued to blaze a trail in that space. He stayed involved in this kind of research from the very beginning. In December of 1996 we presented our first ad effectiveness study, which showed the branding impact of exposure to those static, simplistic ads. I still have copies of those if you'd like one.

That'd be great! I'd love to show them in the book, people would love to see those!

That landmark study then led to the 1997 brand impact study by the IAB, which also demonstrated that Internet advertising could drive brand metrics. At that time, between Millward Brown and some of the other companies that were emerging in the space, there was a lot of research being run. That growth in research led to other companies like Dynamic Logic being born. There's certainly a lot of research out there to support the branding value of the medium, but for some reason I don't feel that has caught on as well as it should. In fact, I find it ironic that the agency holding companies which own these research companies (Omnicom owns Millward Brown, which in turn owns Dynamic Logic) are just as guilty as every other agency in terms of being more focused on the click than they should be. In my opinion, the overemphasis on click-through rate is still a problem.

That's the one thing I imagine I'll hear from a lot of people; that if early on we had taken emphasis off the click things could have been different. If we'd demonstrated more emphasis on the exposure and the effect of that exposure, it might have changed the dynamic. Maybe it would've helped brands to better understand how to use the medium, and the dollars might have flowed from those advertisers rather than the X10 Camera and "punch the monkey" ads. It would be different if the only way to measure a print campaign was if somebody tore it out and went to the store with it. That was the analogy we started with, unfortunately.

I agree, we need to take responsibility for that. The reports that we sent out, and still send out to clients, should have focused on more than click rates. The reports back then were simple. The page view was a proxy for the ad because the ads weren't rotated; they were hard-coded directly to the page. We had clicks and we showed a click rate. We sent these reports weekly and the reports focused on page views, clicks and click rates. Those were the only metrics we had and we were excited about it! Unfortunately, there's been no looking back.

From my perspective, we were in the midst of doing advertisements on CD-ROMs and along came websites. Many of us knew the Internet was going to be a big medium, but I don't think we realized how big it could be or how quickly it would get there. The CD-ROMs were a big portion of what we were doing at that time, yet where are they now? They didn't last long but we thought we had more time with the web and were just excited to have this new medium to play with!

I didn't anticipate broadband penetration to go as deep as fast as it did. The reason banners were small at the beginning was because bandwidth was constrained. We forget that now, but back in 1994 I'd say about half our audience was on networks, either on college campuses or in big companies. The rest was on 14.4 modems, 28.8 speeds were just coming on and wouldn't take over for another year or two. It's shocking to think about it now, but on a 14.4 modem a page with heavy graphics was painful. It would take one to two minutes to load some of these pages! The small ad format was required because of limited bandwidth, which is one of the things that slowed down the evolution to larger ad units. My vision for how big the medium could become was constrained as a result of how slow it was at that time. When you're on a modem it's hard to imagine that this Internet thing would grow really large, really fast. So in my opinion, it's broadband that really drove the massive growth of the web.

Understanding how deeply involved you've been since the very beginning, and the challenges we've gone through to get where we are, where do you think the business will go in the next five years? Do you foresee a challenge or a great opportunity?

The advertising models we're emphasizing at Monster MediaWorks are inline with our two key beliefs about the future of Internet advertising. One is that data is incredibly important. Using data to target, retarget, extend audience; those are the driving factors for our industry right now and we're exploring the unique role we might play in the targeting space. We're building a business around the ability to target really rich data segments that our advertisers are interested in. The other thing we're focused on is building richer experiences for our advertisers, the kind of branded content and sponsorship experiences where sponsors are logically and seamlessly integrated into the user experience.

So with traditional ad units, we think data will carry the day and IAB units will be targeted via data increasingly. On the other side, we see creating richer, more interesting and more intricate sponsorships for our brand partners; the kinds of things that cannot be replicated through data, ad networks, or other venues, but could only be created through a partnership with a first party publisher like ourselves. Those two things are where we are placing our chips, if you will. Sometimes advertisers want to create those deep, interesting, never-been-done-before experiences. We can do that. Other times it's all about targeting IAB units to deliver maximum efficiency and minimum waste.

CLOSING REMARKS

Rick was one of the first to identify the advertising opportunity in this business, and without his involvement things could have taken a long time and gone in a very different direction. If you've ever sold an ad banner or online sponsorship you owe a little debt to Rick. In addition, he has continued to be one of the most animated and genuinely nice people in the business. Thanks, Rick, for being part of our story and for getting in there right at the beginning to help forge the path!

CHAPTER 2

RICK PARKHILL

As of 2012 Rick Parkhill serves as chairman of video crowd-sourcing vehicle, Poptent, a social network dedicated to connecting top brand advertisers and advertising agencies with over 20,000 independent video creators across the U.S. and eighty other countries. The platform provides brands with high quality, cost effective solutions for the development of targeted video assets to be used in both on and offline advertising campaigns.

Prior to Poptent, Rick served the industry as CEO and founder of iMedia Communications Inc., founded October, 2001, which was acquired by DMG World Media in 2005. Rick and his team were responsible for creating and hosting one of the industry's most recognizable, and highest regarded networking and educational events called the iMedia Summits. The Summits serve to gather together agencies, brands and publishers in an invitation-only environment that fosters strong connections alongside deep educational learning. The Summits have been responsible for a host of great moments, but most importantly the quality time that all sides of the business has. Whether poolside or in a conference environment iMedia was, and still is, responsible for the ongoing cross-fertilization of ideas in the Internet advertising business.

Prior to Rick launching the iMedia brand, he was CEO for *Digitrends,* one of the industry's first digital media publications and networking groups. Rick also served as EVP of Softbank Interactive Marketing and was involved in many aspects of publishing content geared towards the growing digital audience including *InfoText*.

Rick Parkhill, what motivated you to get into this business?

When you say this business, I'll define this business as interactive media and marketing. For me, it started in the late 1980s. I published a magazine at that time called *InfoText* that I launched in 1988 all about interactive media marketing; the first magazine for media marketing executives about interactive. Interactive at that time was touch-tone telephone and a little technology called Audiotext that enabled telephones to communicate with personal computers. To me, that was the beginning of the information revolution as we know it today. It was pre-Internet.

That's what empowered interactive media at the time. As rudimentary as it was, it was revolutionary at the time and completely enthralled me. The evolution of media was so exciting; what was going to happen in our lifetime, making the ability to access information that you need on the go, and all the things that are available to us today. In the 1980s, looking forward it was sort of a dreamland for us, and frankly I became addicted to it! I had no choice about what my career path was going to be, I loved media!

I loved reading about the history of media and understanding the evolution of newspapers in our society and the impact that media has on our society, going all the way back to the printing press. I loved just understanding how the printing of books changed the world, and I was seeing how interactive media was going to change the world dramatically over the coming years. To be a part of that, for me, was irresistible.

Has the Internet met your expectations?
Indeed, it has created wild realities that I'd never expected. What I dreamed of in 1988 with *InfoText* magazine, well, where we are today I never would've expected. I can't say looking back that what's happened today ever would've occurred without me taking that wild leap forward and jumping in both feet first to the whole Internet thing. There was no network at that time; it was a lot of independent, local telephone companies. And this was on the heels of the divested AT&T. The telephone companies ruled where you'd be able to access information, who could generate it and who could store it. It was a highly regulated, complicated industry until the Internet came along and completely freed all that up. And none of us saw it coming until around 1993 or 1994.

I was at a trade show called "VOICE." It was a big trade show about voicemail and interactive technologies for telephones in the late '80s. Nicholas Negroponte was the keynote speaker. He got up on stage in front of a bunch of voicemail vendors at that time and said, "Your business is going nowhere in the future, because a thing called email is coming along." And everyone looked at each other and asked themselves what was going on? Here was this very well respected MIT futurist and he is blasting what we do for a living. What's email? I think about what a visionary Negroponte was. Those are the kind of people we have to look at for what's next. They say the crazy things many don't want to hear, but what they say is steeped in intelligence and a well-thought out vision for the future.

So to answer your question, it's fulfilled my expectations and exceeded them dramatically.

When you were first exposed to the concept of email, do you remember how long it took from "email is coming" to email being the norm?

Oh, it probably took at least five to seven years until I had an email address after that. That was in the '80s. I had my AOL account. I established that in about '92 or '93. No one was exchanging documents in the early '90s through email or any other method except a fax machine.

Looking back, does that surprise you how quickly it happened? Five to seven years in the grand scheme of things is not a long time.

Yes, it's true. The rate it happened is what's so astounding. How quickly everybody had to have an email account. I think there were a number of factors that coalesced at the time, which created a perfect storm for the advent of digital, and specifically for email. PCs became more fun to use – the drag-and-drop technology that Apple created was a revolutionary step. My first computer was an Apple classic, a Mac classic with no hard drive. All of a sudden computing was fun. I'd sit up late at night playing with my Macintosh computer learning how to set type and having a ball. I figured out how to publish a newsletter, which was the precursor to *InfoText* magazine.

Prior to that, I was in the finance business providing third-party equipment lease financing for technology vendors. I backed my way into the information business and started writing a newsletter for my clients that I called "InfoText" and then invited advertising in to support the venture. My first advertisers were MCI, AT&T and Sprint. All of a sudden I was the voice of this new industry of interactive media. It was thrilling. Frankly, it's been a thrilling ride for the last twenty-five years now. Every turn has a new element of excitement to it, as though it's a rollercoaster ride. And hang onto the bar because it's going to toss you all over the place. All of a sudden that rollercoaster takes another dip and picks up speed then you're off on another wild ride. It's a pretty good analogy.

That's the way this industry has been, a lot of unexpected turns. Social media isn't something that a lot of visionaries were sitting around saying, you know what's going to happen here in the next five years, social media is going to become the rage and it's going to take over email. You didn't have visionaries that were out there saying that. No one saw it coming. It was the product of a few guys at a university – completely unexpected turns.

It was indeed a bit unexpected. You started out doing a newsletter then went into magazines covering the digital media industry. You got into doing *Digitrends* and then launched iMedia, which turned out to be an integral part of the business for years to come. You've created a very successful group of companies that have covered and editorialized and helped share information and knowledge about this business. Can you tell me how you made that transition from the printed side of the business, with the newsletter and print publications, into the event side of the business?

My training in business really was being a restaurant manager. I was a general manager of a big ski resort restaurant in Mammoth called Whiskey Creek. I did that for six years. I loved it because it was a great business to be a part of. My strengths were that I was a really good host. I loved bringing people together, seeing them have a good time, and meeting new people. What my businesses have been about is developing a community of like-minded people and giving them the opportunity to exchange ideas, meet with one another, do business together, make friendships because that's so much what business is about; the people that you meet along the way and the friendships that result from them. You either sell something to them or they sell something to you. You partner with them and you have these symbiotic relationships. My strengths have been creating a community of people like that and then creating an atmosphere that they were comfortable in.

So inadvertently you created the first social network.
I guess I did, all the way back to Camp Interactive, an event that I launched back in the '90s, which was

definitely a social network. It was a real world social network gathering for the industry.

So it's all your fault.

Yeah, I'll take blame for where it landed, too. I started off with a newsletter that I printed up on my Macintosh, went down to whatever the local printer was and ran off a bunch of copies and stuffed them in envelopes. I actually licked stamps and stuck them all in the envelopes. I was distributing about 1,200 newsletters twice a month, and that was about as simple as it got. I eventually moved into faxing newsletters because that was high tech at the time. We were collecting fax numbers from our audience, hoping that they didn't move offices anytime soon! Every week we were sending a fax newsletter out in addition to our monthly-print publication and trying to use as much of the technology as we could.

We had a dial-in program, where you could dial a 900 number at the time and pay fifty cents and listen to the daily news that we would post about interactive media. We used as much of the media as possible. Some of it was experimental and some was for good economic reason. It was easier to publish electronically than to press ink to paper and mail it, so it was a natural evolution. I still love the print medium and being able to hold a magazine and flip through pages. All the richness of that is such a great experience, but it's going away slowly. I wish it wasn't. The whole iPad technology, it supplants that print experience and exceeds that experience in a number of ways.

So the way my products evolved was just a natural evolution with technology. And it was natural that

Digitrends went away as a print publication and became a website and an email newsletter.

There was a beginning trajectory that was upwards. You saw what happened around the first bubble bursting in 2001 and then the most recent economic recession. How have the ups and downs changed the way you plan for your business?

A lot of what happened in the late '90s was just euphoric. People were becoming *gazillionaires* overnight. There were stars in everyone's eyes. People at the lowest levels at a startup company thought they were soon to become millionaires. It was completely unrealistic. Unfortunately no one stood up and said this was the case, and if they did then no one listened. Everyone thought it was going to go on forever and there would continue to be silly businesses being overfunded by VCs. It was just a false economy that when you're in the middle of it, the euphoria of that kind of gold rush mentality, nobody wants to think about a bubble.

We created one of the biggest business bubbles of all time and that burst around 2000/2001. With the bursting of that bubble, I think it taught all of us a huge lesson about the realities of economics and value propositions. It made us take a closer look at our businesses and think about whether or not they really have long-term vitality. Do they deliver a value to someone or is this a hype business? I think it's just been a natural maturation process. And those of us who lived through that bubble have a better perspective on how to plan for the future.

Do you think the folks who are setting up new companies today give enough credence to how those bubbles built up in the past? Do you think they take it into account when forecasting and building their current businesses?

I think some do, and a lot don't. I don't think you can really over generalize that assumption. I'm involved in an early-stage company today that just closed their A-series round. We've got money in the bank. We've got executives who have been through a couple of bubbles, and who've got some experience on their side. What happens with a lot of VCs and a lot of investors, they are looking to some brilliant, young kid that's got an algorithm that's going to turn into the next Google. And when you talk to the investment community, a lot of them say that; we're looking for the next Google. That's crazy. Look for good businesses.

Not every business is going to turn into a $100 billion business. If that's the way you're going to run your fund, tell your investors that upfront and hopefully they will run for the hills. There are only a handful of companies that ever gain that stature. People have to be more realistic about their business models, and put people on their board and at the executive level with a level of maturity that can do that. Our business suffered a lot by overenthusiastic investors and executives that created business plans that had no merit and no basis in reality. They just went off and spent a bunch of money and did a lot of marketing. They never questioned the value proposition that they were offering to the consumers or business. I think in today's business environment, we have a far more mature industry. We're seeing more adult attitude being applied to new businesses today.

Given that it is now a more mature business, do you believe it's possible to have another bubble like we had in the early '90s?

I don't think we'll ever see that kind of thing happen again. When you look back at the companies and the business plans that were funded in those days, there were some really, really stupid things that raised a ton of money. When you look at them today, it's like what were they thinking? There was just so much money being thrown out. There's a lot more cost and experience and acumen being applied to today's investments than in the '90s. In those days it was, let's throw a bunch of money out there and see what happens. Look at all the things that happened in that decade that were huge winners.

And there was tons of money. Money follows money, and the fact that there had not been a bubble to date, and there had not been a burst as of yet, is what fed the growth. Having had one previously and as big as it was, I don't think we'll ever see that happen again.

I certainly hope not. Let me personalize the discussion for a second. To look back at that period, can you recall maybe one of the bigger errors in judgment or bigger mistakes that you made? How did you change your approach?

Yeah, at *Digitrends* we were part of that whole euphoric bubble. We were in the print magazine business at the time covering the interactive media business. We were publishing *Digitrends*. We had another magazine called *e-Biz* that we launched to follow the e-commerce business, and we thought things were going nowhere but up. We were taking on more office space, more employees, more overhead, committing to printers, hotels and contracts and we got overextended. When our company started going out of business, and our advertisers and sponsors started falling out, we were overextended.

We tried to do too much too fast and ended up paying for it. I talked to John Battelle about this. The Industry Standard was a great example of how you could get caught up in the bubble. John was publishing a book that was 300-400 pages every week because his advertising demand was so high. To keep an editorial ratio that kept your readers meant he had to publish 150 editorial pages to compliment all the advertising he was taking on. If he looked back on it, he should've limited the amount of pages he was going to publish and put the pages up on eBay for auction. This would've kept his book a manageable size, his staff a manageable size, and made five times the amount of money. But he didn't do that. He was in the sort of legacy model of magazine publishing, and you take as many ad pages as people want to give you. So going too fast is dangerous. None of us reckoned that the future would ever slow down at the time, and that was naïve. I regret that and certainly learned a tough lesson from it.

And that's a lesson that you apply to your current business where you've raised the money with XLNT ads?

Absolutely, we've had some minor downturns. iMedia is a ten-year-old business today. If you look at our graph we grew very rapidly in the early days, but we didn't overextend. We didn't launch a lot of new products. We focused on our core business, built our core and then expanded slowly. Then a couple of years ago the slow down happened and we felt it. We just went flat as a result, but didn't drop. We were able to see it coming and understand that we're part of the global economy. Some of our clients are going to be hurting. We're going to have to do smart things, but we saw it coming in advance and took steps to deal with it. It was a small bump in the road, not a weightless dip on the rollercoaster.

I know that you're an avid surfer. What is your trick for balancing the ability to spend time with your family, go out and surf and run a successful business? How do you handle all that?

I'll answer that one with a personal story. You're a dad so you'll appreciate this. My son, Andrew is twenty-two. When he was born he went into cardiac arrest. He nearly died. His lungs filled with fluid. He spent a week in the ICU and I was in there every day standing over this kid and praying for him. I made a commitment to myself, to God and my family that if he lives I'd be a good dad, and I would balance my life. And you know what? He did live! Ever since that moment I've done what I can to fulfill on that promise and I'm glad that I have. I say no to a lot of things regarding travel and opportunities.

I could spend my life on the road in this industry. I've just learned to balance it. I love the business. I don't have to let it overcome my life. I love my family, I love my activities and seeking balance in your life is where you find happiness. I know a lot of people that spend more time in the business than I ever would. But I look at them and I don't think they're that happy. They're working their ass off. They're hardly ever home, their personal lives are kind of a mess. Their personal lives are kind of lived on Facebook. Their relationships suffer. They lack balance in their life. I'm not critical of them. But for me, I have to be at home, I have to be in the water and I have to be with my kids and my wife. And sure, I love the industry and I love working, but it's not what I love the most.

That's a great statement. And I'm glad you brought that up. I know a lot a people pay lip service to what you just said but I think that you are one who actually does a very good job of it.

Thanks, Cory.

When you retire, how do you want people to remember you professionally? I'm assuming you're not going to retire for another forty years, but when you do, how do you want the professional business around you to remember you?

I would like to be most remembered as caring about this business and the people who are active in it. From the very beginning I've loved this industry because it's afforded me so much opportunity, not just financial. The people who are closest to me in life, besides my family are people that I share this industry with. I've made great friends in the industry. If I stepped out and retired, they'll still be my great friends. This business is full of wonderful, creative, big-hearted people. And it's given me so much. I hope when I retire people will think about the events that we've done; that I've facilitated a lot of relationships and facilitated a lot of the growth that's happened in this business by bringing people together and caring about them.

That's a very true statement. A lot of the people that I've met in this business and the great relationships I have come directly as a result of having attended the events you put on. Many have come from direct introductions that you've made. So for that, thank you, I'm sure a lot a people are going to remember that.

Some of the most gratifying things for me are seeing people like Matt Wasserlauf this week. He was able to sell his company for a profit. And I feel if Matt looks at his experiences at iMedia and the people that he met and the way that we may have helped build BBE, I hope he looks back and says iMedia and Rick and Mike and the whole team, were instrumental in helping me get there. That's how I'd like to be remembered.

CLOSING REMARKS

Rick's interview was a special one because he touched on the balance of family and work. This is a difficult concept for many to grasp, and even more difficult to implement, but it's probably the most important concept of all. This business can consume you, trust me I know. I am sitting on a plane right now writing this summation and missing my wife and son (and son-to-be). Never forget, that as much fun as work actually is you have to take time for the other more important things in life. Thanks, Rick, for that reminder.

CHAPTER 3

STEVEN COMFORT

Steven Comfort is currently the VP of business development for Fwix, a service that indexes the web by location, as well as an accomplished home winemaker. Steven has also served as VP Sales for YuMe (an online video network), NexTag, Tickle Inc (now within Monster), and eGroups (now Yahoo! Groups). He has worked at and consulted a number of additional startups, all of which have thrived. His specialties have been running sales teams and identifying partnerships that bring new technologies to media companies and brand advertisers.

Steven holds a unique place in the history of the Internet advertising business, as one of the first media buyers to purchase an online ad banner. The ad banner in its early 468x60 version was validated by Steven and his agency's clients when *Wired Magazine* launched the first commercial website, *HotWired* in the fall of 1994.

His career began on the agency side at storied shops D'Arcy Masius Benton & Bowles (DMB&B) and Messner Vetere Berger McNamee Schmetterer/Euro RSCG. He made the shift to the digital sales side, as many agency media people did in those days, and has truly shaped many deals and brands using the digital medium. His story provides a unique point of view as to how the web garnered the attention of the early brands that jumped in.

Steven Comfort, let's start with a quick background of how the first digital ad buy actually went down.

The first web sales calls were done by Jane Metcalfe, the co-founder of *Wired Magazine* along with Louis Rossetto. She came to New York to meet with some of the media folks that she heard of through the *Wired Magazine* sales team, and this even pre-dates Rick Boyce (*HotWired*'s first sales leader) being hired. The *Wired* sales team was out there trying to sell *HotWired* to their magazine advertisers. They'd come across various agency people who had some knowledge of the web and an interest in the *HotWired* project, which was still on paper at the time.

She came to meet with the agencies for AT&T, MCI and a few other brands. At Messner we had other clients that were good prospects (Volvo and Club Med were also *HotWired* launch advertisers) but MCI was the one that was kind of a no-brainer since it was telco, and she really got my signature based on nothing more than looking at a QuickTime movie and a couple of slides on what *HotWired* was going to be when it launched. There were, effectively, section sponsorships originally being sold There were twelve sections on *HotWired* at launch, each with a small banner sponsorship right at the top. That was as far out as anyone had thought about what the advertisers' participation would be.

It was a three-month sponsorship. We had no ideas about audience size or who would be there. That was the first sales cycle. When *HotWired* launched with its twelve advertisers, it looked like they would just be sold-out forever because there was a right of first refusal for all of the advertisers that participated at the launch, and everyone was planning on staying. I think they realized pretty quickly that they were going to have to change that model if they were going to be able to scale it and bring in more than the first twelve advertisers.

Rick built the first *HotWired* team, which was separate from the *Wired Magazine* sales team, who weren't necessarily enamored with the web. Their priority was selling pages in the magazine.

When you say they weren't enamored with the web, what was there to be enamored with at that point?

There wasn't a lot to see. I remember one of my favorite sites, not because it was a content site but because it provided a utility was Yahoo. It was simply a one-page directory. It was a long scroll that started off with the word "Yahoo!" at the top (an acronym for Yet Another Hierarchical Officious Oracle) then a big letter "A." Then about four companies that begin with the letter "A," then the letter "B" and about four different companies, the web was comprised of almost all corporate and university websites at that time that began with "B." Then the page scrolled all the way to "Z." There were maybe 125 links on the page. That encompassed all the known sites that were worth visiting on the web at that time, and that was where I started my experience.

The whole consumer web was indexed on one page!
All on one page, it was great!

What was the site under "Z," do you remember?
I don't. I don't know if there was a "Z" to be honest. I don't think anyone had come up with a site worth indexing under that letter. There were a couple of letters that didn't have any sites linked to them. I met Tim Koogle, former president and CEO of Yahoo!, five years later in 2000 while Yahoo was acquiring the company I was working for (eGroups), and talked to him about those days. I said, you know, when I was looking at that Yahoo page in 1994, you were leaving a successful software company to take Yahoo's CEO job. Yahoo was a three-person startup that had just raised one million dollars. When I looked at the page I didn't see a business. You must have seen a business. You must have seen something different. What did you see? He said, well, I never knew that it would be a huge business or that it would turn into anything like what Yahoo turned into. But I knew that navigation was always going to be important to the web and that we were going to be one of the keys to navigating the web.

It was a visionary decision at the time.
It was. I think one of the fun things about that time, of being kind of a veteran of that time, is that there was no gold rush. No one got rich off of it. There were no

IPOs. There were no Internet millionaires. There were just people who were interested in the technology. The technology came first and then the important questions followed like, how will the web change my job? – be that an architect or a lawyer or whoever it is asking the question.

What was the process, or how did you go about trying to sell these ideas to the clients you worked with at the time? I have to bet that most brand managers and primary client contacts hadn't been online at that point.

Right, I was just a media planner. Not "just a media planner" like it's a negative thing, but I was a pretty junior person in the agency structure. Most of the people that had any practice with the technology were younger. So it wasn't surprising for comments around interactive media opportunities, wherever they were, to come from some of the younger people.

At that time, a lot of our clients were entertaining the idea of participating in video-on-demand trials. There was a famous one at the time that Time Warner did in Florida, which was very expensive. There were similar ones in Texas that were available to advertisers to participate in. A lot of these VOD tests had maybe three, four or 5,000 users and/or households in the test beds; not a huge number to work with but not a small number either. It was enough to garner some attention and provide some learning.

These tests were very expensive, typically $100,000 to $1 million to participate in them. If you were lucky you would get a learning or two out of those tests, and at the time it looked like video-on-demand was going to be the next big wave of consumer consumption. It's what has now transformed into Netflix and that type of business model.

We evaluated these opportunities as part and parcel of the normal workload we were doing for our clients. I started to hear about the web while writing an internal white paper on interactive technologies in general, and after the second time I heard about the World Wide Web I thought, I need to figure out what this is. I'd heard about it from different software developers. Clearly there were some consumer related projects underway on this "Internet," which I didn't understand. I decided I needed to fill in the gaps about what I knew.

So I started to dive into it in 1994 as one part of a larger matrix of interactive advertising opportunities, within which were Prodigy, CompuServe, and the early version of America Online. You could run text advertising within those environments so they were in the consideration set, along with the video-on-demand, CD-ROMs, etc..

When I examined them all on a media opportunity matrix and asked, what are the capabilities my client would have from a media standpoint and from a creative standpoint in these different test environments? Some clear opportunities rose to the top. Prodigy, CompuServe and AOL provided text opportunities – check. Limited text in the bottom third of the screen, and that's pretty much what they can do. Video-on-demand, there's video – two different opportunities to work with.

What was interesting to me about the World Wide Web from an advertising standpoint was that you could have beautiful graphics, close to magazine quality reproduction. You could do audio. I'd seen a QuickTime movie, which blew me away because it was the first time I'd ever seen video on my computer monitor. I was used to looking at Excel on my screen all day long. So I knew the web offered a lot of possibilities. Although, I also knew we probably wouldn't be doing anything with most of them anytime soon.

In those days it took a minute or two to download a photo on a Mosaic browser and a DSL line shared by about 100 people. Video was going to be a real stretch; it clearly wasn't ready for prime time. But the fact that it was possible, I knew it wouldn't be long. It's taken longer for video to find its way to prominence on the web than I expected. I figured at the time it'd be maybe a year or two before video took off. Of course I was way off and it's taken more like fifteen years to truly take hold.

Looking at the web within this media matrix way it was like, wow, you can do so many things on the World Wide Web! Comparatively speaking, I can probably get a sample size of about 5,000 to look at these media samples just as I could in Florida or Texas (the video-on-demand trials). But with *HotWired*, I can do these things for $15,000 sponsorships, much less than the TV trials. I can work in all these different media types, and we'll see what the response looks like. So it was a lower price tag, a slightly wider geographic audience and different media types to employ in the advertising, which means you can use more of the creative palette. That seemed like a no-brainer.

Our agency was also pretty good at bringing PR to bear or stirring up some type of press coverage for campaigns. For instance, the partners would do things for MCI like take an obscure award – i.e., The Golden Turkey for misleading advertising (that was actually given to AT&T in 1994) – and blow it up into a national campaign.

So being in a new media type with the Internet, and being close to the launch of the commercial web and involved with it early, that would probably be something that was press-worthy. Messner could get some extra mileage out of it. That helped the cause, too, just the fact that it was new for new's sake. Since this was going to be experimental anyway, you really couldn't go wrong. If it fails then say, hey, it was just a test. It was only $15,000 bucks, we saved you $85,000. We were about to spend $100,000 plus on the video-on-demand trials!

It wasn't that hard of a decision. The price tag was low enough and the upside was clear enough to clients that they didn't put up any resistance at all. We were Organic's first clients for *HotWired*'s launch, because we didn't have anyone on staff who knew HTML, and soon thereafter the production went in-house.

After these campaigns ran, were they judged as success-ful or simply as nice tests and some good press?

I think they were judged as successful simply because of the wide spread media exposure that started to come out of it. It's not like the web just blew up immediately and captured the popular consciousness. The business press and the advertising trades were onto it early. I'd say in the first six months of the commercial web – the initial brands that launched with *HotWired* and that were soon with Vibe.com and early CNET advertisers – went from a couple dozen to a couple hundred advertisers in the course of six months to a year. That captured a lot of attention; that was newsworthy.

So our clients got caught up in, not a press storm, but this never-ending, constantly repeating cycle of typically business and trade articles about advertising on the web and how brands were participating. Messner Vetere was a strong player there. And there was very little competition at the time. They built out full production teams internally to do nothing but digital production. Messner was a leader in working with the Avid system to digitally edit TV spots.

Messner was already very good at doing TV creative. Because MCI had maybe 300 different executions a year, distinct executions not just, hey, here's the sixty-minute, the thirty-minute and the fifteen-minute off of the same spot, Messner had become very good at doing all the post-production in-house on Avids and capturing that part of the revenue equation. Most agencies had to farm out that work. It was a very easy transition for such a tech savvy agency to start to capture the digital production budgets as well. The reason the majority of agencies really struggled with making digital even a break-even proposition was because they didn't have the production piece. So it was easy for Messner to turn a money-losing endeavor for most full-service agencies into a break-even endeavor, by being able to build websites for clients and charging them for it. That kept them towards the front of the pack and helped a lot with new business pitches.

From a media planner perspective, at what point did you have that epiphany that this little component of media that you'd played with on the media side, was starting to take off?

Really quickly, within the course of a few months between June and Thanksgiving of 1994, I went from thinking that this is going to be a neat little project to this is revolutionary and could transform business. I didn't see big dollar signs. I just looked at it as the next big media innovation after, say, cable TV, and in terms of a new media form that was being born – a new media type.

It seemed pretty clear that because the hardware was much more expensive then and so was everything else, from getting Internet access to modems, and high-speed connections to the back of the machine to give you a decent Internet experience, this was an upper income media vehicle. It wasn't going to be "access for everyone" for some time. It was very desirable, from a demographic standpoint to advertisers, to reach an audience who could afford to put a DSL or T1 line into the back of their very expensive home and/or work computers.

So it didn't take long to see that digital advertising was going to be a very powerful media vehicle. I would think of some of the gold standard vehicles for reaching high-income people and the web stood out. The idea of having some American Express-type of data on high net worth individuals at scale, that's going to be really valuable. Whether it looks like a Bloomberg system or like American Express advertising programs today, I didn't know what the marketing opportunities would ultimately look like. But it was clearly going to be an audience that advertisers would want to reach. Smart people were getting online quickly and fighting internally inside their corporations for Internet access at their desks. It looked a lot like the early days of Bloomberg where the bankers and traders were making their cases internally: "This is why you need to pay for this system and put it on my desk, because it's crucial to our business, and me getting this financial information quickly is going to be key to the success of the firm."

That's what the web was looking like to me. Michael Bloomberg became the richest man in New York by building a similar system. I didn't imagine the vast consumer web like it exists today, but then again not many people did.

At what point did you make the decision to get out of the standard media buyer side of the equation and into more consulting and helping these companies try to build and grow their businesses? What was the thought process for that?

I like the uncharted territory jobs. The web was clearly going to be a very powerful media type. There weren't many companies that were really trying to address the web just for the web's sake. Most were an appendage to the main business and for me that started off with *HotWired* as an appendage to *Wired Magazine*. But it very quickly broke off into a free-standing entity. And the founders said from the beginning, look, we're not going to repurpose *Wired Magazine* into *HotWired*. *HotWired* is going to be original content that's built for the web for people to consume on the web.

That was very appealing to me. Being part of a creative group that was going to pioneer a new experience on the web was exciting. There was definitely a kind of tone in *Wired* that rubbed some people the wrong way because it was rather preachy or elitist, but we *were* leading. It was fun to create content for the web from scratch. Not really for a new audience, because it's just people consuming media in a different way, but building content for the medium itself was exciting.

I knew the web would be a nice sell to advertisers who were interested in jumping on board and doing things in interactive media. It interested me personally as a young guy with an interest in technology. Professionally, working for *Wired* and *HotWired* seemed like the next logical thing for me to go do. I was always the guy in the media department who was deeply into analytics and spending a lot of time on the research side of things. I was always pushing for more computerization inside the department at DMB&B (now MediaVest). So once this media type sprang out of the computers that I was already interested in, and it became a sight, sound and motion format to bring interactive media to advertisers, that was just perfect for me.

How did your feelings about the business change when this massive bubble began developing and all of a sudden every company was being valued at a heightened valuation? Did your opinion change during that time?

It definitely did. I was up to my neck – happily up to my neck – in business on the web before there was ever an IPO. Before Netscape IPO'd, before Yahoo IPO'd, CNET, before any of these public financings happened I was completely engulfed in the business. The difference is once people started making huge amounts of money, it just attracted a ton of people who had none of the passion that the folks I was working with had. People started coming into the industry because they could see dollar signs. It's natural.

But the crazy valuations were being set in the NASDAQ, and when you're a private company being compared to your peers and your peers are public companies, those valuations are based on something tangible. One startup that I worked at called eGroups was compared to About.com, which was a standalone public company at the time (About.com is now owned by *The New York Times* and eGroups is Yahoo! Groups). We had a really high valuation. But when you looked at the component parts and the assets of each business you'd say, okay this one's private and this one's public. You looked at their unique users, at the type of content that they moved, at their technology and their IP. You looked and said, well, maybe the humans that are running the companies are slightly different but these other components are really similar.

Even though the valuations for some of these companies were kind of crazy, especially looking back on it, the basis was usually on comps. The comps were built on public companies. That's just where the market was, for right or wrong. I wasn't crying too hard when the bubble popped. I wasn't crying a lot of tears for the people that I saw as opportunists, who came into the industry for no legitimate interest more than, "It looks like it's going to pay better than what I'm doing now."

Yeah, I remember a lot of the conversations. Early on the business was full of people that had passion. I

remember learning a lot at every one of those conferences I attended, and I remember **Web Attacks** and
ad:tech growing in the marketplace. I think it was '98,
'99, I went to ad:tech and you could see sharks swimming
in the ocean, so to speak. All of a sudden they were just
swimming around trying to find out which company was
going to be worth however many billions of dollars.

Then the bubble went, POP! Brands like i-Media and
ad:tech that were still surviving, were still trying to
get the people with passion and the decision makers
together. You had the *Click-Zs* and the *MediaPosts* and
their conferences trying successfully to refocus the core
group of people on what the businesses needed to be
so they could grow in a more mature fashion. And the
sharks left the water for a little while. After that period,
into the late 2000s, what do you think were the big takeaways that people had from the previous ten years? What
knowledge was going to help shape the next five, six, ten
years?

When you look at it from a conference perspective, there
are places like TED that are really unchanged that have
aggregated the same, mindful audience. Many of the
people at TED have already made their fortunes. Now
they're really serious about a couple of things; for some of
them it's philanthropy, their pet cause or whatever their
true passion is.

Those are a lot of the people who were there at the
very beginning before there was any money. They were
participating in the early San Francisco web and on the
WELL (Whole Earth 'Lectronic Link, a NorCal bulletin
board that preceded the web). They were the South of
Market web people.

South of Market seemed to attract all the web folks.
They're still here. They're still here working in web companies. Some of them made big money along the way. But these are people who have been unchanged by the weather or the economies and what's happened. On the advertising side the story is much uglier. It's been much more of a crass experience.

The way our business has naturally been tied to agencies has made it difficult. Agencies struggle with making the digital piece break even, much less be a profit center for the agency. That has been such a struggle and caused such friction around the partnership deals between companies. It's been tough on people – it doesn't matter if we're talking about before the bubble or after the bubble – the people that are actually running this digital ad economy. It's hard work. The margins are thin, if there are any margins. We're not there yet in terms of setting up an infrastructure that can work anywhere near as well as network or cable television, or even other major media types. It's not a very efficient marketplace.

How long do you think that's going to take, another ten years?
If you look at the whole pie of all the money in digital advertising, let's just say in the United States, about half of it actually gets delivered fairly easily. The search part is not prone to a lot of friction. There are plenty of moving parts and daily adjustments and all kinds of algorithmic maneuvering, but it's a lot easier to spend money on search than it is elsewhere. So there's part of me that believes these demand side platforms and the more API-friendly exchange marketplaces can

provide a lot more liquidity and stronger, more stable market conditions. But there's still just so much one-off selling going on that I'm struggling to figure out how that gets streamlined.

I think the struggle for meaningful reach is very real. It's part of the reason why there are so many online networks in the world. A major advertiser can turn to one of the broadcast networks today and say, hey, when we work across NBC, plus all of your cable properties and owned and operated affiliate stations, and the wider affiliate network, they can deliver an awful lot for Advertiser X.

It's really hard to go to an entity online and do lots of business in one conversation. There are so few places online where you can go and get really large scale and talk to just a couple of deal makers inside of that media company and then do a lot of business. They're just so few and far between on the web. Advertisers and agencies need to deal with dozens of existing and potential partners to meet the needs of most brands.

If you're a big brand, you're probably using some of the really large reach partners, what we used to call portals. You have search that you need done. Then you work in some other placements. It's the "everything else" that takes up half or more of the time.

And that big bucket you describe, the "everything else," changes all the time; mobile gets thrown into that bucket, video, social media is in there, too.

Something like Twitter shows up that didn't even exist before.

How much do you think businesses have been hurt by just focusing on tactics rather than sticking to a road map and having a strategy for what they should be doing?

I don't think there are enough people or enough managers at Fortune 500 companies with the experience and the knowledge to take the high road. There are not enough clients who have the clout inside their organization to say, we're taking this long view. Most brand managers and marketers have to go and chase the shiny thing, whatever it is that year: It's mobile, it's Twitter, it's Facebook. Most of the marketers chase it so that they can fly a little banner internally and say, "I got us on to Twitter, and now we're doing it – *me.*"

That'll probably never change. People have to justify their existence and have things to put on their evaluation report. Sticking to plan usually doesn't stick out as, wow, that's really innovative. In a marketplace that changes as much as digital, it's hard not to chase the shiny thing. Look at innovation in television. There isn't any, but it's still growing and is still the lead media.

But they stick to a plan.

Oh, absolutely. There actually is some innovation in television it's just not as obvious to us from the outside. I think marketing people have to be on top of what's new. Cory, you do it because it's a hobby, too, but I think it's definitely a "to do" item what to stay up on. In the early days of the web, we used to send around emails to each other saying, "Check out this site. You're going to freak out when you see it." We don't see that much anymore. The thrill of discovery is largely gone, now we schedule time to investigate new things on the web.

I remember a LinkedIn status update a few years ago from my old boss, John Battelle, which read, "Trying to grok Twitter." It meant I want to figure this thing out. I know influential people and early adopters are doing it. There's a big storm blowing up around it. I want to understand this new app.

I find myself doing the same thing. I schedule time to sit down and try to figure out what is going on with new technologies.

What do you think the next five or ten years holds? What is the most exciting part about the business going forward?

The next exciting thing that seems obvious, but it seemed obvious in '95 and it's still not here, is moving it all to mobile, like that now famous Eric Schmidt quote, "Mobile is going to be the number one screen." It's not that one-to-one marketing finally comes true because it's your mobile device. But because it's your mobile device the importance of location and where you are, I think it brings the promise of one-to-one a lot closer. Because we know it's your phone, not the household computer.

You're probably going to be holding onto that device as tightly as you hold onto anything. The same way as you check – do I have my keys? Do I have my wallet? Do I have my mobile device? Okay, I'm ready to leave the house. That's not the same as a desktop machine or a laptop or other ways of accessing the web that we're used to; smartphones, tablets and PDAs are very different. The devices themselves, I'm just blown away by how quickly the products are updating and improving. The quality of the user experience on top of these 3G and 4G networks is awesome.

Unless it's on AT&T–

Unless it's AT&T and you live in San Francisco or New York; I feel so sorry for them, when you think about the Seven Hills in San Francisco or the skyscrapers in New York they have to be the toughest cell markets to get coverage to. Then there are a lot of local regulatory issues with putting up new cell towers, it's really hard to improve. But cell coverage is certainly where they're getting scrutinized.

Absolutely.

AT&T Park, man –

I can't even use my phone in there. You have done a lot of different things, how do you balance learning, doing your work and your personal life?

One of the things that I've done is make sure that I'm working with the right people who are going to trust me to do that, to balance correctly. It doesn't mean that you couldn't micromanage me and that I would resist turning in a timecard that says this is the percent of time I spent doing whatever. That's how a lot of lawyers work, for instance. You say, here are my billable hours against these different clients. These other hours are not billable. What were you doing? Were you jogging? Didn't you come in late this morning?

So part of it is an understanding with the people that I'm working with that I have a long leash. You're going to have to give me a lot of rope because I'm travelling a lot. At Fwix I'm flying off to meet with large publishers because San Francisco doesn't have many. You need to give me the flexibility to determine when I need to be in San Francisco, or wherever else I should be. Fwix operates in seven countries, so I need to be in seven countries and figure out that balance. If I'm not in San Francisco where you can watch me doing my job, then you need to trust me that when I'm in New York, that's where I need to be. If I am in L.A., Sydney or London, that's the most important place for me to be at that moment. And in return I need to get the work done. It's a mutual understanding.

The family stuff is a constant struggle, and largely an emotional one. With a young daughter at home, when I leave for a week she's different when I come back. She has new words and can do new things. That's a really difficult thing to go through as a parent. My wife works, too, so there's a real strain on her when I'm away.

The way I've dealt with the personal part is to schedule more short trips. When I was single, or even before we had a baby, I might do an extended trip visiting two or three cities. Now I do shorter trips, with a quicker turnaround so that I can be home with my family as much as I can. Plus I work well on planes, so that helps.

CLOSING REMARKS

Steven is an industry vet if there ever was one, and his experiences have been valuable to many, including myself. His passion for the business is one of the things

I have always taken away from him. He has spent years investing in the knowledge base of the Internet advertising business. His excitement for the medium has paved the way for billions of dollars in advertising to follow. Certainly if he hadn't made the first buy, someone else would have, but he did and has stayed with it since that fateful day in 1994. Steven doesn't get enough credit for his role and experience in the business, but hopefully this chapter helps give credit where credit is due. Thanks Steven, for everything you've done, the time you've spent with me over the years chatting, and for your endless excitement about this business.

CHAPTER 4

DAVID CARLICK

David Carlick is an Internet visionary, a trusted advisor, and a man who knows how and when to get things done. David began his career with Foote Pacific Advertising and went on to join Structured Systems Group, but eventually left to start what became Carlick Advertising with Adison Olian. In 1993 it was acquired by what was then Bozell, Jacobs, Kenyon & Eckhardt. Their Mountain View office became the Silicon Valley office of BJK&E subsidiary Poppe Tyson, where David eventually moved to become EVP. There he spearheaded their digital efforts.

During this period David's vision expanded to create one of the first online rep firms and ad networks, DoubleClick. He wanted to spin the company out of the parent company as a startup, and in his research with VCs found Kevin O'Connor, founder of Internet

Advertising Networks (IAN) in Atlanta, Georgia, where he and Dwight Merriman had come up with DART, the ad server. They agreed that a merger of their efforts would be the fastest way to dominate the market. When the idea was pitched to parent BJK&E, the parent company decided to fund the merged company itself as a new BJK&E subsidiary. Eventually, additional funding was taken in from other venture investors and DoubleClick was fully spun out to become a public company with O'Connor as CEO. David joined the board of the new subsidiary, and resigned when he departed Poppe Tyson in May, 2007.

Along the way David was involved with some of the most innovative businesses online, including, BigBook (the first online yellow pages), IPro (the first online audience measurement system), Ask Jeeves (the first natural language search engine) and Intermix, which would eventually launch MySpace and sell to News Corp.

David then continued his role of entrepreneur and investor through Vantage Point Venture Partners and most recently with Rho Capital Partners. David's résumé of board seats reads like a *Who's Who* of Internet pioneers and standard bearers, and he has mentored more than his fair share of budding businessmen. He always has time to sit and talk about the business, further demonstrating his passion and joy for it.

David Carlick, what got you interested in the online advertising business?

In '93/'94 we were running what had been Carlick Advertising but was now Poppe Tyson Silicon Valley. My clients started showing interest in the Internet, even before Netscape (the first widely distributed Internet browser). We started doing what I call wallpaper work for them. In other words, they were engineers, and they could put up web pages and such, but they wanted it to look nice and reflect the corporate brand they represented, so we started doing some design work. Our original Silicon Valley design work, for companies like Synopsys, Silicon Graphics, and Hewlett Packard, was about making the sites look pretty. If you're doing online, it's ultimately interaction design as well as more traditional design because you just don't make static pages. You have to make sites that have a function. We built our efforts and positioning around the idea that the web was not about content per se, but about the applications and the interaction that satisfied user needs. The content was just the material for all this, not the machinery.

For examples there were clients like Synopsis, which was a really interesting one for me. Synopsis was in the design automation business, meaning what engineers use to design the chips that ultimately go into products such as today's iPhones and iPads. They had frequently asked questions that had risen out of their call center and with their support department. The concept of the Frequently Asked Questions was bringing up and surfacing ideas and questions that they needed to address. It seemed to make sense to address these through a website. That was an example of functionality that people hadn't thought of before, and we were beginning to work into our work.

Frequently Asked Questions, or FAQs, have an interesting history dating back to when most support was provided by telephone call centers. You can usually catch most of the things that are broken or are a problem for the customers, and that an engineer can't figure out, with the most frequently asked questions. We discovered that if you have those questions and answers documented where the phone support person can find it, they can answer the question efficiently and move on. That allowed the call center to spread out the workload so the new guys were handling the easy questions. If they ran into problems or challenges they would escalate and send the hard ones to the experts on the team, and that way the expert doesn't have to answer the boring ones over and over again.

They had found through trial and error, and based on the ability to execute primitive queries of the Frequently Asked Questions on the website, that they could let their customers use a browser and scan the frequently asked questions and do an initial round of Q&A and have some of their basic questions answered. This dropped their support costs dramatically; one immediate way that B2B used the web early on to reduce hard costs.

It dropped the number of call center people they had to have on the phone dramatically, and even their engineers were going online and doing the work themselves. It seemed to me, as I described it at the time in my report back to my colleagues, as "enlightened self-service." I thought this was great. I saw a parallel in two worlds at the time; customer contact and marketing practice. I knew almost immediately that this is going to be a big deal in the future of marketing and customer interaction.

How did that initial realization that this could be a significant tool for business shape your point of view in determining how this could be an advertising medium, or at least some kind of strong marketing vehicle?

It is not necessarily an Internet idea that got me thinking. What happened first was something altogether unrelated, the fact that self-service gas stations had emerged. This was the early '90s. Instead of having people come out and attend to your car you'd swipe your credit card, put your gas in, take it out and then drive through an automated car wash. At the time car washes were free.

Now what I had done is I'd gone to the gas station, verified my credit card transaction and filled my own gas. I had washed my own car, left faster than I did before and was completely happy for it. With Hertz Gold I'd found that a similar thing happened. I gave Hertz Gold my driver's license, insurance, social security number, my ID. Everything they could possibly ever want to know about me in exchange for never seeing a counter, never standing in line. I would go to pick up my car, and there would be a board. I would go to where the car was noted on the board and drive out. For Hertz it was a huge savings in labor costs to not have people in line or who have to handle the lines. They could have people doing things instead of servicing the customers directly. I, and any other customer, simply cooperated with their computers to get stuff done.

This struck me as largely the future of business in that I thought every business would have to present itself to their customers in a more efficient way, however that way took shape. If you're comparing the features of a car, you would want to do that on a website. If you're looking for real estate, you'd want to do it on a website. That facilitating of communication was what we were doing with our business at Poppe Tyson.

We were business to business largely. We did as much work for our clients below the line as above. We could help them with their marketing campaigns externally, but we could also help them with creating efficiencies in their business. The Internet seemed the natural way to do both from one single point of access to their business.

To me, advertising is measured media, but advertising is also everything you do to communicate yourself to your customer. Some people call it marketing as an umbrella term, but I simplify and view it all as advertising your services. So a business brochure is advertisement. The point of purchase can be considered advertising. The retail support strategy is advertising, and then of course the advertising is advertising. I became immediately interested even before there were a lot of places to put ads in how companies could present themselves to their customers and provide this enlightened self-service in order to be able to improve their relationship. It was the extension of that self-service gas station concept!

It also struck me that there would be a good payback for a car company who spends ten dollars to print a brochure and who knows how to get it into the hands of a customer. If I could get a customer to engage, look through a car site as they prepare to shop for a car, I would have an ROI that I could measure in terms of the analog to physical world of getting that customer a brochure as opposed to getting that customer to go visit a website.

So when you got involved with this business you saw it as a matter of business-efficiency and customer service before you looked at the creative component of it for advertisers.

There was a creative component to it, which is of course the presentation of the website itself. That became an interesting part of the business. And so we came to the view and described it this way; that when you go to a browser and look at information from a vendor, or from a magazine or a publisher or whatever, the whole world is talking content. Everything is content, and that content has to be engaging and attract the attention of the user.

And our view was different. Our view was, when you use a browser and go to a website you're using an application. You're commanding an action through your browser via the application on the server to provide you with results for what you are attempting to do. All my experience in computers had been that people like interactivity. They don't want to watch a movie on their screen unless they ask for it. But they really don't want it to be a TV set, the old "lean back." They want to click here and get this, click here and get that. And so in your applications or your CD-ROMs or anything else, it was more about surfing through the information and then taking time to watch what you'd surfaced up, than it was a presentation layer to imitate radio or TV.

Branding means some things to some people, other things to other people. To me branding is what your customer says about you. That's your brand. If your customer loves you and recommends it, you have branded it. If your customer re-buys your product or service, you're branded. So, yes, I did view the website as being a huge service opportunity for people who are considering your product or service. The interactivity let people find their own way to the information or answer that suited them. It let companies present themselves in a more sexy way. It let consumers be in control.

That is a different perspective but it makes quite a bit of sense.

We embarked on that business and it took off rapidly. It was really exciting. One of the early customers who we did web design for was Silicon Graphics, and it's old history that Jim Clark left Silicon Graphics to start what eventually became Netscape. He eventually discovered Marc Andreessen, right out of school, who had done the Mosaic browser. And while they rummaged around for business models they eventually revolved back to doing some form of the browser as their business, and staging and hosting the servers to serve to it.

They had, for a time, decided their business was really going to be in the server business, maybe licensing the browser to large corporations as a software business. They were going to support publishers, and maybe they could get a revenue share from publishers per paid server or maybe not, but the business didn't happen to go that way. The browser took off and it became a big deal. The server business did well and Netscape all of a sudden found itself in the traffic business, which they really hadn't anticipated.

What do you think would have happened if their first business model had been successful? If their first idea was that they were going to support publishers and manage all the back-end systems and data, is it feasible to say that the Internet would have been a more closed environment? That all the content would have been funneling through one primary player?

No more so than when it was controlled by DoubleClick later on because Netscape would have been, in the end, more of a serving and storage platform. And we were just talking previously, things that make sense don't always happen immediately. So, sure, it would have made a lot of sense for a third-party service to be able to enable the publishers, but the publishers weren't ready for that. Although Netscape signed up quite a few.

For all practical purposes, the major publishers got in later to digital. Time Warner did the Pathfinder site early on but they resisted putting their content online. Magazines all did deals with AOL to have their content funneled over inside the AOL closed garden. That was their big online strategy for some time.

When the bubble burst in 2000/2001 and crashed to the bottom of nuclear winter on 9/11, and as the Internet advertising dollars disappeared because the Internet investors quit funding startups with wacky ad budgets, most of the people from traditional media said, thank god it's over, I'm out of here! They assumed they could go back to business as usual and not have to worry about the Internet thing.

They thought it was just a passing fad and had met its end. What were you doing at that time?

I left Bozell/Poppe in 1997 and took a side trip into an ad targeting deal that didn't work. That was a tough introduction to that side of the business. I joined Vantage Point in '99. I was at Vantage Point Venture Partners funding Internet and new media deals. We did all the work for Toshiba computer systems. We introduced their laptops, their printers, and they asked us to look at digital.

So we look at all the closed gardens of digital for advertising. We looked at AOL, Prodigy, Ziff Davis and all the major players at the time. What they had created was two things. One of the situations they created was their own walled gardens, if you will. In that instance, it was difficult for a brand to own its own space. If you went into Prodigy and put up stuff about your car, your brand looked like Prodigy with some of your car pictures posted up on it.

That part of the Internet didn't seem attractive until I saw the first web browser. The other thing was that Microsoft announced the Microsoft network, which had fourteen publishers signed up. At that same time 50,000 new .com addresses had been registered in that same month. It became clear that there was going to be far too many sites to have an old model work here, that you're going to have to have some other way to aggregate this information together for consumers.

So I was in the lobby at Netscape visiting in the early days and Jim Clark walks by. He says, "Carlick, you know we're doing a million page views a day." That was big at the time, a million page views a day, because the Netscape browser was the homepage for many people. It was the default page. The default page was work we designed on their website, and we designed all the subsequent pages until it launched off into wherever you were going to go, and those pages got people every time they fired up their browser because nobody knew how to change the default page.

And so to the world the Internet looked like Netscape. If you saw the newspapers with all their coverage – "The Internet is coming...It's going to be big"

– in that coverage they would all show a picture of a Netscape screen. They'd show a picture of the White House homepage, which was our work, and they'd show a picture of AOL or something. So the Internet is coming, it's going to be huge. It dawned on me that even with a million impressions a day that wasn't enough to field a full sales force for a single publisher yet. However, if we could aggregate a bunch of sites together, we could fuel a strong sales force. So without doing a business plan inside Poppe Tyson, just with the support of Fergus O'Daly, who is a great guy, I put together a sales team in Silicon Valley and got Netscape to sign up to be the anchor client. I then got twenty more guys to sign up and hire a sales team, and now we had created DoubleClick.

DoubleClick took off, but it was a money losing deal. We had settled on 20 percent or 15 percent commission, which we'd lifted from rep firms. It was a great place to start, but it wasn't going to work in the long run at that scale. The original idea for the business of DoubleClick, as it emerged from Poppe.com, was simply a rep firm. Peter Adams, a young college graduate running IT after three years, came up and said, "You know, we're trafficking all these ads and it's a pain. We should really have an ad server. We should find a way that we can store all the ads and then serve them up and count things like impressions and clicks and stuff."

And that is the birth of the ad server – just like that?
Yep. So we developed one right away. Along the next few months we worked and then DoubleClick was ready to roll out, in April of '94, its ad server. Then I was talking to some venture guys with the idea of

raising money and spinning that out, because I thought DoubleClick was a pretty bad fit for an ad agency. As history turns out I was wrong because 24/7 Real Media was eventually bought by an ad agency. But it struck me as more of a publisher or service provider, so we were talking to venture guys about spinning it out and the talk got fairly far with a few interested groups. When Sprout Group, a guy named Keith Geeslin introduced me he said, "You know, Kevin O'Connor has a company called Internet Advertising Networks, and he's got an ad server and they're in the same business. You should talk to him."

So I called Kevin. Kevin says, "Oh yeah, I know you guys." Because he was a very studious guy on this, we chatted it over. I had most of the publishers and most of the traffic, along with the brand name and the business. He had DART ready to run, where ours wasn't finished yet and his was arguably better. So we proceeded with the discussion of merging the two together and spinning the business out. It made sense and, historically speaking, it was absolutely the right thing to do.

DoubleClick became the de facto ad server standard that was eventually acquired and merged into Google – such humble beginnings.

We agreed, and this process was very instructive for me. It was early in my days of making business dealings. I was terrible back then. I just figured all these things would come to me. I didn't push hard, I just hoped for the best.

But it all worked out.

It did work out. We agreed that we should put them together and spin it out from Bozell, and we had venture guys lined up ready to go. So Kevin flew up to New York one day while I was in California and pitched the idea. To my great surprise the Bozell guys, Chuck Peebler and Val Zammit said, we'll fund this. And Bozell, for one of the few times in its life, became a venture capital firm and funded DoubleClick. So Kevin and his motley crew moved into the Poppe Tyson offices in New York until we could get in another office that we had.

And that was the informal beginning of Silicon Alley?

It was before "Silicon Alley" was coined, but they moved into our offices in a rat's warren and a little leftover space from Bozell until we carved out more space, because Poppe had been growing, and now DoubleClick was growing. We expanded our office on the West Coast as well, down in Mountain View, to include a DoubleClick area and then through an acquisition that we had done on Madison Avenue just around the corner we entered into more space. DoubleClick took over that floor before moving down into their building with the basketball court and all that cool stuff.

Kevin came on as CEO and I went to a spot on the board, and at the time DoubleClick was a small revenue deal. It was a very exciting space but it was small revenue, and Poppe.com was competing with CKS Partners and others, all of whom were doing big business at the time, and preparing to go public, which was my activity through the end of '96.

I had forgotten about that connection between Poppe and DoubleClick, and it's one of the very few times in the history of this business that an agency spun out something that turned into an industry standard. DoubleClick became the industry standard for ad serving as well as for an ad network at the time.

Yeah, oddly enough. I loved the network side, which was an extension of the rep business. It was a publishing business and I was interested in the ad serving side, but without the ad serving you couldn't have created and managed the network. Although it was a tough slog when Kevin first joined up and we'd go call on guys like Sony and try to explain to them that we're going to run their ads on our ad server – not just traffic the ads, but they were going to be part of this network – and there was a great deal of resistance.

It becoming an industry standard happened because of two things. First off, timing; the other is that Kevin O'Connor is a terrific digital and technical business guy. He was laser-focused on what had to be done. He did a great job of growing the product, acquiring a footprint and building upon it.

Midway through the '90s, after I had left the board of DoubleClick, the decision was made that the market was much more excited about the platform serving business – the instance where a hard drive is spinning and money comes out the other side – and less excited about the sales force and publishing business. And so they divested the DoubleClick network.

Some years later I was lucky to join the Ask Jeeves board, right at the bottom of the Nuclear Winter. In fact, my first board meeting with them happened to be the morning of September 11, 2001, which made for a very unusual board meeting, what with the events unfolding in New York. As Ask Jeeves got traction due to, among other things, AdWords and Teoma, the relevance engine that they bought, Jeeves started growing rapidly. They continued doing acquisitions and we wound up buying back from a different party, the old Excite network that had been the DoubleClick network that I had originally started back in the DoubleClick days. It turned out to be a very profitable part of Ask Jeeves and a big piece of their sale to Interactive Corp (IAC).

It's a tangled web they weave, pun intended. That's what happens when you're in the middle of all the different moving parts of this business. You get to see when those opportunities arise and if you can take advantage of it, you do.

That's an interesting point, Cory. I've found over time that there are a lot of people who are better at seeing more things than me. Some things I see clear as a bell, and others I can't guess. I think I looked at GroupOn in '08. I just couldn't see how they were going to get the distribution or the retailers or the business going. I was completely wrong.

You were very early with Poppe Tyson and DoubleClick and then Vantage Partners. In a similar fashion you are still early with your role at Rho Capital. You are able to identify what the components are for success in this business – applications, technology, creativity. You identified an agency model that was successful and a services component for technology that made it easier to operate. You identified the need for the publishers to be united to create efficiencies in monetization and that led to the

ad network model. You even created the model for an ad server, which is literally the backbone of the business now. But now that the business has grown, you are having trouble identifying where you think it could go?

There's a lot to see. If somebody shows me something and I don't understand it, it doesn't mean that it's not going to be great. It just means I don't understand it, and if I try to understand everything, I'll be dead. So if I get something, I get it. In the case of the early Poppe.com and DoubleClick, where we had such a great partnership with Fergus O'Daly, who was such a driver in migrating this stuff from Silicon Valley to New York and making the business happen, I could see the ad network being the solution. My other guys saw the server being a solution. Kevin O'Connor saw that. I didn't see that until our guys had offered one up to us. I could see the services websites being a key thing that companies had to have. That part was as clear to me as could be. So both of those were clear and both happened, but I missed other things. I missed a lot of stuff.

When you look at companies now, and at the companies you passed on, has the criteria that you use to evaluate companies for investment of either money or your time changed?

Yes, a great deal from when I first started looking at deals in '98 until now, almost thirteen years later. Partly the criteria changed because I'm focusing on earlier stage companies, and there's a transformative period in our world now called efficient capital because of things like Amazon's servers-on-demand and storage-on-demand, and the huge advances in programming languages – the

Ruby on Rails and others – that let people be more productive. And the big stockpiles of shareware and things that you can grab off the shelf to integrate in, and the big platforms for integrating applications into mobile; all those things combine in the media/digital media business to make it easier to start companies than before.

We have a company that we funded which has raised a total of $3 million and they do things that in 1990 would have cost us $25 million to do. They got their prototype working on a quarter million to a half million. This changes the whole nature of things. And the beauty of it is, for many of the investors, you do not always have to bet on an institution emerging from this. There used to be a running joke, is this a company or is it a product? Now you can say, is this a company, a product, or a feature for a product? These days there are many companies that may start as a feature and turn into a real product, and that product can turn into a larger company. The real nature of venture and Silicon Valley is reasserting itself in acquisitions. And I say that because more than ever the public companies can't afford to do the R&D, because it comes right off your earnings and public companies are measured by their earnings.

So the stock price rises and falls with the ratio of net income to the revenue dollar. They can buy companies, and that doesn't affect earnings. It doesn't flow through the income statement, at least for a while, until we have to consider the impairment of the asset. So it makes more sense for a company to look around and see the things that matter and buy them, than it does to try to develop five to get one that works when it'll have to come out of your R&D and screw up your net income line. You've seen Cisco and Intel and Yahoo do this, even though Yahoo had real funding money.

So acquisitions are becoming interesting here, and efficient capital makes it easy. So the short answer to your question that I took too long on, is that a lot of times now you can look at something that's exciting but small and not know what's around the corner. GroupOn is an interesting example that I'm not involved with. GroupOn started off with one idea – found this tactic of getting a coupon announcement, found it worked so well that they refocused on that tactic – and that became their strategy. And it's been a great hit.

The same thing is true here. If you read our website, what I say is if you're investing in the early stage of a company you have to be open to what's coming. Chances are the revenue of the company in three years won't be what's in the business plan today, and what you're looking for is entrepreneurs who are able to be quick and flexible and thoughtful at the same time. What that translates to is something new for me – my one strategy is tactics.

What do you mean by that?
My overarching strategy is tactics; you're able to try more things now and find out what people respond to. If you find people really respond to this and don't respond to that, then you can focus on the thing they did respond to. And then when you try to explain why they're responding to this one thing, what you're describing is your strategy.

We have a gorgeous field of bright entrepreneurs who are creating things that an investor at various stages, from seed to angel to super angel to venture, can look around at and find what they're interested in.

So the criteria used to be more heavily weighted towards the idea, whereas now it's more heavily weighted towards the people behind the ideas and their ability to react and respond while having vision.

I think so. I think with my switch towards earlier stage deals, it's people and it's traction. You have to have some people and you have to have some traction. It's very difficult for us to fund a PowerPoint of an idea, even if it's three guys who have done one hundred things in their lives. In previous larger-money early-stage days, you were trying to put the whole ball of wax together. You have a team, technology, a large market, a road map; you're going to do these things and out of this will emerge the next "blank."

What is it about this industry right now that you enjoy most; is it the creativity, the excitement?

I think it's just the unfolding of time. Things are happening so much faster now on many levels. One level is that businesses are coming up, becoming meaningful. Behaviors are changing with a speed that I don't think has happened before. Market caps, like Facebook and Zynga, are being created more rapidly than Google did ten years ago, and that was more rapidly than many companies had done before; all that is happening in a very exciting way.

The opposite side is that as fast as things grow, they ossify. So companies that once were the hard-charging, innovative leaders become stuck in their product line or their ways. Microsoft has a bit of that, and you could infer that even Yahoo has a bit of that, and sometimes I wonder if Google doesn't have a little bit of it from time to time in that as organizations get larger they don't move as easily.

The landscape of Fortune 500 companies has changed quickly over the last century. It's constantly being replenished, and in some ways that's happening faster, and that's enjoyable to watch. The other thing, Cory, it's the people. In a way I'm a people person and the people that I get to work with are just terrific. Even the ones I don't get to work with are pretty terrific.

Since I've met you – and I met you initially a long time ago, but really only got to know you well in the last couple of years – you're a good person to be around because you listen, give great feedback and always have time, which is one thing a lot of people in this business forget to have. I know you're busy, you've got a lot on your plate, but you take time to sit and talk and listen, and that's an art that far too many people have forgotten.

That's a nice compliment. But I could be the proverbial duck; peaceful on the surface but paddling like mad under the water.

Possibly.

It could be a function of age, Cory. To some degree I've no longer decided to be frantic. I can't know everything. I can't keep up with the entire business. I can't even keep up with the trades. I can't even begin to and so you just come to the conclusion; I can't do it in 100 hours and I can't do it in 1,000 hours, so why should I try?

And do you think that perspective changed from twenty years ago, fifteen years ago?

Oh, it's age, too. When I was in my young buck stage of business I was pulling all-nighters and excited about work, and wanted to load up on new stuff and keep up with everything and have more stuff happening. I was known as a deadline junkie at the time. I've since switched it to; *nothing simplifies life like a deadline because at least you know what has to happen.*

That's a good quote, I like that.

It's one of my email signatures.

But the real answer is…it's a funny story. I was thirty-one or something, and then the Osborne computer was being released, which went on to be a $100 million a year business; one of the great innovations, really, the first mass market portable, personal computer. It had a really transformative effect on the industry, and I was just coming into advertising. I was so excited by this whole thing; everybody's going to be using computers, this so matters, it is so life changing, it is so important. I was one of those evangelists. I so believed, "this is important," as if it would not happen without me helping push the wheel forward.

We were going to have a photo session of the Osborne at Bill Arbogast Studio down in East Palo Alto, in what was called Whiskey Gulch, a rundown area where photographers could own buildings, and where you could buy whiskey, which for years Stanford prohibited within a mile of the campus. All of which was torn down to be a Four Seasons Hotel, but I digress. So we got the computer, and then Adam Osborne was going to come down for his part in the photo shoot.

Adam was later and later and later, and I'm keeping the photographer there. It was this beautiful huge studio. Very eccentric character; had shot all the famous stuff in Silicon Valley up to that time for the big brands. Well, not all, but much of it. And so Bill says, "You know, this can wait until tomorrow. I've been through this a million times. Everything seems like it's going to be the end of the world if it doesn't happen, and tomorrow we'll wake up and it won't be the end of the world. Just get over it." I said, "Tomorrow I'll do that, but today you're staying here until Adam Osborne comes here and we get this shot done."

So we did stay and got the shot done with Adam Osborne. But he was right, you know, but it takes age until you get to that point of view. When you're swept up in all the stuff it seems like this has to happen tonight no matter what.

I wish more people could learn that lesson quicker, myself included.

You won't, it just comes with time. Don't be in a hurry to get old, it happens soon enough.

Let me ask you one last question. Looking back at how the businesses progressed, is there any one thing you can point out that you think would've dramatically changed the direction of the business, anything that leaps to mind?

One is the deal that I left Poppe and DoubleClick for, which was a thing called Power Agent. And the idea of

Power Agent – it was too complex and too ahead of its time – was to go after this whole privacy thing. So you would opt in to Power Agent and then you would have a visible shield of your personal identity behind the shield, and in front of the shield would be all your attributes. People could target you by exposing your attributes so that you would be able to turn the entire ad world towards you, much as search does when you explicitly name what it is you're looking for, but passively because you've published your attributes in a way that people can get them to you without knowing actually who you are. Then, not only would you publish your attributes but when advertisers buy you as a target, say today on places like BlueKai, you would own your profile, be your own data owner and get a rev share of what was paid to target you.

People would accumulate points for having the profile out there, it would be a game. And all the deals would find the consumer. We were going to get local deals, George Garrick was with us and he called them "nuggets." All this predating AdWords, of course, and GroupOn but we didn't get it right. We would've had to do different things. Had we managed to pull that off, we might've bypassed the whole privacy, secrecy, stealth thing that we're in right now. People would all be targetable, all get value from being so, and PII would not be an issue. So now we do all kinds of clever stuff to try and figure out whether people are likely customers. You've seen the *Wall Street Journal* fourteen-piece article on it. It is a constant war and misunderstanding of tracking and privacy.

So the whole privacy problem is your fault.

It is my fault.

CLOSING REMARKS

David provides a lot of great insight into this business, and his involvement in so many successful aspects of the business is hard to match. Almost uniformly across the web if you speak to people who know David, they have good things to say and that is a legacy worth aspiring to.

CHAPTER 5

TIM MCHALE

Tim McHale is a gentleman and a scholar. He is the managing partner and editor of *MadAve Journal,* MadAve Consulting and MadAve Mobile. In his current role Tim covers the online advertising business from these three points of view, as someone who knows all three sides and can speak to them as well.

His experience is deep, having acted as media director for a number of Madison Avenue agencies beginning as an intern at Ogilvy & Mather, all the way to serving as chief media officer for Tribal DDB Worldwide.

Tim's foray into the interactive space began with the role of media director at Blue Marketing/ACG and eventually joining Agency.com as VP, Media Services where he was instrumental in merging together the acquisition of i-traffic. Tim held the role of EVP, Director of Strategic Planning for i-traffic. He has worked with packaged goods brands, entertainment companies and a number of successful efforts in the digital marketing space. He believes in the future of the mobile, among other things, and his thinking is widely regarded as some of the most influential thought leadership in the industry.

Tim McHale, what got you into advertising in the first place?

I took a class, Advertising 101, in college and it opened up this whole new idea for me that I had never thought of before. I was a business major and I really liked what I saw in my class. What I liked about advertising is that it was a combination of art and science. I had a creative side to me but I knew that creative in the traditional sense, in terms of being a musician or an artist was not a moneymaker. Advertising helped combine your creative side and your business side to where you can actually make some money.

Then of course, once I got into the agency business it was a whole social dynamic which I fell in love with. That continued until I got into the digital space, and then it became even crazier.

What brought you from the world of traditional advertising into digital?

I was really lucky because I got a call from a friend of mine who was searching for a traditional media director who did not have a lot of digital media experience. That was perfect! What they were looking to do was fill a hole in their services with someone who understood marketing and media overall from a traditional perspective. At the time, as early as it was, these folks knew the Internet was just a media vehicle and the thing that made it different, or the thing that was going to satisfy the agency's clients, was to have somebody on board who understood how the media process worked overall.

It was that back then at Blue Marble, when we had thirteen P&G clients, among others. They were very comfortable with me and my background and we did some really great work together. It was an opportunity to actually be trained on the job while I was being paid for it in a new industry that I knew had tremendous potential. I was delighted with it. It was a much different culture back then compared to what it was in traditional media, primarily because there was a generational divide. Secondly, there was a completely different kind of skill set that was needed in the digital space versus the traditional space. For me it was a great opportunity to bring my traditional background into a digital space, while at the same time learn a completely new language, if you will.

That must have been difficult, being taught a new category and learning a new language on the job when that language had not even been fully written or developed as of yet.

You are absolutely right. It took six weeks to get a campaign up and running with MatchLogic (a leading ad server at the time). That was the primary third-party server and we were really excited about the opportunity to collect data on usage and target audience. At the same time, the tools were extremely basic and ancient by today's standards.

Culturally it was a challenge because traditional media was more of a hierarchical experience in terms of how the agency was created. Here, in the digital space it was a more holistic experience. It didn't really matter what your title was, everyone was in it at the same level and working on the same things. So that took a little bit of getting used to. If anything the junior folks that I had hired who were reporting to me, in a lot of ways, knew more about the digital media business than I did.

That's an interesting thing to think about, how the generational divide didn't factor into the business because the business was so new. Other than having to build the plane while flying it, what was the biggest challenge at that point? Was it applying your experience in traditional marketing and advertising to the digital space and then translating that to clients?

Everything was a challenge because the business felt like it was moving so fast, but ironically it was going slow in many ways because it took so long to do everything. Everything today is shrink-wrapped. Back then you basically had to outsource everything. At that point everything was being reinvented or invented in-house, from banner technology to ad serving to trafficking and reporting and measurement. We were speeding along because we knew things had to be turned around in a relatively short period of time. We had to go through so many more steps to accomplish a campaign, such that the agency had an offsite meeting after I had been there a week to try to draw out a new diagram as a first attempt to create a process. We were dealing with new clients, new people and new technology and without a lot of history to go on. There was a lot of insanity and frustration and a lot of egos at that time. There was also so much money coming from the whole category, not in terms of spending but in terms of evaluations of the different companies. Those valuations made for some relationships that were relatively one-sided. Our clients needed us to do something, but the publishers felt they should be in charge and didn't always want to be flexible because they felt they were a big company already. The egos got in the way sometimes.

So, you had many people who were very young. On paper it looked like they were going to be millionaires in the next six months whenever the IPO took place for their company.

That definitely makes for some interesting meetings.
The other biggest challenge for me was the excitement of the medium compared to traditional media. The digital space was not only a vehicle it was also a channel. Search was a new concept that everyone was trying to figure out. It was exciting to me to understand that not only was the medium going to be used in a traditional sense for advertising and reaching people, trying to get people to convince themselves to buy new products, etc., it was also a vehicle where you could sell things on the channel itself. So that was interesting to visualize in a very short period of time, and communicate to our clients who were further away from the digital space than we were.

In fact, one funny story was that on my first day of joining Blue Marble I was dragged into a meeting over at Ernst and Young. They had just awarded Blue Marble a large assignment to help build out their website, which turned out to be a huge endeavor – they actually put a million dollars aside for media. Back then that was still a lot of money. I was introduced to the client as the "Internet Guru," which was funny because I had not been at the agency for more than twenty minutes. What got me through the meeting was, knowing that the client knew even less than I did. I had, of course, done my homework and learned as much information about the Internet as was possible in preparation for my interviews. That being said, I was really still a newbie audience.

As the "guru," what was the biggest question clients were asking at the time? What was the hurdle getting them to advertise online?

We had not even gotten into the place where we were advertising online. Most companies were just building websites for the first time. One of the really exciting parts of being there was that the clients would have $600,000 assigned for a website, which today is unheard of for that scope of work, but everything cost a lot of money back then. Our point of view on the Scope Mouthwash business at the agency was, why do you need a website for a mouthwash? Everyone knew what Scope was. It had 95 percent awareness already. We came back with the idea of having a viral campaign to take the traditional effort, which was, "Get Kissably Clean" for the mouthwash in their TV spots. We decided to create something on email, which would allow people to send a kiss to the ones you love, kicking off on Valentine's Day. They loved the idea.

We convinced them they didn't really need a website, what they needed was a web tool with the functionality to be able to send kisses out from the site. On the first

Valentine's Day in 1998 the campaign crashed the P&G servers because they had no idea that they were going to get that much traffic.

And that was considered a success?
Oh, that was a huge success. In fact, I think we won an award as one of the ten hottest shops for *Adweek* because of that campaign.

I love how one of the metrics for success was, did it crash the servers? That happened a lot.
Because nobody knew how much cloud space you needed on a server. There was just so much that we did not know at the time. Nobody knew about middleware or load time or anything like that.

You've been involved with many phases of web advertising. What do you see as the watershed moments, or the most important trends that helped shape the business to date?

There was a moment back in 2000 when McDonald's implemented its first digital media campaign. By the year 2000 we were further along than we had been in the previous two years. There was still the bubble that had yet to burst. We took an existing credit of $200,000 they had with Disney and ran a digital campaign, I think for their Ronald McDonald House feature on the Disney Channel – Disney.com, I think it was. That was when McDonald's, a very conservative company, had decided the net was something legitimate. I also think it was when I was working on Continental Airlines, and e-commerce was starting to overtake the travel industry and travel agency business in a major way. That was when it became very clear to me that this was a significant moment in terms of having a medium that would be here to last.

Through 2011 what other big trends have you seen that affected the way the business has directed itself?

Well, if you remember pop-ups they were controversial because everyone was questioning whose real estate the screen really was, whose technology led, whose audience data was being used and which content was really at play. Now we don't really have those discussions. Pop-ups are not standard but you have pop-unders and pop-overs that are pretty much accepted in today's e-commerce field.

In terms of things we see today, I think predictive modeling was a concept that is only now coming into play with regards to some of the properties out there. Targeting has so many capabilities with products like Advertising.com, Audience Science and Tacoda, as well some of the other ad networks, where you can really target through demographic, geographic and psychographic information.

In terms of the latest on the art side of the business, it's video. You have pre-roll and post-roll and you have endemic video campaigns for the web; not a TV campaign that is being refurbished for digital media. There is the argument that you can't take a TV commercial, implement it online and have the same impact. That is a subjective element because some campaigns work better than others. I think video is here to stay and that means you can have a campaign where you have a media planner able to allocate dollars against a video campaign using the TV messaging where it will run on the online video networks – like on Tremor Networks – and generate a mass significant reach.

Conversely, part of the problem was that we made digital media so cumbersome because it did not have the tools in place early on to be successful. Plus there was a whole cultural clash between the traditional people and the digital media people. There was a fight for dollars and turf protection and there was very little cooperation. Today you have media agencies where you see many of the same people planning traditional and digital media. Not necessarily buying the same inventory, but you have a lot more integration and acceptance between how things were done versus even five years ago.

There are so many different technologies available for advertisers these days. You were attracted to the idea of the art and the science in advertising. At this stage, who do you think is winning in that discussion? Do you think art is more important, or that science is starting to gain a stronger, more important foothold?

One of the things I left out was, of course, social media. It is not just the science of the media itself, or the advertising message and the content and the art, but the science is the channel where you are delivering your message. What you have today is a merging between advertising content and PR, and it doesn't really matter where the message is coming from. In fact, it could come from my next-door neighbor's rang on a site rather than just the brand itself being aimed at me through social sharing and user-generated content. I think you are always going to have a division between advertising, paid advertising and user-generated or soft advertising, which is content. At the end of the day it doesn't really matter. What matters is the audience. That hasn't changed between the traditional and the digital medium. At the end of the day, you are selling products and people are smart enough to see a value proposition whether it is through a thirty-second ad, pre-roll spot or some content that they see on a neighbor's Facebook page.

I see the challenge in determining the opportunities for brands to endorse that take on a holistic approach, in terms of the overall messaging, to make sure that each of the channels you can afford to be on is well equipped. At the end of the day we are in the business of specialties. The brand manager who may have a generalist's view and understands the medium enough to get the point will be successful. Fundamentally, it is the messaging that is most important, not so much the science behind the media plan.

Of course the functionality, usability and dialogue of your marketing platform, between the client and consumer is ultimately important as well, and having a strong understanding of integration.

I personally don't think one side will ever win out over the other. You can only be effective if you maintain a strong balance.

Yes. Most people feel that word of mouth is the most important advertising there is. You can spend money till the cows come home, but in terms of advertising what the response is and what people say about you is ultimately the most important element.

Very true. Looking back at the things you've been involved in, what do you feel has been one of your best personal successes in the business?

When I went from the corporate world to becoming an entrepreneur was an important step. From being in the traditional media business, where the giants of the business had pretty much set up all the agencies and there was not a lot of space for becoming an entrepreneur, to where I am now. All of the major agencies were being bought up and all the clients at the same time were being merged and acquired, so the traditional media became a business of giants. When I got into digital media space, you had many different small players who still had that entrepreneurial fever.

There were many roll-ups going on. In fact, when you and I met, Cory, it was because you guys had to a standalone agency, which was acquired by Agency.com. You were at i-traffic, a successful standalone shop, which was rolled up into Agency.com and from my experience it was a little messy, but at the end of the day we all got through it. In fact, being able to survive a roll-up was quite honestly what helped me prepare to become an entrepreneur better than anything else I did. I had to be able to roll with the punches and think three times as fast as I had ever done before. I had to be able to predict outcomes in terms of how my time could be best spent and plan accordingly.

My traditional media background helped me understand how to service clients and understand how marketing worked. Back in 1998, it was the perfect time for me to get into the digital space because digital media was just emerging as an advertising vehicle and I was able to apply my skills there. By 2002 I had been through so much and had really been taught a new trade. By then I had earned my bones, if you will, from being in the digital business for five years. I was considered an old-timer. A few of us got together and created the Oldtimers List, which is still in existence today. Making the decision to become an entrepreneur was one of the best I ever made.

It was scary compared to being a regular paid employee. The excitement and opportunity to live the American dream by being an entrepreneur still excites me and gets me up every day.

Being able to make decisions that influence where your career path is headed is a nice feeling.

It's great. At the end of the day we have a handful of stable clients that are not moving around, and the stability of being in an agency business that is not as crazy as it used to be. Yet at the same time, you are an entrepreneur.

Conversely, what do you look back on from that period of time and think you would have done differently? Or, what was one of the key things you learned the most from, but was not considered a success at the time?

I think the experience of i-traffic and Agency.com cultures trying to mesh together, that was a learning experience. These two companies were so different and I hadn't ever experienced a roll-up before. I had not thought about how important culture was in terms of what made a company successful or not. Here you had two very successful companies between Agency.com and i-traffic and my job was to be in charge of integrating the two. I was one of three people at Agency.com who were brought over and parked at i-traffic.

My loyalties at the time were still with Agency.com because that was who hired me in the first place, and I had been with them for several months. i-traffic was a very different kind of animal because the product i-traffic was selling was very different compared to Agency.com. Agency.com was used to building major websites and i-traffic was used to running advertising to push people to those websites. It was a difficult transition, everyone was feeling the pain. For me it was very difficult wearing two hats at two different agencies at one time because you still had two successful companies that were resistant to becoming one. That was the biggest learning experience I had that I would not have judged a success at the time, realizing that at the end of the day your business is only as strong as your culture.

I remember that stage well. That is when we first met!
Yes it was. One of the exciting parts about the business, though, was going to all the conferences. Once I was able to understand the digital media space and culture that was found in digital, I thought that camaraderie in the beginning at these conferences was just so dynamic and so exciting that it really made me feel like a part of something larger than just a job.

One of the recurring things I am coming across doing these interviews is that the business itself was driven at the very beginning by a very select few. There was a small group, almost an inner circle, who were really passionate about this business and driving it forward. Over

the years that core group has continued to grow and expand and evolve, but surprisingly there are still a lot of the same people in it. That is one of the more interesting things I am seeing about this business; as much as it is about technology, it is about the people.

It is absolutely about the people. It is now a legitimate media property so you don't have people leave the digital media space to go back to TV or into another business all together. There is stability now and you are going to see careers flourish and have people stay in this space for a long period of time.

What is the one thing that has gotten you most excited about where the business is headed?

Video is going to be an exciting part of the future and social media. I think we are looking at mobile as the next big medium. It's funny as the screen gets smaller the dynamic quality of the functionality gets larger. I am talking to you on my iPhone, which is also a computer, which is also a smart phone, which is also a refrigerator magnet if you want it to be! I think it is another business that is going to reinvent itself with a whole new skill set of people and a whole new understanding of how to measure it. It will be based in part on the digital media space overall, but there is a whole new technology and paradigm and a quality with mobile that has nothing to do with the past.

I can't really predict the future that far out, but I do see mobile as the ultimate media property. Maybe in five years you have wristwatches that function as a digital media property. Until that day comes the mobile medium is going to be where the action is. In some ways you can see there is still very little money going into the media space overall for mobile. The quality and the potential are there and the audience is willing.

New is basically what wins the day. My personal motto, and that of *The Madison Avenue Journal* is, "You're either new or you're through." That might be a good place to end it, because that is really what it is all about. Whether it is the technology, culture or the individual that gets up every morning and wants to make a difference, you have to be new.

CLOSING REMARKS

Tim's interview got me thinking about the ride that was the early period of this business. There were so many different ways to get to the end goal of leading a successful team and influencing great clients. Tim's was about a baseline of experience and desire to take that experience into uncharted waters. His experiences in the business allowed for a combination of maturity and innovation that not many other people had at the time.

I take away from this a sense of never resting on your laurels. Don't get complacent and don't get stuck in a rut. Never be afraid to take what you know and jump into something you don't know, because when you get out of your comfort zone you learn and grow. True maturity is not about understanding everything, it is the wisdom that stems from knowing what you're limitations are and testing them.

CHAPTER 6

SARAH FAY

Sarah Fay is a veteran of the media services industry. In her two decades of experience, she has developed and implemented groundbreaking new models for advertising and media and become a well-known voice in the advertising industry on the topics of digital marketing and media integration. She has helped to build one of the most recognized digital companies in the world through a combination of acquisitions, new business wins and organic growth.

In her role as president of Carat Interactive and then president of Isobar, Sarah orchestrated the successful acquisitions and merging of several companies including Lot21, Vizium, Freestyle Interactive, Molecular, iProspect, Ammo and Bluestreak. Sarah is also responsible for launching Isobar Mobile, a highly regarded mobile marketing entity.

An industry thought leader, Sarah initiated several ground breaking studies including "Born to Be Wired" (2003), which examined rapidly increasing Internet use by teens, and "Never Ending Friending" (2007), which considered the increasingly vital role of social networking as a component of social behavior and also calculated marketing ROI for Social Marketing campaigns. Sarah has been widely quoted in such sources as *AdAge, Adweek, DMNews, B2B Marketing Magazine*, *New York Times, Wall Street Journal* and *USA Today*. Additionally, she regularly addresses audiences at major marketing conferences and participates on a number of company and industry boards.

Sarah Fay, let me start from the beginning. You were involved in advertising, what got you interested in digital and online advertising?

Well, I was specifically in high-tech advertising. I was a partner at an agency called Freeman Associates, which specialized in planning and buying media. We were a media agency for companies in the high-tech sector, including AOL, which we considered to be high technology at that time. AOL was a challenger to Prodigy and CompuServe (actually Steve Case hired us back in 1992) and we covered the spectrum of technology companies from consumer tech, all the way through to Enterprise Computing.

We followed the technology trends very closely, and were exposed to new technologies as they were emerging. One company that hired us was called BookLink, owned by David Wetherell, who later became CEO and chairman of an incubator company called CMGI. No one would ever remember them today, but they were launching the second browser (after Mosaic) into the marketplace. The physical launch took place at the trade show, Comdex and we arranged for free distribution of the BookLink browser software through publishers such as CMP, Ziff Davis and IDG. The reception to this distribution was wild. I had never seen a product take off this quickly. It was so popular, so hot, and all of the publications were covering the advent of the Internet.

These were very early days for the Internet, but the topic was high on the radar of *PC Magazine, PCWorld, PC WEEK,* and all of those publications. David Wetherell, as the client, sat us down and preached to us about what the Internet was going to be. He said, "This is going to be a major marketing platform." So we got a glimpse into the future from someone who really rocked the market eventually.

CMGI had a great rise and, of course, fell during the .com bust, but our exposure to and involvement with that company made us early believers in the Internet and what it would mean for advertisers. Because we were in the high-tech sector we had a lot of clients who were tuned in as well, and interested to experiment and try banner advertising which we were more than willing to accommodate, primarily because we were fascinated by it. It seemed like the Holy Grail of media. With the offer of perfect targeting, and immediate user-response mechanisms, you would know immediately how well you did in getting the interest of the user. It was the perfect direct marketing vehicle. As AOL's agency we managed all of their subscription media. That was very PR focused, too. We were always looking for the next big thing we could do to generate a better response. Interestingly, it was a really long time before AOL adopted online advertising. They were the last to let us do it!

They were sending out those CDs back then.
Yes, we were carpet-bombing the world with those CDs. We found that the farther forward in a publication you could place the CD, the better response you would get until finally we were asking for the front cover. So we were the ones who invented that front cover spot for the CDs, and funny enough it improved the sale of the publications, too.

We weren't making a heck of a lot of money from online advertising services back then, but we were learning a lot. We were bush-whacking like the rest of the world. In fact, when we began we weren't even using ad serving; we were buying on a site-by-site basis. We were manually placing and tracking the returns. It was a very cumbersome, manual, slow process but we were dealing in fairly small numbers anyway. Little by little we started to grow our online media volume and become more sophisticated in our approach.

This was the pre-.com boom, so we really got our feet wet and learned a lot before the Internet craze hit. When it did, we were one of the few places you could go to have somebody deal with your online advertising. That was an exciting time for us. We took on a lot of .com business. We worked with Smarterkids.com, Audible; we started to get into a lot of consumer areas. We were still positioned in the high tech space, but justified this business by saying; well it's really technology because it is a website.

We were determined to keep our position as a technology-focused media company. Until one day we got a call from Think New Ideas, which was one of the new digital agencies, to say that they were pitching Gillette and they needed us. They were losing because of a weak media story and wanted us as their partner. I originally said no, Gillette was clearly a consumer account and we were decidedly not in that space. But they begged and we ended up saying, well, okay, what do we have to lose? One week later we had the Gillette online media business!

Then we partnered with another company called Viant, another early web build agency. We won the RadioShack account, which eventually became one of Carat's biggest accounts. It was exciting times. Because we got in early we found ourselves at the forefront of a hot marketplace, and we had credibility and license to go into any account that was building and looking to establish itself in the digital space.

You were integral to people figuring out how to utilize the web as a marketing tool. You were building websites, executing advertising, and buying and placing media. You also started to lead the discussions for how the larger agencies were going to start thinking about digital as well. You started to go to the larger Madison Avenue companies and teaching them how to do online. What was that transition like?

Well, timing is everything, right? The timing of the boom and the bust made a lot of people successful or unsuccessful, and it happened to help make our success. Freeman Associates folded business to Carat just as the first wave was building, and we rode that wave all the way through our earn-out. Business was just flowing into the agency community. There wasn't a single agency I knew of that wasn't doing extremely well. I felt like I was running around with a basket, catching money falling out of the sky. I just had to get there fast enough. Online was a differentiator for us, as we held a very strong position relative to bigger agencies.

We could help companies in the Internet space with offline advertising, and we could do the online advertising as well. We were one of the few that did both at the time. That was something unique about us that helped us get more business.

Carat may have preferred to acquire a company that had already become a big national player in the digital space, but the boom drove the valuations of these companies into crazy levels, and Carat wouldn't swallow the prices.

It so happened that while they were looking around, we were building our online business and it didn't go unnoticed that we won the RadioShack account. It also didn't hurt that as a result of our win, the RadioShack account was delivered on a silver platter to the rest of the Carat Organization. I mean, that account came to Carat without a review; $300 million dollars in TV and print. So Carat management was like, hmm, there seems to be something here. We absolutely do need a digital arm for the company, and you seem to be doing that. Why don't you write a business plan and we'll invest in it?

So we wrote a business plan. They made the decision to invest in Carat Interactive, and we air-lifted about twenty-five staff out of the Newton offices into new, cool offices that were befitting a digital agency right in downtown Boston on Newbury Street. Of course right after we signed the lease the whole market came to a halt.

The CEO during that time at Aegis PLC, Doug Flynn, was something of a risk taker and had nerves of steel. He believed in this digital thing and was going to hang in there right through the lowest times of the .com bust. He had a lot of critics in doing that, but we were bound and determined to make him proud anyway. Even though the market wasn't what it was supposed to be, we had to find a way to make the business work.

The original plan was to launch an online media agency in the same model of Avenue A, the biggest online media agency at the time. But most of Carat's businesses were traditional accounts that were going to come along slowly in the digital space, so we couldn't rely on that business coming in quickly. Carat Interactive had to stand on its own two feet and be able to win accounts without our parent company, which meant we needed to be full service; we needed creative, we needed search engine marketing. Because online media budgets disappeared for a while in 2001 and early 2002, we needed to offer services where the majority of the executional budget came to the agency in fees, rather than just offering media where we could charge a small commission against media budgets.

We had to react very quickly to the marketplace when the .com bust happened. We were like the little engine that could. We still had the investment dollars from Aegis to sustain us through the really dark times, and during that period we connected with the community. We built the brand, aligned services, made a couple of acquisitions, because when the market changed we were able to be opportunistic and do some acquisitions that we wouldn't have otherwise been able to, for prices that Aegis was happy with. And we came out the other side of the bust a lot stronger and in a position to gain business and win. You probably remember when we acquired Freestyle. We were on an upswing at that point and that helped fuel the momentum.

First you'd purchased Lot21, then Freestyle.

Yep, the Lot21 acquisition was final at the end of 2001. We also purchased Vizium. You might recall Vizium, which was Alan Osetek and Manu Matthew. That was a brand that Aegis ended up keeping and they launched their alternative media brand as Vizium.

And then a year or a year and a half later, we acquired Freestyle in mid 2002. At that point we were winning accounts as a full-service digital agency, and it's interesting because online and traditional media were two completely different worlds. There was a community of digital marketing professionals, and a community of traditional media professionals, and those two worlds didn't come together very often.

Carat Interactive was well known in the digital space, whereas Carat itself really wasn't for a long time. So we built a brand on our own within this big company and the majority of our business was the accounts that we brought in as digital accounts. We spent a lot of time evangelizing the traditional accounts and trying to get them to accept, understand and adopt digital advertising. That probably didn't happen in a big way until around 2000, maybe 2004.

I remember Adidas, as an example. In the early days we would contact the Carat account lead on Adidas and say, you really should consider doing an online component for such and such a program. And they would say why don't you tell us what you would do with $300,000? So we would create a multi-faceted plan that offered different opportunities to engage and measure. And then they'd say, hmm, what would you do with $40,000? And we'd sigh and say, okay, we can do *some* things. And then they'd say, you know, it's really just not enough to make the effort. That happened so many times, but we finally had a breakthrough, which was really a watershed event for that account when they launched the "Impossible Is Nothing" campaign.

Originally there was no budget allocated for digital advertising and we had a big job convincing them to dedicate some cash to digital media for "Impossible Is Nothing." But it turned out incredibly well. We ran the video spot of Laila and Muhammad Ali boxing in a ring together. It was the most successful homepage video spot on Yahoo at the time, with approximately five million views and a couple million visits to the website. There was this reverberating effect, globally, all around the Adidas organization. The digital element of the campaign was considered such a success the U.S. Adidas person in charge of the program received a Global Marketing Award from their internal global marketing organization for innovation. All of a sudden Adidas wanted to incorporate digital into all of their marketing programs.

That was right around the same time that a lot of the traditional accounts started buying into digital media. That put Carat Interactive in a good position for campaign integration. There were so few examples of online/offline integration being done well that you could be proud just for having the digital people and the traditional people in the same room knowing what's going on, on both sides of the of the organization. In the best situations we would have programs where there was true strategic integration across the multiple touch points. Adidas became one of our best examples, but there were many others.

I'm curious if you think the business itself has gotten to a stage where most agencies or brands are truly doing a good job of integrating?

Most areas of media specialization are so "siloed" it can be very difficult to synchronize all campaign elements. Even in the best of situations with the best of intentions, it's difficult to do. Media tools are emerging, or being refined to make media integration easier, more possible. Campaign management tools that help measure and manage media buying in real time are creating single points of control, which not only makes integration easier, but it requires strategic oversight that understands and modulates spending across all the mediums.

I do think advertisers who really get it are starting to use TV and offline media as catalysts to create a social movement. We are seeing more and more incorporation of Facebook, Twitter, mobile applications and things like that, into offline advertising. So by combining mediums together advertisers are demonstrating the power of integration and the ability to create a much bigger effect.

It feels like the complexity of the business has created a situation where we require technology in order to manage all the different facets of marketing and therefore, the integration of online and offline is very dependent on technology. Is that accurate?

I think technology will continue to be a big key to integration. Data and technology will show us the returns on advertising, and help to identify how the best results can be achieved. It is a big challenge to consistently use data in the right way to achieve better advertising results. Just the human push to get people together, and have everyone understand what the various elements of the program are meant to do, is a huge effort. It's hard enough to even identify one person to write up the strategy, so everyone is singing from the same song sheet. I think that we have a new strategist emerging which is someone who has both media and creative planning skills; someone who has oversight to all elements of a communications strategy, and a decent understanding of the digital elements as well as the offline.

That's still very tricky in any situation because there is often confusion about who owns the strategy. Take Pepsi as an example. They have lots of agencies, and traditionally the agency that has always owned the communications strategy has been the TV agency or the creative agency. Pepsi has actually changed its process so any one of their agencies can submit an idea that can become the core communication strategy for a campaign. They don't necessarily write everyone else out of the script when they select a winning idea, but that becomes the lead idea and the lead agency. I personally think that's a great approach. It levels the playing field and allows the generation of more and better ideas.

Beyond the strategic overtones of where the business is headed, you see brands starting to use offline media to drive a social action online. Do you see that as a significant trend that's going to drive the business forward?

Definitely, Carat was talking about paid, owned and earned media from the time we conducted the "Never Ending Friending" study on creating ROI through social media. We coined the term "The Momentum Effect." You could create more value for your money if you could inspire people to carry your brand's message. But this wasn't necessarily easy to do. Creating a great thirty-second spot isn't easy either, even if you spend a million dollars shooting it. You've got those same kinds of bets going on in social media. People have to figure out how to package up the owned and earned media in ways that can be counted on to deliver, rather than making big creative investments that may or may not work.

I don't believe big brands can rely on just social or digital media alone to drive demand for their products. You can't get the impact with digital only. But you can make your budgets work a lot harder by making digital and social media core to advertising strategy.

As ever, an advertiser has to develop great and relevant messaging that will appeal to their audiences. Even more importantly, advertisers need to think of their messaging like a publisher thinks about content. If an advertiser's message is ever going to turn into earned media and get passed from consumer to consumer, it has to be entertaining, interesting, useful or some combination of those three things. If a brand's message offers some benefit to the viewer, then social and digital can extend the reach and longevity of the program that starts out as paid media. I think that's where much of the marketing battle will be won or lost in the future. As Antonio Lucio, the CMO of Visa recently said when addressing an ad:tech audience, "Recommendation is the new advertising." And consumer sharing is certainly a form of recommendation!

Over the last ten years, what has most surprised you about this business?

It never ceases to amaze me how long things take. If you had asked me in 2000, I would have said mobile marketing would be huge by now. I thought digital TV buying would've been in place at scale by now. I was projecting far into the future when I said these things would be established by 2005. And 2011, I thought by then for sure. I don't think anybody saw the whole social revolution coming. I never imagined what that would become. Whoever heard of Facebook? When did I sign up for Facebook, maybe 2007? It was a professional experiment. For a full year I was posting for the benefit of my professional colleagues to see how Facebook worked, and look at what that's become. I always knew the consumer was in control. I understood that there were blogs, and people were listening to each other more than they were to advertisers, caring about each others' opinions more than advertising messages, but I never thought it would turn the industry on its head, and that has definitely happened.

You're surprised mobile and digital TV didn't take off as quickly as expected, and I agree with you. That being said, we're talking about a span of less than ten years,

and they're probably still very fast growing mediums compared to what we're used to. When you look at traditional TV and print, the Internet exploding exponentially every single year, and now watching something like Facebook, which has fast become one of the biggest market capitalized companies in the world in a span of five years, maybe we've gotten impatient and greedy at the same time.

Maybe. I have to say that I really did predict the face of mobile would change based on the devices we carry. Whenever people pooh-poohed the idea of getting a message on their phone, my answer to that always was, well, today you think of it as a phone, but tomorrow it's going to feel more like a computer, a little mini TV, radio or, I don't know, all of those things together.

I paid a lot of attention to what the futurists predicted. I used to go to technology conferences and listen to what the analysts had to say about the "home of the future" and how technology would change our lives. The fact that digital has permeated our lives in all kinds of different ways doesn't surprise me at all. I really believe that's going to continue to change exponentially over the next decade; that it's going to be even bigger change than what we've had.

I read a great book written by my friend, Emily Green called, *Anywhere,* which predicts the mobile marketplace will dwarf the Internet by adding trillions to the world economy versus the billions brought by the Internet. And it's all going to come from an upgrade to the existing infrastructure: faster broadband, cheaper access, more wireless video, richer experiences over wireless devices. We are still in the early stages of mobile usage, and as it gets better mobile usage will become much more prevalent in our lives.

When you get on your computer what's the first site you end up at?

Email then Facebook, because that's my other email. Then I usually get my news feeds, so that can point me to any number of places where the news I'm interested comes from. I bounce around, in terms of what my media company du jour is, to get the news.

And if I were to ask you that same question ten years ago?

It probably would've not been digital. I was nowhere near the digital addict I am now. I would wait until I was at work before I looked at anything.

The way I start my mornings these days is definitely with email first, Facebook second, and mostly I read my RSS feeds third. But then I go to PearlJam.com, that's my fourth site of the day.

So you know your passion area.

It used to be my Yahoo page, but that was ten years ago. Before that it was probably my AOL homepage.

Maybe there will be some amalgamation – like a lot of people are into FlipBoard now – that puts everything into one spot.

CLOSING REMARKS

Sarah has been a thought leader and influencer in the business since it began. In addition to winning awards and recognition over the years, she exemplifies how one should handle oneself in business and is a role model for many people throughout the industry. What I took away from my interview with Sarah, as well as my time working under her at Carat, was to always believe in your ideas and pursue them through to the end. By doing so you will continue to learn and grow as a professional, and growth is what keeps you relevant in this business. No matter what role Sarah has taken in her companies she always is relevant to the business, which is no small feat.

CHAPTER 7

DOUG WEAVER

Doug Weaver is a highly regarded strategist and opinion leader in the world of online advertising. Over the past ten years he's worked with over 350 leading companies, including Yahoo!, *USA TODAY,* CBS Interactive, Dow Jones, WebMD, National Public Radio, ESPN, About.com and *The New York Times.*

Online marketing and sales people know him through many different venues. He's a frequent moderator, host and speaker at the iMedia Summit series, author of "The Drift," an online newsletter that reaches nearly 7,000 top industry executives, and he's trained thousands of Internet salespeople through both public and private sales workshops.

After a fifteen-year career in print advertising sales with companies like Hearst and Condé Nast, Doug became the advertising director for *Wired Magazine* in

1994 and sold some of the web's first ads on the company's *HotWired* site. He then served as VP of sales for Firefly Network, a pioneering company in personalization, targeting and community. Doug was elected to the board of directors for the Internet (now Interactive) Advertising Bureau and managed the development of both the IAB Road Show (the organization's main presentation to marketers) and the IAB Professional Development Series. In 1999 he received the first IAB Service Award for commitment and contribution to the industry.

Doug Weaver, you've been involved since the very beginning of the Internet ad business. You were involved in those first days with *HotWired*. Talk a little about those days.

Well, just to put a fine point on things, I would say I've been around since the very beginning of the *web* ad business. The reason I clarify that is because there was definitely previous activity around sponsorship deals and things like that at the closed BBS systems: AOL, CompuServe and Prodigy. However, the real beginning of the advertising business came in October of 1994 with the launch of *HotWired,* which was *Wired Magazine*'s digital publication. It wasn't really a digital version of the magazine. It was a unique digital product under the Wired brand and was the very first website to accept advertising.

What brought you into the web business? What was intriguing about it from the very beginning?

I was drawn in not by the web ad business per se, but by *Wired Magazine* and the promise of the digital revolution.

That sounds a little hackneyed now but it really was quite compelling.

I was recruited. I was working for Condé Nast many years ago as a career magazine seller, and out of a combination of curiosity, ambition and self-interest, I decided to go to work for *Wired Magazine.* I was employee number one in New York for them and probably employee number thirty in the company. I took a leap. It really was a magazine job and while I was filling out my paperwork to be their advertising director and open their New York office, they said, "Oh, by the way, you are going to sell ads on our website." I said, "Great! What's a website?"

I backed into it and the tail ended up wagging the dog, and that really led me into the digital ad business in a big way. I never looked back.

When you started bringing those out to the clients, what was the reaction?

It was interesting because the way that we priced the ads on the website, it really was finger in the wind. This was before the invention of the first ad server; before the invention of the first analytics program. So there was no way to count anything.

We would call on accounts like Volvo and Club Med and AT&T, MCI, and these were all fairly tech-savvy customers for their day. We would say, you should advertise on our website. You should be here and take out one of these sponsorships. But at the end of the day they would ask, what would we get for our money? We would say, with a straight face, you get a month. We will put your banner ad up on the site and you will be the sponsor of the 'Digital Alchemy' section, or 'On the Road' or

'Signal' or some other section of the site. It will go up on the first of the month and it will come down on the last day of the month. They said, great, what would that cost us? We said $15,000. How did we come up with that? That was what it cost to run a page in a magazine at the time, so we were really just putting a finger in the wind on pricing.

You have any idea what the traffic was back then?
Zero, we have zero idea and there was probably pretty close to zero traffic. The reason why they all did it was the cool factor and also the opportunity to learn, and be perceived as part of that community. So *Wired* and everything digital at the time was just white-hot and we benefited from that.

Where *Wired* later struggled was that they had essentially built a model based on the cool factor and then had to wade into the land of accountability later on and had a tough time with that.

How did that part of the business progress and how was your experience with it?
It was absolutely amazing. We were always in the business of selling ads in the magazine and also selling ads on the website. So the next couple of months, I would say my job as advertising director for Wired Ventures and the de facto spokesman for *HotWired* in the East was to be on just about every panel that took place about anything digital or web over the course of the next six months. Everybody wanted to hear what we were doing. We had the playing field to ourselves for quite a while because it

was going to be about another four or five months before Yahoo launched. It was going to be another year and a half before the first commercial ad server came to be. The Netscape IPO happened about a month after the launch of *HotWired.*

We were the big fish in the pond for a little while and for the sake of our ego, it was a great place to be. I am not sure how much real science was being done but there was an awful lot of evangelism.

You mentioned Wired Ventures because it had *HotWired,* but then they expanded pretty quickly and had other properties to work with, right?

Yeah. So Wired Ventures, Jane Metcalfe and Louis Rossetto, the founders of *Wired*, had a pretty grand vision for it to be a multimedia company. In fairly quick succession they launched Wired Books and published three or four book titles. *HotWired* was out there. There was even a foray into Wired television going on at the time in the CNET model of a combined web and TV company. It was pretty early stuff.

Louis Rossetto just recently did a pretty amazing retrospective out in San Francisco and gave some great history on just how many different irons they tried to put in the fire. It was quite an ambitious company.

They started putting more digital assets together like HotBot and some others.

Yes, exactly. Initially there was a real desire on their part to be the authoritative editorial voice of the web. Of course, as you know the web thrives because the web is unruly.

They quickly realized that the more we try to control this, the more we are going to be an island in the sea in the middle of this big web, so they decided they wanted to get into the search business, hence the launch of HotBot. At that point, InfoSeek and Yahoo and some of the other players just had too much of a head start, and they never really got the traction with the HotBot product.

I remember buying on HotBot for a while but it was eclipsed relatively quickly.

It was fascinating because *Wired* really helped to create and incubate the environment, whereby some of the massive IPOs of Netscape and some other players, but they themselves did not really benefit from it. At least not to the extent that one would think they might have.

If you could speak to yourself back then, what advice would you have given yourself?

What I would probably say is number one, be really ambitious, to the point of being unreasonable. Because I think that part of the business side of Wired Ventures, many of us were always trying to conform the message and the vision and the ideas that were being talked about in the magazine, trying to sanitize them and moderate them for the appetites of the existing advertising community. That was probably the wrong thing to do. Instead we should have been incredibly ambitious and thought about how we could completely revolutionize and reinvent advertising; that was the mission Google ultimately fulfilled years later. I would challenge myself to think bigger thoughts, re-imagine how any of it can be. Ultimately, that was the outcome, or I should say that *will* be the outcome.

Do you think some of the decisions made back then, how the advertising should be displayed, tracked, measured, reported, had any lasting negative impacts? Do you think that we overcame those in a good enough time, in a good enough fashion so that the business was able to continue to grow quickly?

No, I don't think so. We have been living under the weight of many of those decisions for many, many years. For starters, we carried into this era a lot of assumptions that online was a medium just like print or broadcast was a medium, or cable was a medium. Those were bad assumptions. I don't think of the Internet today as a medium. I think of the Internet as the grid into which everything else plugs.

So the Internet ought to be the trellis on which all the other vines grow. That is number one. Number two, the idea that the role of advertising was to somehow be a transportation vehicle to sort of push people off to web-sites – fifteen, seventeen years later we are still living with that and it is an absolutely dead idea.

Here we are in a consumer-driven medium that is all about the consumer exercising their will and being in charge and holding the mouse, yet we are constantly try-ing to push them to the locations where we want them to be. It is bad business, bad science.

It is amazing to think about what the web, and business today, would have been like if it had started as a social medium.

I actually spoke about that in a speech last year at iMedia. I said when Tim Berners-Lee invented hypertext and effectively created the web, for the first couple of years of its existence the web was exactly that, a social medium. Pretty much everybody who was on there was part of a fairly closed community of scientists and intellectuals and artists and writers and they all knew each other. They commented on each other's stuff and traded links to each other's work and so forth. It was pretty amazing.

In fact, in the earliest days of the web there was very little thought among marketers and agency people that the web would ever be anything with regard to advertising. It was seen as too esoteric and too strange. It was really after the Netscape IPO that everything changed. Then it became a huge land grab and went from being the web of people to the web of pages. Everybody started creating these little digital cities and suddenly we had to try to populate them and get people to go to these dumb websites that we built.

That became the beginning of the decline of the web's potential. What is exciting to me about the whole social era of the web is that it's kind of like, back to the future. It is the return to the Web of People. That is hugely exciting.

You keep referring back to Netscape and the IPO of Netscape as a watershed moment.   In the '90s, what were some other watershed moments?

The launch of Yahoo and them coming into their own was pretty huge. InfoSeek, a brand that was recently sold for scrap for two thousand dollars, was a pretty big player before Disney bought them. They launched essentially the first pay per click model and I think that ushered in an era. The size of the payout to Yahoo, the size of the payout to Netscape, the land rush mentality and then combine that with the quick hit, easy money thinking behind InfoSeek, suddenly you develop all the ingredients for tulipmania. Suddenly you had people starting to come into the space with the expectation that we are all going to have a payday, we are all going to get rich, and we began to lose sight of building at that point.

What about once we go past the 2000s – the Internet bubble bursting and then the renaissance of the business – what were some watershed moments of that period of time?

Well, I am not going to answer that question directly now but I may back into it. Here is a tidy way to think about it. A good friend of mine, Charlie Thomas likes to say that it breaks nicely into three phrases.

The time from 1994 until about 2000 and the first Internet bubble was the age of the website. It was all about people building websites, huge land grab. It was the construction boom of the web, and then we had our first chastening moment.

We had the first meltdown and obviously the September 11 aftermath put a big chill in everything. At that point the business redefined itself and said, alright, what we need to do is make a business out of this. We need to build the infrastructure for advertising and messaging and figure out a way to get the right ad in front of the right person at the right time, and start to think about audiences and so forth. That period lasted another seven years, right up until about 2008. Then we had our next meltdown.

We had our next major economic event. Those have a cleansing and rejiggering effect on our business. It causes everybody to sit back and take stock of who they are and what they are doing. We always come out of those events differently than we went in. So the next phase, the one we are in right now, is this marketing era. It is the idea that we have spent all this time and money and effort figuring out how to put an ad in front of a consumer. But that is not all there is. That is not even most of what there is. If you look at the Internet, the best we can say about it as an advertising medium is that it is okay. It is pretty good. The creative is pretty good, the measurement is pretty good. The old adage, an Internet ad is never going to make anybody cry, is probably true. But if you think about it as a marketing medium it absolutely *rocks*.

Now the challenge is really going to brands and embracing all the marketing tasks they have in front of them: customer relationship management, publicity, the overall audience development, the research along with all of the communication elements. And really embracing the whole thing with them, that is really exciting. That is the era we are in now.

You're calling out that there are three distinct periods of the web marked or bookended by major economic activity. One is the bubble bursting, another is the recession. You're also saying the first stage of the web was as much about publishing as anything else ad-driven and growth-driven through the penetration of technology. The second area is intangible. There is some advertising, some publishing; it's a bit of a mix. But the third period is really

about marketing and the growth of social as a tool for consumers, and CRM as a tool for businesses allowing the whole infrastructure to work better. Is that right?

Yes. If you play that out further you would say all the work that is being done right now in the area of hyper targeting and geo location targeting of advertising and behavioral targeting, we are trying to sharpen the razor just that much further. Many people think it is all going to be about more targeting. Well, I happen to think more targeting might actually just be the last gasps of the era that is fading away.

You would go on to say that the ad business has not been as successful as the marketing business is going to be.

Exactly, look at all the things that are happening out in the marketplace. The agency business is struggling to define itself in this era. They are still trying to retrofit the old models of payment, accountability, services and business models. They are trying to make that fit for a business that is much more expansive. You have publishers, agencies and marketers all switching roles. I do not mean to sound like Bob Garfield here but it is a pretty chaotic, wide-open environment that we are going into now.

You do a really good job and I have told you many times that I think the writing you do is spot on, insightful and extremely well-written. In order to be able to write the way you write and formulate the opinions, you have to stay on top of a lot of different things. This business changes so quickly, there are so many things to read about and stay "in the know" on. How do you stay on top of all the changes in the business?

The short answer is that I use the customer that is most vital to me as my filter. Whether you are navigating an agency business or a service business like mine, or any other business in this environment, the thing you have to be good about is understanding who you serve. In my case it is pretty simple; the people I serve are the EVPs and SVPs of advertising or media sales, the chief revenue officers at the publishers. I certainly read a lot of stuff, but that's the thing I get the most out of.

I talk to them. I hear what is happening in their worlds, where their businesses are struggling and where they are succeeding and what customers are asking them for and so forth. That becomes a really important filter for me. It helps me to develop a sense of what is real and what is important versus what is background noise. What it has helped me do frankly is also turn down the volume around some of the things that are just vastly over-hyped in our business. I hear constantly, everyone is talking about DSPs and real time bidding and on and on and on, and I just wonder why that is what we are excited about? Shaving another eighth of a point off the cost, or adding another eighth of the point to the click right, is that going to get us there?

I agree with you on that one. I feel many of those people are spending a lot of time trying to define the difference between splitting hairs.

Exactly, one of the key problems with our business has been that it has gotten very self-referential. It is almost like the pundit on CNN and MSNBC and Fox News, all watching each other's shows and commenting on what each other say. A lot of the world doesn't care about any of that.

There is a lot of news being made, but there are many just talking about the news.

Talking about how other people are talking about the news. You know what I try to do? I try as often as possible to deflate things and boil them down to their core elements and give people who read what I write some actionable things that they can do. Give them an actual perspective, clarity around the issues as much as I can offer it, and present it as what it is. It is my point of view. It is my distillation and my take on what I see happening out in the marketplace and fortunately, I think many people have found it valuable.

How often do you find yourself in a discussion with someone debating a point of view that you put forth and trying to see what the other point of view is?

I wrote a paper about four years ago called "The Oreo Doctrine," which basically said our business is going to fall down into two different spheres of influence. There is going to be the transactional side, all about right ad, right person, and right time – essentially the plumbing side of our business, which will be dominated by a handful of quants and scientists. Then there will be this marketing side, which will be the business consulting, problem solving and solution-orientated side of the business. That would be really a very separate practice.

What has been interesting is that I have heard from many people on the quant side come back to me and say, whether someone from X+1 or a number of different technology companies, "Yeah, we know that you are pretty down on our side of the business and you don't really believe in the technology side of the business."

But that's not my point of view at all. I don't look at it as an either/or kind of a world. I don't say that one is better than the other, only that they are different and there is going to be a place for both of them. It is very often just elaborating on that point of view and that vision for the business, and people come to understand that we are not all that far apart.

I have no idea whether that was lucid or if I just confused the issue even more.

No, it makes sense. There are two sides of a coin for a business. There are people who are really good at one side or the other. Very few are good at both. It takes a special kind of brain and a special kind of mind to get into the quant's side of the business, and I think it takes a special kind of mind and person to be on the marketing side of the business. I do not think there is a lot of overlap, they can co-exist quite peacefully.

If I were running a major publisher or agency or brand these days, the way I would be looking at it would be, okay, so how can technology help me save many creative man-hours? How can technology take a lot of the transactional stuff out of my way so that I can invest my human capital more meaningfully to allow people to really use their brains, talents and souls in creating value? One definitely feeds the other.

I interviewed someone recently who is struggling to answer that same question. They are trying to find ways to use technology to commoditize half their business so they can focus on the creativity and the solution-oriented side of the business. And that's how they want to differentiate themselves going forward.

Pretty good strategy.

On a more personal side, what still gets you excited about this business?

Every day! What frustrates is that I look around the business and I see so many people who do not realize what they are in the middle of. I see people whose view of what we are doing is so narrow that they do not realize this is like the printing press. This is like fire, it is that big.

What excites me about the business is that we are in a cycle of permanent dynamism. This is never going to stop changing. This is never going to settle down. It is never going to become a mature marketplace. The nature of digital technology says that as we invent we speed the pace of invention. You have new players, new ideas and new companies coming into the mix every day. I see this from a standpoint of, wow, I lived in the world of analog media and I sold magazine ads and was part of that world for a number of years. How lucky am I that I get to be a part of all this and have a front row seat for it! If you can't get excited about what is going on in this business, then I think some perspective is in order.

The innovation and refreshment of the business is what gets you excited the most.

If you go back just a few years people were saying, break up MySpace! They are going to dominate things. Now MySpace is an afterthought. Now people are saying Facebook is just a juggernaut and Facebook is going to be the next great company, and maybe they will be. Maybe they already are to some degree.

If you go back about twenty years, the single biggest brand in computing was Commodore. If you go back fifteen years, the dominant player in search that no one would ever overtake was InfoSeek, followed shortly thereafter by AltaVista.

Neither of which exist anymore.
We are sitting on top of this era of absolutely massive invention. To answer your question even more succinctly, this marketing era that we are in now is particularly interesting because we are seeing the vestiges of the advertising business finally start to fall away and we are being challenged to be digital anthropologists. We are challenged to say, let us follow the consumer. Let us see how they are really living their lives, how are they using all these digital tools to inform themselves, entertain themselves, communicate, share and shop and everything else.

Then let us figure out how we create value for brands, for media brands and retail brands. How do we create value within that life that they are living? So it is no longer about, hey, they are going to come to our website and we are going to show them an ad; but rather, they are going to live their life online, or at least a substantial part of it, and it is going to be there with them. How do we create marketing value in new ways that fits within that lifestyle? That is a pretty cool theme.

You said that we are moving into this marketing stage of the web and the shackles of advertising are falling off the web. If I were to fast-forward, do you think that paid advertising is going to be an essential part of the web, or do you think it will be gone?

If you take the word 'advertising' out and you put in the term 'marketing,' 'paid marketing,' I think it will be a huge part of the web. The shape of advertising itself is going to change pretty dramatically. I just don't think it could survive using the advertising ethos of the 1960s and '70s, which is I have a product to sell, I have a message to put in front of you to make you buy that product, here it is. Whether that comes in the form of a banner, a fifteen-second pre-roll spot or what have you. I think that part of it has to atrophy and fall away.

Are Digitas and Turner going to be working together in some ways to create value for Unilever? Yes, but I don't think anybody right now has any clue what that will look like ten years from now.

Seventeen years into a business and we don't know what it is going to look like in ten years. That makes it a lot of fun. That is in line with what you were saying about what gets you excited about this business? I think that is a big part of it.

One of the things that I have been known to say over the years is, the only people that really worry me are the ones that think they have it all figured out, like, this is *the* model. It may well be the model that will get you through this economic cycle and the VC community, or the banks might buy into and it might make you rich. I think the smartest people in the world, the smartest in business – Bill Gates, Mark Zuckerberg, Sergey and Larry over at Google – are constantly reinventing their businesses. They are constantly challenging themselves. Reinvention is a core part of their corporate identity.

So I look at these tiny players in technology or with different media, models and so forth and I see them acting as though their business model or value proposition is handed down by Moses on Mount Sinai. I am thinking, guys you have to figure out some flexibility here.

I agree.
The last thing I would like to say is I really relish the idea, the opportunity to be a part of the intellectual engine for this business; as small as my part of it is. The kind of thing we are doing right here, talking about the future gets me excited all over again.

CLOSING REMARKS

Doug Weaver is one of the most influential people in this business, and he continues to do it with a smile and a passion that I rarely see anywhere else. He mentors sales people for a living and some of these people emerge as stars in the business. He has provided me with some of the most important thought starters of my career, and has helped me to become the professional that I am.

I met Doug in my very first year in this business when I was a young, green, somewhat egotistical media planner. He was a patient man, putting up with my passion disguised as authority, and he has always allowed me the honor of his time and his consultation when I was faced with questions that I didn't know how to answer. I hope you see from his interview the intelligence and the perspective that he brings to this business, and are able to take away from it a fraction of what I have. Doug is the definition of a gentleman and a scholar, and I thank him for being involved in this book.

CHAPTER 8

JOE MANDESE

Joe Mandese is editor-in-chief of *MediaPost* and routinely covers the advertising and marketing industry with a keen eye and a knowledgeable point of view. Joe has been covering the business with *MediaPost* since 2003, and prior to that was Media Editor for *Advertising Age,* another industry must-read. Joe has sat down to discuss the trends and vision shaping the industry with some of the most influential people in our industry, and his input has surely helped shape the direction that many successful businesses have taken. His role at *MediaPost* has also led to conferences and industry research that many people consider the standard. I was lucky to have had the chance to sit and chat with him on his perspective on the business.

Joe Mandese, when did you first start covering the Internet ad business?

It was probably before the Internet, because remember, it's a continuum. I'm a trade journalist who covers media and at some point, the Internet became meaningful media. I've always looked at it from the point of view of an outsider chronicling something. I would never consider myself an insider. I never drank the Kool-Aid. I always tried to stay emotionless and detached. I'll give you a little history on it, because it might give some perspective on how the trade publications covered the development of the Internet.

I was always somewhere in between the digerati and the media traditionalists, because I think you have to keep an integral view of the media. I first started covering interactive media in the late '80s, but it really took off toward the early '90s when some of the agencies developed interactive media practices. The view was, it's neat, we can interact with it, there are creative possibilities but we don't know what to do with it.

At the same time, you had these big media companies talking about creating interactive media platforms, whether it was the Warner Amex's seminal QUBE system in Columbus, Ohio or later when Time Warner launched its Full Service Network in Orlando. Then the telcos came into the business. They all looked at it from the point of view of walled garden, closed infrastructures and TV systems that would be interactive and create all this commerce and content interaction with consumers. But they never became anything more than test beds. Big advertisers and agencies would get involved and rarely put any real

money into it, but they would test interactive advertisement and content.

Then, in the early '90s there were some agencies that
were experimenting with other platforms. Ironically,
they were really CD-ROMs, or interactive kiosks. And
in my opinion, it was really the interactive kiosks that
started to become the beginning of the mindset of how
agencies thought about what would become online
and Internet advertising. The best example of that, I
think, was Martin Nisenholtz who had been at Ogilvy &
Mather. He's the head of *Times Digital* now. Back then
he was playing with these little kiosks trying to figure
out how you communicate in an interactive advertising
environment.

The thing about kiosks is they were in close proximity
to things. In the beginning I don't think agencies knew
what to do with it. So Martin was in this little annex
of Ogilvy & Mather, downtown on Park Avenue South,
in the basement cobbling things together. His idea and
vision was if we can figure out how to create an interaction with the consumer around advertising it's a whole
new ballgame. That started to progress through the
early '90s, then came online services, like CompuServe,
Delphi, Prodigy and ultimately AOL. I'm not sure when
Madison Avenue jumped on. I was at *Ad Age* at the time.
We became an early content contributor to Prodigy.

I became actively involved in programming it, creating content for it. At first it really sucked. It was very
flat text and took twenty minutes for a simple graphic to
load line-by-line through these modems. But you could
start to feel the idea of it, like, wow, we can instantly
transmit content to people. We came at it from a trade

perspective, but the idea was there and I did think the trade was a good barometer for what we'd ultimately have with consumers. Certainly the tech trade titles were the earliest adopters. To a certain degree, the advertising trade press, too.

We started with fax-based newsletters because that was the technology of the time. A lot of individuals started to get fax machines and we started doing daily faxes. That evolved into early commercial online services. The rest is history, but from my perspective there was a progression going on. Along came this thing called Mosaic and the graphical interface that was the true beginning of the World Wide Web. All of a sudden you saw a whole new way of conveying content that was much more intuitive.

I'm not sure where the real rallying cry happened but I think most people would attribute it to the famous speech that Ed Artzt, the chairman and CEO of Proctor & Gamble at the time gave. I think it was a 4A's conference, and most people would say it was his rallying cry that got Madison Avenue to jump on the Internet. And then someone, I think former 4A's President, Burtch Drake sent me Artzt's original speech, and he never actually used the word "Internet," which is funny because even I quoted him on it over time. But the truth is he gave this rallying cry that, basically, advertising media was going interactive.

His cry got agencies to start thinking about it in a big way. And the industry started forming all these committees and groups like CASIE. The FAST Summit, and all these initiatives to accelerate the way advertisers and agencies thought about interactive media and particularly online media, started creating protocols and guidelines, standards and best practices, around how to convey all this stuff. It was a very exciting time because nobody knew what to do with it, but there was a lot of energy there. It was interesting to watch from the outside. Some agencies ran with it and made it a centerpiece of what they wanted to do. Others kept it in those basements. I remember hearing David Verklin, at Hal Riney & Partners at the time, talk about it at a conference, and he articulated really well. He said, depending on the agency you talk to, they were pushing it into other practices.

They didn't know what to do with it. Some were pushing it into what would be publishing groups – magazine buying groups or content groups in agencies. In the case of Hal Riney, at that time they looked at it as a form of brochureware – catalogs and collateral pieces. So it made sense to place it in the catalog unit. In Hal Riney, that was the unit which was responsible for developing online and Internet advertising. The best examples I saw of it were actually what I would've called boring units in agencies. They were B2B shops or industrial agencies like Poppe Tyson, which was a division of Bozell. Poppe Tyson was famous because it incubated DoubleClick. People there got really excited about this because they understood the one-to-one ability of this medium. From a B2B or industrial market point of view it was very powerful because you could finely target and have more efficient communication. It could replace direct selling in a more efficient way. And you saw this going on in other agencies, too.

I think Freeman & Associates in Boston, where Sarah Fay came from, ultimately got acquired by Aegis. They were B2B groups and tech-focused shops really. They started to take root. Their successes started to build on other successes. They ultimately got acquired or absorbed into bigger agency holding companies. That's where, in my opinion, the practice started. It was still coming from a very prosaic point of view. I don't think there was really an understanding of what creative messaging was yet. It was just experimentation, trial, trying to do things. At about that time I was at *Advertising Age*, and it was really interesting to watch.

Trade publications, especially *Ad Age*, set the tone and the agenda for the industry to a certain extent based on what they covered. I was a media editor and was covering interactive media, writing about Martin Nisenholtz and everything. There was some switch that got flipped at some point at *Advertising Age* where the publishers and my editors really didn't want to write about anything else except the Internet. We were obsessing about it.

There were issues at *Ad Age* where it would've been hard to find a story if it didn't have something to do with the Internet, and this is back in '96. It was interesting to watch how the trades continued to cover it. And that contributed to this huge buildup of Wall Street capitalization and financing, and a lot of the money was from these .com brands.

We all know what happened from there, the .com bust. It's important to know it wasn't just irrational exuberance, though it is certainly part of what happened. There were other things going on that I think people forget about. Part of the buildup to 2000 also was a function of Y2K, because there were a lot of incremental budgets created in corporations, specifically to upgrade their technology. A lot of that money did get diverted into online and digital media development, so there was a lot of money flowing at that time for something that had nothing to do with the Internet. It was really around Y2K.

When Y2K ended, when that entire infrastructure got rebuilt people had new computers, new systems. It actually created a vacuum in the market. Part of what happened with the .com crash was the disappearance of a lot of incremental tech spending. It was this irrational exuberance bubble that busted on Wall Street; these ridiculous multiples on .com businesses that had nothing more in them than a domain name, some content or commerce concept, and traffic counts. That was the whole goal: make consumers aware of it. Push into this thing and the rest will follow. It was a very heady time.

But it started to unravel. Then, of course, the economic recession of 2001 didn't help matters. But that's when I, as a journalist, started flipping the other way. I said, wait a minute, you guys are overreacting in the opposite direction now. Just because this stuff had a hiccup doesn't mean it's not really important. It is going to change everything. So it was about that time that there was a lot of good thinking going on in some of the big agency holding companies. That's when the real first class of the digital native agency started to be created and they were entrepreneurs.

A lot of them were renegades who left Madison Avenue agencies and created their own shops specifically to create Internet advertising, and were more creative minded. At that time you started to see true online advertising emerge. It was clunky display ads, banner ads at first. Not a lot of rich media, very static. But people got the notion that this medium could generate a lot of eyeballs. That was a classic way of thinking about advertisements but it didn't really unlock the underlying value of interactive media. It was just putting ads alongside where people happened to be looking at stuff. Over time those banner ads got richer, and now they're in-banner video. Soon they're going to be high-definition video.

There was an amazing concept that I think is really important, told to me by Ira Carlin, who was media director of McCann-Erickson before they unbundled their media services. He was also running one of the first interactive agencies in a holding company called ThunderHouse, which was a unit of Interpublic. He had this great diagram that showed the Internet. It was a spoke-and-wheel diagram that had all these things in the wheel: commerce, content, interactivity information, customer service support. The center of that wheel was the Internet, and Carlin's view was that the Internet could be anything. It's just a matter of what you want to post in there.

I'm going to digress to one earlier anecdote. I think it's an important one to remember because it relates to what Ira was saying. When Ed Artzt did his rallying cry, the industry reacted. At the end of that year there was a big summit in New York, which was the beginning of the initiative. They had this one-day conference in New York at some big theater and with lots of presentations about what the committees were doing to create standards. At the end of the day they had a press conference with Ed Artzt who sparked the whole thing. There were a bunch of reporters in the room and they were asking him, "So now that we know what this Internet thing is, what is P&G going to do with it? How are they going to transform it to advertising?" And what Artzt said really kind of blew my mind. He said, "We see this as a better way to interact with customers. I see it as a way to accelerate customer support. It's a better form of an 800 number." It was interesting because he sparked Madison Avenue to start thinking about making this investment, but didn't really see it as an advertising medium.

At that time the perspective was more prosaic, which was that this thing would give you an interactive feedback loop with your customers. Today if you look at what a lot of big companies are using the Internet for they're using it to monitor what their customers are saying about their brands and then reacting to it, it has come full-circle. Going back to Ira Carlin's spoke-and-wheel chart, for me it said if the Internet could be anything, what is it? It's really just a giant bulletin board that you could post things on. You can post any kind of content up on it, and somebody else with a computer browser can come along and grab it down. Then it's just a matter of how good the browser is, how good the bandwidth and the content.

In the beginning the problem was that the bandwidth wasn't there. The technology infrastructure wasn't there. People had ideas for doing things that they couldn't execute. What Ira said to me back then, which I didn't fully grasp until today, was that the Internet was not designed to do a lot of things everybody says they want to do with it. But it will get there. They will retrofit it. It was not the right system or architecture to build what people wanted. But there were critical masses forming around it, and things like digital compression and increases in computer power, because of Moore's Law and all those other things like improvements in screen technology and fidelity, would ultimately allow you to convey any kind of content across the Internet. The funny thing is we're there now. Cloud companies like Amazon and Akamai have actually built that out. And now devices are getting better and more seamless. It's fun to come from that original point and see what's possible now. In a way it's varied because now people have a blank canvas. They can really do anything. The trick now is ideation, just having great ideas.

Those were the major milestones I look at. I was always on the outside looking in as a journalist. I've never made an ad, never created marketing or an advertising business plan or strategy. I write about them. But what's interesting is that we journalists have an objective perspective.

When I left *Ad Age* I worked for a consultant for a while, Jack Myers. We were involved in some early Internet strategies. Then I went into Inside.com, and *Brill's Content* and PriMedia, and then I came to *MediaPost*. And that was actually a really important thing for me because *MediaPost* was the first ad trade publication created to publish on the Internet. It forced me to focus on the Internet a little too narrowly at first. The Internet needed focus, but it needed to be looked at in the broader concept of marketing and media.

One thing we did back then, we started creating channels for using information. We had our digitally focused publications, like the Online Spin Board and *MediaDailyNews,* which was mainly about online and digital media. Then we spun a lot of that off into *Online*

Media Daily, and focused *MediaDailyNews* on the over-all marketplace. I thought it was really important to look at it from all the silos. If you fast-forward to today *MediaPost* publishes more than fifty publications daily and all focused on different things.

What's important is the Internet is all of these things. We don't get heavily into commerce, which is an important part of the Internet because we're focus-ing on advertising and media communication. What I like about the *MediaPost* approach is that we get to look across all these things and see it from different vantage points of the industry. That's really impor-tant to me. I went from thinking the Internet is just a piece of this bigger puzzle, to the idea that it actu-ally had some of everything. I started to contradict my own thinking, and part of that is simply critical mass. When enough people are doing something it supplants all other logic.

I want to go back to search because it is important. It was my boss, *MediaPost* founder, Ken Fadner who articu-lated this best for me early on and made me understand it. That the real power of Google was they created an organ-izing principle around search. If you look in Google's mission statement, it doesn't say anything about search advertising. The mission statement is that they want to manage the world's information and use technology to do it better. Search was the mechanism for doing it. The creation of AdWords, and creating a market struc-ture so that advertisers could go in and create a market around buying key words, terms, and consumer content, created a financial market that supported the creation of better search capabilities for consumers. It was the perfect win-win. It wasn't intrusive to the consumer and it allowed them to have a better navigation experience.

Search was the first real financial model for the Internet. It created a boom for growing the Internet. I do think it took a long time for brands to understand how to use search. I also think it took a long time for them to learn how to use conventional forms of advertising communication online. With banner ads and click-through rates it took awhile for the industry to come along with Attribution Analysis, to understand what led up to that point. We're still working through all of that, but now with bandwidth improving, more rich media experiences and video coming into play, I think the Internet has become similar to traditional media in terms of brand communication. But it still hasn't been fully tapped.

This notion of interaction, co-authoring, co-storytelling and listening to the consumer is really hard to do, and it's exciting to follow. What's going on now with social media is as big an inflection point for Madison Avenue as what took place in the mid '90s, with Ed Artzt's rallying cry and the overreaction of the industry. It's the same thing. I'm starting to hear from a lot of agencies that they don't really understand what to do with social media yet. They don't understand the implications of it, but they know it's going to change everything.

The agencies that develop the models, going forward, will win the day, or else they'll be out of the game. What you're seeing now with some big agency holding companies is they're trying to get their minds around social. There are some smaller specialty agencies coming up, and more importantly, some new entities that you wouldn't even call agencies. Platforms or service providers are creating the infrastructure that is allowing brands, marketers and agencies to interact with consumers on social media platforms. It's a very exciting time because the script has yet to be written. If you believe all the hype, social is going to be the game-changer, and it is the way people are going to communicate going forward.

I'll give you one last personal anecdote about *MediaPost* because I also think it's instructive. We have a really good technology team for a trade publisher. We're not Microsoft or Yahoo, but we do a pretty good job. Our president, Jeff Loechner who is a visionary, built everything about *MediaPost*. The whole industry is moving around in a new direction and it's this new technology or platform that's going to change everything. Think about the way we publish, primarily through pushing email and newsletters to registered users or creating pages for people to browse on or search for. Well, about five years ago, Jeff said, "This new thing has come along that's going to change everything. It's called RSS, or Really Simple Syndication. Everything's going RSS. That's how everybody's going to get everything." And the truth is RSS is a pretty amazing technology.

I'm not sure why it hasn't caught on in a bigger way. It is a very important technology that is fueling, informing and distributing content. There are things that people don't even understand about RSS, but they're getting it that way, whether it's through an ad or something else. The point is that Jeff would change the way we think about what we do every eighteen months or so. First it was email and search then RSS, then blogging took off. Everybody had a blog. The consumers were now the content creators.

It was user-generated content and a lot of publishing platforms are better than the CMS systems that the biggest companies have and even *MediaPost* use. Basically, we've had five or six of those inflection points and one of them, most recently, was social media or Twitter – the world of the microblogging. Right now it's probably Facebook, and why we have to adapt and shape our system around this infrastructure to do a better job. In truth, all these things are important. But the other truth is, eighteen months from now it will be something else that will become equally as important. Technology progression is never going to stop. It's always going to change.

A while back we were trying to come up for the theme for our next OMMA conference, and struggling to figure out what the big theme was in our business. OMMA is an acronym for Online Marketing, Media and Advertising, but I think it's important to realize that it's not just online anymore. One idea we had was to take the OMMA logo and put a slash through the "O"– make a statement – because the Internet is just a way of talking about a site or a group of platforms that people use to interact with, and provide data and information and experience it. Part of it is online, part is mobile, part is social; a lot of it is through what would now be called web-browser-based content. Some of it is things I don't quite understand myself yet. I know that eighteen months from now we're going to be calling it something else. I'm trying to put words around what these companies like Spongecell and Pictela do. They don't even know what to call it. If you spend time talking to Pictela co-founder, Matt Straz and walk through their pitch, they're calling it stuff that I believe is wrong. They call it a "brand content platform." Branded content is a whole other thing.

What they really are is this new pipeline, this new way of displaying information in a very rich way, very dynamic way. I think you're going to see this everywhere. Every piece of real estate, whether it's a person's hand-held screen, their iPad, their browser-based computer, their TV, their over-the-top Netflix account through their wireless network into what we used to call a TV, whatever it is.

A really smart guy, Cory Treffiletti, once showed me a nifty chart that showed future penetration curves for digital media. It was created by Carat about five or six years ago and showed the penetration of digital to all media. I liked it because it recognized that all media was becoming digital. There were different curves, but even magazines and newspapers and Yellow Pages, and all these things we think of as being tactile, text-based media, were becoming digital. If you look at where we are now in 2011, a lot of them are on those curves. Of course new digital media have come along, I mean, there wasn't even a mobile line in that curve.

What makes me personally excited about covering it is that I'm always learning. I am doing my own personal venture right now. It's not in trade publishing. It is in publishing, of sorts. It's a consumer thing and I get very excited about it. All these things I've been learning at *MediaPost,* and from talking to people in the industry, get me very excited about the potential for anybody to do anything. That barrier to entry has gotten pretty low. If you have a great idea you can execute it. The thing I tell my partner is that whatever we do now, whatever we invest in will become irrelevant in eighteen to twenty-four months. The technology will have changed by then. The core CMS and information architecture stuff will still work, but it has to adapt.

What you just ran through puts a great wrapper around the whole business and the progression it's seen, but you're the second person this week to tell me that a lot of the pundits and early people who were proclaiming that this business is going to be important, predicted the interactive component of where brands interact. What they were predicting was the advent of social media, but it took fourteen or fifteen years for social media to take root. Why do you think it took so long?

There are a lot of reasons. One, is it was completely antithetical to the original Madison Avenue model. Part of that's reactionary if you want to stop that impending change from happening because it's going to destroy your business model. A year or two ago I spent some time with Brian Wieser, now CMO of Simulmedia, but who was then the chief economist for Interpublic and, by default, for the chief bean-counter for the ad industry. If you go back to the original Harvard manifesto that Mrs. McCann endowed, that created Bob Coen's job for half a century of tracking ad spending, who was then succeeded by Wieser, it had this very narrow definition of what advertising is. It's this book that was written in 1948. When I went to college in 1979 or '80, I took Advertising 101 and one of my professors said this is what advertising is. It's a very narrow definition. Social media can't possibly fit into it.

So I spent this day with Wieser; he called it a "social sojourn." We ran around New York as he was trying to understand how to factor social media into his computation and his analysis to determine its role in ad spending and ad economics. As we went from this expert to that expert, I was posting on my BlackBerry during cab rides and blogging it. It was a fun, interactive process and at the end of the day when Brian came up with his rationale, it was that social media is not advertising. It does not fit into the Madison Avenue construct.

Now, do I agree with him? No. I think the problem is that we have these labels for things and that's how we think of everything. That's the way human beings are. You need reference points. I really think this is the biggest thing in the industry right now. It's what we are trying to figure out how to bring to life at OMMA.

I do think in those inflection points, where whatever we come out of in the next eighteen months to two years is going to be completely different. I don't think most agencies really see it yet, in part because it didn't fit into the original construct, how we defined advertising. The other thing is you had to let go. There was that great Association of National Advertisers conference down in Orlando a few years ago where another P&G CEO, A.G. Lafley used this line that pretty much summed it up; "It's time to just let go."

That was the year that Coca-Cola got reamed by the guys who took the Diet Coke and the Mentos thing and created this social, consumer-generated interaction that blew their minds. And what was Coke's original reaction to that? Let's sue the bastards. Then they realized, oh, we can't sue our consumers. In fact, they love our brand so much they want to play with it and do stuff. It took Coke nine, ten months or something like that, to figure out a strategy and how to react to that. In the meantime, their consumers were all over YouTube, all over their own MySpace and Facebook pages with this thing. Eventually, Coke got it right and figured it out; we need to go with the flow. This is a good thing. We need to let the consumer take control of our brand. So that lead to this ANA conference, and Lafley said, "It's time to just let go."

Well, we can't completely let go. But we can in some places and not others. I think that's what the industry is trying to figure out. Our behaviors are pretty much the same, no matter what technology or platform comes along. What happens is that new technology and platforms will allow us to behave the way we want to behave. The truth is we, as consumers, were always in control of the message, of how we perceived the brand. We were always in control whether we turned the channel or not. Even if the TV was on we were in control whether we perceived the ad message or not. I don't want to get into a debate about subliminal advertising or latency effects, but the reality is the consumer always processed the message the way the consumer wanted to.

Great communicators can influence that. They can get them interested, excited, titillated, make them think about something. It was about four or five years ago that the Advertising Research Foundation started doing some really interesting research, some of it related to neuroscience. The understanding of how the brain works has been very important in the last four, five, six years. I'm actually very excited about that and working on some other projects related to it.

The ARF started thinking about this notion of co-authoring and co-storytelling. It always took place, even in linear media, like magazines and newspapers. The great visionary message creators, David Ogilvy or Bill Bernbach, and their clients came up with very powerful messages to tell their consumers something. But the consumer always brought their own baggage and reshaped the message. How that came out in social dialogue might have been very different than how they shaped it in the beginning.

That's very exciting to cover right now. We covered one epic story for the last ten, twelve years, and now we're going through this new period. We had our *MEDIA Magazine*'s Agency of the Year Awards recently, and were recognizing all these great and innovative agencies. I got up and said, here's the thing, for the past thirty years I've been a storyteller. Most of the stories I've been telling have been pretty prosaic and wonky stuff about some guy winning an account, or some guy making this media buy. But when you come right down to it, I'm telling stories about people.

The biggest story going on right now that we didn't see coming is this new industrial revolution. Chris Anderson said it best in an issue of *Wired*. They set up the whole idea; the things that make this industrial revolution different than those that preceded it – whether it was trains, planes or automobiles – the industry that's being transformed and revolutionized right now is the one that is a proxy for our entire society. You and I deal mostly with that part of that society that involves commerce, but all of the ideas of our society and everything we think is shaped by media, recorded by media and reinforced by media.

These things that are changing now are radically changing everything about our world and how we think as human beings. If you want to play that out on a political landscape or the global affairs landscape or, you name it, the milestones are like when Twitter helped fuel the Iranian revolt, or what's going on in China. These things are really powerful. It's the same lesson applied to every brand and marketer, which is basically what I said at our Agency of the Year Awards; "You guys are the new revolutionaries. You guys are all trying to think about how to use this transformation to make society better and more effective. Now, you're doing it mostly from the point of view of commerce. P.T. Barnum said, 'You can only sell a bad thing once, you can't sell it twice.'"

You've got to have a good product. You've got to have the goods. You've got to communicate it well. I have a very idealistic view of this, but I do think it's going to make society better in the long run. It's really scary. I don't think anybody controls it, that's why Madison Avenue doesn't like it.

CLOSING REMARKS
Joe Mandese has a passion for how media affects consumers, and consumers affect media. His coverage and personal insights have been valuable to a whole generation of entrepreneurs and professionals. I hope you enjoyed his points of view!

CHAPTER 9

GIAN FULGONI

Gian Fulgoni routinely provides a wealth of insightful presentations detailing the status of the Internet advertising industry in his current position as chairman of comScore Inc.. Gian has led the area of research for this business since 1981, where he was president and CEO of Information Resources Inc., a leading market research company. Gian led IRI through a period of dramatic growth, going from $2 million in revenue to over $500 million per year.

He is a fixture on the speaking circuit for events such as OMMA, ad:tech and the 4A's conferences where he summarizes the data and research behind the trends affecting Internet advertising. comScore is responsible for the backbone of the industry's efforts to garner more brand dollars and is one of the core companies responsible for the growth of the business as a whole. In addition to the influence of comScore, Gian is a wonderful, charismatic gentleman who is more than happy to take his time to talk with anyone about the business.

Gian Fulgoni, your background is a unique one. It's all about research. You were president and CEO for IRI. When did you decide to make the leap into the digital space?

I had been the president and then CEO at IRI for close to twenty years. The Internet got my attention in '99 and intrigued me in the context of basically what I had done at IRI, which was to build the scanning data systems that are used by the Consumer Packaged Goods (CPG) industry to track their sales at retail. When I looked at the Internet in '99 everything was in full bloom. E-commerce was exploding, and I realized that while there were a couple of research companies that were measuring audiences (NetRatings and Media Matrix), nobody was measuring e-commerce. I did a back-of-the-envelope calculation to see, in the offline world, how much money marketers spent on audience ratings data across all traditional media: Nielsen TV, Arbitron Radio, MRI Print, etc.. And also how much money they spent on ratings versus how much money they spent trying to understand how consumers buy products and services and what drives their purchasing. The answer was that they spent four times as much on the latter than they did on the former. So the research money was going toward understanding buying behavior far more than it went toward understanding audiences.

This gave us the idea that maybe there was an opportunity to build a company that measured both online audiences and how people bought products online. And if we were able to do that, we would have a unique research offering. That drove the design of the comScore system, from the sample size and panelist recruiting requirements to the data collection and storage technology. It was all determined by what we had to do to capture the buying behavior. As an example; on average only about 5 percent of the people who visit an e-commerce site in a month will buy something there, which means that 95 percent of the traffic that you'd get out of an audience measurement service is really not relevant to the buying measurement.

So whatever the sample size is that will give you the visitation data accurately, you have to multiply it by twenty if you want to have the same degree of precision for measurement of buying. That was the basic message, which led us to conclude that we had to have a million people in the United States under measurement. That then shaped everything: the panel recruitment methodologies, the incentives, the data collection technology, the scalability, the data warehousing, the analytical systems and everything else. That's what drove it. I think we executed against that plan pretty well. We did run into two unexpected challenges that happened pretty close together. One was the implosion of the Internet, the bubble bursting, and the second was 9/11.

Both of those events for comScore, as a startup business, caused two things to happen. It caused our sales curve to slow down dramatically, while the cost of building the business didn't change. It basically increased the cash burn rate and led us to have to do probably two more rounds of financing that we would not otherwise have had to do, which led to more equity dilution and all of that unpleasantness. On the positive side, we discovered the scope of the data collection system we built to capture e-commerce turned out to be a major advantage for us, because we were able to also measure all kinds of other consumer activities that we never anticipated happening on the Internet.

I don't think anybody foresaw all the myriad ways the Internet would be used today by consumers to do different things. From a research perspective, the bigger the sample size you have the better you're able to measure those activities. So a system that was originally built for e-commerce was also able to capture all of the other activities that emerged, which put us in the driver's seat in our market segment. The scale of the technology we had to build to capture e-commerce, and the flexibility that we had to build in it also turned out to be big advantages. I don't think anyone has ever seen anything as dynamic as the Internet.

Almost every day you wake up and there's something new happening, which is good and bad. It's good in that it gives you another opportunity to measure something. But it also opens up opportunities for other people to come along and stick their nose into the tent and try to get a piece of the business. What we found is that the more flexible and scalable your data collection architecture is, the better you are able to handle this Internet thing. It moves at lightning speed. It's kind of a funny story in the sense that many of the fundamental decisions that we made a decade ago, in terms of technology scale, flexibility and efficiency that were focused on e-commerce, have turned out to be major competitive advantages in the myriad other things that we're measuring today.

So you did a very good job of laying the groundwork for the system that would become the backbone of measurement on the web. What were some of the most surprising developments that you witnessed, which forced you to go back and revisit your methodology?

Probably the biggest, single change that we've had to make is to recognize that there are some things that happen online where website server data can add value to our panel data. Panels are terrific for measuring people behavior, but it can be challenging to build out a large enough panel of work users. You have this massive atwork access of the Internet that hasn't shifted to home as broadband has been installed there. To this day half of all consumers' e-commerce buying is still done from work computers, so measuring online activity from work computers remains very important. But it's difficult to get third-party measurement software loaded onto enough work computers. The IT folks aren't too happy about it.

So for a bunch of reasons, about two years ago we decided that we would bite the bullet and figure out how to integrate the server-side data (which measures traffic from all sources) with panel data (which is best for people metrics) to get the best of all possible worlds. We call it Unified Measurement. In doing this we had to account for the impact of cookie deletion, which causes huge inflation in unique visitor counts in server data. If a computer revisits a site where it received a cookie, but after the computer has had its cookies deleted, the site server counts it as new unique visitor.

Today, about 30 percent of Internet users in the U.S. delete their cookies in a month and do so about five times on average, so the degree of inflation in unique visitor counts is huge. But if you can adjust for that by integrating the server data with panel data, which can tell you the cookie deletion rate, you can come up with very accurate estimates of the number of unique people visiting a website from all locations. This also allows us to estimate visitors from mobile devices and Internet cafes, which are very important sources of traffic in some parts of the world. We now have about 90 percent of the top 100 publishers tagging their server data for us. It's allowed us to provide better, more accurate audience data. That was a big change.

The other change we realized, as watching video online exploded, was that because of encryption and distributed video players it was really tricky stuff to track. You had to have the cooperation of the video site itself to help with tagging and all of that, otherwise there's just no way to measure it all from a panel. That was a big surprise. We thought we'd be able to do it with a panel alone, but that turned out to not be the case.

One other surprise we learned early on, the Internet isn't called the World Wide Web for nothing. We realized, looking at some comScore panel data in 2001 that 30 percent of the traffic to the big portals such as Yahoo, AOL, etc. were coming from people outside the U.S.. When we built our panel, we let people who were living outside of the U.S. join, so we were getting a measure from day one of how much traffic was going to the big U.S. sites from overseas. I remember when we looked at our data and said, wait a minute, 30 percent of Yahoo.

com's traffic is coming from international visitors. How can that be? As we looked into it, we realized that 60 percent of the people in the world who spoke English and owned a computer lived outside the U.S..

At that time the bulk of content on the Internet was on U.S. sites. So even if you lived in Timbuktu you could just type "www.yahoo.com" into your browser and go there. That was another interesting piece of learning that also turned out to be an advantage for us, because we built the comScore panel to be global from the beginning. And so we've been able to very quickly adapt into measuring the global Internet; we measure forty-three countries today.

Cory, you've started businesses and I'm sure you've seen this as well; as much and as carefully as one plans, you really need some luck along the way. There are things with the Internet that have happened that you never could have expected. Maybe one of the real lessons is if you want to be in the Internet measurement business, flexibility and scalability are two of the most critical things you can build into your systems, because you never know what's going to happen.

Things change quickly. One of the watershed moments for the business was the standardization of the impression counting methodology. Can you talk about how you and comScore were involved in that effort? How it came to be and where it ended up?

Around four years ago, as our data measurement technology was seeing all the information that was coming down to the panelists' machines, including the ads they were receiving, we started building out a service to report on the number of ads that were delivered by publisher and then broken down by advertiser, type of advertiser, etc.. We called it Ad Metrix, and it's been very successful for us. Then one day I got a call from one of the largest CPG advertisers, and the gentleman said to me, "Need your help with something. In the TV world there's a thing called a 'make-good,' which is that if the network doesn't deliver what we were promised in the upfront buy, if we don't get the audience according to the TV ratings data, which means that we didn't get the ad impressions delivered that we paid for, then there's a make-good in the form of additional ad impressions provided free. What we've discovered as we've begun to move some of our branding dollars onto the Internet is that there's no such guarantee on the Internet. We'd like you to measure several of our campaigns and tell us which demo segments are receiving the ads." This was about three years ago.

So they tagged their campaigns and ran them, and we measured which comScore panelists were getting the ads. They had also given us their target audience criteria. One criteria, was that nobody outside of the U.S. should be getting any of these impressions. Lo and behold, for the first campaign we looked at, half of the people getting the ads didn't even live in the United States. Then when we looked at frequency we started to realize that the frequency was way higher than what was intended and the reach was way lower. That led us to ask, why is that happening? Then the light bulb went off, and we realized that there were two drivers of the problem.

One was cookie deletion. The ad servers kept pumping impressions against the same machines, thinking they were new ones because the cookies had been deleted. That lead to over delivery of frequency and then correspondingly, under delivery of reach. The second issue that was happening is that the cookie-based targeting is not the same thing as targeting against a person. Let's say a woman is on the machine and she goes to babycenter.com, an ad gets delivered and a cookie gets put on the machine. Well, fine, but what if sometime later her husband is on the same computer and an ad is delivered against that cookie but this time through an audience buy? The ad server is not delivering it against the woman now; it's delivering an impression that was intended for a woman but delivering it to a man. That's what was causing some of these demos to go out of whack.

As we looked further into the issue, we realized that the geographical problem was sometimes just being driven by a lack of process and discipline, and stupid things – for example, somebody forgetting to turn on the IP parsing switch! The industry was moving so fast and the discipline, the process, wasn't as tight as one would like.

I think this led to the first post-buy reporting that now is on its way to becoming standard in the industry. It's also being recognized that it's no longer sufficient to do the analysis after the campaign has been delivered. It's necessary to do close to real-time reporting, which is reporting back in a time frame that allows the agency and the ad delivery company, whoever it is, to make adjustments and tweak the plan if it turns out that the delivery isn't going as intended. That was a valuable piece of learning for us about the realities of online advertising.

Once the counting methodology was laid into place and the definition of an impression was standardized, you would imagine that would've taken care of a lot of the discrepancies in reporting between different data sources. But even today there are still a lot of discrepancies in reporting. Do you think the industry is going to get to a point where those discrepancies become a non-issue?

We could certainly improve it, still. An example is a survey done about a year ago by a company called Collective, asking 400 agency and advertiser executives questions about their use of ad networks. One of the questions was, "Do you use the click as a measure of ad effectiveness?" And 65 percent of the people they asked said, yes. When you look at the age of the respondent, they found that the younger people were much more likely to use the click than the older people. So we've still got this educational challenge out there, but we could improve things.

There is this difference between the audience numbers you get from servers and panel data. Servers count cookies and panels count people. That difference has been mitigated significantly by the work that we've done integrating the two. It hasn't made panel data look like the server data and won't because you've still got cookie deletion inflating the server data. But it's narrowed the gap and increased credibility of the third-party data. In the media industry bigger is always better, and I think you're always going to have the temptation of quoting bigger numbers, which will lead to some degree of different numbers floating around. As time has gone by, we've learned more and more about what's counted right, what's counted wrong. And I do think that things will continue to improve. Will it ever get to perfection? No, I doubt that, given we're talking about people, human interaction. I doubt it'll ever get to that, but I think we've moved in the right direction. A lot of education has been done and a lot of learning has been obtained. I think it will continue.

I know that comScore has pioneered a lot of research to support and provide information on the relevance and the efficacy of advertising online. Do you think that online advertising has become more effective over the last ten years? Do you think we've improved at driving brand metrics, such as awareness and consideration and intent?

Yes, we'll gladly accept some credit for the learning that our research has provided. For example, the click isn't the way to do it, blah, blah, blah. But a couple of other things have happened that are really important. Moving from a static banner to rich media and then to video gives you a richer palate and you can do more things, you can say more things, you can communicate better. It's opened up recognition that the Internet is more than a direct-response medium, that it can also be used as a brand-building medium. We're still in the infancy of that, but there's massive upside as the rich media and video palates are used more and more.

One thing we've just realized, we put out a paper this week called, "What would Don Draper do in a Digital World?" We looked at more than 100 consumer-packaged goods online advertising campaigns, and we identified the elements in the digital ads that were leading to success and compared them to television. We did this through a business unit we recently acquired called ARS. If you look at the traditional component drivers of success for branding advertising in television they are included in digital creative at a far, far lower rate. But when they are included, you get higher sales lift. However, what is included far more in digital ads than in TV ads are pricing and promotion information. It's almost like the Internet is the new print. This is especially true in the CPG industry.

What we're finding is that the CPG ad campaigns that are quickly lifting sales at retail are the ones that have pricing and promotion information in them. It's almost like the industry hasn't yet gotten to the digital branding applications. They've been more focused on the short-term drivers of sales, which are price and promotion. I thought that was all really interesting stuff. And so looking forward I'll lay out one future scenario, which is not good news for the newspaper or magazine industry. The print newspaper industry has been buffeted by a whole bunch of stuff from losing the classified business to a lot of auto advertising going online. At the same time print readership has plummeted.

If the printed newspaper industry were to lose the weekly CPG grocery pricing listing and then the Sunday FSI coupons, it would be a big problem. I suspect that's the next thing that's going to hit them because you can communicate pricing information so much more efficiently on the Internet while getting a higher reach. The evidence is now beginning to emerge, and I think our study here is one of the first to show it, if you stick price and promotion information into an online ad, even in a banner ad, you're going to get some sales lift. It'll cost you a fraction of what you'd pay to put that in a newspaper. And think of what you could do with rich media.

Think of what you could do with video. You could have it all. You could have a branding medium and kind of short-term price promotion communication medium, which to me, when I think of price and promotion and coupons, I always think it's more akin to direct-response type advertising. It's not branding, it's a communication of an immediate incentive to buy the products. So I put that into the direct-response bucket, but in CPG those direct-response dollars are still going to print. If they come online, it's going to be a massive boost to the online advertising industry.

On top of it you've got all of the branding dollars that haven't shifted to digital as of yet. With rich media and video I think the Internet will increase its share of that spending. It's exciting to be in this business.

Maybe one of the issues that we're struggling with is the amount of inventory that's available. Maybe Facebook will solve that for us.

They have a lot of inventory available, that's for sure. comScore puts out studies and research papers and findings that you come up with, how long does it usually take for the industry to see widespread adoption of the findings that you pull together?

I always tell our people to think in terms of frequency, because you cannot just publish a finding once. We put out a lot of stuff and some of it gets lost in the clutter. I think there is a frequency response curve in our world that just goes on and on and continues climbing. You just have to keep pushing the results of the study. You repeat it. You keep educating. I'll say don't worry about repeating the same bloody thing, this is a dynamic industry. People are busy. They've got a lot on their plates. To get through to all the constituents is just not going to happen with a frequency of one.

We've got to keep pushing it out. The temptation is to think that it's going to happen much faster than that, and the reality is that it doesn't. I ran a little experiment on Twitter. If I put out a tweet and then look at the re-tweets as a measure of the interest that's generated, I can keep putting out the same tweet throughout the day, throughout the week, throughout the weekend, and I'll keep getting re-tweets, which says it's like a fire hose. There's so much stuff that's being communicated in the digital world that it's easy to miss something.

You're hitting a different audience.

Different times of the day, different days of the week; frequency is key, at least in our world and what we've experienced. Maybe that's true for online advertising generally. Maybe it's easier to miss an ad online than it is on TV. Maybe frequency is more important than reach.

Nobody gets upset when they see the same commercial running a couple times in a program, so why would they get upset when they hear the same set of data a couple times?

Exactly, or maybe they didn't see it the first time, or second time or third time, right?

You've mentioned reach and frequency – comScore talks about a lot of metrics, some of which are more endemic to the web. How important do you think it's been to

date that the web can be measured in the same metrics as traditional media and then built upon?

It's very important. I've heard some people say that with data-driven targeting, reach and frequency are irrelevant. That, to me, seems idiotic. Even if you're able to target with 100% precision, are we saying that the number of times that you communicate that message doesn't matter? I could accept that in a very accurate targeting world that reach is no longer the issue because you're reaching your target audience. But there's still a question of how many times you have to communicate your message. It's pretty clear in traditional media that the communication of a message often requires more than a frequency of one to persuade somebody.

So whether one's talking about the Internet or any kind of medium, the challenge of persuading somebody has been proven in traditional media to be a function of how often you say it. That said, it's what you say that's really critical. You start from that. The work that we've done at ARS says that what you say is four times more important than the media weight you put behind it. Fine, but that doesn't mean that the number of times, the frequency isn't important. It also doesn't mean that the reach isn't important. Because even if you're targeting very accurately through the exchanges and all the other stuff, nobody's going to convince me that they're reaching the entire population of prospects. So you need to know what percentage you reached. Did I reach 10 percent of the entire target segment that's relevant for my product at this point in time, or did I reach 80 percent?

The simple fact is if you don't know how many of them you reached, you don't know how much you should be spending.

Exactly, same as with frequency. It gets even more compelling when you say, well look, if you're a media planner and you try to figure this stuff with television and the Internet and the other media that you've got, you need some idea whether you're reaching the same people or different people. Somebody could legitimately ask; do we have these single-source databases that allow us to do that today? And the answer would be, no. So you've got to make some assumptions there. But any media planner worth his salt would still be working with some assumptions, such as, if I overlay a TV campaign with an online campaign am I boosting my reach? Or am I just delivering additional frequency to people who've already seen my ads? You've got to have some idea to put the plan together.

Even before the Internet, go back to when it didn't exist, you had print, you had radio, you had television. As I recall, since I was alive in those days, reach and frequency were critical to look at across media. Why would it be any different today with the Internet even with great targeting? I think that some of these realities of life are true today, every bit as much as they were true before the Internet. It's easy in the Internet world to believe that everything is different.

We used to think a company didn't have to make money. That was the mantra of the early days. We found out that was wrong. Then in the offline world, the more recent mantra was that every American should be able to own a home. Well, yeah, but maybe not every American can afford to own a home. So let's face that reality, there are certain economic truths and maybe certain media truths that transcend change.

I was quoting Ted McConnell at P&G when I said, "One of the critical things as digital emerges is that we've got to be really focused on the truths that transcend change." In other words, don't think that just because the Internet has come along that everything changes in the way that advertising persuades people to buy Product A versus Product B, or that people will stop watching TV. We're still dealing with people and there are still universal truths about them. So that's another challenge for the Internet, to think in terms of how to integrate into a multimedia world because television is not going away.

CLOSING REMARKS

What Gian provides in his role, and what is seen in this interview, is that data is valuable. It is especially valuable for a medium that has not yet matured! It may feel like Internet advertising is a big business but it is still growing, evolving, and it's clear that where we are now is not where we'll be in two years.

Gian and comScore have maintained a focus on the growth of the business by proving results. And for the business to continue to succeed, we need to see results. More advertisers need to get beyond the click and to surface the metrics most important to them. Then the industry can see the accurate data, extrapolate that out to other categories and prove the medium is effective for most all advertisers

CHAPTER 10

BRUCE CARLISLE

Bruce was a pioneer in the digital advertising world, making the move to San Francisco in 1995 and launching SF Interactive, one of the first digital ad agencies, back in 1996. SF Interactive grew to become one of the largest, fastest moving digital agencies with such clients as Netscape, VeriSign, Snapple, Morgan Stanley Dean Witter and HP. They were a creative powerhouse leading the development of many formats of rich media, and eventually integrating media planning and buying into the mix.

In 2003 Bruce sold the business to Butler, Shine & Stern in Sausalito, combining to create one of the most innovative cross-platform creative shops in all of the U.S., and since that time Bruce has remained an active marketing consultant with his company, Digital Axle. Most recently he has been spending his time with the startup of

Conference Hound, an online brand dedicated to providing the most user friendly site for professionals to search for and find conferences, conventions and trade shows.

Bruce Carlisle, you've been part of this business for a long time. Tell me how you got into it.

I got into the business in a very backdoor way. I was the play-by-play radio announcer for the hockey games at St. Lawrence University. This meant that I also had to sell, create and produce radio ads for the local banks and pizza shops to support the broadcasts, which is how I landed on Madison Avenue after graduating. I spent thirteen years working for big New York ad agencies. I had the good fortune to work closely with Jerry Della Femina and Louise McNamee at Della Femina, McNamee, which was exploding in the late '80s. They made it up as they went along and had fun doing it, and that's where my entrepreneurial bug has its roots and where I learned an awful lot about the chutzpah required to start a company and an agency. I then moved to Washington, DC where I started a marketing services agency inside a big Washington, DC public relations firm, which at the time was called Ogilvy, Adams & Rinehart. I was there from '91 to '95, and from about the time the original Netscape browser was introduced we started thinking about putting the public policy clients that we had online because money in Washington comes there to be spent.

As a communications firm we thought the Internet was going to be a pretty interesting place for the trade associations, which are the big communications clients in Washington, DC to communicate their mission and their goals. So we started building websites mainly for trade associations in late '93 or early '94. I kept walking by a bookstore near my office on K Street in Washington, and seeing copies of *Wired Magazine*. It seemed like everything was happening out in San Francisco, and at the time my life was changing in 1995. I got divorced. I sold my house. I quit my job. I threw all my junk in the car and drove to California and got a job with Working Assets as their first director of online media and marketing. My job that first year was to build a website that, frankly, doesn't look a whole lot different in terms of its vision than the *Huffington Post* looks today.

Time passes and things don't necessarily change!
I spent a year there, and during that time I got invited to a meeting at Organic. At the time the players were all down around South Park. During that year Working Assets conducted an ad agency search and discovered that the ad agencies we talked to in San Francisco were fundamentally nowhere in terms of online and digital. When I went down to Organic my sense was while they were doing really cool stuff, they were coming at everything from a design perspective, which wasn't that surprising since most of the South Park companies had really fallen out of the CD-ROM business.

Coming out of that meeting I had the sense there was room in the world for somebody who could talk about the Internet more in terms of advertising and marketing as opposed to general branding. At one point during that first year Rick Boyce, the sales guy for *Wired,* came over and showed me this thing called a banner. We actually used an ad agency (ironically the agency I later sold my agency to, Butler, Shrine & Stern) to make a banner. I think we were one of first to buy banners online as a client.

The way that Organic approached the business was really about websites. The way they talked to their clients was not the way I had grown up. I had been classically trained to speak to the clients I've had at places like Ogilvy and McCann Erickson in New York City. After a year at Working Assets, I decided there was room in the world for something that looked and acted like an ad agency but understood digital marketing; something that fit halfway between and ad agency and what the Organic and the other South Park companies were doing.

That's really how SF Interactive was born; we consciously put the company halfway between the north financial district, which is where all the advertising agencies were at the time, and South Park. It was no accident.

What kind of clients were you working with back then?
Two of our first clients were Netscape and VeriSign. We did not have a media capacity early on. We were much more of a creative shop, and we collaborated with MediaSmith. They did the media and we did the creative for probably the first year-and-a-half of our existence. What put us on the map was that my two partners, Alejandro Levins and Drew Carpenter and I somehow got introduced to Netscape. It was within a year of their IPO, and they were the hottest company on the block, the Google of their day.

We went down to Netscape and convinced them we knew how to do banners. They were building up a huge battery of internal creative resources for their net center portal, and after winning that assignment we, as a three-person shop, essentially got to walk around doing business pitches saying we're doing the online advertising for Netscape. At a certain point we actually brought MediaSmith in and collaborated with them for some period of time working on Netscape. Another early client was VeriSign, which was a client of SF Interactive right through to the day it got sold, and it was really one of the bread and butter clients of SF Interactive.

We started working with them before they had their IPO and were still in a small flip-up building in Mountain View. At a certain point, sometime in 1998, we decided that we had the wind at our back. The .com money was starting to get spent. We were getting lots of calls. We found it easy to get publicity. We'd gotten written up in *The Wall Street Journal* in the first three months we were in operation. And we discovered to our surprise, that venture capital firms were actually telling their new companies that they ought to come talk to us.

We decided that we would take the jump to try and become a bigger agency, and that we would go into media planning ourselves. So we hired a senior leadership team that included a creative director and director of account services, Russell Quinan. Then Rob Middleton became our media director, and we started rolling.

Everything kind of snowballed. We just started getting client after client. A really big early client was Women.com. Another was Discover Brokerage, which had been Lombard Securities and later became Morgan Stanley Dean Witter. We went out and talked to Ken Gilbert, a former colleague of mine from my advertising days in New York, and became the agency for digital with Snapple. We picked up a lot of hip new startups in the Bay Area. We did the first website ever for Jamba Juice. And that's a good sampling of how it all took off.

Do you remember pre-2000, the mid '90s into the late '90s, what kind of results you saw from the advertising you were doing for brands back then?

I think the most striking thing in the early days were the click-through rates. They would blow people's minds today. When we were doing internal ads for Netscape they were doing routinely five, six, or seven percent click-through rates. We built, as far as we know, the first HTML pull-down menu ads for Women.com, where people could do the pull-down menu and click into a content area where they wanted to go. Those got phenomenal click-through rates, some as much as 20 percent mainly because of the novelty. Nobody had ever seen anything like that before.

Another thing that was pretty big, we worked on an HP project where Goodby, Silverstein was our client. This was when Rob was still at Goodby, so he hired us. Between Rob and our creative team, we negotiated the first full-page takeovers. We had, in *USA Today* for example, the four sections that would come spitting out of a printer, which was wild stuff for the time. And HP just dominated the major portals on the Internet for one day; this was the first time it was done. I think what we got the most attention for was that we did a lot of things first.

I recall many of the campaigns you refer to quite vividly, because at i-traffic I remember looking at all that stuff and thinking, oh, we've got to try and beat that. What

was the sales process at that point? How difficult was it to get these things created and executed?

Well, it wasn't always terribly profitable. What worked well for us was that my partner, Alejandro was a real champion of the technology team. We always had technology people in the room as fundamental parts of the creative process. Nothing really got concepted unless there was a technology person in the room and a media person. The whole idea of taking over the website and making things happen on a page required a media person and a technologist to tell you what to do. So some of the cooler stuff we did was because of that, and in those days publishers were willing to try just about anything.

We had the capacity to really push the envelope creatively. And so we could go to clients and say, our creative people would like to do this, and here's a demo of how it works because we could get our technology people to demonstrate it. I'm always careful about claiming too much to be "first" in certain things, but there's an awful lot of rich media things that later turned into companies that came as a result of us pushing the envelope. The real driver was the fact that we had coding people, writers, art directors and media people working together in the room. That was a real advantage we had in those days.

The people you had in the room that created the opportunities, the creative, media and technology people, it was unique to get all three different aspects of the business in the room at the same time. Where were you hiring those people? To be able to find media people and creative people and technologists that all had some understanding of the web at that point was difficult.

We had a very young staff. We encouraged exploration. Rob's media team had very few people who were more than one or two years out of college. Very few people were constrained by the past. We had some really good engineers who were into the idea of the web as a marketing and advertising vehicle. They were thrilled to have somebody ask them what was going on instead of us just dumping orders on their queue. And I give a lot of credit to my partner, Alejandro, who was just a phenomenal people person and the tech people's champion.

We were able to recognize that was the way we were going to be better, particularly when we started. Early on we had Michael McMahon at Left Field as competition. We really didn't compete against Organic and those places. They were building big huge websites, which wasn't our game at all. We were building branded websites and focusing on advertising. The way we differentiated and the way we were known was through creative, but it really was a good marriage of creative and technology and media.

Given what was going on, what was one of the biggest hurdles to being successful pre-2000?

We were actually very successful pre-2000. We were profitable. We were growing at an amazing clip. We paid an excessive amount of attention to people issues. There was a culture of overt communication. We had this ridiculously good culture where people really liked working there. And no growing pains, that I can remember, compared at all with the shrinking pains. More often than not the growing pains would be a failure to deliver on time because we didn't have the resources.

I'm pretty sure there were places where our media recommendations probably weren't as good as they could have been, because the people doing them were too weeks out of school. I'm sure we left a lot of things unexplored, and there were a lot of pain points that came from clients. You would promise a client something in good faith. You'd run into a lot of problems. The client didn't care or understand why. You were learning and trying to do something great for them, but they were upset. And it wasn't because we weren't paying attention or didn't have the resources; it was because nobody had ever done it before. A lot of my job at the time was actually running interference with clients and protecting our people from them.

Does anything else from that period stand out in your mind?

Oh yeah. When we started out I decided we needed some promotional materials. We went out and bought thirty SF Interactive mugs, and we noticed that every Silicon Valley startup that we went to pitch had a kitchen. We used to just leave a couple of mugs in the kitchens every place we went because they'd always bring us into their kitchen. For some reason all these companies were really proud of their kitchens, which were funded by startup money. We'd just leave the mugs and hope someone would call us.

Sometime we'd go dashing off to Silicon Valley from our office in the city; we'd fill up the coffee mugs with coffee and drink it in the car. When we were done we'd chuck them in the back of my car. Well, we got to this first meeting with Netscape and were so excited, we thought it was such a big deal, that we forgot to bring fresh, clean beautiful mugs. I drove down to Mountain View with Drew Carpenter. We got into the parking lot at Netscape. It had this huge beautiful fountain in front of it that's now VeriSign. We were about to go into the building and I said, "Oh, we forgot the mugs." Drew looked into the backseat and said, "Lots of mugs in the backseat!"

We stopped the car in the parking lot, got out, grabbed about six mugs and proceeded to rinse them in the fountain. We went into our meeting, we won the business, and left six mugs washed from their fountain in their cupboards. That was our lead gen campaign.

I'm sure that they'll be happy to know that you basically gave them all E-coli.
Sorry, that's one of my favorite stories.

Do you remember any campaigns, banners or efforts you saw on the web that were impressive to you at the time?
There was such and onslaught of new, cool stuff coming at me. I think the emergence of rich media was pretty impactful. I wouldn't say any specific campaign. There was a technology – you'll probably remember it – that was one of the early push technologies, where you downloaded this app and it messed up everybody's network. But it would actually push news onto your desktop.

PointCast.
PointCast, that's it. We did a couple of campaigns for them, and that was just amazing stuff for those days;

the idea that you could push content into a little piece of somebody's desk as opposed to getting there more actively through a browser. What was going on then was the browsers were getting better and better, so you always had to dumb down your sites. My main memory is that people were building really cool stuff on the latest browsers in their office. And I, as the executive, would constantly have to say, "Yeah, but it doesn't work on my client's daughter's computer."

And we used to see that not just on our stuff, which we tried to avoid, but on a lot of competitive stuff. Just keep people going for broke creatively and creating things that didn't work on 90 percent of the computers out there.

I remember those issues. The technology was definitely a hurdle because the penetration of really good computers in the marketplace was so low at the time.

Bandwidth was a huge factor. Everybody was doing dial-up 28K modems.

Let's talk about post-2000. At that point you've gotten SF Interactive to a certain stage in its growth, and sold the business to Butler, Shine & Stern. You've stayed very involved in the business from a consulting and marketing strategy perspective post-2000. What have you been doing since then?

SF Interactive grew amazingly fast. We grew incredibly profitable on our own, and during that period nobody in the investor community really recognized that digital agencies were fundamentally not scalable revenue businesses. Sapient, Razorfish, U.S. Interactive and companies like that were going public at insane valuations. What was also going on, and we got caught in the middle of it, was that the traditional holding company ad agencies were trying to catch up. They were making acquisitions and trying to figure out how they were going to get on top of this digital world because they had paid no attention to it for far too long.

We became a very attractive acquisition opportunity for all the holding companies to the point where, late '99 and most of 2000, I acted more like an investment banker than the head of an agency. We had private equity firms, WPP, Omnicom, IPG and random investors showing up at our door, one after the other, trying to cut a deal with us because we had gone from zero to $12 million profitably in under four years. We were over $100 million in terms of media billings.

We came very close to doing a deal with Ogilvy, which was close to my heart because I had started out as an assistant account executive at Ogilvy. I had worked for their CEO, Shelley Lazarus, when she was a management supervisor. Unfortunately it took them so long to get their act together that by the time they got the deal in place we were being offered a far better deal by a private equity firm and we took it. We raised $10 million. In hindsight it was the easiest thing in the world to do at that time. They let me and Alejandro take some money off the table, and we were going to be the next Razorfish.

That was our goal and we opened up offices in Washington, DC and New York City. We closed our $10 million financing about six weeks before the NASDAQ peak and then it cratered. The next two years were brutally difficult. We had two or three really large national clients – Morgan Stanley, Dean Witter, Snapple and a couple of others – where the core agency had made acquisitions, and had gone out to the clients and said, hey, come on back home we've got this interactive thing covered.

The big blows we suffered were less about .coms going under – we certainly had our share of those – but more about three or four of our national brand clients reconsolidating under the umbrella of their original agency. I spent two years slicing the company by more than half, and we lost a good chunk of really good people. The history with Butler, Shine & Stern is that Greg Stern and I had worked together at Ogilvy in the early '80s. He was part of my inspiration for moving out to California. I'd visit him sitting on a dock in Sausalito starting his own company, and decided there was nothing wrong with that picture. We had a number of conversations about joining forces and finally got to a point in about 2003 where they, like everybody, were having their own .com issues. They needed to be perceived more interactively. I felt it was important to do the right thing for our investors and our people and stabilize things.

So that's what drew us to put the two companies together. I stayed for a year and helped out where I could, and we brought a fair amount of business over with us. In terms of revenue, we were roughly the same size at the time of the acquisition. I think it worked out incredibly well for BSS, and as far as I'm concerned it worked out fine for me because I was able to put the thing into good hands.

Greg and I are chatting next week.

You'll get different perspectives. My perspective is that Greg, and I'm sure he won't admit this, needed to bring his two creative partners kicking and screaming into the digital age. They took the pieces and parts of us that worked for them, which was not all of it. They just wanted nothing to do with media on the digital side; they were all in on the creative.

So post-sale and post-bubble, what have you seen in the last five or six years that's most impressed you about where the business is headed?

More than anything else is the bifurcation of media; the fact that new channels with their own models just keep popping up. I also think that over the last four or five years the value of the case study has decreased. I started to believe that because you were successful doing a social media campaign over here, with a certain set of tools and strategies, it by no means guaranteed you'd be successful over there with mobile or video.

I think the pure fire hose of media channels is astounding, some of which are paid and some unpaid. And the fact that they work in different ways for different segments of your audience; there are now different demographic groups with not just different media behaviors but with media behaviors defined by fundamentally different sets of media. And by that I mean, as an example, younger people who don't even use email anymore.

It is interesting how the different generations are adopting new pieces of technology. The question is, do they end up all merging their experiences, or are we watching

the evolution and death of some of the things that we're most used to at this point?

I have no idea. That's what keeps me in this. I love the fact that it changes all the time. I think it's really hard to be an agency or marketing advisor right now because the universe of opportunities you don't know grows larger than the universe of stuff you do know. I think predictability has, in a lot of ways, just gotten worse. I've seen it with some of the campaigns we've run. We've done one thing that worked great for one demographic, and then stunk the place up with something else.

Having been around the business as long as you have, you start to understand how to react in situations where you don't necessarily know what the outcome is going to be when you launch.

Yeah, and a lot of my consulting starts with, let me tell you what we're not going to find out. Let me tell you that after a month of doing this you're going to hate it and want to fire us. But after three or four months you're going to be really happy. That comes from experience.

On the flipside, if you're twenty-four or twenty-five there's a lot of stuff that just comes intuitively and in ways that I can force myself to learn, but that won't ever be intuitive to me. And that makes it hard to be an agency.

When you are raised in that environment and everything is second nature to you, it's not a matter of seeing trends but a matter of understanding how they live that life-style. Nowadays, I feel when we try to analyze what the different generations are doing we have to look at it from an outside point of view and that's hard.

When I started my media career as an assistant media planner at Grey Advertising in New York, there were six media vehicles and always had been six. It blows my mind, the volume of channels and the differing models. And having been around this now for close to seventeen years, it's important not to get too caught up on whatever fashion of the moment is. PointCast is a great example; push technology was going to change the world in 1997.

CLOSING REMARKS

Bruce's insights into the business, and his experience, have been immensely helpful to a number of people. What I take away from his interview is to follow your gut, stay focused on the business you want to be in and be sure to empower your people to succeed. Allow them to be creative, to pursue ideas, and they will take you to very good places.

CHAPTER 11

JEFF MINSKY

Jeff Minsky has more than nineteen years of experience advising Fortune 100 companies on how to get the most impact from their media budgets. He spent the majority of that time focused on emerging media and specifically the web, working with such companies as DeWitt Media, Ogilvy, and most recently NEXT, a division of Ogilvy's Ignition Factory.

In 2000 he led the 4A's initiative to create Standard Terms and Conditions for Internet Advertising, leading to a landmark agreement between the 4A's and IAB which, amongst many other highlights, established the concept of sequential liability and third-party ad server numbers as the basis of reporting.

Jeff has been a mentor to many and a friend to many more. He publishes a weekly newsletter to his internal teams and clients, "The 10's" that gives readers a glimpse of the cultural changes of U.S. media consumption, and brings a quick glance view of the top media/advertising stores of the week.

Jeff Minsky, if I think back my first day at an ad agency was your last day at the same agency. When I came in you were already doing things in digital. What was your attraction to the digital side of the business?

Well, my life could have gone one of two ways, and it went the digital side. But it could have gone a completely different way because, for my bar mitzvah, I wanted a moped. Had I gotten that moped I might be motocrossing, or who knows. I might have been – what do you call the guy that fixes all the motorcycles up? A mechanic! But no, I instead got an Apple II computer for my bar mitzvah. I'd always had an interest in technology from way back. I wasn't a major programmer, but I always had this interest in technology.

When I graduated college with a degree in economics I wasn't exactly sure which route I wanted to go, but I had roommates that had had internships in an ad agency. They brought home free magazines and I thought, hey, that's cool, let's try that. After a year of going between some really strange – and that's a book in itself – different types of jobs, I got a call from a company called DeWitt Media.

To this day I am not 100% sure how they got my résumé, other than possibly from my college. I interviewed and was fortunate enough to get a job there. And I remember the first moment that I worked there for the same person that you did – Peter. I walk in and he throws this huge book of spreadsheets in front of me, and it was a *book*. It wasn't a program. It was a book of spreadsheets called a SQAD book (Standard Quotation and Data) and he said, "Here, pull out all these average SQAD costs," which literally were hundreds of numbers that I had to take a pencil and write down. We had computers but were still segueing there, and it was just the most ridiculous process in the world.

I remember that Gene DeWitt was still on DOS when the world had three years ago switched to Windows. Finally he ended up going to Windows, and I remember the first little inkling of digital that I had at DeWitt. I was working on the MasterCard account and Gene asked me to do a survey of online services. At the time Prodigy was the leading online service, followed by CompuServe with this upstart called America Online, with a whopping 400,000 subscribers at the time. There was rumor that something called Internet in a box was going to come out, but that was six months, even, after I'd done the survey.

Anyhow, I was doing this overview of online services and I'll never forget the feeling I had when I got onto AOL and saw that people were there all hours of the day and night, chatting away. And this is back in the wonderful 1800-baud modem world, if you were lucky to have 1800 bauds. It took close to two and a half minutes for a basic screen to load. But seeing that people's eyes had to be on the screen – at that time there was no way for digital to be background noise, you had to be looking at that screen – that kind of captive audience, to me, was a much better opportunity than some of the things in software or in traditional media. That's where I sort of fell in love with it. I said this is going to really gain attention in a way that other media just cannot do. So that's how it all started, and that's when, after the MasterCard project, I started doing some digital. And that's when the Internet started to really roll out and Netscape, as a browser, emerged.

I had some basic meetings with Neil Weinberg, who was at a company called Internet Connections or Interactive Connections, and he showed me around all these servers and said, this is the future, and I got the bug.

I wasn't just doing digital back then but all sorts of non-traditional media, and I remember taking a ride with Gene. We were going to see this 3D theater that had opened up, the Sony IMAX on the Upper West Side, and Gene said, "Jeff, what's your future look like? What's the future of this digital thing?" I said I imagine a day where there's one centralized computer in your household that's allowing you to connect all your other computers onto the Internet and get your media served across the board. That was actually the one thing I was right on. After MasterCard I started doing digital for Discovery Channel. I remember doing something with ZDNet, and that was about the time that I left.

Most people in this industry stay at their first job for a year and then hop around. I was at DeWitt for six years. It was family. It was the best education anyone could have gotten in terms of understanding media, and as you very well know, there were lots of personalities in that place, for better or worse. But if you could survive it, it was a phenomenal training experience, and I have to say probably better than what most people get today.

I agree. I was there for a year and a couple of days, actually, but I remember learning a whole lot that year I was there.

And you were there when things had already started to change a little bit. In addition to the Internet, people were still talking about interactive television. I think it was 1994, Time Warner VOD Orlando trial, and what we heard is that they had people in trucks pushing in VHS tapes if somebody ordered a movie. So that was their digital experience back then. Nowadays, obviously, we've achieved better than that. You wouldn't think twice about VOD now.

When you left, did anyone give you advice? I remember when I left Vickie sat me down and said, "I really wish you'd stick around. I don't think this Internet thing is going to last. It's just a fad." What was the reaction when you told them you were going to leave to go focus on the Internet?

About a year before I left we had lost MasterCard for whatever reason, and Gene said, "Don't worry, you're on Discovery, your job is safe." So I felt very good about that and worked on Discovery for a year. And then I got a call from a sales rep. Remember when you saw me only for a day? Back then not only was I digital guy but I was out-of-home guy, and I had a specialty in marketing out-of-home. I had worked on MasterCard's World Cup sponsorship and had done a lot of outdoor for Reebok and for MasterCard. If you remember, Discovery around Manhattan had telephone kiosks with LED lights that told you the time and date of the show; I was the one that started them on that. And they did it for five years even after I left.

When I told them I left, for about three or four days I didn't hear much of anything. I was between jobs. I was taking a weekend going to Cape Cod; I had not had a real vacation in about five years. The day before I leave for vacation, Gene calls me into his office. Now you may remember what that was like, we still call it "WOG-ing," (Wrath of Gene). So he calls me into his office and he says, "Sit down." I'm thinking, oh god, what's going to happen to me?

He sits down and he writes down a title. He writes down a salary, which was about 25k more than I was being offered at Ogilvy, and in the title is SVP, AMD Director, or whatever it was. He says, "Stay." And I looked at him and I said, "You're Evil." I said, "You've just turned what was supposed to be the most relaxing week I've had in five years into the most hellacious." Back in that day, at my salary range, 25k made a huge difference. I was living with two other people in an apartment on the upper west side. That alone could have gotten me my own studio or more. There was no wrong answer.

I took the week and had lunch with Gene when I got back. I said, listen, Gene, if I'm just going to Ogilvy to go to a different agency, then I'd be stupid to not take your offer. I said, I'm not leaving to change agencies, I'm changing careers. To be honest with you, they have IBM and if anyone's going to start investing and growing the Internet space, it's going to be Ogilvy and IBM. And your clients will get there eventually but they're just not there yet. I said, so this is me changing careers, and he respected that, I think. We shook hands. He was very pleasant and wished me well.

I don't change jobs just for the sake of changing jobs unless there's a life reason to do so. For me it was, I found something I had a passion for. I couldn't really take it to the nth degree at DeWitt at the time, but I knew that I could take it somewhere at Ogilvy.

So when you left for Ogilvy and got to work with clients like IBM, what was their outlook on the digital media business and where it was going?

The first year I was there I was still part of the non-traditional media group. It wasn't a separate digital team. It was the same job I'd had at DeWitt thrown together, in that I was still doing out- of-home big event type things as well as Internet. That was back during the 1996 Olympics. And that was one of my first things I planned there, the Atlanta Olympics.

I'll never forget one meeting that I had at IBM. Their whole approach and sell was this idea of e-business, and that was their whole platform; we're the company that's going to help change your business into a new business. I walk in with my recommendation for the Atlanta Olympics campaign and I say, okay, where's your projector? Where do I plug in to show you the stuff? And they go, oh, we use acetates. So here we are, the company who's promoting a business, and I had to go print out acetates to be able to show my presentation. The cobbler's children have no shoes, as they say. It was going to grow because, as with IBM it was a self-fulfilling prophecy.

The Internet is built on servers. In order for there to be the demand for more servers, you need to have content.

In order for there to be content, someone has to fund that. So the first year that we were doing it, it was with the eye towards, let's find all the places where we can add value in and really drive some interesting adjuncts to our campaign. We were making it up as we went along, and that was the first year.

The second year I remember Mary Ann Capanetto, one of the main IBM clients at the time, and William Absten, the media director over at Ogilvy, saying that we have to look at the Internet as an advertising vehicle not just as something fun to play around with and maybe drive business. We still have to hold it to fundamentals, and so we have to drive the CPM down and look at what it's going to bring to our plan overall. At this time there was no comScore and no real way to measure the reach and performance.

One of the first things I did, and one of the things I won an award for when I was at Ogilvy, I was the Al Gore of search, with the first real major search campaign. We'd have people that were buying a keyword here, a keyword there, and this was all pre-Google. This was the Yahoo, InfoSeek, Excite, Lycos and AltaVista days, and I'll never forget that we had talked to IBM about literally blocking out, for competitive advantage, the entire lexicon of tech words. From 'laptop,' to 'computer,' to 'server,' to all the brand names like 'AF400' or 'OS2,' or whatever IBM was trying to push.

There was a campaign, right around the time that Windows 95 came out. It was IBM's OS/2 campaign. I remember it vividly because it featured a very interesting face. In fact, the name of the campaign was "Faces," and it was just quotes about why OS/2 is so good and why it's better than Windows 95, etc.. So we decided we would do some fun conquesting, as they would call it these days, and we bought the words 'Microsoft,' 'Bill Gates,' 'IBM,' 'OS2,' 'Windows 95,' and 'Windows.' Again, this is pre-Google. This is pre text links, but every time someone searched they would see an IBM ad with the "Faces" and the claim. That was the best use of new media from 1996; virtually every time Bill Gates typed his word in he saw an IBM ad. We expanded upon that.

I knew Jeremy when he was at SoftBank. In fact, Jeremy and I shared a bond because he had worked at Ogilvy prior to me being there, but he'd gone over to the sales side at SoftBank, a Japanese company that was repping many Internet companies in the U.S.. He called me up one day, "Jeff, I'm not working at SoftBank anymore. I'm going to work for Rich LeFurgy over at Starwave." LeFurgy, who later became the first president of the IAB, was the head of Starwave, the official developer for the ESPN website. The next day he called me again, "I'm not working there anymore. Anil Singh just made me an offer to be the first sales guy reporting in to him at Yahoo." I said, "That's cool. When you settle in come see me."

Neil and Jeremy come into my office, and they think they're there to negotiate a two, maybe three month deal on the order of ten to twenty keywords. But we literally blocked out the entire lexicon of technology terms, and I remember one term in particular that IBM wanted called 'cryptolope.' I'm thinking, what the hell is a cryptolope? Nobody's searching 'cryptolope.' Cryptolope, as it turned out, is an encrypted envelope, which is a security type thing. I will never forget the look on Neil's and Jeremy's face when I said we want to block all these terms, like two hundred terms, for the year. Anywhere you could search you would see a banner come up with IBM on it if you were searching a tech term. And the responses were great. These were the days of six to eight percent response rates.

Awareness is high that IBM and Microsoft are strong online. Anderson & Lembke, Compaq and a few others were advertising back then as well. But again the tech industry was all self-fulfilling. Fund this content, let content grow, and at the end of the day more people will go online because there's more content there. The more people to go online, the more servers we'll need, and we'll still be selling our business. At the same time that the Internet's growing, you still had AOL growing by gangbusters, and one of the things that I did in '95, '96, maybe even '97 was the infamous Deep Blue versus Kasparov chess tournament.

Again, there were very few areas within AOL and on the web that were doing a lot of traffic. But we did a big area on AOL for the tournament, and then the one that we did on the web was a deal with WarnerBrothers. com. WarnerBrothers.com, at that time, was one of the more heavily trafficked sites. What we did was the first use of cartoon characters and animation on the web for a product. We took Bugs Bunny and Marvin the Martian and Elmer Fudd, and they ended up playing chess and promoting the live event for the chess tournament. That won, I think it was an Effie at one point. No, it was the ANA Award.

At the same time the web is growing, AOL was growing at an even faster pace because it was a simple person's web. And a lot of clients at that time were doing golf course deals. AOL's sell was, if you announce publicly that you've signed a deal with AOL, your stock price will go up by 20 percent. At that time it did, because Wall Street was really ignorant about how to value all this stuff.

There were some clients that just wanted to do deals, where they said, okay, we'll spend $15 million with no clue what they were getting for that money. And part of the problem was that AOL used a couple of tactics that today no planner worth their salt would allow them to get away with. No matter what your deal was they would dump the majority of the inventory into email and into chat, charge a ridiculous amount of inventory for the endemic, or for the real premium value stuff, and just a dollar CPM to bring your overall CPM into what you were looking for. Except there were two issues with it; no one wanted to buy that stuff to begin with, it was untargeted, and they were using server pushes.

This is the one thing that I still think planners don't pay enough attention to. Let's say you have a $15 million CPM that you want to pay on generally premium stuff, for an impression that would be there for the entire exposure time of that page being up. But then you have AOL that, every eight to ten seconds, would rotate the banner while charging the same CPM. It wasn't fair but planners overlooked it. It was blissful ignorance or selected attention, but I started fighting back against that, and one of the things that I fought back against was this idea of bottom line CPMs.

We brought in one client who shall remain nameless, whose deal we were doing from scratch. Since we were doing this from scratch I went ahead and took all the learning I had of all the tricks I knew and was not going to let them get away with it. I was giving them line-item byline-item to negotiate CPM to a proper CPM, up until I got a call that someone in senior management at the agency had used their contact. AOL complained that I was slowing things down. Yes, I was – on purpose. So this person agreed to the bottom line CPM, and that was one of the main reasons I decided to leave, because I'd gotten them to a place where they had to negotiate correctly and my own side ended up pulling the rug out of that negotiation. So that was one of the challenges.

I should mention one other thing with AOL, an interesting side note. Again, I was a media director on digital for IBM at the time, and had been trying to get in touch with AOL so we could look at and explore opportunities for IBM with them. I had been bringing senior people in to meet with Mary Ann, our client, but could only get the attention of a junior level sales rep at AOL. I said, no, I really want to speak with Myer Burlough, who was at the time the head of AOL sales. So after a month of trying to get in to them, I get an email from an AOL screen name, J-E-F-L-E-A, or something to that effect. He says, "Mr. Minsky, I think this was meant for you – you'd like to see this. This was forwarded to me by accident."

That junior level sales guy that I had been dealing with had mistyped the screen name that he was sending an email to and sent it to the wrong person, and in the email it says something to the effect of, "Myer, I hate to bother you with this, but this Jeff Minsky guy over at Ogilvy, who has a exaggerated sense of self importance would like to meet with you. I don't know if it's worth your time or not," blah, blah, blah, blah.

So I called Myer after getting this email and said, "Yes, could you please tell Myer that despite my exaggerated sense of self-importance, I still represent IBM and would like to get in front of them?" Within three minutes I had a phone call back and we were having brunch on Sunday on the upper west side. To which Myer says to me, "Jeff, I will always go around agencies. They slow things down and look at things too carefully." I said, "That's fine, go around me. They'll always send it back to us to analyze." That's exactly what happened over the years.

And I wonder what happened to that salesperson.

I don't know what ever happened to him, and Myer somehow escaped jail, but a number of AOL sales guys did not. But that's another story in of itself.

That's a different book.

Yeah, and again, over the years I ended up having to come in and was asked to fix and put value into AOL deals, and the problem wasn't AOL for getting what they were getting. My core blame was with Wall Street, and part of that goes into another story.

Being at Ogilvy we were very fortunate to have blue chip clients like Kodak and IBM and American Express, although we didn't handle their digital. We weren't really mired in .coms at the time. But our first .com was WebMD, and they were in a battle with Doctor Coop, and would look at the comScore weekly numbers specifically to see if Coop was up that week, or they were up that week. And they thought, and were right probably, that depending on who was up that week would reflect in their stock price. So they started dumping money, if they were behind, into bottom of the barrel cost-per-click networks.

Back then the bottom of the barrel was really bottom of the barrel, Asian pin-up sites and things like that. And we warned them. We told them not to do it but they continued, and then Doctor Coop would spend more money so they would be up, and WebMD would spend more money so they would be up. At the end of the day, that's a pyramid.

That's not sustainable. That was a house of cards ready to fall no matter what. And sure enough in 2000, that's when the house of cards fell. Every company playing that game – let's take our VC money, spend it on cost-per-click networks just to show Wall Street more eyeballs – wasn't realizing that quality counts just as much as quantity.

A lot of people were doing that back then.
They're still doing that today. If you look about at some of the networks, even with exchanges – and I know exchanges put targeting and behavioral data to make it more qualified – they're still missing the major point of what we've learned over fifteen years plus. That is, the Internet changed the dynamics of advertising to show just how important context is.

The frame of mind of the consumer at the time that they're receiving the message is important. That's one of the main things we have learned from every bit of research that we've done, and every bit of analytics on all the campaigns is that contextual relevance is far more important than behavioral targeting. Behavioral targeting is still better than pure demo, don't get me wrong, but contexts trump that.

I agree. Based on your background and all the things that you've seen and been involved with, if you could go back knowing what you know now and identify one or two things we should have done differently as a business, what would you recommend that it be?

Well, I would have invested in Google, that's the first thing. That was my one big mistake because I didn't quite understand the whole thing about Google and thought, who the hell needs another search engine? We had twenty of them.

Something that Greg Stuart from the IAB and I have had one difference of opinion on, that's threaded the past eight or ten years when we were all trying to get our definitions straight of what defines an impression. What defines a click? What defines a view, and how is research done? The major argument that I had with Greg is that Greg was about consistency over accuracy. We have to remember the IAB is a biased organization – biased towards sellers. They do not represent the Internet like they're supposed to be. They represent a very important but biased view of what Internet advertising should be, balanced by the 4A's that does the same thing for the agencies and for the clients. When they come out with standards, they're usually compromised standards. They're not exactly what we want and they're very good to work with. In fact, in 2000 I wrote Version 1.0 of the

Terms and Conditions with Lisa Baldwin who was over at Modem at the time.

So our definitions should all be consistent, but they don't have to be 100% accurate. I was all about accuracy which will lead to consistency. So even if it takes a little bit longer and we encourage them to adopt new technology that they didn't have before just so we can get an accurate measurement, then that was more important than consistency. Consistency is very important, but at the end of the day you'll get that if you're accurate. The problem we have now is that we're consistent, but we're inaccurate, and we're getting more inaccurate by the moment because the systems to be able to track mobile, and to be able to give me an accurate number of exactly how many people play FarmVille, CityVille, Angry Birds or whatever, don't exist. And now that the Internet is spreading out to all devices it is more complex.

We could have completely addressed that fifteen or ten years ago. We would have been a lot better positioned if we were about accuracy and had a clear definition on everything. There's still a lot of loosey-goosey numbers out there that billions of dollars of decisions are being made on.

What about the Aspen Group?
So in the late '90s a lot of people led by P&G and their FAST organization tried to put together a conference to get the industry kick-started, to be able to develop Terms and Conditions so we didn't have each agency writing their own and we could actually have a standard we could look to, to do business. But no one could get their act together and it wasn't getting done.

There was a conference that many of us had been invited to, initially called Digitrends and then eventually called iMedia, now part of DMG. And this conference would bring buyers and sellers together. So at one point we suggested that we get all the buyers into a room and without anything collusive being done, talk about some of the issues that were affecting the industry.

We formed an informal email list – Yahoo! Groups list, whatever it was called – called the Aspen Group. We kept in contact, and this email chain that went on for about six months led to the input that Lisa Baldwin and I put together to write the standards document for the 4A's. Mike Donahue was very supportive in taking our input from this group and writing the Standard Terms and Conditions for the 4A's perspective, which we then took from as a division of the 4A's.

We didn't do this on our own in collusion. We took the 4A's and negotiated it. Mike Donahue called it "the all-nighter" at the 4A's media conference in New Orleans back in 2000 or 2001. And at that conference you had Richy Glassberg and a whole bunch of folks from the IAB. We were negotiating on behalf of the IAB with us in the 4A's, and at the end of that evening – I think we finished negotiating at two in the morning or something ridiculous – we had done something that had never been done in any other medium. We had gotten the sellers to agree to allow us to put the terms of sequential liability into our Terms and Conditions, in addition to many other things.

Sequential liability was important. The Internet was the first medium where we were able to put the concept to use that you can only sue the people who have the money. So if the client has to pay the agency, you can only sue the agency not the client if the vendor doesn't get the money. If the client has not paid the agency, then the agency is held harmless and the only recourse is for the vendor to go after the client. That was exactly what we needed to get the Internet kick-started. It was a huge win for the industry, and since then sequential liability has found its way to standards and decencies across various other media types.

I'll always be able to point to Version 1.0 of the Ts and Cs and say, I co-authored that and helped change the course of how business is done. So at the end of my career if I ask myself, what have I done for the industry? To me that was a proud moment.

You have many proud moments, and a lot of influence in the business overall. Whenever I had a chance to listen to and talk with you I've learned from you. I've been able to watch you do what you're doing in the business, and it's been great.

I appreciate that. I just happen to have been at the right place at the right time and found something that was part of my passion point since I was thirteen.

To your earlier point, what Vickie said to you, to say that the Internet is not going to change things and digital is not going to take off, I never, and this should be very clear, said that it would take off at the detriment of TV. I love television. I think the fact that we still spend upwards of $2,000 to $3,000 to buy a TV set indicates that TV is not dying off any time soon. The business model is going to change. But the idea of co-viewing experiences, or watching big experiences on a big set while leaning back is something that I do believe my kids and my grandkids will be part of. Where they get that content and the nature of that content are two different things, and I think that's where it's going to change.

CLOSING REMARKS

Jeff has been a trailblazer in the business for many years. I was lucky enough to have met him on my first day in the business, and maintained that relationship for seventeen plus years. He has been influential in a number of ways, but what I take away most from him is the necessity to have standards in the business. Standards make it easier for new entrants to come into the business, lowering the bar for some while giving others something to overachieve against! Standards are of crucial importance and help serve to destroy any obsolete set of standards that may have been laid before it. Remember the 468x60 banner? That was a standard but the industry realized that it needed to go away.

I also take away a simple idea, that to be success-ful requires a personal interest in what you do. Jeff had an interest in computers, which could have easily been diverted to an interest in a moped but fortunately was not. To achieve success do what you love, or at least what you like; when you invest so much time and energy into your career better to enjoy it than be miserable. This business was built on the backs of people who loved it, and it still continues in that manner.

CHAPTER 12

JACK MYERS

Jack Myers is a veteran of the media business who has spent more than three decades as one of the industry's leading visionaries and economic forecasters. He currently serves as a media economist and chairman of Media Advisory Group. The Media Advisory Group invests in early stage companies that advance and support the media ecosystem and represents management teams in the sale of media companies with value of more than $100 million.

Jack speaks internationally on transformative business strategies, and publishes the weekly "Jack Myers Media Business Report." He also curates MediaBizBloggers. com, an open thought leadership platform for media, advertising and marketing professionals. Jack has authored three books on advertising and received multiple awards, including the George Foster Peabody Award for Journalism, the Crystal Heart Award from the Heartland Film Festival, and has been nominated for both an Academy and Emmy Award.

Jack Myers, you began the "Jack Myers Media Business Report" around '84, is that correct?

I started my company in '84 and have published a variety of editorial products since then, but as a subscription only report, we launched that in March of 2009. The Jack Myers Report, in one form or another, has been around since 1984.

What got you intrigued in covering digital media and the Internet?

My whole career has been built around anticipating trends and studying technology as it impacts media, advertising and marketing. If I've had a particular competence or skill, it's been accurately forecasting the impact of technology on our business. I may have accelerated the speed with which I thought change would take place, but contextually I've been pretty good at visualizing the future.

What led me to leave CBS in the early 1980s was I believed that cable had a strong future, and CBS was not investing in cable. So I left to become active in the cable universe. In 1993 I wrote a book called, *Adbashing: Surviving the Attacks on Advertising,* at the exact same time the Mosaic browser was being introduced. I wrote extensively in that book about the impending impact of interactivity on the future of advertising in media.

I've always been focused on the value of interactivity to the media and advertising business no matter what technology fostered it. With Internet browsers, it became clear that the Internet and the web were going to have an increasing impact. By 1998 I was fully committed to a focus on interactivity and the growth of digital media.

Do you remember what some of the early warning signs were for brands, and what intrigued them about the web as a viable tool for advertising?

Before the web I think what really spurred an interest in interactivity in '97, '98, '99 and 2000 was interactive television. In many ways interactive television has not progressed much beyond where it was in the year 2000. Digital has sped past it and been on a super highway, while interactive television has been in the old country dirt roads.

Advertisers, agencies and media companies began taking interactivity seriously as a result of a lot of the developments that came along around '98 or '99 in interactive television, and then transferred their interest over to what was happening in the Internet as it became obvious that Internet opportunities were going to be much more valuable than those that were being offered by various interactive TV companies.

What do you think the hold-up has been about interactive television versus the web?

Interactive television has primarily been restricted by the cable operators' decisions to avoid interoperability among the cable boxes from company to company and from cable operator to cable operator. It's been a focus on limited interactivity and maintaining their core subscription products around content and around Pay-Per-View, and to a limited extent, On Demand.

In 2003 the cable industry made the decision to stay with their dumb set-top boxes, which meant a seven to ten year amortization process before newer interactive boxes would be distributed widely. We have new set-top boxes with true interactivity coming into the industry right now. The industry made a conscious decision to avoid the introduction of digital interactivity, which allowed the Internet and TV connectivity to explode.

Seven to ten years, so you're talking between 2011 and 2014 or so?

Yes, before 2014.

Do you think that's when we're going to see a lot more interactive television coming to the forefront?

We're seeing it. We've seen it with the investment by six cable operators in Canoe Ventures, which even though it had a slow start, focused on creating interoperability for interactive offerings. More importantly, we're seeing that the consumer electronics manufacturers are building in WiFi and Bluetooth to enable the television to link directly to the Internet, and that's creating a competitive reality that forces the cable operators to be much more focused on what they can do internally within their own systems to embrace and expand interactivity. We are seeing a great deal of two-screen technology and content developers, focusing on the synchronous marriage between the television and mobile devices, the television and tablets, the television and computers. Social TV and TV commerce are two huge growth businesses.

You mentioned the consumer electronics companies are integrating web vehicles into the televisions and onto their devices. Many are being done in the app space because they've begun integrating apps into television sets. Do you think the app space has made that bridge clearer to people?

Absolutely. I envision in the future we'll turn on our television set and up will pop our apps as opposed to the guides that we see now. And people will control their apps sitting on their couch with simple gesture recognition, without even a remote control in the long-term future. That technology already exists and is sophisticated enough to work.

Put Microsoft Kinect on steroids and take what you see with the iPad and the app lite model and build that into your television. Whether Internet delivered or cable operator delivered, we've got a radically different vision for the future of television.

You help brands understand where things are going to go from a media perspective. To do that, you have to stay on top of current trends and current developments in companies. How do you prioritize and stay on top of all the different things that are going on?

It's a process that's been developed over years of trying to gather a lot of intelligence from a lot of sources. Listen to smart people when they talk. See what's happening at the trade shows and draw some logical conclusions out into the future. I'm somewhat of a sponge. I soak in as much as I can and then try to find the common themes and patterns and form logical conclusions.

When I was at CBS from 1976 to '82, I was responsible for new business development, and as part of that I started paying a lot of attention to technology because I thought that would open business opportunities. At the time, CBS was not necessarily the best place to do that but I learned early on that you have to pay a lot of attention to advances in technology, understanding that the changes in our industry happen very, very slowly, but they do happen. Technology is the lead force that allows you to anticipate what those changes will be.

I talk to some people and they tell me they try to focus on certain categories of technology. I talk to others and their response is basically they don't sleep. It's amazing how people balance all the learning that's required to stay on top of this business.

There's a fine line between trying to stay ahead of things that are happening and falling behind on certain things. When you try to stay on top of too much you inevitably fall behind on others. The difference between what I do and what a lot of people do is I don't necessarily drill down deeply into specific issues or business opportunities. I'm not running a business in the nature of a media company or an agency. I'm not responsible for a narrowly focused part of the business that I have to stay ahead of in order to be successful. So I'm more interested in the big picture patterns that emerge and therefore don't have to be concerned if I miss that little nugget for a few weeks, or a few months, as long as I'm picking up on the ultimate trends that I see evolving and emerging. I'm also looking, for the most part, twelve months, twenty-four months, thirty-six months, ten years down the road as opposed to being concerned about what's going to happen next week.

Were there any trends that surprised you over the last six years? Any that caught you off guard?

I anticipated social media but I thought it was going to evolve more out of gaming and the virtual worlds, like Neopets and Club Penguin and those types of social activities. With the success of myYearbook, console gaming and the social gaming sector, along with virtual currencies I believe that business is fulfilling its promise.

I was into Facebook when it was still .EDU. I saw that coming, but how rapidly it has evolved into the greatest social influence of our time could not have been anticipated. I also believed Twitter would be successful. I published an interview with Biz Stone weeks after it launched. Mobile has evolved a little more slowly than I would have anticipated, in terms of it being a valuable advertising medium. I think we've still got a ways to go on that one. What surprised me more is how slowly the industry has embraced online video, and that YouTube has not moved more quickly to evolve into a viable advertising medium.

Do you think that part of the slow evolution of online video has been a combination of the lack of true quality programming and the abundance of user-generated content that's been witnessed in the video space?

Yes, but YouTube and Google have been very slow to define advertiser-friendly content around user-generated video, and developing more traditional channels and formats. They are now moving in this direction and it could have a dramatic impact on the business, primarily by reducing the cost-per-thousand and cost-per-view of online video advertising. I think there probably could be any number of compilation and aggregation plays out of the YouTube space that Google, for a variety of reasons, has not yet really developed or focused on. Traditional media models in television are still very strong, and the traditional thirty-minute or sixty-minute program model is still very strong. It's unlikely that's going to collapse and be replaced by the two- to three-minute video model. They will co-exist.

A primary reason why online video has been slow to evolve into real business is that we still have the twisted pair of copper wires coming into the home and that slows the delivery. As 4G and wireless distribution of TV into the home becomes more viable, we will experience a dramatic shift in the home video experience.

So you think mobile is potentially a good boon for online video?

4G wireless is a huge boon for online video, yes.

That definitely makes sense to me. I think more and more people are starting to access video through their devices, not necessarily from their computer, and it's becoming an entertainment platform in and of itself. After 2000/2001 when the bubble burst, did you think the business was going to recover in a quick manner?

I never believed that the bust was a long-term collapse of digital media. That was an illogical conclusion out of the bust. I gave a speech in 2000 comparing the Internet boom to the tulips in the Netherlands, but pointing out that the technologies and interactivity were not going to go away. There continue to be huge investments made on the assumption that if it's built, advertisers will support it. But the amount of money that is available from advertisers is relatively stable and cannot support all the VC-funded digital companies competing today. So we may be in another mini-bubble.

If you're not bringing a superior product to the table versus what marketers have available to them now, then you're not going to grow and succeed. I think social media is a hugely superior product for marketers, but I also think it draws primarily from promotional and direct marketing spending as opposed to advertising spending. Mobile, especially when combined with GPS, delivers enhancement capabilities. Online video distribution, when combined with quality content, will be huge. I also believe that the traditional legacy media, for the most part, are pretty well positioned to capitalize on a lot of these trends.

I don't consider Facebook to necessarily be the greatest new marketing opportunity since television but it has massive social and cultural impact, which marketers need to learn how to appropriately exploit. They can capitalize on social media opportunities with TV programs like *The Biggest Loser, American Idol,* programs that people are passionate about, and media content that people are already engaged with. That's more relevant than putting an ad onto a Facebook profile page.

Do you think technology drives the consumers and how they interact with media, or that consumers drive how the technology is adopted by the media platforms?

Apple introduced the idea of apps, but it was consumers who embraced and drove the business. I don't think anyone at Apple necessarily anticipated that apps would be as fundamental to the business as they have been. Consumers take technology and design it to meet their interests and needs, and I think there's a lot of technology out there that falls flat because it doesn't really meet consumer needs or interests.

Apple started this whole app revolution. They created the iPhone, and part of their operating system was they wanted to have the system run on applications, and then consumers really took it and ran. Now we're seeing apps integrated into television sets, into your car and your refrigerator. It's one of those situations where the adoption of the platform is driving the rest of the electronics manufacturers and publishers to find ways to create the interface for their application using this new model. It's a "what came first, the chicken or the egg" kind of a question, because when you start to dive down into what drives that adoption, is it the industry as a whole? Or is it the consumers who point at stuff and say, "I want that, I don't want that"?

Ultimately it comes back to the consumer; you can't anticipate adoption rates. People really defined what Twitter is all about. Twitter is more content but the capability has been defined by how it's being used in Iran and Egypt, and as a marketing tool, as opposed to it being how people originally envisioned it, as a way for people to simply communicate with their best friends and family.

Who would have anticipated that Twitter would change societies, politics, global relationships and impact on the way people live?

You get a chance to talk to a lot of people in this business. You mentor many people in this business. What are some qualities you think make someone successful in this business?

Number one is passion. The people I know who have been successful in this business love it. They love being a part of it. They're passionate about it. They care about it. Historically, being successful in the business required to a degree, conservatism, and you look back at the history of television, radio, newspaper, magazine, business models, they're relatively unchanged for the last fifty or sixty years. Success has been driven in the traditional parts of the industry by adhering to the legacy models and not challenging them.

The growth and success in the last ten years has been by adapting those same legacy models with new distribution technologies. So we've got somewhat of a conflicting set of universes in our business. We've got those who are responsible for the business and tend to be more traditional and conservative, and those who are responsible for innovation and creativity, and for advancing the state of the industry. They've been people who had a passion not for media as much as they've had a passion for what's possible. How can you tap into the technological opportunities that are out there?

Whether it's going back to David Sarnoff and William Paley and Leonard Goldenson and the early innovators in television and radio; or today, there's Jeff Bezos and Steve

Jobs and Mark Zuckerberg, who have a vision and pursue that vision to whatever extent they possibly can, and let the business models follow and adapt to the technology, and the opportunities to the revenue streams. But the revenue streams have been almost secondary to their passion and their belief. On the business side, it's been those who are fairly conservative who understand the traditional models, the legacy models. That's very slowly changing.

When I talk to Sir Martin Sorrell at WPP and Nick Brien at Interpublic and Rishad Tobaccawala at Publicis, there's a different attitude and approach and vision. There's a return to the focus on the business model. What are the possibilities for business growth and renewal, rather than technology adoption? And there are business developments taking place that evolve out of a love and passion for the advertising and media business, rather than out of concern for how Wall Street is going to react. A perfect example is Les Moonves at CBS, who had to focus on Wall Street but whose decisions have been driven by his passion for quality content and his concern about audiences.

If there's a danger to our business today, it's that VCs invest without a great deal of understanding of the business models that are likely and possible, and invest in companies that are unlikely to have value for another decade, if ever. But they expect results in three years. We have a lot of early stage companies that will not be given the time they're going to need.

Some of the VC people might argue with you, but I agree with what you're saying. I think a lot of people don't

necessarily dive into what the reality behind the business is going to be and that has caused some of the issues when we talk about bubbles; whether referring to the bubble from ten years ago or, if you are correct, that little bit of a bubble developing now.

People do seem to invest in things without always thinking through how the consumers are going to react and what the business model could be as far as consumers are concerned. What you're saying has merit.

Thanks.

Are you an early riser or a night owl? How do you get stuff done?

I'll typically work until eleven, midnight, 1 a.m., and then I'm up 6:30 or 7 a.m.. I don't consider myself either a particularly early riser or particular night owl. I'm fortunate that I'm able to write my reports fairly quickly after gathering the intelligence. So I'm able to produce and publish content with both quality and quantity.

In addition to providing a wealth of content, your content makes sense. You think things through and grasp a lot of subjects faster than most because you're used to looking at them with that 30,000-foot view.

A lot of that is from having listened to a lot of people over the years, so when someone says something new or different for them I recognize it and I can acknowledge it and understand what the change is. When I hear Sir Martin Sorrell of WPP talk about the importance of content ownership and how they're building their future business models around ownership of content, I recognize the importance for WPP and the industry.

That's something that's been gestating within that company for over a decade, but the fact that it's now bubbled to the surface and is coming out as a major initiative for the company is a sea of change, and it will have ripple effects on the industry. Sir Martin makes a lot of comments, but if I'm able to hear them, synthesize them and communicate what was said that was truly different and important, it has value to my subscribers.

What motivates you?

I truly love this business. Talk about passion. I grew up building crystal radios and digging behind the set of my TV to try and figure out how it worked. I owned one of the first transistor radios. I grew up in the town where GE manufactured radios and was part of the first teen focus groups GE had on transistor radios. I had one of the very first transistor radios ever manufactured, and it never left my hand. I loved both radio and television, majoring in radio/television at Syracuse University. All I wanted after college was to work in radio and television, and I did. I'm very fortunate that I picked an industry that doesn't stop advancing. In a lot of ways it hangs on to its legacy models but keeps getting better and more interesting.

CLOSING REMARKS

Jack writes prolifically, he volunteers his time to Syracuse University, mentors hundreds of young people, and engages with many entrepreneurs to help them think through their ideas, all in the hopes of seeing the bigger picture. Listening to Jack's POV on this business, I am reminded of two things. First, success follows passion. This business is filled with people who are brimming with passion. If you're not passionate about your business you can never succeed.

The second thing is to get out of the weeds and see the forest for the trees. If you are mired in the details all day you could miss the bigger picture. Check things off your list, but try to sit back and think things through or you could spend too much time diving into work that won't return the highest benefit. When you are capable of seeing things from a strategic view you can better prioritize, follow the trends, and apply them to what you do best. If you are fortunate enough to spend time with Jack, or anyone else at his level in the business, count yourself lucky and make great use of the time!

CHAPTER 13

MAGGIE BOYER FINCH

Maggie Boyer Finch kick-started her career in advertising at the age of sixteen, interning for large, traditional ad agencies. This quickly led to the discovery of Internet advertising and a passion for digital media. In 1993 she moved her life to Silicon Alley, where she and two other media entrepreneurs launched a small digital media agency called iballs, which eventually rolled up to help form Avenue A. Avenue A rose to prominence and grew into one of the largest, most successful online agencies in the world, eventually becoming Razorfish, as it is known today. During her tenure with Avenue A, Maggie led the development of online media efforts for many brands, helping blaze the path for most of the online advertising you see today.

Maggie eventually became VP of media, and general manager of aQuantive, the holding company that owned

Avenue A and Atlas DMT. During this period she also played a leadership role in the formation of DRIVEpm, which grew to become one of the leading ad networks serving direct marketers online. When Avenue A was acquired by Microsoft, Maggie continued her growth and development as chief of staff for APS and general manager for the Publisher Tools division within Microsoft.

Maggie took a break, in her own words, to start a family and recently rejoined the ranks of the digital entrepreneurs with her new company, King of The Web. Maggie's role throughout the life of the industry has been significant, as that of a leader and influencer.

Maggie Boyer Finch, you're a veteran of the online business and definitely of the online ad business, how did you get started?

A bit haphazardly, I suppose, as a lot of people do in their careers. I started out with an internship courtesy of an aunt, who was working at Wunderman Cato Johnson. I encountered a world of traditional agency inter-workings, which affirmed my infatuation with advertising but inspired me to seek something more. WCJ's focus was on direct-response, specific-to-print television and a little bit of radio. This gave me a good foundation from which to grow. But frankly, I spent a lot of time ordering pizzas for meetings. Still, I managed to find time to pop in and out of the different groups: creative, media, sports marketing, DRTV and newspaper.

I really got a good flavor for all of the DR channels at an early age. There was a moment in time, and I can't say exactly when or where it was, that Young & Rubicam and Wunderman decided to form a digital media group.

Back then it was just called the Email Group. We would buy some email lists or be on message boards and that was about it. There were a handful of people in New York, and one guy in Chicago who comprised the digital media team. The guy in Chicago was Paul Marin, and he was a creative. He needed a media partner and was kind enough to involve me. It seemed like a great opportunity, and so it began.

At the time I had a boss who thought this was a gigantic waste of time. But I, somewhat secretly, pursued the opportunity despite his lack of enthusiasm. When we landed some budget from H&R Block to do an email-based promotion, my boss was noticeably agitated about the waste of time that the Internet fad was creating. More importantly, he couldn't believe any client would want to spend money online. H&R Block wanted to spend $10,000 on email, which was probably $10,000 out of maybe a $10 million DRTV budget. But still they were excited about it.

So I grabbed it and ran. I met with companies like Juno, who were just starting to socialize CD-ROM marketing concepts. It was hard to find the right media partners, since the media outlets themselves weren't entirely sure how to sell digital media. In the end, this little campaign for H&R Block was awkward. It was geared toward young people and so obviously off-brand; in some cases you got an email inviting you to a nightclub to listen to a band, and I guess you had your taxes prepared afterwards or something. It was sort of a bizarre relationship but it actually worked.

So that's the first online campaign that I ever did, and it just kept trickling in like that for a while. Established brands would show up with one-off projects or whacky ideas, and Paul and I would make it happen. The conversations were minimally sophisticated with senior marketers saying stuff like, I want to try this email-thingy or that Internet-thingy. I think Paul had the only Internet connection in the office, and I would go sit at his desk to surf chat rooms or learn how to use email.

Then suddenly things picked up pace. NY had a growing digital media team, so I took a trip to the New York office and met with three or four folks brave enough to jump ship from their traditional media planning jobs. Despite the risk it was killer to be given some autonomy for the first time. In a world where "Mad Men" style hierarchy is hard to break into, I was loving this burst of empowerment. I also loved that it was uncharted territory, that it needed definition, and that the pace of growth seemed unstoppable! Out of nowhere, Yahoo popped up as a powerhouse and that was a transition point for digital advertising and for me.

Yahoo decided to create an online portal for the average person, a friendly point of access to the Internet. I remember while at Wunderman, talking to Softbank Interactive who was the rep firm for Yahoo at the time. They came in on a sales call and brought Jerry Yang with them. It was a very casual meeting. I brought my boss and we demonstrated that we had some real advertiser interest at our agency. Jerry talked about something called "hot words." These eventually morphed into what we now know as 'keywords' or 'search.' I remember thinking, this is so cool. Within about a month or two it was an impossibility to talk to Jerry Yang anymore.

It just grew so quickly after that. Did I mention that I loved it? And from there, there was no looking back. I never returned to traditional media. That was the beginning for me.

Then you ended up being part of this really large agency that was breaking the barriers down and getting larger brands involved in the business. How did you get into that position?

The segue to Avenue A and aQuantive, later named Razorfish, was a fast on-ramp. I went from sitting at 2 a.m. press checks and listening to an account executive teach me how to choose the right shade of pantyhose for a client meeting, to launching Avenue A's media division in a short span of time. Things moved so much quicker in the world of digital media. Organizations were nimble, young, flat and smart. Campaigns went up in days and results came back in minutes. Some would later argue it was a bit too fast.

After the Wunderman experience I moved to New York and met up with Michael Cohen and Steve Klein, who had the idea to launch a small media agency that was completely digital. It was perfectly brilliant, and the three of us built this little business called iballs, which we thought was really witty of course...eyeballs and impressions.

It was witty!
Really, it wasn't that witty. The people who prank called us and said, "Is this Big Balls?" – they were the witty ones. So a lesson learned in naming a company or brand. But

really it was insane, within months we couldn't keep up with the pace of business, primarily from companies that hadn't existed three months prior but now had massive amounts of money to spend. Of course I'm referring to the .com boom. There was a fair amount, maybe 30 percent to 40 percent of companies that were traditional businesses who were just early movers and shakers such as JCrew.com. They were an early digital company, as were many catalog businesses.

The others were companies like N2K, Music Boulevard, and a number of other Internet businesses that have since disappeared through acquisition or meltdown, but at the time they were flush with cash. At iballs five of us sat in 500 square feet and churned out media campaigns, full of 468x60s. The 468x60 size quickly became a standard ad size, but not without some pain. We were cold calling on companies and saying, "Can we put this image on your website? It's roughly this size," and the easiest thing to do was place an image at the top and bottom of the page, which was roughly 468x60.

We doubled the size of iballs overnight. And in about a year and a half the industry was enormous. It was like a rabid dog foaming at the mouth. My schedule as a young person was to get in at 7 a.m., crank out banner campaigns until 8 p.m., then hit industry parties until 2 a.m.. It was fabulous and draining.

Keywords (search) were always part of the media mix, but most of the money was spent on ad banners, primarily 468x60s. A good chunk of a media planner's day was spent standing by the fax machine waiting for hundreds of pages of click-through reports to come back from dozens of different websites. Each site had different reporting formats and ways of measuring impressions and clicks. We only thought about hits and clicks at the time. After receiving these infinitely long reports you would manually enter all of the data into a spreadsheet in Excel. That was how we first measured performance. We've come a long way.

That was the extent of the media business back then. It was rough around the edges but still full of transformational promise, stuff traditional media could never do. And the ad spend just kept growing, and we could barely keep up. At that point there were probably only several hundred of us digital media people in the entire world. We were a small conference at best. We concentrated in New York and SF, and most of us were pretty young so naturally we all went out after work. I can't remember who started it, maybe it was Tom Hespos, but I'll never forget the Internet Drinking Bureau.

The IDB!

That constituted half of the world's digital media talent, right there in one bar every Thursday night. We had a community! As soon as you fired those performance reports off to your customers, you'd go out to some $250,000 launch party every night of the week. Not just on Friday nights or Saturday nights. No, every night of the week there was another one. Snowball! Tripod! You went partly because it was a work event. The people at those parties were the knowledge trust. Anybody who knew anything about what was going on in digital media was at those functions. The community was strong. In fact, as you're writing this book, I bet you find that a lot of those same people are the knowledge trust today.

But to be honest, we mostly went to those parties because it was a blast. And who wouldn't want to go to a party where Wyclef and Yoko Ono were emceeing a small get together hosted by Sonic.net?

Yes, there are a lot of the same people still at the core.
It's a testament to the pace of evolution in digital business. Without that evolution and change, those really smart people would not have stayed engaged all these years. It's yet to hit a point of stagnation. Contrarily, ambitious young people going into TV, print or radio advertising in the '90s felt like there was little room for growth. There were always going to be hundreds of people that got there first and little chance of finding something undiscovered, because nothing was really changing.

Digital business is changing so quickly that smart people keep coming in droves, and the new guy can be as smart as the old-timer. There are loads of opportunities for young people.

The path to Avenue A was like that for me. As all of these online businesses popped up, more companies were built to service them. One of those companies was Avenue A. At the time I'm not certain Avenue A knew what it wanted to be. Before I joined the team, I believe they were testing out the ad network model. But at some point the agency model prevailed, and that's when I started chatting with the founders. Short story short, I joined in '98 to build and run the media buying and planning discipline. Shortly after Avenue A purchased iballs. The iballs offices became the agency's New York subsidiary. They really adopted iballs and we grew into something bigger and better. Those were the very beginnings of Avenue A.

I like the term that they "adopted" you.
They really did. Avenue A, even though they were still trying to figure themselves out, was smart and ambitious! At iballs we were smart and scrappy. We were getting stuff done, and I give us loads of credit. But the founders at Avenue A, when I met them I said to myself, these guys are thinking big. They were creating their own technology. They didn't like the technologies that existed, so why not? Back then there were only a couple of companies in the ad serving business. Can you remember the names of them?

Like Adknowledge?
Adknowledge was one. There was another one.

MatchLogic?
MatchLogic was another! I remember them coming in to pitch when I was still in New York. They pitched the idea of paying for technology to track ads. I had an army of people that were just pulling in faxes and inputting impressions and click data into Excel. The ad server idea sounded pretty awesome. But when I got to Avenue A and saw what they were up to, it blew all of these other companies out of the water.

The vision was so holistic. It was technology coupled with all of the services of an agency. We put these pieces together under one roof. We challenged the idea that we were measuring the right stuff at all. We even went to the first digital media conference in a gorilla suit and named the gorilla ROI (Roy) trying to get people to remember the importance of R-O-I, not just clicks and impressions.

This all sounded too good to pass up. They were a passionate, smart group of people that had two really important characteristics. One, a complete lack of knowledge about traditional media, which meant they weren't at all afraid to break the mold. Two, they were technologically driven. They wanted to turn the fundamentals of the media business into a technology business. Technology was more efficient and accurate than people in many ways, which freed humans up to tackle other problems, like custom analytics that demonstrated unparalleled value from an agency.

This made the value of banners and buttons and links and search words crystal clear. We created many of the necessary tools for valuing online advertising. We weren't the only people doing this, but I believe we were the best.

This is one of the reasons that I wanted to do this book in the first place. This is a great example of a company, in Avenue A, where the story could be lost. You had iballs, the two companies merged, and Avenue A continued to grow and dominate the space for a long time, maintaining its brand and eventually turning into Razorfish. There's a whole generation now working at Razorfish who have no idea any of this ever took place. They think Razorfish has been around for forty years.

You're so right. Just a couple weeks ago I bumped into a young guy in my office building and we introduced ourselves. He works at digital commerce business in the upstairs office space. I asked, "Have you been in that company long?" He said, "Oh, yeah, but I launched my career at Razorfish," and there was an earnest look of pride in his eyes when he said it. I thought to myself, that's so cool. But I just said, "I love that company."

You didn't say, "I helped start that company"?
No, I was proud on the inside. It was a nice moment. There are many of us that have had this experience, knowing that you were part of the genesis is enough.

You left for a while, right? You got out of the advertising side of the business, but you're still in the media side of the business, so you have a unique perspective. What do you think is going to shape the next five or ten years of the media business?
It's a tough question because I don't feel like a media expert anymore. When I checked out of all the digital media stuff I really checked out because I went and got knocked up with twins, and that sort of threw me for a loop! But I do have a unique perspective.

I watched an industry get its shit together. People were tackling tough stuff like, what's the efficacy of a pop-up ad? What seemed like a basic question was actually heady stuff. How do we address ethics in digital advertising? How do we mesh reporting systems, new and old? How do we marry elements from three or four industry sectors into one? And while we made great strides in our maturity as an industry, there was plenty more change afoot.

When I went on my first maternity leave, it was at the moment Google launched their AdSense program. In the time it took me to have some babies, Google had literally taken over the digital advertising world. It couldn't have been more than six months.

I felt like I couldn't recover. I felt like I picked the worst six months to procreate. What once was a portion of a media buyer's job was now an entire chunk of the industry, dedicated to managing keywords on Google. That was it. So I took the opportunity to reflect on my career path and made a shift to help my colleague, Scott Howe, on the publisher side of the business. He was launching aQuantive's first publisher business, an ad network called DRIVEpm.

As a side note, we made the shift from calling the entire business Avenue A to calling it aQuantive when we decided to sell products to other agencies, competitors. The Atlas Technology was too valuable to only make available to Avenue A, so a second business was born, Atlas DMT. Avenue A and Atlas were then housed under the company name aQuantive. I think it was Sean Finnegan who first voiced a concern about buying technology from a competing agency. He was pissed off about the shift to a holding company name and felt it may disguise something more sinister. (It might not have been Sean, but I'll stick to my story since he's a good sport.) Anyway, Sean was upset and felt we may be trying to pull the wool over his eyes. If he purchased Atlas Technology, suddenly, his top competitor was taking money from his pocket and possibly benefiting from his data. It was a valid concern, so we went to great lengths to compartmentalize the Atlas ad serving business from Avenue A's agency business. Hence, the holding company aQuantive was born. This was also useful when launching DRIVEpm, the ad network.

I remember that issue coming up often.

A lot of people were mad about the Avenue A, Atlas relationship at first, but over time we earned the trust back. Anyway, I came back from maternity leave and made the shift to helping Scott with his fledging ad network business. I mean, heck, we had a technology, we had an agency so why not throw caution to the wind and start selling ads? Scott launched DRIVE with an amazing team, and when I came back from leave he enticed me to come and play.

Working on the publisher side of the business I quickly learned how hard it was to be on the other side. It also showed me how complicated the publisher business was. After all those years buying media, I thought I understood my sales counterparts, but I was wrong. Too often I looked across the negotiation table and thought, what's so difficult here, man? Just give me the price in need, I'm about to give you a bunch of money.

It's not that easy is it?

DRIVE gave me amazing perspective. Just the rigor of managing a sales cycle, the complexity of establishing demand when ninety percent of your inventory is unsold is daunting. When you buy unsold inventory and arbitrage it, you know every publisher's dirty secrets. It's a complex and fragile ecosystem on the sell side. I had totally underappreciated this. Publishers had a far more complex business than the agencies ever had, ever. This experience was like finding the missing piece to a puzzle you've worked on forever.

I think a lot about that career transition, about classifying myself less as an agency person and more as a media person. We have enjoyed a buyer's market for so long that the advantage was never really in the publisher's court. Publishers had to be profoundly smart to survive that market climate, which made me realize the tide would eventually turn.

I think publishers should focus on selling more creative products. That means everything from social to video to targeting, and everything in between. The industry just lit up, again, and I can't imagine that's going to slow soon. Social media is the new 468x60. Oddly, social media allows us to build media plans that don't spend a dime. There's this new dollar-less media world.

In a long-winded way, I'm expressing that the pendulum has swung again. It's not swung too far however, things are more balanced than ever. It feels like we've matured and there's healthy tension on buy and sell sides. The pace of innovation has escalated again. Ads are morphing. Young media mavens are learning some of what we already know, but also teaching us new tricks. Overall the pie is still growing.

Gone are the days when agencies bundle up their spending clout and make ridiculous demands. But similarly, publishers do not roll in piles of ad dollars without proof that advertisers are benefiting. I keep thinking we might see the upfront come back, but I know it's sort of fool's gold, you know?

That train's left the station. I also think gone are the days of having to get all your reports through a fax machine.

Thank god. I will say, though, we used to use the thermal fax paper that came in a big roll, so it was possible to realize a decent high by hovering over the fax machine long enough.

Yeah, and then you'd have to go find it because it would all roll up.

Exactly, and you would spend the first twenty minutes just trying to flatten the paper out without smudging the ink. I don't miss those days.

You know, when you're not interviewing me, I'd be curious to hear where you think it's all going. I'm sitting in all these social agency pitches lately for King of The Web, and it's fascinating, the technologies they're using and the campaign cycles that last only a few days. We used to brag about turnaround times of thirty days. They're like, well, a social media campaign is roughly 48 hours – totally different.

CLOSING REMARKS

Maggie was part of the founding team of what eventually became one of the leading digital agencies, Razorfish. Her work in the early days and her leadership in the industry are responsible for much of the foundation that has set the stage for the current levels of growth. What I also found interesting is that she was able to take time out to have a family and jump back into the business without skipping a beat! Many people worry that once you're out it's hard to get back in. But when you are passionate and smart, jumping back in is just a matter of getting back up to speed on the newest developments!

CHAPTER 14

RISHAD TOBACCOWALA

Rishad Tobaccowala is currently chief strategy and innovation officer at VivaKi, part of Publicis Groupe. Rishad is a visionary in our industry, consistently pushing forward the business, innovating in the advertising and marketing category, and leading great minds down a path that provides clients with actionable insights that improve their performance. During his time with Publicis he has held the positions of CEO at Denuo as well as president of Starcom IP. He oversees and unites the strength of holding company assets such as Digitas, Starcom MediaVest, Razorfish and Zenith Optimedia as these agencies blaze trails for their clients. Prior to Publicis, Rishad was the founder of Giant Step and the Interactive Marketing Group at Leo Burnett.

Rishad is an avid early adopter of new technology and has shown repeated ability to help brands take advantage of that technology to engage with their consumers. He is a heavy traveler, speaking at conferences and with clients all over the world, and his leadership has helped develop and influence some of the most impactful people in the business of online marketing.

Rishad Tobaccowala, thank you for taking the time to chat today! You're a busy man so let's get started. You were very early into digital, having founded the interactive marketing group at Leo Burnett back in '94. What attracted you to the digital marketing space?

I came at it originally from a direct marketing background, in that my previous assignment at Leo Burnett had been in direct marketing. I quickly realized that the data collection and segmentation that occurred in direct marketing could be very powerful if applied properly. However, the cost of actually executing a program tended to make direct marketing not very viable for most clients because of the cost of buying names, the cost of production, the cost of mailing.

At that same time I was also interested in technology. As I began to see things happening in the early days of America Online, etc., I thought, hey, you've got the power of direct marketing without a lot of the cost structure and with the ability to be far more creative than direct marketing. And that's what originally brought me in, which is a combination of technology and creativity to take what was direct marketing to another level.

And in those early days were you capable of identifying all the different analytics and the components of track-

ing and measurement, to be able to bring the direct marketing into digital space, or did it take a little while?

To a great extent it's still a work in progress. What began to happen is others came at it from a direct approach. My previous background prior to the last assignment in direct marketing was brand marketing. And while to a certain extent relative to brand marketing there were a lot more metrics, many were not necessarily appropriate.

In those early days it was things like clicks on an ad that most advertisers were looking at, but there was also the ability to do pre- and post-measurement of people who had come to your site or destination. In '94, '95, online marketing was really about Prodigy, CompuServe and America Online. It was not about the World Wide Web as we know it today. Just around then is when the Netscape browser was being developed. And it wasn't really till '96 or '97 that it began to become more of a World Wide Web approach. In those days, on things like America Online we did some really unique campaigns. We took McMom's, which was the online and direct mail program targeting mothers that McDonald's was running, and we ported it over to America Online (AOL). We created a great initiative called Oldsmobile Celebrity Circle, which was a way we put together message boards, a virtual showroom and a live talk show every night on America Online. In that way we took over the sign-in page every night from 8 p.m. to 9 p.m.

We did not necessarily take part in the first actual advertising deals, but one of the more interesting first forms of advertising on the web was *Wired*. In fact, two, three days ago I was just talking to Rick Boyce who was also one of the early pioneers. Rick and some of the folks from Giant Step, as well as folks from Leo Burnett and I developed a sponsored show on Wired.com called "Packet." What we found particularly attractive was that you had new forms of engagement. We were early on so we were pioneers and there were no rules. We had new forms of metrics and measurement to play with, and because these were new programs we did pre-post analysis as well. We examined clicks and the number of visitors.

But also, when you were pioneering in the early days, one of the big things that we would get was a lot of publicity. Almost every one of these programs was covered in *Wall Street Journal* articles. Our clients enjoyed it because, also, there was no way to know how to price it and we took advantage of that absence of information. Even when we participated in the early days of America Online, even America Online didn't know what they had. Two years later when we withdrew from those placements, the other brands that tried to take over the same content and marketing opportunities had to pay twenty times as much as we did. So one of the things I always tell people today is if you pioneer, it's not as much about being shot with arrows in your back as leading with spears in your front.

This whole idea of pioneering being bad and brands being hesitant is because you're scared. There's no reason why you shouldn't pioneer. One of the key things we learned, and I continue to learn, is go early, go fast, otherwise go to sleep.

That's a good motto and one I think a lot of people did live by initially, at least for the first ten years of the business as things were changing so quickly. What were some of the early challenges?

There were three areas we had to spend a lot of time with. The first was selling the medium. Today we don't have to really sell the medium. In those days we had to sell online. Nobody was on it. There was also a challenge to access, 56K were considered a fast speed for a modem. There was no broadband. And relative to television, which has always remained a critically important part of the way marketers have thought of things, the feeling at the time was that we couldn't do as many things online as we possibly can with other media. The audience just wasn't there, and the access and experience was poor. Brands were questioning whether it would have any scale. And why couldn't they do the things they could do on TV? Obviously on 56K broadband you couldn't do streaming video. That was one of the biggest challenges.

The other challenge was to build a case of how to measure it. Once you began to measure it, there was some issue as to whether we were measuring the right metrics.

The third issue was how not to take traditional advertising and just put it online. What we were proud about was taking something like Celebrity Circle Oldsmobile, and questions about usage and activity, which would eventually be referred to as "engagement." We wanted to know when they had the greatest traffic so we asked an old fashioned question; what's prime time on AOL? It turned out that primetime on AOL was 8 p.m. to 9 p.m., or 9 p.m. to 10 p.m. Eastern, not surprisingly because that's when people are home. In those days there wasn't much connectivity at office.

Second, what do people spend all their time on? They were spending time in chat rooms and on message boards because those were two unique things. So we said, how do we combine chat rooms, message boards and primetime? And we came up with a show, International Creative Management and ourselves and Oldsmobile, where you'd come in every night and have a famous celebrity who would chat with you in the Celebrity Circle. And as you waited for them you'd have this little showroom of cars from GM. What was unique, were message boards where you could leave messages, including messages criticizing the car company that were answered. This wasn't like boarding over a print ad. We were utilizing message boards, we were utilizing chat, and we were utilizing the fact that you needed to have new things every day.

We were very proud of that. "Packet" on *Wired* was about pioneering thinking, and Monday, Tuesday, Wednesday, Thursday, Friday we would have a different article, which was put up from *Wired*. Then we would have interactive banners, which were new at that particular time, where you could see what was happening with the cars. One of the big things that we were proudest about is we eventually sold on, look what you can *do* with it, rather than how large it is and what it is.

Because from those days, and I continue to believe this, you sell something new on art and justify it with numbers. You could never sell anything new based on numbers. Later on when a whole bunch of people came into the industry, we tried to sell it through numbers. We then found ourselves selling numbers, which were not actually very pleasant. We were selling click-through rates.

When you were pioneering, you were initially selling the business based on art not numbers. Do you think the business has slipped now and we're primarily selling it on numbers and data? Do you think there's still a component of art to selling the business?

I still believe the business really is about art, but science is more important than it was. In the old days we tried to think it was about size, but what we were really selling was art. Today we have size, but we have balanced the art part and the science part of the business. The science part clearly is more important. Google is all about science. It's about bid optimization, performance measurement, and it's about a whole bunch of things related to data. But if you actually look at Google, a lot of their future is about display advertising and creative video via YouTube, etc.. They have bet big on the Android mobile operating system, and search being mobile, and that's got a lot of mathematics and engineers and algorithms. But a more important part of their future is tied to display.

It's about what do you do with one of these platforms, like Yahoo or Google. How do you make them more interesting? How do you make YouTube the next Netflix and what are the creative things you can do on YouTube to garner more of an audience at any given time? There's an art and a science to it. And it's not just science as people at Google or some other people think. In fact, if you skew too much to one side, which is all left brain, and to a certain extent that's what Google did and their results are terrific, you're going to have new things emerge through the right brain and science. An example of that is Facebook; maybe my friends can point me on how to discover things rather than through search. Now some people think it's all about "friends." But if you actually look behind Facebook, it's a bunch of amazing engineering and data.

It's always about a combination of art and science, and I'm always concerned when anybody says it's exactly one side or the other. Because the reality is it tends not to be one-sided. It tends to be a balance. When I was running a company through the downturn we never had a layoff. We continued to grow, which was unheard of, and that was because I kept one singular focus. And the focus number was how many people are coming online, and how many people are getting onto broadband. I knew things would recover and they did.

So from 1999 to 2002, while the world was going to hell in a handbasket, more people were getting broadband, more people were coming online. I would put up a chart which detailed the real numbers and the random number generator. I considered the NASDAQ to be the random number generator and I would say to clients, you do not make decisions on a random number generator. Look what real people are doing. The hype was creating a situation where we were focusing on the extremes, and the extremes are not how you build a business. For example, when people thought of social media in the last few years, they thought of Facebook. Facebook is an important part of the social graph, but Facebook is not *the* social graph.

People basically think Google is search. No, no, no, Google is dominant among traditional search. People are increasingly discovering through Facebook and Twitter and lots of other places. That is becoming a component of search that Google does not currently own. I think one of the things this industry recognizes and needs is people who keep a sense of perspective of what other people are doing, and not necessarily what venture capitalists are placing their bets on or what people in the media are writing.

That's a very good point. We do tend to get a little caught up in ourselves, don't we? What are people doing right now? How do you see people using their time online? What's the overarching trend behind how they're approaching the content, and how is that affecting the advertising being laid into it?

The most impactful development over the past 100 years until a generation ago was the invention of the internal combustion engine, because it changed society and culture. Today we have something even more impactful and that is the external connection engine or simply the connection engine. This is how we describe the eco system built on the Internet. We call it the connection engine because people use it to connect to discover, connect to transact, connect to share and connect to express themselves.

Interestingly all of these primary actions are merging together now. In the old days you could say a discovery engine was Google. A sharing engine was a blog and then it became Facebook. An expression engine was MySpace and Facebook. A transaction engine was Amazon. But today on Facebook you can transact, you can buy stuff, you can express yourself, you can share. You can do all of the above. Clearly you're discovering new things there as well. All of these actions are merging together but consumer belief is the fundamental change you have within this connection engine. People are sharing, transacting, expressing and discovering. They're doing it and it is effecting, it is changing their beliefs and mind-sets. So they're now expecting less and less arbitrage of information. They expect to get all the information and process it themselves.

There is also an unwillingness to wait. Networks and movie companies are finding it impossible to manage time windows. People are getting use to an on-demand world where they want it right away. The connection engine also serves to eliminate distance. They expect responsiveness and accountability immediately from companies. But most importantly, most of us are now marketing to ourselves. So how you facilitate self-marketing to people is becoming important.

Those are some pretty significant changes. Instead of marketing to people you want to facilitate self-marketing. Instead of segmentation, where you take large audiences into small audiences, you now take audiences of one and you make them into larger audiences. So they're aggregating audiences in order for you get large enough groups of people. Google's a great re-aggregation engine. I want to find 30,000 people who type in the word, 'Toyota' and speak to them.

The other thing is you're going to have to talk to both the users and the surrounding voices, which many people refer to as the influencers. A heavy user and a heavy influencer are not the same thing. A heavy influencer happens to have great impact, especially as an advocate or a detractor, about how a product is bought and sold. These are fundamental shifts and changes to marketing, which basically means our client organizations have to think about organizational design, incentive systems, measurement systems and talent instead of just freaking out about what their Facebook strategy should be.

So how does that affect an advertiser's role? Do they have a role in that environment?

I think advertisers have a tremendous role. My underlying belief is that marketing is about understanding customer requirements. And it's not my definition but it's *a* definition by Philip Kotler, who wrote a seminal text book on marketing. Historically we've not paid much attention because consumers did not have as much control and power as they have today. Today we have this environment that I call the "people's network," and it's more powerful than any network to date. The people's network is not only that I can express, but I can connect with people and get information.

So if marketing is about understanding and meeting customer requirements, and customer requirements and customers are getting more powerful we have to find a new way to market. You no longer can market a product through brute force of just pricing, or through brute force of logistics or market domination. You have to understand the new landscape, glean insights and develop ideas. Learn what people want and then engage with them. And do not forget that people engage with things that are creative. They don't engage with numbers. Behind everything lies the math of how to do things and measure, those are the numbers. That is the science. However, the honest truth simply is people use Google because it's fast, simple and usually works for them to get what they want. It's not because there's some big fat algorithm. And increasingly as people game it, it works less and less. The art is what gathers the consumer, the science delivers the experience.

The other truth is, if it were just numbers there would be no Apple Corporation. Pound for pound, ounce for ounce Apple products are 30 percent to 50 percent more expensive than anybody else. But you know what? They're magical. And that is what marketers do not comprehend. People choose with their hearts and then they use numbers to justify what they did. Understanding what people want and then putting together the right balance of art and science is what marketing is all about. It's not about message distribution anymore.

You've been a thought leader for the industry for a long time, and have lead successful large companies that helped shape the way advertising has been executed for brands and for customers. Is there anything, looking back, that you were surprised about or that really caught you off-guard?

I've been caught off-guard all the time, but usually I've woken up in time. I can think of two things right off the top of my head where I missed the extent of the big impact. I didn't miss them completely, but I clearly missed the beginning of them and so we had to play catch up.

First, I missed search, and the only excuse I have, besides the fact that I'm incompetent, is that it came about not from branded marketers or Fortune 500 advertisers but from the long tail. The original search advertising was basically people who were advertising little to none, or advertising in the Yellow Pages. That wasn't where I was paying the closest attention. It wasn't that we completely missed search, but we were behind search. We intended not to be behind in gaming, not to be behind in social, not to be behind in video, not to be behind in most things digital, but we were behind in search.

And right now, I don't believe most in marketing has completely got a grip on how the people's network, which is my definition of the social graph, will change marketing over the next decade. Some earlier implications are that you may want to pull back on advertising and promotion and put more money into products and service support, which is part of marketing. If you have a superior product and superior service maybe that will be more important than your distribution dollars and advertising dollars.

Don't get me wrong, you still will need advertising. One of the things that I found is if I blog and I don't tweet about it, nobody comes. So tweeting is my advertising. And in my case I can't afford anything else so I just put out a tweet. If I had a larger budget I would do a promoted tweet, optimize my blog for search, etc.. But that's advertising. At VivaKi we are betting our company on the link between paid, owned and earned connections. I've helped write our strategy to incorporate this reality; we believe clients are looking for "ideas simply and efficiently delivered across paid, owned and earned connections."

That's the new frontier. It's not analog and digital. It's not above the line and below the line. It's paid, owned and earned. We've tended to understand paid. We've tended to understand owned. Everything from client stores to websites to content falls under owned opportunity. Earned is sort of new, but it's really just a new name for the impact of word-of-mouth but now it's scalable. In the past, PR was one element of earned. Defining the link between paid, owned and earned is what's become important. How do you plan across them in aggregate? How do you think creatively across them? How do you measure across them? Those are the interesting challenges.

So you're saying the earned element of marketing is what really gets down to creating the balance you were talking about between the art and the science of marketing.

Yes, that is the end goal of the balance between art and science. And there's a lot of science and there's a lot of art. And in many ways the future of marketing is waiting for marketers of the future. I know I'm not good enough because you need a different type of renaissance person, someone who understands and can execute them all. And we're training them so the people in our organization who are eight to ten years younger than I, those are the ones who can solve these challenges.

That's encouraging!

It is. They are developing the skills that are necessary. They've grown up with this and they have lived this environment.

So if you acknowledge that Internet advertising seems to have really launched around '94, you could say that we're close to standardizing the core part of the business, the paid part of the business. How long do you think we

have before we truly understand how to standardize the earned piece of the business?

What tends to happen is we standardize the past and innovate the future, then you have to connect to the past for scale, and innovation is where the fun comes from. My guess is we're going to standardize very quickly when it comes down to the earned space.

Do you think standardization hinders innovation?

I think it creates systems where one or two players become the leader, and innovation comes from the startups. When a couple of companies become the dominant player, what they do becomes the standard. That was the network effect in the algorithms behind search, and that was Google and Microsoft. You're seeing the same network effects, I believe, in social media. You're seeing it in Facebook, and to some extent between Facebook and Twitter. I would say in the United States people basically believe a social media campaign tends to have online, maybe three or four elements: a Facebook element, a Twitter element, a blogger outreach. And then something to do on your own website, and you're off and running to the races!

But social is far more complex than that and will impact everything from CRM, to legal to organizational design and service delivery. And it definitely is not just about getting "fans." When it comes to social, as an example, it's easy to get a fan but what is the value of a fan? That is something we will standardize sooner rather than later. I don't have many friends but all of a sudden I have 1,400 "friends" on Facebook. When people say, "I've got a million fans," I say so what, I've got a million mosquitoes. What does that mean?

Consumers feel and believe if they become a "fan" or "friend" of yours that they need to be treated special. That's a very interesting question – how should you treat these people differently? Is this just a simple CRM platform, what's happening with most CRM platforms? Most CRM platforms are being automated and outsourced. Could you actually have an automated out-source response to Facebook and still have a fan? If it's a content distribution platform, well, Coke has, I don't know, 25 million fans. That's fantastic. But they have two billion people who drink their stuff, so is 25 million fans meaningful?

You come at these questions from a very creative and logical perspective. What do you do to maintain your creative thinking and approach to all these different issues and challenges that face the advertising business?

The first is I do not lose focus on the fact that this is eventually all about people. I do not let the technology and mathematics get in the way. By the way, I revere mathematics and I revere technology. I have a math degree and I like technology, though I couldn't write a line of code. But I don't let that overcome the fact that this is eventually about people.

The second thing is I'm continuously questioning what I believe. If I believe something strongly, I build a case why the opposite is exactly true to ensure that I have thought through the angles.

The third is, I'm continuously learning. I get up most days when I am not on the road at 4:30 in the morning and spend a couple of hours reading, investigating and visiting things online that I have read about or heard about. It may be topics I need to know more about, examples of online marketing, or perspectives and points of view. One advantage of learning is it makes it harder and harder for me to simply dismiss things. Most people who dismiss things don't even know what they're talking about. For me, I don't dismiss but I ask; where is this likely to go, and I formulate an opinion. It's curiosity and embracing new ways of thinking.

Then I try things. I tweet and I blog and I Facebook and I use LinkedIn, Four Square, Quora and lots of digital services and tools. At the same time I'm a traditionalist. I read my newspapers if I can on a plane. Not on my iPad but the old fashioned way. I have a Kindle but I like books. I like the smell and I just like writing on them. And I like having them all over my library to look at and to remember. I like seeing movies in a theater, so I'm innately analog though I embrace digital with everything. And I say, okay, why do I like this versus not liking this? I routinely question myself. I listen to what clients have to say. I listen to what other people have to say. And the last thing is I actually have reverse mentors, which is I've got lots of people within my company and outside who teach me different things. These people mentor me on games and on music and on technology. They say here's what I should know about. And since they take pity on me, they spend a lot of time training me. In many areas it's much easier for experts to train me than for me to train myself.

And finally, I believe in some key realities. You've got to be comfortable that there is a consumer behind this, or a person or human being, or whatever the right word is. And you've got to be comfortable that you are in the business of selling stuff. And there has to be a business model. If there is no business model then you shouldn't be around. And so once you say that, or you're speaking that from a frame, it allows me to simultaneously engage with a client and say, "You who are a senior person and who sometimes might be a little confused, I'm about as confused as you are. But here's how I sort it through and here's what I think we should do." And then they say, "You actually aren't completely sure but you built a pretty good case, so we'll do it," which is better than me running around saying, "I have seen the future! Let me show you the way." After all, who the hell knows? But the good news is, at least eight out of ten times we've been right. And the other two times we figured it out very quickly so avoided having our clients get into any disaster.

CLOSING REMARKS

Rishad's interview leads me to thinking about how difficult it can be to be a visionary. To be visionary you have to be able to spot trends, identify their application to a specific category and be willing to listen to *lots* of stories. When you are trying to anticipate the future you have to wade through a high volume of people telling you what they think, what they've created, and find those that have value in your eyes. As the saying goes, you have to squeeze a lot of lemons to make lemonade, and that is especially true in the world of online marketing.

That being said, Rishad also reminds me that one of the best ways to be successful is to surround oneself with talented people. Rishad admits that one of his strengths lies in finding smart people and putting them all in a room together. Rishad's teams have fostered some of the industry's leading thinkers and doers. Some of the strongest talent in the business has worked under Rishad's wings, and that is a sign of success in and of itself. So if you are looking for success in this business, don't be afraid to work with people who push you to be better. It's a surefire way to drive success in you!

CHAPTER 15

MITCH JOEL

Mitch Joel is president of Twist Image, an award-winning digital marketing and communications agency (although he prefers the title, Media Hacker). He has been called a marketing and communications visionary, interactive expert and community leader. He is also a blogger, podcaster, passionate entrepreneur and speaker who connects with people worldwide by sharing his marketing insights on digital marketing and new media.

In 2008 Mitch was named Canada's Most Influential Male in Social Media, one of the top 100 online marketers in the world, and was awarded the highly prestigious Canada's, Top 40 Under 40. Most recently, Mitch was named one of iMedia's 25 Internet Marketing Leaders and Innovators in the world. *Marketing Magazine* has named Twist Image one of the Top 10 Agencies in Canada for two years running (the only digital marketing pure play to make the list).

So, Mitch Joel, let's get started at the beginning. You got involved with Mamma.com pretty early on in '99. What brought you into this business?

My online business happened long before Mamma, which is weird to say. I was actually a music journalist and I was publishing music magazines, but the story of my life was I grew up in a family of four boys and my parents were, I'd say, lower-middle class. Instead of giving these big birthday presents they would buy one thing that we could all share, and as soon as technology came to be, whether it was the early version of Pong or Atari 800 and stuff like that, that's what they did and we would all share them.

So I had a computer in my house really early. I remember having to buy a modem in the U.S. because they didn't even have them in Canada yet. Canada is always a little bit behind, and being really into technology I just couldn't wait. In fact, when I started publishing my music magazines in the late '80s, I put them online. And online back then was really immature; this was the early days of the first web browser, maybe even a bit before then. It was to the point where there wasn't even an ISP in Montreal where I live. I had to call long distance and pay long distance charges into Toronto log-on to what was then the Internet.

I was involved, and I really felt it from those days because being a magazine guy, my life was spent going to the corner newsstand every week and hoping that there'd be a new issue of *Rolling Stone* or *Rip,* or whatever it was that was hot at the time. Suddenly I would log onto this page and get all the content I wanted, fresh and updated. I remember one of the early sites I would visit was All Star Music. It was the nascent days for the web and the kinds of sites that were being developed were simple, but I would be blown away that there would be new, fresh news about the music world every day. Maybe only four items or whatever, but it was there. That to me was a staggering realization that if this thing goes, and I felt it would, it was going to change everything I knew about media and publishing and marketing.

So going from there to editing a local paper, that had an online presence, too – that was important – to then joining Mamma.com and helping build the sales team there; I'd been involved in the online world almost from day one, but this was a big step. I remember seeing that first banner ad on *Wired* magazine, so for me it's been a long road.

You definitely took the hard way to get onto the Internet. If you do a search for me online there are some who think I created the first online magazine ever, because back then there was just absolutely nothing to compete with, and most of those have died and there's no record of them anymore. I jokingly tell people who think I became this sudden phenom on Twitter or something, that if you go back and look at the archives on my blog from 2002, there are over 3,000 posts already. That's a long hard way to be an overnight success.

You're a fifteen-year overnight success.
That's about right!

So you showed an interest in the business. How did you get into the advertising side?

Being a person who produces magazines, two out of the three are actually free magazines, and the way you make money on a free magazine is advertising. Advertisers come because there are a lot of these magazines out in the marketplace and they have each garnered an audience. I knew the model really well; the more people you could put this message in front of, the more value it had to a brand or to an advertiser. So when it came to the online world, looking at how I was going to monetize it at the time, the same model seemed to make sense online. Other people were proving this to be the case so it made sense. It was working for the online magazine websites that I saw and then it was something we helped Mamma. com to explore. Back then at Mamma we had CPMs to work with because we didn't really have pay-per-click per se, as it was a bit before that model took flight.

Mamma was long before Google and Overture and all the rest. But what we had was the ability to put banner ads up and target those banner ads based on searches and demographics for users. So if you were looking for something medical, we could put a WebMD banner up there if we hard-coded it into the actual search algorithm, which is a whole other story that talks about how early the days were of the Internet back then. We knew that the more relevant ads you put up in front of people, the more value they had and so it was this natural fit.

The challenge with online advertising then, and a little bit still to this day, is in figuring out if we made the right call. Was the right thing monetizing pages off of putting an ad in front of someone's face? I'm not sure, but it was the traditional way that we've morphed into the online world.

That's a running theme because a lot of the people that I'm talking to had been involved in those very early stages, and one of the things I'm uncovering is there were decisions made about how to monetize the platforms through banners and skyscrapers, and a lot of those things were being considered at the time. Almost universally, if they could go back and identify a different way to do it they would.

I have been jokingly saying that the mistake we made was we let Madison Avenue come in. I think it's a natural mistake, meaning we have these guys out in the valley programming and really thinking about a product, whether it was the early days of Yahoo, Google or even Mamma, which was a meta-search engine – sort of like what AOL, Yahoo were trying to do but able to produce a better result – and the people who see the opportunity are the Madison Avenue types, because they're constantly looking for places to put a message in front of a consumer. So anything that gets a semblance of an audience is interesting to them.

I often wonder what would've happened if we didn't let Madison Avenue in and instead turned to the marketers, not the advertisers. We forget that advertising is a subset of marketing. Marketing is a much bigger world in terms of an industry and capabilities and things you can do, and I think we are rectifying the path a little bit now. You see this in terms of how online marketing works, how great Google AdWords is, as far as I'm concerned, in affiliate marketing and things like that. So we're seeing this minor self-correction in the business, but I do wonder what it would've been like had we looked at the marketing capabilities versus the obvious sort of slap-an-ad-on-it advertising attitude.

Do you think the business would've been less driven by the advertising and more by subscriptions?

Yeah, that's a possibility. We would've gotten to a result that looks something more like Google AdWords sooner. And when I say "Google AdWords" I don't necessarily mean text ads on search, as much as I think of the model for integration. One, it's non-invasive. Two, it's highly relevant based off of what you're searching for. And three, it is self-service based on actual actions taken rather than estimated exposure. You only pay if someone clicks. Google doesn't want inefficiencies there. If no one's clicking they want you to either change it or get off. All of those elements are very counter-intuitive to advertisers. Personal advertising models make up something more interesting, and slightly more unique.

I don't know if it's about going from advertising-based content to subscription-based content, because you have to remember in the early days it was very much subscription-based still. You still had to buy-on to an ISP or an AOL at the time, too. I just think that new models would've been explored. For instance, somebody who owned a Google might've said, is there a better way than just putting a flashy banner ad on this content? I think the people who spent the time thinking about that are the ones who benefited.

The truth is we can say what we want, but advertising, in terms of banners, still works to a certain degree in terms of marketers wanting to pay for that attention.

How do you think marketers view the web now as opposed to ten years ago? Do they view it as an advertising vehicle, or as a marketing vehicle?

I don't think it's changed much because they fundamentally still see it as an advertising channel versus a marketing opportunity. It's the same old story; you walk into a chief marketing officer's office and say, "I've got this really sexy search engine marketing report to show you. However, behind door number two is a football helmet for the Dallas Cowboys because we can sponsor the stadium and have a box there." Where do you think they're going to go? It's pretty obvious what they're going to do. We're human beings. We're attracted to the shiny bright objects and tend to go with the things that are more fun and clever. But we live in a world where most people's first brand interaction comes through search. So what does that say about us as brands if we're negating that? We have more traditional values based into our system as marketers, or we're not paying all that much attention to it?

I just have this feeling that if we can take a better, more holistic marketing perspective of the business, things go very well and the performance is there. The brands that do are the brands that are winning. What are they doing? They're building databases. They're building intense and interesting CRM programs. I always say the brands that are doing social media well are the ones you never hear about, because they're not the sort of Bellwether, YouTube, Mustafa, Old Spice type campaigns. They're the brands who have a great blog that get all of the industry's attention, or they make their content that much more shareable. Or they open up and allow people to review and say things on their site and do things to engage with the brand. Those areas, to me are what make brands successful.

And part of making the web work for a brand comes from realizing it's not just an advertising channel, it's a media platform. It's a place where you can publish text, images, audio and video instantly, for free to anyone anywhere in the world. You can execute with amazing targeting. You have amazing analytics that can give you tremendous insights into your audience. The minute we can rise above the sheer advertising capabilities, which are there and they're immense, those are the cool things I like marketers to look at.

You bring up an interesting point, Mitch, in that the most effective advertisers and marketers online are the ones that you don't necessarily notice. They're just a part of your day, a part of your landscape.

It goes back to the analogy of the football stadium versus the SEM campaign. How many brands do you deal with day-in and day-out who are just so understanding of their key performance metrics, and maybe even web analytics in general, and then go into the minutia of search engine marketing and actually know what they're cost per acquisition is for a new customer? And they know what they're willing to spend and how it will perform?

The truth is we know thousands of them. They're just not the big name brands that we typically want to see mentioned in a *MediaPost* or *Click-Z* article. I call them the "head downs." Their nails are dirty they're digging their hands in and really using those analytics to win.

Do you think the business has changed in that we've become more dependent on the analytics and less on the creative idea?

I've been on this kick recently, and a lot of it has to do with a close friend of mine, Avinash Kaushik who's the analytics evangelist of Google and has written two books. One is called, *Web Analytics an Hour a Day*. The other is, *Web Analytics 2.0*, where there is this beauty in using the analytics to drive creative. I know a lot of times it makes marketers gasp, especially more traditional ones, but if you think about it from a pure ideation standpoint it makes a lot of sense. If you know that these are the directions in which your customers engage and react, why not create messaging to that end? Doesn't knowing create a better platform to be a hyper-creative brand and do something unique there?

The flip side is this classic Steve Jobs line; "You can't ask your customers what they want because it's not their jobs to tell you what they want." And although it's a very ego-driven thing by a brand that touches so many of our hearts, it's a powerful message, too. Those two worlds have to collide. If you know what you're doing isn't working, and you're doing nothing creatively to adjust or to tweak that, that says something.

You can say that when you're creating products that people drool over and want the second they see it, versus the rest of the world of marketing. You can't say that if you think people just aren't resonating with your advertising and marketing. I believe there's a healthy balance to be had there. The challenge is we're not stocked with the right pedigree of marketer that sits down and is able to really look beyond the analytics and pull out what

Avinash calls "the insights," to have truly actionable items you can derive from there to deliver true results.

We used to live in a world not long ago where there wasn't a lot of data and the data we had was hard to manipulate and hard to use. Now we're in the same position where the data we have is hard to manipulate and hard to use, but that's because we have too much of it. The machines can't handle it. And so I do work with big financial institutions and telcos, and it's funny, when you start getting into the personalization of this data and the real digital CRM stuff, they're challenged because the computers don't move fast enough. It's going to take three days to pull that data.

It's fascinating to sit back as a marketer, who remembers the world prior to digital, thinking, wow, we used to want to kill for this data and now we're at a point where we have so much of it, it's almost choking our systems.

It's almost the process paralysis idea, that you get so much information that you just decide to shut down.

It's normal. These days we have shelf lives for CMOs that are between eighteen and twenty-four months. We have shelf lives for agencies that are sometimes even less than a year. Are you going to be the guy to do the 180-degree turn? Are you going to be the woman to do the 180-degree turn? It's hard to say. A lot of people don't want to pivot and would rather proceed based off of what they know, and put a small set aside for experimentation. You go look at media usage and consumption, where consumers are, and you just overlay that with where ad spend is going. Where is the rationale on that? How is the web at 20 percent of total estimated spend, sometimes less, even possible?

Through the period of time that you've evolved, what technology or company has come up that surprised you the most?

Don't you feel that it's everything? I remember when eBay first came online and I thought, oh, an online auction, how come I didn't think of that? And then look at something like YouTube, and say, really? In a 2x2 screen with majoring buffering issues, shaky cam, terrible audio, bad lighting, in a world where you can get a forty-two inch plasma for $600, this is the future? I always say, I'm not a futurist I'm a *present*-ist, and I always refer back to that YouTube model for exactly that example. I saw YouTube very early and thought, who cares? Why would anybody like this? So for me anything that's new is exciting.

Even thinking back to the early days of Yahoo, AOL and Google, and of Sergey and Larry being very adamant about and hyper-focused on search. I was in search and I'm sitting there saying, but how are you going to monetize this? Their response was we're not going to worry about the monetization. We're going to focus on getting people great search results. I didn't know how they were going to make money, but I obviously missed that one.

And then look at what AOL and Yahoo did. They kept adding and adding and adding and creating the portal model versus what Google did. It's now 2011 and it's really interesting to see what transition took place, what happened to the portal model and how people's interest shifted. I also think that the social media effect will be big. Bigger than all of us really know or think.

Part of it has to do with a line that I constantly say, and said earlier, where suddenly we have this platform that's sophisticated yet simple enough for anybody to have a thought and publish that thought in text images, audio and video instantly and for free to the world. It's not just a broadcast now. People can take that content, share it, do something with it, comment on it, add their own or create to it. So when people ask things like, is blogging dead? Is the web dead? Is it all mobile now? I still go back to that fundamental idea that things haven't completely blossomed yet.

The subtitle of my book is, "Everyone is connected. Connect your business to everyone." That, as a sort of pretense, has still not come to total fruition but I believe that it will.

If I had to guess, I'd say that what excites you most about this industry is the rapid rate of change.

I talk a lot about the rapid rate of change and then the completely slow rate of change. If ever there was a moment in time where I developed an interest in quantum physics or time loopholes, or whatever sort of science jargon you want to throw at me, it's when I look at the web. As fast as technology moves, it still moves really, really slow. Again, looking back at the web and interactivity and now twenty odd years in, a lot of brands still grapple with this. You're right in the sense that I tell people it's a marathon, not a sprint, but you're sort of sprinting in the marathon because you've got to keep pace with things that move really fast.

The other instance where I get a lot of pleasure is in thinking about my favorite title for myself, which is Media Hacker. Some people see hacking as negative, I see it as a positive. Taking things and putting them together in a fast prototype manner, seeing how they work, tossing out what doesn't, moving forward with what does, and then developing over time that iterative process. That part to me has been the most interesting, the media hacking part.

You look at the constructs of traditional media from where it was ten, twenty, thirty years ago, to where we are today and it's staggering. I don't know how you feel, but there isn't a day where I don't feel overwhelmed. I come in and look at the brands we're working with and I think, what do you do in a world where you can do anything? And so it's both an amazingly powerful moment and a totally frightening experience as well.

It sounds like that's also the biggest challenge of the business itself; since you can do anything, how do you focus on what you should be doing?

I don't know if there's an answer to that. The truth is that you look at the business objectives, and this is where a lot of people fall down because they're more interested in ROI as a title than an actual goal. I learned a lesson by hearing Richard Binhammer over at Dell talk. Someone asked him about social media ROI and he said, "We have to remember it's not just an accounting term, but it's something that applies to the entire organization." So when you ask, what's the ROI of your marketing, it doesn't make all that much sense because the context of ROI has to be based on everything. So you look at business objectives.

When brands come to my agency, Twist Image, and say, this is what we're trying – we want to be on Facebook, we want to be on YouTube. We go back to ask them, what are the business objectives? What are you looking to do this year? What does your outlook look like? What's your cost per acquisition? How much does it cost? We look at all that. For us it's about the strategy, and the brands that really win are the brands that tie that strategy holistically together. It's the whole ecosystem, the brand ecosystem, the digital ecosystem. We ask to tie into all that and then effectively drill down into the tactics.

I have a lot of respect for brands that ignore Twitter, only if that's part of the strategy and that strategy they're currently employing works. So for me it's way more about that versus the more generic attempt to be all things to all people? Because the answer is, you can't watch everything. The web is going to work for some brands, it won't for others. TV will work for some, it won't for others. It has to do with the strategy and the creative message together, in unison.

How far out do you think brands can truly plan a strategy in the digital space, given the rate of change?

I don't know that you can. I think the answer is you can probably do a year or two out. When it comes to digital you have to embrace an iterative process. You have to know that although we're seeing something out of the gates, we're going to do this on Twitter. And this type of online marketing over here, there's a star caveat next to that that says "based on the analytics and what we learn as we go."

I think part of it is you have to be willing and open to work in the iterative process that allows you to do that pivot that we were talking about earlier. The challenge with that is most brands don't want that. They want to commit and then take a look at the research at the end of the quarter and see how it did. I don't believe that to be real. I think the real time web is when brands start looking at their web daily and in terms of really what's working and what's not. Because the truth is you can kill it. There's nothing wrong with killing it. And I think that the idea of killing those sacred cows, although it's a very cool business term, is actually a practical execution of the digital world.

You can basically start over on a regular basis, can't you?
Well, you can make a decision that says we're going to be doing this on Twitter, and then actively realize within that engagement what consumers really want, how they're connected, if it's working or if it's not. And if it's not, kill it. I don't think brands look all the worse for it. I think brands look all the worse for when they're not communicating what they're doing. So for example, I had this thing on Twitter called, "The Business Book Review," and it was just a 140-character quick little business book review, and I realized it wasn't working for me here, but someone else was doing it well so I killed the sacred cow. I said in my last tweet, "This is being done already over here, follow it."

We tend to forget that the amazing thing about the web, at a rudimentary level, is for most brands it just makes you more findable. If someone is looking for something that you sell, you want to be findable. Starting there, as a pretense, is actually a pretty strong place to be. If you can tie that into a strategy, in terms of how you're rolling out marketing later, develop it and get results, more power to you.

As your career has progressed you've gotten to talk to a lot of people, interact with a lot of people and influence people. Who's been a big influence for you?

I was very fortunate in that the current CEO of my company – I have three business partners now – is the person who was formerly chosen to lead FCB at the time, a leading direct marketing agency in Canada. He built this company up from zero to multi-office, multi-city, hundreds of millions of dollars in billings, etc., etc.. When I was growing up – because there's a bit of an age difference between us – a lot of my friends at a university who were in marketing or advertising went to work for FCB, and I had a lot of respect for those guys, it was Mark Goodman. We became friendly through a bunch of non-profit things we had gotten involved in with industry associations, and had an ongoing dialogue and friendship that eventually led him to join the company after he left FCB.

It was amazing for me to have a mentor become my business partner, and to this day still is. My other two business partners were more peers, but were also a huge influence because I see in them a lot of the stuff I'm just not great at, and I think they see in me a lot of the things they're not great at and together it works.

If you think in terms of the generalities of the world, I was always a fan of Tom Peters and how he thinks creatively about business. I wouldn't say independently, but the four guys who put together the *Cluetrain Manifesto* have acted as mentors to me, just because the content within that book. Work by people like Seth Godin had a profound effect. I remember reading *Permission Marketing* prior to it being in print. I'd met Seth through an Internet World event or something and I just knew from the moment I saw him speak that he was the type of marketer I was and wanted to continue to be. It was almost like someone had finally said what I was mumbling to myself in offices my whole life.

And it's funny, because a lot of my peers, and I include you in that group, are tremendous mentors to me. I think of the early days with the early online advertising world and of you and Bryan Eisenberg. I think of Ivan Ashcausik and Tom Hespos. I follow, I read, I pay attention and am just inspired by people. I even look to the more contemporary people. I think of Tara Hunt who wrote, *The Whuffie Factor* and her perspective that she brings to marketing. Charlene Oley, Clay Shirky, Dan Ariely; there are so many interesting authors and thinkers. And because we live in this multi-media world you see and can consume so much of it. It's strange because being a guy who does a lot of public speaking I've become friends or acquaintances of a lot of these people. It's not like you just read a book and sit twiddling your thumbs waiting for the next book in two years, you have this constant engagement because you're following on Twitter or reading their blogs or checking out their articles. I actually tell people often that a lot of times my mentors are people I've never met before.

It's interesting because in having this conversation with you and with some other people, this business to the outside world is very much a technology-driven business. But when you talk to the people in it, it's a people business.

It's funny, because even as you said that I'm thinking, *oh, I should mention the guys,* because I do my podcast called, *Media Hacks,* which includes Hugh McGuire and Chris Brogan and Chris Penn, and Joe Jaffe who comes in once in a while, and Julian Smith and a whole bunch of other people. People say, oh, this Internet thing and this Facebook thing is really bad for civilization because we're all just going be sitting in front of these terminals and never have any human interaction. I'm like, *what?*

I think about C.C. Chapman. When I was trying to figure out podcasting, I remember Joe Jaffe did an interview with C.C. Chapman about podcasting years and years ago. Now we're 300 episodes in, so we're talking a long time ago. And I remember saying to Joe, "I'm thinking about podcasting." He said, "You've got to speak to C.C." And so I'm chatting with C.C. through Skype or email, and then we meet a year later at the first pod camp, which was like a meet-up of podcast nerds. It was like we'd been friends for so long that we had this strange feeling, not that feeling of, it's great to meet you, but rather it's nice to see you again.

You know things about them just because you're following one another and you care; some of it's public, and a lot of it's private. But you're right, I think fundamentally at the end of the day the reason I get excited even about digital as it is now is just the social aspect of it all. I call it real interactions with real human beings. Like, Cory, the way you and I met was fully digital. We happened to luck out and meet a couple of times in person and through those interactions get to know one another. And so we became closer because of the physical meet-ups that we've had, but we were actually really close regardless.

I've been trying to abolish the IRL (In Real Life), because I don't believe that when you're online it's not real life. I think that you have different types of interactions now, and that because of technology we have a new layer of interactions. But I believe that we live in a very connected world and that's an opportunity if you can feel comfortable expressing yourself and connecting in a human way.

I agree completely. I've read all the things that you write and some of the people you mention I've read regularly, and I value those opportunities to sit and talk and listen to people face-to-face after I've gotten to know them in the digital sense. That's one of the beautiful things about the business, and I see that the advertising business has benefited substantially from that. Because the pace of growth of this business, and the way that we've all distributed and syndicated our ideas, we've learned by osmosis by just being online. You couldn't have done that without the Internet.

Look at our world. Forget the marketing world, look at the advertising world. If you were running an advertising agency fifteen years ago and had an awesome strategist and a super creative ECD, you would never let them speak publicly about how they think, how they operate, how they come up with ideas, what their thoughts are. Now if you don't do that you can't even build your business. That's a huge tectonic shift in how we operate as an industry. A guy like me sharing exactly how I think about these digital channels, very blatantly and publicly the way I do on my blog every day, you would never do that – that's the secret sauce, why are you giving that away?

What we've realized is that in sharing this information many things happen. One is it makes each one of us smarter and better, and the truth is at the end of the day all of that smartness doesn't account for anything unless you can execute. So that's where the world really changes. And if people ask, what's coming next? I think that's the next thing, the execution. It's interesting to see a lot of traditional agencies bring in the right people or develop the right competencies to do this, a lot of the specialty boutiques as well. To me those are the big things that are coming soon.

It's still exciting business and that's why we're doing this book, so people won't forget about all the excitement that came before, or about the companies and the people and all the different interactions they may have not even known about at the time.

Here's the basic thing I tell people. Let's not forget that the ways in which we connected, was we would take these computers and plug them into the phone line – the phone line! Talk about the worse plug you could choose in your house to get some information through, and that's what we did. And so when people say, wow, I can see it's still pretty primal right now, I say, it is.

Remember, the Internet was never meant to be an advertising media channel. We put that layer on top of it the minute we saw any component of commercialization there. That doesn't mean that we're ever going to be able to figure out how to do it right, or how not to do it right. We're going to see in the end what this looks like. But we're working hard by taking very traditional ways of advertising and putting them into a channel that it was never meant for, and as a channel evolves, it keeps changing so dramatically that it's not the same. For example, is the phone predominantly the same way it was when it was first invented? – Yes. Is TV, radio, print? – Yes. The Internet? No. The Internet looks nothing like the Internet did a year ago. Newspapers, they looked the same 200 years ago. Okay, they have color, different sections, but they look the same.

CLOSING REMARKS

Mitch Joel is an intelligent guy and if you have the chance to speak with him, take it. His passion for the business is unique, and he gives everything he has to it. Mitch exemplifies why this business is, at its core, a people business. He lives and breathes digital media; he talks about it, lectures on it and writes about it.

His path is a unique one, but one you may have heard before. He followed one passion (music) to another passion (the web) and along the way created a career! If you are looking to be successful in any business, no matter what it is, find what you love and create a job around it. If you love it, it won't feel like work and will flow seamlessly into all aspects of your life. If you want to be successful, emulate Mitch by tapping into your own personal passion. That will create a beeline path to success!

CHAPTER 16

SUSAN BRATTON

Susan Bratton is the co-founder and CEO of Personal Life Media, Inc., a multimedia lifestyle brand providing entertaining and authentic personal content to socially conscious adults. As a publisher of direct-to-consumer online information products, the company provides automated platforms for information product publishing to serve experts who deliver virtual workshops, downloadable training systems and support programs via blogs, web audio, video and ebooks.

Renowned for her impressive breadth of business relationships in the media, marketing and Web 2.0 World, she treasures talented individuals with unique perspectives about digital marketing, which she ably showcases in her weekly podcast and blog, *DishyMix: Success Secrets from Famous Media and Internet Executives.* She is the creator of two books on interview techniques, *Talk Show Tips:*

72 Secret 'Master Host' Techniques, a system to teach podcasters, radio and TV hosts; and for information product marketers, *Masterful Interviews: Creating Profitable Content,* how to prepare, produce and promote their work.

A highly regarded digital marketing entrepreneur, she sits on the boards of a number of technology companies including ZEDO, Inc., 1-800-FREE-411, aka Jingle Networks, Collarity Inc., MerchantCircle, Newsforce Inc., and Powered Inc., as well as the board of the Silicon Valley American Marketing Association. She is a founder of two industry associations, the Internet Advertising Bureau (IAB) and the Association of Downloadable Media (ADM). She is also co-founder of the Bay Area Interactive Group (sfBIG).

Susan Bratton, you started a company back in 1986 representing a number of print publications selling advertising. How did you get sucked into the digital world?

I was an early adopter of the Internet in my publisher's rep firm business. I had networked all my employees' Macintosh computers myself and we ran our business off of a centralized database. I realized the power of the interwebs then, even though we were struggling to use arcane technical interfaces like FTP and bulletin boards. This was the pre-Netscape browser era. As a tech enthusiast, I quickly realized the value of emailing my customers as an additional channel to drive more sales.

During that time a friend of mine got a job at a company called the @Home Network. He was staying at our house while he was working there because he was from Marin and this company was in the Silicon Valley. He was willing to make considerable sacrifices to get a job at @Home and that intrigued me. They had an impressive engineering team assembled, first tier venture capital and a breakout idea. This was a Silicon Valley superstar startup in the making. You could just smell their future success. I knew choosing a well-funded startup with a solid team of experts could be my chance at making millions in an IPO versus squandering my career working in a company that didn't give stock options.

My husband, Tim, with whom I now run Personal Life Media, had already started his first company at age twenty-six and had an IPO. It seemed crazy to work for any company that didn't offer stock.

Lo and behold, they needed someone with advertising and technology experience to run sales for their media business. I had been selling advertising that was marketed to technologists – the publications I represented were video magazines and computer graphics magazines. At the time we were doing multimedia on CD-ROMs. For example, one of the magazines I used to sell advertising for was called, *Multimedia Producer.* That was the world from which I came. It was a very simple leap for me to know what worked in the CD-ROM world could work in the broadband world.

I understood how movement and multimedia on the computer could be a very compelling way to tell a story and sell products. I knew that @Home was a company that could succeed. If anyone could figure out what this broadband opportunity was in the online advertising space they could do it. So my job at @Home was to invent broadband advertising. They hired me, gave me a laptop and said, okay, figure it out.

I worked hand-in-glove with the content and editorial team and the design and engineering teams, and we co-created new ad units that took advantage of high-speed digital transport. That was how I transitioned from print advertising to digital and broadband advertising. I took two experiences, an understanding of ad sales and experience with multimedia, and repackaged that knowledge into next generation media types.

How fast were the speeds at that time?
Because most consumers were dialing up on 9600-baud modems, our 10-megabit data transfer rates for broadband pipes were blistering!

That seems like a snail's pace versus these days.
Fifteen years ago most people were on AOL with 14.4 mode.

Do you remember the kinds of ad units you were creating and how effective they were?
We created an ad unit called the BBox, which was essentially today's IAB medium rectangle. And the BBox, or Broadband Box, was an ad that was optimized for the ratio of a video screen. It was a 4X5 image. You could take video and pop it directly in there. The most successful ads we had were video ads whereby people would walk into the ad and start talking to you. Back then, these ads were riveting and got massive click-throughs. These innovative ads might take you on a journey to different website destinations or run a television commercial inside. Those kinds of units pulled very well

for marketers and excited them about the potential for emotional advertising delivered online.

We targeted Fortune 500 brands very early on, and a lot of these big brands wanted to have emotionally evocative campaigns. For example, the Interactive Brand Council at Unilever worked very closely with us because they knew that broadband was one of the things they were going to need if they took their television mentality to the Internet. So they were very interested in doing pioneering testing even against a small audience. It took us a couple years to get to a million customers in broadband or addressable households.

We did a lot of pilot programs and a lot of testing of different ad units using larger file sizes, richer graphics, more animation, the integration of video, multiple images, banners in which you could interact. Now we call that rich media. Fifteen years ago that word hadn't yet been coined.

That's interesting because what you were doing is a lot of what has now become the standard but only in the last five years or so.

We were setting early standards in advertising excellence. Even as we acquired Excite we were pushing ahead. We bought Excite to have a larger addressable audience in narrowband that we could upgrade to broadband. And we bought Excite for the search engine technology. This was pre-Google, and Excite and AltaVista were the main search players. We merged our tiny broadband sales team into the larger narrowband sales organization – about 250 people sales, marketing, research and ops professionals – and continued to focus our collective attention on rich media. We worked with all the rich media vendors at the time to be the leader. Yahoo and AOL controlled larger audiences than we, but they were not as focused at the time on next generation advertising models. AOL, specifically, was focused on their dial-up audience and they couldn't offer rich media.

Our media industry differentiation was the ability to scale rich media advertising. Where we got caught in a negative business spiral was that although @Home had targeted the Fortune 500 brands, Excite, which was ultimately the bulk of our revenue because with that brand, we had the audience, but the sales focus had been on getting the easy money that was flowing freely from all the new .coms. When the dot bomb occurred, the Excite narrowband online advertising revenue channel didn't have enough traditional, stable big brand budget revenue to keep afloat.

So if you had the crystal ball what would you have done differently at that point?

It was predictable, the hyper-fast growth of .coms and their ultimate lack of sustainable revenue when the VC funding dried up. There were two things that happened to the Excite@Home business. The cable companies wanted to vertically integrate, to squeeze out the @Home middleman. They wanted to build their own networks, provision their own modems to their own customers, and to own their own broadband portals. The cable companies stopped paying @Home's bills and they starved us out and stole our technology. Excite's narrowband consumer site was planted so firmly in the .com revenue stream, that we made an unrecoverable error by going for the short term cash of VC funded advertising revenue instead of taking the time to do the long term work it was going to take to get ad revenue from Fortune 5000 brands. When the market started diving, we couldn't make up the lost time for doing a half-assed job going after the short-term .com revenue.

The mood had been, go, go, go, go! Go as fast and as big as you could grow it. "Go big or go home!" That was a Silicon Valley rallying cry at the time. There wasn't a lot of executive latitude around growing long-term sustainable relationships.

And that became one of the casualties of the .com collapse.

I learned a few hard and important lessons during this time. Business accelerated very rapidly in the late '90s. I was in my mid-thirties at the time and I learned how to manage through change; rapid, inexhaustible, never-ending, unceasing *change*. This week we were doing a product launch, next week we were buying a new company, the third week we had to do a major deal, the fourth week we were holding an event, announcing a pivotal milestone.

I recall spending a lot of my management time assuring the younger team members that it was okay and that for the foreseeable future business was going to keep accelerating, evolving at this rapid rate.

I remember having an epiphany where I realized that I was no longer managing my emotions through rapid change, no longer feeling insecure about all the change, ceasing to feel nervous about it; it had become a way of being instead of a disruptive situation. It was standard operating procedure. One day I simply realized, when there was a week that went by where nothing changed, and I thought to myself, wow, I'm suddenly feeling like I might be addicted to change. And I'm so used to it now that it's almost the way in which I exist in this massive, constant, chronic big change world. In the late '90s we lived in a business climate, in a culture of chaos and change. Change became the status quo.

Do you think it's possible that one reason the .com bust happened was that most people had not become comfortable with change? And the landscape was changing so dramatically, so quickly that most people could not keep up?

Actually, no, I don't think that's the reason why the dot bomb happened. I think it happened because there was too much venture capital put into ideas that didn't fly. VCs were getting external validation from the market for funding zany ideas. There was a lot of cash for trial and error going on, and when it was determined that a lot of that experimentation was not panning out successfully, the VCs pulled their horns in, closed their purses, folded their arms and took their funding away. That started the chain reaction, because it was a very incestuous pyramid scheme of business development deals across the industry. When that started to falter the whole system collapsed.

I remember that timeframe well. In a single year my team went from having the entitled attitude of, what are you going to do for me today? To, please, please, please don't lay me off in the next round. People went from total and complete focus on themselves to, what do we need to do to keep this company afloat? It was a very interesting time to watch the reactions of employees mature from a selfish to a group dynamic, coming together to try to hold the business off from failure.

What were some of the good things that came out of that period?

Well, certainly the exuberance and the fast market growth gave a lot of people an opportunity to see what it was like to put together, fund and grow a company. Many of those entrepreneurs went on to do a better job in executing solid business strategies in their subsequent companies. As serial entrepreneurs, many of these early employees got another chance or another couple of chances with follow on business. They'd established connections with VCs. They got their startup chops. VCs publicly stated that having a failed business was no longer a *bad* thing for an entrepreneur. A failed startup became a badge of honor, a notch on one's belt. It was perceived as something that was a natural course of things in the world of entrepreneurs. People realized that when you started with a business you were starting with an assumptive model that was conceptual, and that you were going to figure out the ultimate revenue model over time. The business wasn't expected to look like what was funded, but it was going to work because you, as the entrepreneur, were going to make it profitable.

There was a level of wisdom that came from those early rapid growth and fast failure situations. Agile development, releasing beta applications, market testing concepts quickly, shipping 1.0 versions of software – all this came from those fail-fast early boom-boom days.

When the dot bomb occurred I stayed on to lay off my team of hundreds. I could have bailed, saved myself the heartache, but I stayed on through the thin, sad downward spiral to closing the doors, because I wanted to be there to lay off my team with as much dignity as I could muster.

During that year I'd be grocery shopping and a person would come up to me and say, you laid me off and I can't find a job! They were angry at me. Grown men sobbed like babies when I let them go. It was collateral damage from a total crap market situation, and I did my best to navigate the negativity with as much grace and professionalism as I could cultivate. Net-net the dot bomb was horrific, depressing, gut-wrenching, but it required work that needed to be done and I did it.

What I learned most was how little resources a company could spend and still stay in business. It helped me become a real miser when I funded Personal Life Media myself. That and my husband is a born cheapskate, which is why we've been able to run our business ourselves with zero funding.

Everyone got laid off. I laid off my VP Customer Service and she laid me off. We locked the doors, threw the keys in the mail and went and drank a bottle of Chardonnay together. What a day that last day was; the end of an era, truly.

Then there were no jobs, none. I golfed and cooked for a year after September 11th, 2001. I went to work in sales part time for a company selling Internet sweepstakes and contests to Fortune 500 consumer brands. I worked for six months straight and was no closer to getting an order after six months than I was the day I started at that company. I never closed a single deal. I worked my butt off, using every sales technique and strategy I'd ever learned in my life. I had been consistently a very successful sales person. There was nothing I could do to close a deal.

The entire company didn't close a deal for six months. Perhaps they got a re-up on some existing business, but zero new deals in six months in a VC-funded company – that's *painful.* The market was a brutal wasteland at the time. It just reminded me that the lead times for budgeting, when you work with those big brands especially back then, were significant. You would have to wait until their next fiscal year to get your deals done. So I wondered how long it was going to take to close the gap between when the big brands would really venture completely into the Internet, which was inevitable in my mind. Those of us in the online advertising who had been exposed to the potential, all knew big marketers would realize online marketing was a massive opportunity. But that sleeping giant was taking a very long, Rip Van Winkel kind of snooze.

During those next two or three years the ad sales teams in the industry worked very tirelessly, very quietly, very diligently to move the Fortune 5000 brands onto the Internet.

At what point did you start to feel things were on the path to recovery? At what point did you start to feel the tipping point towards positive thinking again?

Only three or four years ago did I get the sense that the online media industry, and digital marketing in general, had become a foundation, not just something marketers were testing. There wasn't a lot of "there" there until just a few years ago. Google's Search Engine Marketing solidified advertising as marketing budget line item, and gave online media the accountability that was required to get the attention of the big budget brands. Even so, there were a lot of companies with new marketing technology offerings that were being pitched to brands and agencies, and they were not fully baked.

I can remember a job I took in 2004 selling a platform, and it wasn't real. I got there and six months into it realized I was still selling something that hadn't actually been built and wasn't shipped. Yet when I took the job I was told that it was a finished solution. I discovered the work was all being done by hand in the backroom by the engineers and the designers. It wasn't actually a functional working product.

I wasn't toiling alone in the vaporware ether. In the startup world it's not unusual to be in a company where there is no "there" there yet. That was the time when people were starting to build the next generation of platforms and solutions and technologies to leverage things like high-speed Internet access, and the number of people coming online, and the move away from AOL and the increase in search engine technology.

The mistake I made was not kicking the tires thoroughly enough on the company's offering. I fell in love with the concept too fast, and I didn't vet the engineering team enough, or the competitive landscape. I learned my lesson to be very careful before going to a startup. I learned the questions to ask first.

I exited that company because I could associate the Susan Bratton brand with vaporware.

Throughout your career you've been involved in doing two things: helping put together and lead ad:tech, and organizing various conferences. The industry has looked to you and those groups for information on the future. You've been one of those people who others look to for positivity and leadership, so it's ironic that you didn't really feel positive regarding a recovery until just a couple years ago.

It took ten years for the Internet to be a fundamental part of consumers' lives and therefore, marketers' budgets. Search gave online marketing accountability, rich media gave it emotion, social gave it personal value and mobile gave it 24/7 access.

So you felt good about search but you *really* feel good about social and mobile.

Search is a factual, cut-and-dried service medium. I personally prefer more creative mediums, like video and social content integration. Right now I'm into persuasion marketing and studying copywriting, effective storytelling, writing dialogue, using video sales letters, webinars and putting significant focus on conversion optimization of my websites.

That creativity is currently being expressed in interesting ways, through the interaction between consumers and brands and consumers and consumers.

Definitely.

You said that you help people manage their way through change. This is a period of dramatic change. Brands are becoming more involved in a very personalized, very

social medium. What kind of things do you advise them on now? How do you advise them to deal with social?

I seldom consult anymore. Mostly I get paid to keynote conferences, if I'm doing anything outside operating my own business. I'm fully consumed with Personal Life Media. It's a solid, scalable business that brings Tim, my husband and co-founder, and I a lot of joy. I spend time growing our business because it's a real culmination of the thirty years of the publishing, technology, marketing and consumer web services experience we both have. I'm leveraging my past to create my future.

Speaking of experience, I have programmed more than twenty global events for ad:tech, more than a dozen IAB events. I've programmed over six hundred panels and more than a thousand industry speakers. I've been to pretty much every one of those big shows and spent a lot of time with a lot of people who do the speaking in our industry. It gave me a very wide purview of what's happening in the industry, so that I understood what was happening in search and broadband and social and display and different kinds of ad targeting, and ad networks and exchanges, mobile and social and all of the latest technologies. I had to know a little bit about everything to be able to program a conference that was broad enough to encompass all of digital marketing. That's background for this insight.

A few years ago I spoke on a panel at the San Francisco Bay Area Interactive Group event and I noticed, in talking to people at that event, that the younger people seemed to really understand the products they were selling from the company at which they worked. But they didn't really understand how it fit into the greater panoply of offerings in the digital marketing and media space.

The first Internet ad sales people came from traditional marketing and advertising. I used to know nearly everyone at the industry events. Now there was a new raft of young professionals who didn't come from traditional, and they didn't have classic marketing training or exposure.

To early people who came from traditional marketing and started the Internet, leveraged the technology and the concepts of traditional marketing in media, and melded them together into a new way, marketers could reach their customers. We had to know about everything that was out there so that it would all fit together and be rational. Young employees untrained in traditional marketing can mash-up ideas and offer a fresh approach, but they still need training.

Guzzling bubble juice, that's what I call this syndrome of youngsters with no training entering a growing market. Sure, you can blow bubbles from your mouth if you drink bubble juice. But if a more experienced person shows you how to blow air through the bubble wand and make bubbles, your mouth will be happier. We need to continue to train our A-players in classic marketing fundamentals. What's a value proposition? How do you manage the halo effect of multiple media channel exposure? How do you conduct reliable market research? There are a zillion important fundamentals we, as the old curmudgeons, need to download to our up and coming next generation.

People do need to have a better worldview of how what they're selling or offering fits into the bigger picture. And a lot of people don't have that because it seems that

everyone is learning how to focus again. And that may not be a good thing.

Yeah, you have to do both. You have to go out and learn the bigger landscape of your market *somehow*.

I agree with that completely. In addition to that what are two or three other qualities you think an individual has to possess in order to have success in the industry, the way it is now?

Make sure the product's real when you go to work for the company. The second thing is that there *are* crazy people in the world. And I've been involved with other companies where they look like they're really good and then you realize there's a person within the senior leadership team who has a screw loose. If you see that you have to say something. People won't believe you at first and then it will come to dawn on them that there's a problem person in the organization. A lot of people do a lot of codependent coping for very bad behavior in industry. I want to give people a sense of self-confidence, that if you think something's wrong or weird or lacks integrity, isn't a quality work, is doing the clients or customer a disservice in the short or long term, *you must speak up*!

Many workers, especially women, get caught because they see a problem but they don't have a solution. Maybe they haven't had experience in that particular situation, or they're young and know that what's occurring is not right, but they don't have a better way. So they keep their mouth shut. I want to encourage people to say, you know, I don't have a better idea but maybe we could all get together and brainstorm some alternatives. Because these are the things that I see wrong with what's happening here now. I don't think that conversation happens enough. I think we're often afraid to speak up or we feel too inexperienced. Or we aren't bought into the company's success and are instead only focused on our own political existence and safety. And so I would encourage people to speak up, state problems *even if* you don't know the solution. Come together to make things right within your organization.

Next, make sure that you're solving the right problem. I started two industry associations. One worked, one was a bust. I was with the original founding team of the Internet Advertising Bureau, and that was an extremely successful industry association and continues to be. Then I started the Association for Downloadable Media when I got into the world of podcasting. As iPod sales were exploding, I started an association to help podcasters come together and monetize their content.

What I didn't realize is that's an industry primarily made up of hobbyists. They don't focus on monetizing their content, they just like doing their shows. I was trying to create something to help people who didn't want to be helped. So that's another question to ask yourself, are you putting your energy into something that people want, or are you selling something somcone made up that people really don't want?

That's a very good point.

There s this wonderful saying, it's a presupposition from the study of NLP (neurolinguistic programming). A presupposition is a core belief around this idea of how we learn and communicate with each other, and it's stated as this; "There is no failure, only feedback." That means the only thing you're doing when something's not working is getting another data point. It's just conversion optimization, to speak in the language of our world. It just tells you that what you're doing isn't right *yet*. Try something else. Try and make what you're doing better.

My failed first attempt at running an ad supported podcast network didn't work. It was not a scalable enough business, not big enough, not enough listeners, not a lot to work with – I could have a million downloads and it's not enough to monetize. Selling advertising is a time-consuming, detailed occupation. Sponsorships come and go. It's not a consistent business. Advertisers have a very fickle attitude toward campaigns. The next-new-shiny-thing mentality is hard on a small business that relies on ad revenue.

I call that desire by marketers to land-grab new audience clusters, to try the latest marketing technologies, "the technovelty effect." We didn't want to be in a market buffeted by technovelty churn. That takes deeper pockets. We'd have to raise funding. We didn't want to be indebted to venture capital, we wanted total control.

Instead, we killed that business model of monetizing podcasts and started charging real money for our content by publishing home study courses. We took the ideas that were working –we're good at creating content people want – and changed our model. Now we sell online information products. We have an online membership site. People buy into our membership site and learn communication skills that instantly enrich their lives, make them more money, get them the love and intimacy they crave. Whether it's how to speak up with power and influence, how to have confidence at work, or how to connect with your lover, your husband or your wife in a deeper and more intimate way, or to have a conversation with yourself about your life goals or what makes your life meaningful. Relationships, intimacy, goal visualization, personal authority; it's satisfying to teach skills this valuable and that have such a significant, positive impact. Our customers love us. It's a gratifying, satisfying and pleasurable business.

And though we're a publisher, ours is a business of conversion optimization because it's all marketed online. It's a consumer web service, which are my roots. But it's about personal growth, which is what I want to be doing in this world. Helping people make their own lives better and the lives of the people around them better by being better communicators. So I used all that huge range of my digital experience and applied it to the thing I love, which is creating great content for which people are happy to pay.

So it's been a wild fifteen years in this business, to go from making up new ad models, to the laying off 250 people in a single year, to the wasteland when all I could do was cook and golf, to bad starts with products that weren't real, to CEOs that literally died. I was in a company where, unfortunately, the CEO passed away. I was in another company where the CFO was delusional. And I was the one that spoke up about it. I launched an industry association in an industry that didn't want it. I failed in my first attempt at a publishing business; podcasts are not profitable, but information products are. Give people what they want.

It's been a fun ride. And Cory, I thank you for the opportunity to look back at my career and share the pitfalls with your readers so I might prevent others who follow behind me from making mistakes that are easy to avoid if you know what can go wrong.

My pleasure. Through the years that I've known you – and others say the same – I always come away feeling better having interacted with you, because you have so much energy and are so inspiring. It makes me want to ask you; what is it that inspires you the most?
I'm inspired now to create a scalable business model that generates revenue that makes people happy and successful. That keeps me going. I've always been very revenue focused.

Right now I'm focused on learning copywriting, storytelling, neuro-marketing and persuasion strategies and how to structure marketing communications to convert prospects to customers more efficiently. I have to keep up with technology, sure. We use online advertising, PPC, SEO, email marketing, dynamic landing pages, conversion analytics – so many technologies and tools it would make even your head spin.

And now in my current professional evolution, I want to be able to write headlines, ad copy, landing page copy, website copy, and auto-responder copy that resonates with people so deeply that they're moved to take action to better their lives.

I've always been one of those people who likes to communicate and educate. Going all the way back to @ Home when I was teaching big brands about what broadband meant, it was really a process of education. And being the chair of ad:tech, it was teaching people about all the great things in our industry. And even today at Personal Life Media, all of our online books and programs, the twenty titles that we have, they better people's lives and teach them new skills.

So ultimately, at my core, what makes me excited is sharing insights, techniques and ideas that better other's lives. Even on my show, *DishyMix,* which I've been doing every week since 2005, teaches something new to my listeners in every episode. I get to interview the most amazing, insightful, wise experts and thought-leaders and see what they know that I can tease out on behalf of my fans and followers. Doing *DishyMix* keeps me learning something new and I get to share it with thousands and thousands of listeners worldwide. That's satisfying!

CLOSING REMARKS

Susan is energy incarnate, and if you have ever had the privilege of sitting and talking with her you come away better for the experience. She has been a role model for many in this business, and her influence is unmatched. From Excite and the IAB to Personal Life Media, she continues to spread positivity and influence people in the right way. Thank you to Susan, for everything she has done, and please keep it up!

CHAPTER 17

TOM BEDECARRE

Tom Bedecarré is CEO of AKQA, a global digital marketing firm that uses innovative ideas and technology to deliver results for the world's leading brands, including Coca-Cola, McDonald's, Nike, Unilever, Visa and Xbox. AKQA has more than 900 employees in San Francisco, Palo Alto, New York, Washington, DC, London, San Salvador, Amsterdam, Berlin and Shanghai. Recognized numerous times as Digital Agency of the Year, AKQA was recently named one of the World's 50 Most Innovative Companies by *Fast Company* magazine.

An enthusiastic entrepreneur, Tom was also a founder and CEO of Citron Haligman Bedecarré, San Francisco's largest independent advertising agency and a leader in launching Internet brands. His influence on the business includes the infrastructure of the agency landscape, the quality of work delivered for marquee brands, and the fostering of talented individuals throughout the business.

Good morning Tom Bedecarré, CEO of AKQA. I'd like to start with how you got your start in Internet advertising. What was the beginning?

Some of the earliest things we did were for a game startup called Rocket Science Games that Steve Blank started and hired us for in 1994. We started our agency in 1990. I started on Madison Avenue at Ogilvy & Mather in New York in 1981 then came out to Ogilvy San Francisco, which at the time was just being rebranded. It was Ogilvy & Hal Riney and became Hal Riney & Partners. I was there for six years. And then some fellows from Hal Riney and I started our own agency in 1990.

We wanted to be a creative boutique like Goodby, Berlin & Silverstein. Those guys had left Hal Riney the year before I joined. We saw them growing up as an agency and being successful as a standalone boutique in San Francisco. There was another agency called Mandelbaum Mooney Ashley that was comprised of some young guys who worked for us at Hal Riney, but left. We thought, well, geez, if Jeff Goodby's doing it and Ken Mandelbaum is doing it, we ought to do it, so we started in 1990.

I don't know exactly where it happened, but somewhere in the early '90s we saw companies like Red Sky and Organic emerge in San Francisco and we felt a little bit like we were missing a train that was leaving the station. I remember some of the first times we ever talked about building a website for somebody it was for Rocket Science Games. I'm sure it was maybe a one-page site that we built for them and I remember Kirk Citron was very cognizant of Mosaic. When Netscape went public we bought one share of Netscape as kind of a symbolic gesture that it was going to be an important turning point in our business. That would've been '95/'96, so I guess being in the advertising business in San Francisco was hard to escape what was happening. The startups that were happening in the Bay Area were everywhere and they were exciting, but for the longest time we felt like we were on the outside looking in.

At that point you started getting into the web development business and doing a lot of site development. Is that correct?

Not really, that was kind of a one-off that we did. I do recall it was very early on and most brands didn't have websites, however, Steve Blank had started up a number of companies and Rocket Science Games was intended to be a very cutting edge video game developer. For the most part, we were doing traditional media and it was really later in the '90s, probably '98 and certainly '99, that there were lots of .com startups showing up on our doorstep. Mostly out of necessity we started doing online advertising at the time.

These startups had lots of money, they also had a lot of urgency to be first movers in the marketplace; to win the first mover advantage, and to go out and start spending money on advertising they needed help. They would show up with a checklist: We need a name, a logo, a website, some banner ads, a billboard on the 101, a TV commercial, a radio commercial. How much of that stuff do you guys do? It might be a young, freshly minted MBA that had sold the business plan to somebody, had no marketing department, and of course our answer was, we do all of that.

So we just forced our way into doing that for a number of startups at the time. Evite was a client, Homes.com, there was an online drug store called, More.com. There were a whole slew of brands coming out in the late '90s, and that's when we started doing online advertising. It wasn't for our traditional advertisers wanting to be in digital, it was for startups coming out of Sand Hill Road with money, an appreciation of the Internet and wanting to have online advertising be part of their launch package of marketing.

Was there a turning point where you really saw that online advertising was a viable, interesting business on its own?

Again, at the time, we were very frustrated that we had missed the Internet, that the Internet and .com had already left town without us and this was probably in '98, '99. We were always a profitable company as an agency and we had grown at that point. We were the largest independent ad agency in San Francisco with more than 100 employees. We were the West Coast Agency of the Year in *Adweek*. We had a lot of momentum, but I was jealous of Red Sky and Organic and the other folks – Razorfish had arrived and all the other interactive companies were doing great.

Somewhere in the late '90s we started meeting with Karim Sanjabi at Freestyle and Bruce Carlisle at SF Interactive and Kate Thorp at Lot21, and anyone we could meet because we thought, maybe we should buy one of these smaller startups. We thought we were sort of the big dog. We had a lot of revenue, made a lot of money, had a reputation as a top creative agency in town – our path was acquisition! And when we met with those people they thought we were smoking something, because they had very high expectations about what they were worth. I think back then Kate might have even thought she was going to go public with Lot21. They had very high ambitions and we were just an ad agency. What could we possibly add value to with what they were doing? It's sort of ironic that we outlasted all of them. But somewhere late in that period, we saw an opportunity to bring marketing skills and advertising skills together with online skills and that looked like a path to success.

There were a number of online ad agencies that had started, but we felt a lot of the larger companies that had gone public, were more focused on web design, web development. They came at it from more of a technology and a two-dimensional design standpoint. Even back in '99, and certainly 2000, we felt that the convergence of video and Internet would mean you had to have story-tellers and editors and people who understand advertising and marketing, combined with people who understood technology, and that that would make a powerful combination.

So it was back in '99 that we started pitching the idea and had a meeting with Mark Kvamme who was founder of CKS, and by this time, was a partner at Sequoia Capital. We told him of our aspirations, about how we thought that this idea of being a marketing-driven, creative-driven, front-end design-driven, complement to what was happening with Scient could be successful. Scient was a company that Sequoia had funded, so they knew the space. Sapient and Razorfish were good examples; there was a lot of momentum at that point with these companies. Some had gone public, had multi-billion dollar market caps, and we thought that there would be a future where the kinds of skills we brought would be equally valuable.

And so the next thing you know we had a term sheet from Kleiner Perkins and Sequoia Capital about making an investment in the company. Then in 2000, as it turned out, Sequoia was helping to launch a private equity fund called Francisco Partners and the relationships were transferred over to Francisco Partners where we met with Neil Garfinkel and Ben Ball from Francisco Partners. Over a period of months we negotiated an investment from Francisco Partners and from Accenture, which at the time was Anderson Consulting, to make an investment in this goal of bringing a creatively-oriented, marketing-oriented, technology savvy services firm together on a global scale.

We took a private equity investment in 2000 and bought a company in Washington, DC called Magnet Interactive, which was one of the original web developers on the East Coast, and an online ad agency in Singapore called TheAdInc. And then in 2001 we partnered up with AKQA New Media and so by that time, we were a pretty large company. We had this large investment backer and thought it made sense for us to call the combined company AKQA.

How you tackled the business at that time is that you approached it from this more mature, fully integrated

**marketing services perspective rather than online adver-
tising and web development. You were looking at it as a
holistic purpose.**

Well, I think integrated marketing is now what everybody
talks about, and it's taken for granted that everything is
integrated. It's taken for granted that that's your sales
pitch. I just went on the Goodby, Silverstein website and
they call themselves an integrated agency now, which I
find fascinating. Back then it wasn't obvious. If you
talked to the Razorfishes, Organics, Red Skies in San
Francisco, they were about technology and maybe two-
dimensional design. If you spoke to Goodby or Hal
Riney and other ad agencies, they didn't really want to
have anything to do with ".com." For them that was a
passing fancy. They didn't want to have anything to do
with technology.

I grew up in the Bay Area. I went to school at
Stanford. One of my best friends called me up one day
when he brought home an Apple I computer that he
bought through the Homebrew Computer Club and it
was a piece of plywood with some boards from Radio
Shack soldered onto something. It was one of the first
computers that Apple made. We always embraced technology. We wanted to be involved in technology and just
saw that sooner or later video and the Internet were going
to be an important combination of skills to have.

When I went to London and met Ajaz Ahmed in
2000, he had started up a new media agency that was all
about online. It wasn't about convergence. It was about
online web development. He shared the same view that
it was all going to be converging and we thought that
was the obvious thing. So that's what led us to put the
businesses together. It's funny because everything blew

up in 2001. After the bubble burst and after 9/11, all these companies were being sold and closed down. Scient was closed, iXL was sold and closed, marchFIRST went bankrupt. Razorfish sold for, I think, $8 million or $10 million to SBI.

The companies that we had tried to emulate were all gone, but somehow in that we hung on to our key client relationships. We had been hired in 2001 to be the online ad agency for Visa, which ten years later is still one of our biggest and most important clients. We were doing work for Nike, which is still one of our biggest and most important clients. A lot of the client relationships we held onto for ten years, but it was important to have some clients and some revenue in 2001 and 2002, because that's when a lot of companies didn't make it through the fire.

We came out the other side at the bottom. When everything went bleak we decided that it made sense to focus on digital and let go of the integrated part of that, as everyone was paying lip service to integrated by this point. Part of it was we thought digital would be a differentiator between us and the other ad agencies. I think it turned out to be a good call. At the time it wasn't obvious that that was the right solution, but that was what we chose to do.

You started out preaching, storytelling and being creatively driven and some of the agencies these days that are successful have caught up to that message. You did something else interesting; you looked at advertising and marketing as more than just putting banners on the Internet. You guys were creating front-ends for Xbox and doing some really interesting things that other agencies

were envious of. How did you start pitching those opportunities, and when did you realize that those were going to be an extension of the advertising and marketing business and that you needed to be in that?

I don't know the exact answer to that. Certainly now we talk a lot about how product design and experience design is so interwoven into marketing experiences and marketing communications, and that customers are much more interested in the application that's going to add some value and utility and some entertainment in their life than they are necessarily watching a thirty-second TV commercial. It doesn't mean they're not watching TV, it doesn't mean TV advertising is dead. We think there's a real value add to create interesting experiences.

So the piece of work that we've gotten most recognition for in the last two years wasn't even an ad. It was a piece of software we developed for Fiat that helped measure CO_2 emissions. It helped people manage their car driving to lower CO_2 emissions and save money on gas.

We have a curiosity about things. When we went to work with Fiat to see how their cars were made, what the functionality was, how technology is used in the car, we noticed they had a Microsoft product that they developed together. It's essentially a Bluetooth entertainment center in the car. There was a USB drive in the car and that got us excited. Our guys were asking, what's the point of the USB drive? It's primarily to put MP3 music into the car so that you could play music and obviously it was Bluetooth for the phone so you get hands-free driving. Their question was, what can we take out of that? Fiat said, well, I suppose anything. It's connected to the computer that's running the car. It's like a Windows operating system; you can pull anything you want out of it.

So our information designer said, well, if we could pull out all this driving information maybe we could build an application that would add some value to their marketing proposition, which is being the greenest car company in Europe. So how could we help create something that would support their "We're the greenest car company in Europe" positioning? The answer to that was we can measure braking, accelerating, fuel consumption, mileage, put all those things together and then come up with some training tools; such as, you're braking too much or you're shifting too high or too low, you're stopping and starting too much. Whatever it is, so that you can moderate your driving behavior, lower the CO_2 emissions, save money, etc..

That's now in millions of cars throughout Europe. We now have an iPhone version so that it can be done wirelessly. Originally you needed a thumb drive that you would pull the data out and put it in your laptop. Now it can all be real time through your iPhone. We also have a fleet version so someone who's managing a fleet can do the same thing at an enterprise level.

There's a curiosity in the people who work here. And whether it's curious about the design of a user interface for the next generation of Xbox or something else, why don't you let our guys take a crack at it? What is it that this car can do with data and what can we do? It's those kinds of questions that our team asks that lead to those kinds of breakthroughs, not Tom and Ajaz sitting in an ivory tower divining what's going to be the future.

We both kind of bet our companies in terms of merging them together ten years ago. It's mostly been growing ever since, with the exception of things blowing up in 2001.

The people that you hired are really what drive the business. You are about a thousand now, so you were hiring a lot during a period when these people didn't exist. How did you go about finding them?

Well, we've grown a lot of them. There's a huge number in our team that have been with the company for ten years. I just recognized two people in the company that have been with the company for fourteen and seventeen years here in San Francisco. So we do have a core pool of people who were adventurers in the '90s that wanted to do something different, be at a different kind of agency, involved in technology earlier, and certainly there were people that left. Just like we've ended up with these really dedicated people that enjoy technology, there were people who left.

Here we were a very successful ad agency in San Francisco and I announce to people that we're going to change our name to AKQA. We're going to shift our focus to being a digital and integrated business, and people that I liked quite a bit came into my office and said, I didn't sign up for that, I want to work at an ad agency. I'm going to New York, I'm out of here. I'm going to somebody across town. There were people who were incredulous about our changing our name. I remember vividly, because I would say, listen, the company was called Citron Haligman Bedecarré, I'm changing it. I can let go of it, so you ought to be able to let go of it.

Recently one of my friends who had left eight or nine years ago came in and said they wanted to thank me for the opportunity that they had to work here. That it's meant a series of progressive promotions and opportunities in their career, and having AKQA on their résumé has opened doors that wouldn't have otherwise been opened. This person was actually taking on a lead digital marketing role in a company who said he wouldn't have had that opportunity without AKQA. But also that he had been wrong and I was right, that he just hadn't seen it ten years ago when I saw it. And not that I even would have remembered, but this person reminded me what a hard time they gave me ten years ago about changing what had been a successful formula. I think that that's part of the challenge in this business, is to reinvent yourself and keep finding new things to specialize in.

We launched our mobile division five years ago and had been focused on how we can bring more value to clients and mobile for a long time. We bought a search engine company almost four years ago. We're having meetings right now about what we need to do to reinvent a company that's grown fifty percent in the last two years. I think that's part of our success is our openness to being a changing, evolving organization over time.

The agency model and agency business seem to be having a lot of challenges thrown at it right now. What do you think are some of the options for the agencies to pursue to reinvent themselves?

Well, I think the advertising agency business has gotten itself into a pinch. They've unbundled services so that all the media is now in the media buying companies that have a lot of power now in their relationship. Most ad agencies didn't embrace digital, or made a failed attempt to embrace digital. They may or may not have a digital offering right now, or they may have a sister company within their holding company that provides that service. But most, I would say, don't have a strong technology unit incorporated in their business. So for an ad agency right now there are problems. They don't have media buying and planning. They don't have analytics, as that's going to be with the media people. They probably don't have a strong digital group. They may have a few digital gurus around. They probably don't have a technology team in the room. I just don't know how you can survive with a bunch of aging TV copywriters. I don't think it's a business model. You can take a look at the public data; the large agency networks have had a very tough two years in '08, '09. They showed some modest growth in '10. I doubt they're up to the 2007 levels again.

It's critical to have media *and* analytics in the business. It's critical to have technology, software engineers and information architects in the business. It's going to be very difficult for traditional ad agencies to catch up.

What do you think about the trend towards automating a lot of that business, the DSP trading desks and the things that a lot of the agencies are doing?

Well, it cuts both ways. I think that those large media-buying groups, that obviously have a lot of clout and volume scale going through the business, they can add technology to save money and maybe be more efficient. I still think that clients are looking for strategy and are looking for guidance and how to allocate their dollars.

The one thing about technology is that it works for the little guy as much as it does for the big guy. If we have smart people and the same kinds of smart tools, it eliminates some of the advantage that a buying group might have in network television.

There's no question that if you're OMD or Group M or Initiative, when you're talking to ABC or CBS, then you have a hell of a lot more clout than if I called them up. But once you start getting people using technology where they're doing trading, buying and placing online ads, the distinction between big and small is diminished. We don't have an enormous media operation, but we are picking up business against the big guys.

So future-wise, assuming the rest of the playing field is level, do you still see creative storytelling and having a strategic component as essential for agencies in order to separate themselves, pitch business and win?

Well, I think there's a lot of complexity in online marketing now. That complexity confuses clients. Having been in the business for a while, it's gone from where people just want to do online advertising so they could tick the box and say, "We have banner ads in our buy," to a very complex set of issues that need to be resolved around, what are we doing with paid search? What are we doing with mobile advertising? What are we doing with banner ads? What are we doing with video online?

It's confusing to clients. They still have their full range of traditional media that they're managing. And instead of digital being maybe one component, digital itself has become very complex. It's one of the reasons why everyone is always talking about the delta between where people spend their time consuming media and where our advertisers spend their money advertising on media, and the fact that there's this big gap. I think Mary Meeker just pegged it as a $50 billion gap of displaced money outside of online advertising.

A part of that is that clients aren't accustomed to how they measure it, how they buy it, how they allocate between the various media types, and understanding what's the ROI of all these different new opportunities.

Do you think that the business is going to get simplified, or the rest of the landscape is going to get more complex?

We're only getting more complex. Media doesn't tend to go away, there just tends to be new media added on top. I think there's a big push for having better analytics and better people to interpret the data. There's a lot of talk about easier to use and simpler to understand dashboards so that information can be processed. I think there's a merging as all media becomes digital, and the distinction between a traditional ad agency and a digital ad agency will diminish.

In one area in particular there are lower technology thresholds, so there's a real dog-fight going on right now for social media because digital agencies like AKQA are heavily involved in social media. PR agencies want to get involved in social media. There are a few social media startups. They're not really significant at the moment. And then ad agencies that sort of missed the boat on the web, and missed the boat on search and online advertising, all the sudden see, hey, I can do a Facebook page!

And so there's more of a sense that this is something they're not too late for.

I think there's a huge push by the traditional agencies to get involved in social media. We'll see where it all nets out, but it's quite a mosh pit when you go to clients and they've got PR people and customer service people and legal people and marketing people and community managers and all kinds of people fighting over who's going to control social media.

How do you stay on top of all the trends and information in the business? What are you reading and how do you maintain some focus on what you read?

I think it helps to be in San Francisco. It certainly helped when the business was started to be here and to see startups and to follow them. I try to follow what venture companies are investing in because I think they're an early warning system of what companies are going to come down the line. I try to attend a couple of what I'd call venture-oriented conferences every year where new companies are introduced. One of them is called "Under the Radar."

Being around Silicon Valley and knowing a lot of people that I've known in the business that have gone off and started other businesses, I think it helps being plugged in and networked in here to be aware of what's happening.

The flipside of that is we're a global business. We opened an office in Asia ten years ago. We've been partnered with our London colleagues for ten years. We just opened a year ago in Berlin. We moved to Shanghai four or five years ago. Having a global network means that we're constantly learning about what's happening. Five years ago when we launched AKQA Mobile, the mobile market in Europe and Asia was much more developed than it was here and there were learnings that we could bring back to this market.

There's always interesting things that are going on in China that you wouldn't otherwise see here. If you look historically, when the market went to hell in a hand basket in 2001, a lot of people closed every office that was outside of the U.S.. We've consistently had a big portion of our business outside of the U.S., and so it allows us to keep our eyes and ears open on trends that are happening not in the U.S., not in the Bay Area.

CLOSING REMARKS

Tom has been one of the leaders of the web business, not just Internet advertising, in San Francisco for a number of years. His team paved the way for agencies in the digital space to get into more than just banners and websites, and I have always viewed AKQA as a premier example of the kind of work worth doing.

CHAPTER 18

SCOT MCLERNON

Scot is currently chief revenue officer for YuMe, a video advertising platform that powers much of the online video represented on the web. Over the last twelve years Scot has built and led three very successful web advertising sales teams with the last two of those years dedicated to CBS Interactive. Scot's sales teams have frequently been cited by Forrester for highest revenue per sales person, four years in a row while at *CBS MarketWatch* won "best business and finance site to advertise with" and have won the acclaimed ASPY award as Best Overall Sales Team on the web.

Throughout his career Scot's been touted as an industry thought leader and evangelizer that's constantly pushed the web's advertising capabilities. In 2000 he introduced day-part advertising to the web. In 2001 he publicly (and controversially) de-emphasized the value of reported clicks in a campaign. In 2002 amongst the ad recession, Scot created the At-Work Brand Network, a group of like publishers and competitors built to rival the size and reach of the major portals. In 2003 he founded the Seller's Forum where twice a year over thirty of the top brands sales VPs share and work out industry issues for a day, in an open but moderated forum. In 2004 Scot co-founded the Bay Area Interactive Group (sfBIG), which remains focused on educating and networking the Bay Area's interactive marketing community.

Hello to Scot McLernon, Chief Revenue Officer for YuMe. According to your LinkedIn, you're also VP of sales for Corralitos Ridge Vineyards.

Very proud to be that.

Let's start at the beginning. You got involved in this business with Quote.com, correct?

No, actually, the path really goes like this. My very first interactive role was in Pacific Bell Interactive Services. We were one of the very first companies to embrace interactive, building touchtone phone applications and technology; "If you want this service, press one, if you want another, press two." And you could go through a whole menu and not actually speak to a human being. That was pretty revolutionary at that time. So credit us, or blame us I guess.

Through that role I met Rick Parkhill who gave me my first job which was truly web-based. Rick co-founded Interactive Marketing Inc., which hosted one of the first trade shows with space online, as well as a trade show floor at the Hilton here in San Francisco. That show was called, "Web Innovation." I sold sponsorships for the online and physical versions of the show and that dates back to 1995.

What kind of audience was there for the industry at the time?

Anything that had to do with the web was exploding, or so it seemed. The online show had good traffic and the physical show had developers and potential developers virtually standing outside of the door waving money in our faces saying, "Just let me in. I just want to see what it's all about." It was mostly "about" HTML then. The show's content was directed primarily towards content creators and application developers of web pages. We were even featured on the *Today Show* at one point. That's about the time the switch really got turned on and the web looked like it was going mainstream.

Shortly after that the show was sold to Softbank Expos. With that change, came the opportunity to join Softbank Interactive Marketing (SIM), the web's first powerhouse rep firm. It was an easy decision since Parkhill's partner at the time was Andy Batkin and Andy was also the CEO for SIM. We actually represented Yahoo before Yahoo even had a sales force, amongst other great sites like Netscape and the Ziff-Davis Publications. That was in 1996.

Along that path, you're watching the beginnings of an industry and seeing the beginnings of advertising on the Internet. At what point did you say, "I know this is

going to be successful, this is where I'm going to focus my attention"?

Well, I was thrilled to A) have a job, and B) have a job in something that felt like it was making a difference. Meaning that it felt like *everybody* was really getting excited; Netscape went IPO in '95, Yahoo in '96. I thought if the investment world is paying attention to this then I should certainly be paying attention and there seemed to be a lot of really smart people getting involved.

At the time there was one other very large consideration, my new budding family. I had to ask myself, and my beautiful wife, whether I can put this much risk into a new career while raising a family? It didn't take long before there was no looking back.

Andy created a very cool job for my two colleagues and I, we were the Internet Strategist Group. Our sole job was to focus on anything "beyond the banner." Innovation and integration were born!

So you recognized the business was going to grow and saw this great opportunity. Tell me how you got into the *CBS MarketWatch* side of the business.

It was due in part to a little bit of frustration with the rep firm model. Basically the rep firm model is to take a smaller publisher that is moving up the ranks and help bring them revenue success. Then if their page-view growth and revenue growth dictates that they need their own sales team you're time is up. Ironically you can get fired for doing a good job. In the case of Yahoo, our lead publisher in our lineup of great sites said, okay, thank you very much, Softbank Interactive Marketing, we've got it from here.

After we parted ways with Yahoo, I started to take a look at this model and I thought, all right, wait a second. I need to be one of these guys on the publisher's side that fires the rep firms. So I found a position at Quote.com to be their national director of sales where I was able to build a sales team for the first time on my own. We had a couple of guys on the West Coast, couple guys in the East, and we went with that traditional staffing model of AE's, account managers and planners. That was '97. It was during my time at Quote.com that I received an email from a long time friend, Larry Kramer that said, "Hey, I like what you're doing over there at Quote.com. In fact, you're getting in my way."

At the time he was running Data Broadcast Company. They were kind of out on the fringe at the time. Interestingly they had a rep firm selling some advertising for them, just banners at the time so they weren't doing very much with the site innovation-wise. They were still trying to figure it all out. DBC made most of their money at the time with hand-held quote machines, and they were putting a little bit of financial information up on their website. They were getting some recognition, though and a couple of awards, but they certainly weren't getting in the way of Quote.com.

So I wrote back, "Hey, thanks, but Quote.com is first to market, I'm hitting my numbers, paying my mortgage and so everything's good." He writes back, "We're about to change all that. Click here." I click on the link and up came CBS MarketWatch. He said, "This is gonna launch in a couple of days. You decide."

I thought, this could *really* be something, with all due respect to Quote.com and its first-to-market status.

I listened to Larry and what he was planning on doing and, in my humble opinion, it sounded as though he was going to first and forever change the way the world received its financial news. It was the start of the financial news revolution, it became the way we learned about what stocks were doing and why they were doing it.

It was the story behind the quote. IBM is up a point and a half, why? Our journalists in real time explained why. Larry took me through his ideas and said, I'm going to go build a newsroom and I want you to build a sales team out of your own model. You've been doing some cool things over there at Quote.com. Do that and a lot more over here, and let's get as many sales people as you want and let's get creative. And Larry drew a line in the sand. He said we absolutely, positively are going to be advertiser supported. *The Wall Street Journal* drew a line in the sand and said we absolutely, positively are going to be subscription supported. And with that *The Wall Street Journal* essentially allowed *MarketWatch* to happen.

It all happened because Larry believed Dave Callaway could have a staff of seventy-five journalists and that I could have a staff of twenty-five sellers, and that together we would be able to pay for those journalists, keep the lights on and provide the very best financial news that you could get. And he was right.

So between *MarketWatch* and *The Wall Street Journal*, you guys were the first major brands to duke out the free versus paid subscription model.

To the best of my knowledge. Look around today and the ad-supported model is the norm. I think you'd be hard-pressed to find many subscription models that are successful out there. And the *Journal* did a terrific job of it. We ended up charging for newsletters, so that was a third piece of business for us, but for the most part it was all advertising supported.

We had another line of income, which became absolutely critical to our success – content licensing. But that really became the two companies that, as you said, duked it out.

A long time ago you and I had a conversation, I think when I was back at Freestyle, and the thing that sticks in my mind is that you guys were really picky about the advertising you would accept on *MarketWatch*. The conversation specifically was around a Budweiser campaign that you were running, where you allowed them to do these really interesting rich media units where there was a beer pouring from the top banner into the side skyscraper unit. At the time there wasn't anybody doing anything that beautiful, as far as online advertising was concerned. So the fact that you really were pushing the envelope on the rich media side and balancing that with playing against *The Wall Street Journal,* with their paid model versus your free model, how much did advertising really work into the business model behind *MarketWatch*? How much did the advertising factor into what the overall revenues were going to be?

There was one other factor at play during that time, the .com downturn. We as an industry needed to think differently, especially as it pertained to our ad units. It was about that time that our editor likened the downtown area of San Francisco to that of a Wild West town that had just been abandoned and the tumble weeds were rolling through the streets and he said, "In San Francisco's media gulch nobody's ordering the Opus anymore."

But if you think back, we give all the credit in the world to Louis Rossetto, Doug Weaver and the group at *Wired* for creating the banner. The idea of a 468x60 pixel banner at the top of a page, supporting all that content, and the page being built to actually scroll away from that advertisement was ultimately flawed. And it wasn't until the .com implosion that everything blew up and our backs were put against the wall. When your back is against the wall, quite frankly, and your family could go hungry, that's when you do your best work. That's when all of a sudden everybody gets creative and everybody sits at the bargaining table.

Some of the best relationships that I still have in the industry, such as my relationship with you, were born out of those days, '99, 2000, 2001, where we all got across the table and said, okay, we're the ones that are left, now let's figure this thing out. And that's when a lot of things happened. That's when PointRoll was created and a lot of great companies were launched.

Kramer and I quickly realized that to survive we'd need to get creative and while some of the ideas were perhaps a bit intrusive, he and I eventually compromised. Particularly when you factor in that when I arrived at *MarketWatch* in '98, Kramer said, "We don't have advertising on the front page. Look at *The New York Times*." He showed me the print edition. "There's no ad on the front page. Look at *The Wall Street Journal*, there's no ad on the front page. We don't do ads on the front page." And that was the first time I walked out of his office a little torn and a little bloody having lost a debate with him. Several years later, when we eventually sold *MarketWatch* to Dow Jones, the entry to the site was a beautiful eight-second interstitial advertisement – some evolution, don't you think?

The concept of front-page advertising may have first come down to survival and then down to a conversation around a much better topic; what part of this million dollars don't you want? The Budweiser idea was really born out of a challenge. It occurred to me that when you're Budweiser, arguably one of the biggest advertisers in the world, and certainly the biggest in the beer business, you get pitched *everything*. But we had an opportunity to pitch him on something that had never been done before, and something he'd never seen before. That was why so many of us got in the industry in the first place , because you actually felt like you could get up that morning and do something new.

It's become an industry joke that each RFP wants something that's never been done before, but we actually went in with something that Bernie Plassmeyer and his colleagues had *never seen before*. The idea of day-parting, owning the Friday afternoon read when people are either, A) going to the pub and having a Friday night happy hour, or B) on their way to the store to pick up their packaged goods for the weekend; we could reach consumers at 4:00 on the East Coast, then 4:00 in Chicago, then 4:00 in Denver and then 4:00 on the West Coast and we could do it with creative that you mentioned. The bottle would roll across the page, or pour from above to down below.

I took one of the ideas from some television creative during the baseball playoffs. As they came back from commercial break and you were looking through to the players warming up on the field, the Budweiser bottle rolled across the screen leaving the Budweiser logo superimposed on the screen for a moment.

And did they buy it right off the bat?

Well, if you know Bernie you know he doesn't impress easily. That afternoon I think we impressed him to the point where he gave me a verbal and a caveat, he said, "Give me a reason that I need this right away." We needed to go back, sharpen the pencil, and I think we gave him an exclusive. We gave him a period of time that he would have this and we wouldn't sell it to anybody else. Bernie was great to work with. He was a no BS kind of guy. If he wanted it he wasn't afraid to tell you. I miss him, in fact.

So you did get the sale right away.

Yeah, and that proves to me that when people tell you there is no budget I never believe that, I believe that the idea isn't good enough.

That's why you're a good sales person. That's why you lead good sales teams.

Thank you.

You were getting involved and pioneering a lot of this rich media. You were doing some interesting things with brand name advertisers and had a big brand to work with in CBS. How did you avoid the allure of stuff like pop-ups? How did you avoid fads in the advertising business that could've generated a whole lot of revenue at the time?

I'd love to tell you that that was something I believed in, but it was something that I learned from both Larry as well as from Dave Callaway. Larry with his original idea of, we don't have ads on the front page, and Dave Callaway being the executive editor. Dave was always my credibility check. I'd bring him an idea or a mock-up and if it made him sigh then I knew we'd maybe gone too far.

It was in the early days of *MarketWatch* where I went onto the front page, went through the eight-second intro message, and then an advertising supported stock tracking tool came across the page in the look and shape of the back of a UPS truck, where the door opened up and it showed you the stocks. It would open and close when the stocks refreshed. Then last but not least a little Pepcid French chef floated across the page. This wasn't exactly a clean, well-lit user experience at this point, and if a typical pop-up had come up I probably would've fired myself as Head of Sales. It was at that moment that I said, okay, maybe we've gone a little too far here, we need to ratchet back.

I give credit to Dave Callaway for what became our stance on intrusion versus interruption: good advertising can be mildly intrusive, but it can't be interruptive. I love that philosophy. I took it and I ran with it. I owned it and I instilled that into our sales team.

I'll give you the example. When you came to the homepage of *MarketWatch* we'd ask of you to watch, for eight to ten seconds, a very nicely done flash ad. In return you would get great financial news and, by the way, we're not going to ask you to do that again until the next day. We put a frequency cap of one on all of those ads. So then you've got free run of *MarketWatch* without any pop-ups, certainly with relevant and nice, clean, well-lit, safe environment ads on the sides of the pages, or maybe in the middle of the page as a 300x250. But it was pretty easy for us to make the decision that we weren't going to interrupt people's experience with an ad in the middle of the page that pops up at you versus something nice and clean and classy for eight seconds as you enter the doorway.

And those drove brand engagement. Those drove the kind of metrics that your advertisers were looking for, right?

Entirely. It was very easy for us and that's when we came out with the announcement about click-through rates. We felt like there are so many more metrics we should be discussing other than click-through rates, but let's provide advertising that produces that kind of resonance, that kind of engagement, that kind of brand lift, purchase intent, all the things that Dynamic Logic started to offer at that time.

Over the years you've trained and managed very successful teams, and done training for people in online ad sales. What were the things that you looked for in the people you hired in online ad sales in order to be successful in the business?

I would love to tell you there's a background part of the formula. I can't tell you where successful sellers necessarily come from. Many have agency backgrounds – there's more of what they shouldn't be than what they should be. I still believe in ideation. I still believe in relationship selling, in consultation, in sitting down at the table and actually building something that works on behalf of our client, and I use that term "our." I believe that the agency and the publisher actually share in the client.

At the end of the day we all answer to the client. Those kinds of characteristics, relationship selling, consultation, ideation, those are all things that the best sellers on my teams have always had a propensity for. And those are the strategic parts. The tactical parts are they have to be absolutely awesome at blocking and tackling. They have to be absolutely awesome at organization. They have to know that you can't be a one-hand wonder. You can't be Milli Vanilli, or whatever that was. Didn't those guys have one song?

And it turned out it wasn't even there's.

It wasn't even them, right? But you have to be consistent and not the gunslinger that cracks the big deal, rides that out for a quarter, and doesn't have anything in the pipeline for the next quarter. So the people that understand, that consistently building that pipeline, those kinds of blockers and tacklers who are building relationships for the long-term and are consistent in their behavior, those are the folks.

The background, if there's any indication, lies in doing the grunt work at an agency. Actually getting the ball and chain tied to your ankle, to your desk and grinding out twelve- and fourteen-hour days at an agency and starting off as an assistant-media planner, something like that, real junior position. Because there's no real training program for this business other than the agency life.

If you can get yourself up to speed on media and digital media by doing that grunt work at the agency level, that's almost like getting your MBA in media.

So you come out with your Bachelors of Science or your Bachelors of Arts and your business degree, that's terrific. But what does that do to prepare you for the world of digital media? Nothing, but if you put in eighteen months to two years inside an agency, now you've got a path into the digital world and maybe into digital sales.

Plus, by that point, you're probably frustrated with the agency business and ready to make a change.

So I'm told. I'm not one of those guys but of the hundreds or so terrific sellers that I've known, either through a training level or through hiring in my own sales teams, I could point to at least a dozen that have agency backgrounds, that have gone on and really been successful. There are a couple of folks that went back to the agency world because they couldn't handle the rejection of being a seller and other things, the pressure of carrying a quota. But for the most part, I could tell you that that's a pretty terrific foundation.

You talk about people having to be able to sell using relationship selling and how important ideation is. How important did you think an understanding of technology was?

Believe it or not, I think that's a little over-rated. For instance, you can be a pretty terrific watch salesman without understanding how that watch is built. You know the catchphrases; you know that the Swiss movement is built on seventeen jewels, etc.. For instance, Ad Operations has reported into me for fifteen years and I really don't understand the ad serving system. I don't really understand it forwards and backwards. I've sat with my ad operations team because it's a little different here at YuMe than it was at any of the other stops along the way where we were selling display advertising, and video advertising is very different.

I sat with ad operations traffickers for two hours just recently because I really want to understand what that looks like. But how that technology actually works – certainly you need to understand what cookies are, how the web is built and formed – you can still kind of scratch that surface and know just enough without actually being a technologist or an engineer.

I agree. Some people in this business, and I count myself as one, know enough to be dangerous but we don't know how it works necessarily.

What's more important, for today's sellers, is to understand what their competition does and what their clients do. Another fascinating part of this career is that there is *always* something we can be doing to make ourselves better. We can learn something else about our clients, what they do and why they do it. How can you credibly recommend an ad solution for your client if you haven't credibly demonstrated knowledge for their business?

I recently saw a print advertisement in an airline magazine that included a picture taken in an airplane from about fifteen rows back and all the lights are out on the plane, all the overhead lights above the seats except for one. And you can see there's this guy hunched over his laptop and that he's working. And the phrase is, "There's always somebody working harder than you." I'm sure there are, but there aren't many.

That's a little frightening isn't it?
Yeah, but in this industry you work your ass off. And so this comes back around to the technology. I don't think you need to know anymore about the technology than enough to be dangerous, but you can always be learning more.

You should also be relatively well-versed at all the things that are in your newsletter and in *MediaPost* and in *Ad Age* and in *paidContent.org,* and everything that goes on in our little eco-system that continues to evolve and change seemingly every four, five, six months and maybe four, five, six weeks. So that's why there are always so many working harder than you. These days on the plane I've decided, no cocktail. No glass of wine. No movie. I've got stuff to do.

As I talk to people there's one overarching theme, which is that this whole business to the outside world is all about technology, but to everybody in the business it's a people business. And the advertising and marketing side is a people business. I want you to explain your view-point on that and if that's the allure to why you're here.

To me the greatest thing that happened when I came back from UpStream was getting back in the saddle of leading a sales team. And leading a sales team is truly about all the various parts. I'm surely not comparing myself to Bruce Bochy or any of the great managers in baseball, although I do think that putting together a really fabulous sales team is much like putting together a great baseball team. You've got some veterans, some folks that you're bringing up through the minor leagues. Here comes your Buster Posey, you sign your Aubrey Huff. You've got a couple of utility infielders and your veterans and the batting coach, all these various players. And when it all hums, when it all comes together it's a pretty amazing feeling.

I'm really struck by how many great people we have when I attend events: sfBIG, iMedia the IAB events. I'm truly struck by the depth of the bench in this business. The competition right now is fierce. I know my competitors are trying to take my money, but I can still be great friends with many of them, even Jason Krebs from ScanScout, Tremor. And it all goes back to the days when we created the At-Work Brand Network. That was an example of when I reached out to my competitors to actually join forces. Another example of back in '99, 2000, 2001 when the world imploded, you do your best work.

I reached out to *USA Today*, which arguably was trying to take my money. *New York Times* arguably was trying to take my money, Weather.com and *CNET*. And I reached out to the leaders of those teams and said if we join together and all sold our front pages to the same client that would be the news around the web that morning. Amazing relationships were built out of that. You're not going to see that in radio. You're not going to see that in television. I don't think you'll see that in print.

I think those kinds of different ways of looking at it were what built the business. Ideas like the Seller's Forum, a classic example of how terrific relationships amongst competitors are formed. That really was a result of John Durham and me sitting down with a couple of other people. I think it was Riley McDonough and Loraine Ross, and actually having discussions about challenges we all shared as heads of sales things, some of which by the way we're still dealing with. The four of us sitting down in co-opetition – I can't imagine the heads of sales of, you name it in traditional media, sitting down and having that kind of conversation. Then turning that into not just four, but twenty-four heads of sales all getting together in a room under the auspice of, we're all in this together, let's make it a little bit better.

So yeah, the incredible friendships and relationships that you end up making is a real added bonus to the career.

It doesn't happen in a lot of businesses, but it definitely happens here. I know from my perspective that's been one of the most fun things about it, is that you meet such smart people and share ideas. I met you many years ago now, and I met Mr. Durham and all these great people that I'm now getting the chance to interview. I learn a lot from our conversations. That gets me excited and that keeps me getting up every day and coming to work. When Doug and I got together to create Habitat, when we finished our first Habitat people from the audience stood in line to shake our hands. People were standing in line to say thank you for helping change their lives. Change their lives! I couldn't believe it. And when that was done, when the last person left and we sat down with a glass of wine just completely physically and mentally exhausted, we looked at each other and I was just so proud of what we created. It truly was a matter of making people's careers better. And I can't think of a more admirable profession.

But people make fun of us because we're only selling pixels. We're trading pixels, but there's a lot more to it.

We're not curing cancer, by any means, but there's a lot of people who are making a living in this industry and to have them say thank you for taking them through a couple of days, as was the case with Habitat, or as a sales head helping them move their career along a little bit, that just feels phenomenal.

CLOSING REMARKS

Scot McLernon is one of the special people in this business; the right mix of experience and cowboy willing to try something new. He never backs down from an idea, but he rarely jumps into something crazy, always giving an idea its due time, its due attention, and the opportunity to succeed. He blazed a path for the innovation in online advertising during his role at *CBS MarketWatch,* and continues to do so in his role at YuMe.

He adds color to the world around him, and if you are one of the lucky people to work for him, his energy and skills are contagious (I asked those who work for him, and they all agree). His impact on the business is far and wide and I thank him for taking the time to be involved in this book. Thanks, Scot!

CHAPTER 19

DAVE YOVANNO

David A. Yovanno is currently the president of Mediaplex, a division of ValueClick. Dave is a seasoned senior executive having served as COO, GM and EVP for ValueClick, a successful, public online advertising company, and as CEO for Gigya, a successful social technology SaaS company based in Silicon Valley. Dave also served in the United States Navy as a Lieutenant and CIO. He is a graduate of The George Washington University in Washington, DC where he earned his bachelor's degree in marketing and master's degree in healthcare administration.

Dave's passion is building and leading teams toward exceptional productivity and achievement. He enjoys developing and executing business strategy, establishing strategic business relationships and solving the problems of growing companies. During his years in the industry he has been responsible for leading many of the initiatives that have shaped the ad network landscape and are emulated by many other networks today. His career has been focused, demonstrating how successful you can be working with one or two companies and working your way up the ladder over time.

Good morning, Dave Yovanno. Let's start with how you got into the business. You were product director for St. Joseph Health System once out of college, and then a Lieutenant and Chief Information Officer in the U.S. Navy, which I don't think I knew.

Yes.

My father-in-law is a retired Navy SEAL.

Is that right? I was actually training for that in college and decided to go the business route. I was ROTC in college. I decided later in my academics that I was probably going to want a family at some point and didn't think the SEAL track would be a good way to go for that.

Well, he managed it and did it well. He served a long time as a SEAL and has a wonderful family as well.

I respect that. That's great.

I graduated college in 1994, and I was training up for a more traditional career in business. I actually selected healthcare administration because that was a really good business route to serve, and I was expecting to be on active duty time to pay back my college tuition. They paid out $120,000 for my college, the Navy did. I was looking for a business track that could help me transition to civilian life as soon as my commitment was over. Though I got lucky, in the year that I graduated they were still down-sizing from Desert Shield, Desert Storm, so they didn't need active duty people, and they gave me an option to go away with no commitment. I actually felt like I was obligated to something and so I gave them the option to call me up for active duty time within a four-year period of me graduating.

So when I graduated college I went on to get my master's degree and then did an administrative residency with a healthcare system, and started getting into IT project work. Then the Navy called me up and said, "We need you to serve some active duty time." I'll save you from that story, but it was really good experience. My point was going to be that my friends and I in college were planning for traditional careers as lawyers, accountants, etc. and it wasn't until my senior year that the Mosaic browser hit my school. It wasn't until that time, 1994 that the market started to develop for the Internet. Until then, it wasn't really a career path people would think about.

I had a computer lab my freshman year in college for the first time. We were the first class to have a computer lab. It was WordPerfect 5.1, with the blue screens. I really got into computers at that point. I hadn't at all up until that point. I took to it so much so that after my first year in college, I worked two jobs during the sum-mer so that I could buy my own computer, and I would stay up all night just learning applications like Quattro Pro and WordPerfect. That next year I used it a lot.

I saw the Mosaic browser come out my senior year in college and designed my graduate program's first website when I was a graduate student. That was in 1994/95, but it was just a hobby at that point, something I geeked-out on. I still didn't realize that a $20 billion industry was about to be created. I had no idea. I was just personally interested in it. I was tinkering with it. Not so much as a programmer, more as a super-user, I guess you can say.

Had I gone to school on the West Coast I probably would have seen the trend at least three or four years before I did. I was at George Washington University, and the technology trends hit the East Coast later. Nonetheless, once I saw the trends happening, I was like, this is cool!

I was bored doing IT work both with the Navy and with the healthcare system. I didn't get excited about a stodgy, traditional career; nine-to-five, where you go to work and you work on very large projects and don't see the direct tangible impact of your work. It just wasn't exciting. There was something about the Internet that called to me as being so groundbreaking and revolutionary, and by that time Yahoo had gone public. Netscape was out there, AOL, and you could see that it was starting to become a real market. And I said, I have to find a way to get into this.

I had a contact who gave me an introduction to interview at ValueClick. It was funny that I only interviewed with one Internet company, but I was very fortunate to start my Internet career with a company that was well-run, that had a good business model. Most Internet companies at the time were burning through cash and poorly managed, and could never establish a sustainable, scalable business. ValueClick was different. It had a seasoned executive management team, including Jim Zarley who is still CEO, that didn't give into the hype and wanted to build a sustainable, scalable business. Almost nine years later I was still at ValueClick, and it was one of the companies that had survived that whole transition and shift in the business from 1998 to 2004. So I considered myself to be pretty fortunate for that opportunity.

When I came in to ValueClick there were about ten of us that started on the same day, and already they had about forty to fifty total employees. ValueClick did about $22 million or so in revenue that year. They were about to go public, and I was right alongside people who had traditional careers in publishing and marketing. I think because of my IT experience I came in as a director of advertising products, which was essentially a product management role. But what was great about the Internet at the time was that it really set a level playing field.

Here I am coming from a military background, healthcare IT work – what was amazing about the Internet was that everyone was starting from the same place. We were all creating something from scratch, nobody had experience basically. It was almost a negative if you had other media experience. It didn't matter if you were in a band, if you were running a healthcare company, if you were working for some big shot advertising agency, it didn't matter. Everybody was starting from level zero, because this whole thing is brand new and there was no track record to speak of. It was the Wild West and it was a land grab to establish your business. If you were passionate about the revolution that was happening, understood Internet basics, were hungry and driven, you could build something.

That part was extremely exciting to me. It created so much opportunity for people like me who were somewhat technically oriented. I'm not a programmer. I understand technology, how things work and can put things together to create business value, but I'm not an engineer. I took computer science classes in college. I became more product-oriented than engineering-oriented. I think that was an advantage because when I joined ValueClick, DoubleClick had invested about $85 million into the company before ValueClick went public, and I was hired to help ValueClick migrate their ad server to DoubleClick, which ultimately never happened.

Because of my IT and product experience I was tasked to run that project. After three months we called the project off for a hundred reasons, but mainly because DoubleClick's technology couldn't allocate properly for a CPC business. DoubleClick could only allocate based on an ordered number of impressions in their system.

We had just gone public, we raised about $100 million and had $85 million investment in DoubleClick, so we had a bit of a war chest established at a time when the first Internet bubble was starting to burst. At this time we were still growing. We outgrew our office space; we had desks in the hallways and had the classic growth chaos going on. After the DoubleClick project, ValueClick gave me $100,000 to go spend on studying our competition. I channeled the money through my personal banking account to make media buys on ten of our competitors and I analyzed all their stuff. I put together this matrix and evaluated everyone in the space. As a CPC business we felt cheap and like the redheaded stepchild in the industry. We wanted to not just keep up, but also get bigger and better.

So I ran this project to study the landscape. I studied Advertising.com, (called Technosurf at the time) E-ads, Engage (which was Flycast); ten of our competitors. I got a handle on their UI, their systems, what they sold, their collateral, their pricing, their agreements, what they said about ValueClick and other people in the space. After a two-month project I came back to the sales organization and I gave this presentation.

I came up with this matrix based on fifteen criteria, scored everybody on a scale of 1 to 5 and had a weighted distribution. I created an analysis that said, granted I'm biased because I work for the company, but it's hard to argue that we don't rank at least 3, if not number 2 on this list. I actually ranked Engage number 1, for a lot of different reasons. The sales team was so amped after the session they put me in charge of sales. If you could show any level of competence, of knowing what the hell was going on in this industry, they'd give you responsibility and that happened time after time within ValueClick to the point where, within a couple years, I was the General Manager for the media business unit.

I had a couple of other experiences where we had figured some things out. Things like optimization, including how to share a site ID in the click string, where an advertiser could share results with us. It was a big problem that we were able to solve which really helped the business grow. I had a couple milestone achievements like that, along with strong financial results for my division, which helped raise my executive position in the company. We also had had a great executive leader in Jim Zarley, who was an incredible mentor for me and the other leaders of the organization, to make sure that we were investing time and resources in the right things, and weren't burning cash like the other guys. It was one of the few companies that knew how to run the business as a business, and we didn't fall into the whole hype of anything. I'll give you a couple stories on that.

This was the end of '99, early 2000 we had six sales people with their feet on the desk, wearing shorts, wearing jeans. You would have a ten-minute phone conversation and get $100,000 IO over the fax. It was that easy. We had to turn our sales people into business development people to go buy clicks because we had too much demand, not enough supply. That was the environment I walked into. There was such a bubble at the time that there were all these companies who raised money, that part of their pitch to be acquired was, look at all this traffic we're getting to our website. What they were representing was that it was organic traffic, but the reality is they were buying clicks from companies like ValueClick.

So you'd have a company that was about to, or already had raised a huge sum of money that would just buy clicks from us. That was it. There was nothing real about it, it was just clicks. So one of the early assignments at the time I was doing this research, was we knew that the bubble wasn't going to last. All these orders were coming through but they couldn't be sustained. I started getting concerned about the quality we were providing as a product. We figured out how to detect the geo-location of the traffic, and in studying our traffic flow with what we were delivering as clicks I found a good percentage of the clicks that we were generating for our advertisers were actually coming from Korea. I remember going into the senior management's offices and said, "Look at this!" And their response was, holy shit, we didn't realize that was going on. And we had just gone public.

So the very first acquisition that we made as a company was a company called Straight Up, which was a small $1 million acquisition. It was in 2000. What that company was about was placing a pixel on the advertiser's landing page so that we could get some feedback as to what's the quality of this traffic we're generating for them. Then it was just a matter of time for us to correct how to improve the quality of traffic. We had no insights into this. The technology wasn't good enough then to know where these clicks were coming from and what was happening once the click got there. It was just important that we fix it, so we fixed it.

So think about what happened, 2000/2001 timeframe, everything came to a screeching halt. We had the big bubble burst. In fact, we went public on a Friday in March, 2000, came out at nineteen, and everyone's running around the office thinking we're going to go to eighty-six. We went as high as twenty-one, I think. And then everything came down to around nineteen, eighteen, seventeen; we were like one of the last companies to go public. And then everything else just came down from there. That's when the whole industry got corrected.

What happened from an advertising standpoint at that time, was there were two types of companies who basically kept the light on for companies like ValueClick and a bunch of others. Casino-on-Net and other casino advertisers, and Providian's Get Smart credit card offer. It was those two industry segments that kept us alive. We had Casino-on-Net paying us over $1 million per month to run banner ads to get people to make a fifty dollar deposit and what-not, and this was the source of our ad revenue, because all the cheap .com bubble money burst.

We weren't getting those crazy click orders anymore. All of a sudden now we've got real advertisers who have a real business they are trying to feed with real advertising, and that became the new challenge. We also had to train our sales team on how to actually sell, we did that from scratch. I brought in professional training for that, set-up Salesforce.com and I think built an incredible sales culture over several years. But we really had to provide value at the end of the day for our clients because the casino guys weren't going to keep feeding us money if they're not getting deposits and those people are not profitable for them at the end of the day.

One of the things that happened with the casino relationship, I noticed a trend. They would start with a budget of millions at the beginning of the month, and then right around the 20th of the month they'd start pulling back their budgets, saying "you're not performing." Then they'd shut us off for the last week, week-and-a-half, and then they would restart us in a couple of weeks and it was the same cycle. We'd start strong, they'd start cutting back, cutting back, and I remember coming to these guys and saying, look, we've got to fix this. I've got a wide network of thousands of sites, tens of thousands of sites. I need to know which ones are working for you and which ones aren't so I can get this consistent level of fulfillment for you.

Their response was we don't share data with anybody. These guys were based in Tel Aviv. So I hopped on a plane with my colleague, I was the GM of the ad network at the time, and got face to face with these guys. I didn't realize it was a 200-person company. These guys were more advanced than anything that I've seen even still today. These guys would pump out one hundred new variations of display creative every Monday. They'd move the twinkle from the top left to the top right in one variation, changing colors, etc..

Anyway, I'm standing across from these guys on the first day and they say, look, we spend $15 million a month on advertising and a good chunk of that with you. You're the first company that has ever come up to see us. So we were there for four days and I told them I wasn't leaving until we solved this problem.

I honestly believe it was that project that came out with the first innovation of how an advertiser can pass a site ID in the clickstream back to the publisher or ad network, and have them track that to some level of performance. The win-win was they were going to feed us back an index, nothing proprietary, just an indicator of performance. They weren't going to send us back the actual value and deposits or things like that. They created their own index performance route and then could pass that back to us by site ID, which is what I needed. I needed to know what sites were working and which weren't, so I wasn't wasting inventory. Once we solved for that it really helped grow the rest of the medium. Companies like Avenue A soon built their own form of a similar index mechanism.

We took that innovation to everything we did; our credit card offers and some of the other performance guys, so that we could get back to this consistent level of spend. It was important for us to have that kind of innovation during that period because the only advertisers that were spending money were ones that actually had a business model behind it. It was primarily those two types: casinos guys and the credit card guys.

The other innovation that was happening at the time was, and I'd be surprised if I'm the only person who mentions this, but it's the company GoTo.com, which became Overture. We were talking about putting those companies together, ValueClick and GoTo.com, and I remember looking at it and saying, I pay to get listed? That can't last. That's not the organic Internet, that's incentivized traffic. What did I know? But if that innovation didn't happen, I firmly believe online marketing would not have become an industry.

There's a great video of Terry Semel being interviewed by *The New Yorker* at the Newhouse School that gives you good background on what it was like for the Big Four at the time, before Bill Gross' sponsored listings model. He's telling this story about how Ted Meisel from Overture came in and pitched him this offer; "I'll guarantee you $10 million this year if you just give me the top five sponsored listings for searches that are conducted on Yahoo." Terry Semel's telling the story, he leaves the room and he's joking with his colleague outside the conference room, "I'm acting like I'm actually thinking about this? Is he freaking kidding me? Hell, yeah, we're losing money hand-over-fist, I'll take that deal." He comes back into the room and says, all right, we'll take it.

Ted Meisel leaves the room, calls MSN, AOL, everyone else, basically says we just signed Yahoo $10 million guarantee, you want in or not? He basically locked up all the major portals, one after the other. Google still pays

Yahoo to this day, which acquired Overture for the patent. Google wasn't making money until this model was created. Search has become such a lion's share of the marketing dollars online that if that model wasn't created, I don't think we would've become an industry. That deserves some place in your notes on the history.

Ad networks have always gravitated more on the performance side of marketing than probably other models, but what I realized was that in order for us to be successful as a business, we needed to have a really solid foundation of direct-response deals, especially as a public company. Those campaigns are the most predicable. Going after pure brand business ebbs and flows, it's much harder to predict. You'll have a big campaign, a big win, but you can't guarantee it's going to be there next quarter or next year. The brand stuff still has the longest way to go.

Another side story about the ad network model that I found interesting was there was a one-page website at the time we were doing our ValueClick investor road show, called Hamsterdance.com.. It was wallpaper, animated with this hamster dancing around with annoying music. It was a one-page website and had a banner at the top. There was nowhere else to go on the site, but if you wanted to click a link it had to be the banner. It had the highest click rate, over 1 percent click rate on that banner. The executive team was using that website as an example. I can't believe we went public with that in the road show. It just seems crazy to me looking back on it now.

It's interesting because a lot of the things you're talking about are outlining what eventually becomes the

standard for the ad network business. That's exactly one of the reasons I think this is a good book to write, because the ad network business is a large portion of the overall online ad business, but nobody understands where the ideas came from. Hundreds and thousands of people who work at all the different companies, including ValueClick – now the number one or two ad network online – have no idea that all the technology, and all the processes for the business come from such humble beginnings.

Yes, exactly. I feel bad for the biggest publishers on the Internet. I just came from an OPA event in New Orleans. You've got *The New York Times, USA Today* and all the big sites on the Internet who have always struggled to maintain a level of brand advertising and tried to justify high CPMs, but they're only successful at selling maybe 40 percent of their total inventory. Maybe 50 percent if you're lucky. There's so much of their inventory that goes unsold, that the ad network business model made a lot of sense. What we created at ValueClick over the course of time with the ad network model was; how do you maintain that balance of being friendly with those guys, but not create channel conflict with them?

Advertisers wanted transparency, they wanted to know where they were running ads; however, big publishers didn't want advertisers to know that you can access their inventory through an ad network. What we invented was a position that said, I'm not guaranteeing any placement, but I'm guaranteeing you won't run outside of this list of publishers. That was the balance I personally helped create at ValueClick, and most ad networks started to operate that way. That seemed to be the right balance, between top brand publishers and ad networks, to help those publishers fill more of their inventory at the highest possible CPM. If completely blind, advertisers are willing to only pay a small CPM. But if they can at least see a list of sites that they are going to run on, they're willing to pay more.

Partial transparency.

It's partial transparency. Now with the real-time bidding and demand-side platforms, it's bringing transparency to a whole new level. There is a lot of control for the supply side about disclosing their brand; however, price is fully transparent. And to get a real marketplace going, the publisher has to be willing to sell at both very high and very low prices. It's hard to say if this model will scale for large publishers. The technology has evolved tremendously over the past few years for publishers to participate in these marketplaces, and the only thing stopping real-time bidding growth right now is the publisher's willingness to make their inventory available in that fashion. Maybe private exchange is the answer. It just creates a lot of channel conflict for their sales teams.

One thing that's important to realize is that you look at the major channels of where money is spent online. The reason that the Overture story is so important is that search is the primary channel of where money goes online, hands down. Then you've got channels related to display, email, maybe mobile, maybe social, search and the low-hanging fruit on the performance side. I think growth is leveling out a bit. You see the projections for display increasing, which is really exciting. I just hope that Google doesn't take up the lion's share of that market also.

You and a whole lot of other people.

ValueClick was a great experience for me because it wasn't just a display business; it ultimately became a very diversified operating company. We acquired fourteen companies during my almost nine-year tenure there, and these were companies that were experts in email, shopping comparison, some elements of search, ad serving technology with Mediaplex and Commission Junction and Be Free, with affiliate marketing, which is just a great mix of all different types of Internet marketing businesses, that was just exciting experience to be exposed to all the primary marketing channels online.

I know from the media side and the marketer side of the business, that ValueClick has probably the single most holistic solution for an online advertiser. They're not necessarily always the sexiest business, but they're probably the most stable and most effective business for a company that's trying to do performance marketing.

We had made it through the first phase of the market explosion, right? So this was late 2000, early 2001, the industry was in a really rough spot. Thanks to our experienced management team we never got into the hype, never from day one. Even though we were right in the middle of it, when we went public we never got too far ahead of ourselves and our core business. Our CEO had started and exited a number of businesses, but they were always businesses that generated 20 percent operating margin and were growing at least 20 percent a year. That was his magic formula and our goal from the very beginning. His view was, how is DoubleClick Media going to make this work? When they generate 30 percent gross margin, that means to get to 20 percent operating margin, you can only have 10 percent operating expenses, it's just not possible. The media model of DoubleClick didn't last. They couldn't give the business away. So here are some of the things that we ran into.

Once we passed that first phase of battening down the hatches, controlling costs, improving the quality of the product and the value that we're delivering so that we can keep that foundation of direct-response advertising, who were the only ones spending money online at the time, once we got toward the end of that period, we were in acquisition mode to help fuel our growth as a public company. Our initial targets were companies that didn't have the ability to survive, that were still operating in the bubble heyday. One of the first companies that we came across was Mediaplex. It's a classic story. The CEO of MediaPlex was on the front cover of *Fortune Magazine*, and on paper was worth hundreds of millions.

After the .com bubble burst, and after our deal to acquire the company, he netted a fraction of that. He and the company had just given up, and it created a good M&A opportunity for ValueClick. And I don't know if you've been to the old ValueClick offices in San Francisco, but it was a beautiful office, right across the Embarcadero, right under the Bay Bridge. Mediaplex had an open tab at the restaurant below, so Mediaplex employees would just go down and rack it up, because they were part agency, part ad server. Employees would go down there and have dinner on their way home and it was on the company's tab. They had a kegerator in the refrigerator in the back kitchen. They had a VP of Karma. They had speakers throughout the office channeling ambiance music. It was just ridiculous. And this was 2002 this was still going on.

When ValueClick came across this company they had started a cost control turnaround with a new CEO; however, they were burning close to $2 million a month. It was clear they were going to be in trouble. They'd just given up. We paid something like $40 million for the company, and they had close to that in cash in the bank. So, we got the company for a steal. It was almost the exact same story with Be Free, which was ValueClick's first acquisition in affiliate marketing. That deal was in the $128 million range. They had close to that in cash in the bank also. It was crazy. It was like we paid nothing for those businesses.

It basically was an even cash deal.
Right, and we come in as a more humble, practical set of business operators, and Mediaplex was cash flow positive in about two months just by turning off the beer keg and canceling out the checks at the restaurants. It wasn't that hard, same thing with Be Free. I think the leaders of these companies had just gotten ahead of themselves during the whole .com explosion. When it imploded they didn't know how to handle it. They didn't want to give it up.

There was so much chaos going on it was like they couldn't get people to buy those companies. We just came in there and picked them up. There were many opportunities that we passed on also. We could've bought Ask Jeeves for about $50 million but we couldn't do that deal because we were doing the Be Free deal. There were just too many deals we were doing at the time. So we definitely leveraged our position of cash, and having made it through the first rough period, we kind of laid the foundation for the next phase of growth in the industry.

You witnessed, for lack of a better term, the rebirth of a whole category, a whole business? ValueClick was in many ways leading that rebirth, from a financial perspective, and you learned a lot during that time. What was the most important thing you learned then that you apply to your business now?

I just went through a session with the team at Gigya and said, look, I've never had to go through a situation professionally where I've had to do layoffs, and the reason for that is that you're always weeding your garden. And so this is just part of the mentoring stuff that I picked up mostly through my time at ValueClick, where if somebody's not an A-player get them off the team.

Typically when you're making those calls, you're asking yourself why you didn't do it six months ago. When you're experiencing high-growth, one of the things I've learned is that you don't want to get too far ahead of yourself. It's important that you have a plan and a budget. That you're going to achieve so much revenue, you're going to keep your cash burn capped or your net income at a certain target rate. And if you're not on track for that, okay, maybe one month you can consider that an anomaly. If it happens in the second month, you need to be overly aggressive in correcting it. All open positions are frozen. If somebody is not an A-player, they're gone. We're not even going to debate it. You're going to over-react to those things, that way you're protecting yourself.

We've had a couple offers out there into some people recently and I've said, you know, I think it'd be great if we can bring these guys on, there's no question that they're qualified, but we need to rescind that offer. We're not going to hire that person just because we're trying to keep things in balance. When you're the leader it's a hard decision to make, but it needs to be very objective. You've got to stay within a limit. And the impact on your team can be extremely positive. It can be extremely rewarding to see how much you can accomplish sometimes with less.

Maybe every quarter, or every six months do a due-diligence check to make sure that you're really on budget, on the plan that you're expecting. We had to do that a couple of times at ValueClick, what we call battening down the hatches. Make sure you're not getting too far ahead of yourself, because you don't want to be in a situation where you're overextended on cash. As a public company the lessons are even more fierce, because if you tell a group of analysts on your quarterly earnings call that you're going to do something, then you absolutely have to do it. So it's better to under-promise and over-deliver, always.

Analysts are basically listening to what you're saying, and they're putting together their own forecast based on that. If it's all hype and you under-deliver on that your stock price is going to go down. It's the same thing that applies in a public sense, as much as it applies in a private sense in terms of how you're managing your finances, especially in an early stage company. That's a big one. The other thing is that your product needs to provide real value. If you can't back-up your sales pitch with real results, you're not going to create long-lasting value, your business won't scale and you won't get that renewal. You're just not going to succeed.

I think managing people has changed a lot, especially with social media. Nobody likes to be micro-managed. I had an absolute awesome time with the team at Gigya. I was with them for over two-and-a-half years, and it's just amazing when you set these audacious goals and you've got your key metrics for what will determine success in the company, like how many clients you're signing up, or how many implementations are going live, or how many renewals are you getting, or how many opportunities is the sales development team creating. Those were the four key metrics in the company.

People are coming in here, not to hide in a cube and do personal things at work. They're here working on the business, and driving the business forward to hit these goals. The metrics are visible right out in the open floor. And if they're not, then there's not a role for them here.

That's the way business is today: get an A-team hired, set your goals, set your metrics and just go. Don't micro-manage. Embrace an enormous amount of trust. I see a lot of that in workplaces today, especially early stage companies. Gigya has a very open office culture. I didn't have an office; my desk was in the middle of the open floor layout along with everybody else's. Everybody hears everybody. And the focus is on the business. If somebody needs to leave early or work from home, I trust and know they're still working on driving our metrics forward.

As companies get bigger things get managed a little bit more old school; where you need to be present in the office more, or you're a little bit more micro-managed, or if you were working from home, people didn't quite trust you maybe. I think that's the challenge for companies as they grow. How do you grow and keep a startup culture? A sixty-person company is much different that a 2,000-person company, but I want to figure that out. You know, a good benchmark in this respect is Netflix. They have great culture at scale and that is something I aspire to create.

It sounds like you've definitely ridden a wild ride. You have so much experience and have faced so many different situations, and all within two companies. When I look at somebody else's résumé for the same period of time that you've been in the business, I might see six companies or seven companies, and you've got two. There's something to be said for maintaining stability and loyalty to a company, and having it be returned.

I'm a big fan of that. I don't know if it's my Midwest background coming from Cleveland, or the time I spent in the military – and I think the military teaches you a degree of humbleness. I've always had a very hardworking, loyal work ethic. I've always had a job since I was fourteen. Some of that is innate to me, but I agree, I think there's something to that. I like forming a team that you spend so much time at work that if you don't have that loyalty invested in work, you're not going to accomplish big things.

I don't care if you're a big company or a small company you've got to give it your all. And those people have to be people you enjoy spending time with, and who create drive for you. You have to want to impress them and earn their respect. If you like them you want to work harder. It can't be a nine-to-five job, just putting in your hours and can't wait to leave. It really needs to drive you. What drives me every day is trying to continue to maintain and earn respect from my peers. These people I work with, I want to show these guys that I'm contributing, that I'm smart. I want to set the pace and lead by example.

I'm expecting them to do the same thing. I love this next generation of people coming into this industry. I'm having an absolute blast with these guys. I posted a job recently to a service we subscribe to that sends the opportunity out to thirty or forty schools within a three-week period. I personally interviewed 100 people, via a thirty-minute phone call. I was the initial screen. I quickly create a filter that prioritized; the cover letter, above a 3.7 grade point average, and just what they sound like on the phone. I turned it over to my head of business development, and we basically had six people start within a three-week period, which is great.

We locked them in a room for two weeks and taught them everything we've learned about online advertising and technologies for the last decade. At Gigya I had members of my management team come from DoubleClick, Quinn Street, we've all had successful runs at other companies, so we just put everything that we knew together in a training program, and trained these guys. We're raising them in our culture, and we've turned these guys loose, and it's been phenomenal what these guys are already doing. The way they are using these different systems like Salesforce and Marketo, how they generate emails, they've become experts. These guys need to write a book.

They know how to create opportunities for a sales organization, because these guys have become experts in variations on email subject lines, the body of the email, the use of the systems, how we use Jigsaw in coordination with all of this. We generate 10,000 prospects a month with the various whitepapers that we write. These guys are setting up 360 opportunities for our sales organization in a month, and 10 percent of those will close in a two-month period. These guys have become animals, and they've taken our original system to another level. I don't even know what's going on over there, it's become a science. They passed me up on all this stuff, which is fun to see.

We're making some investments in that next generation. Honestly, if I was coming out of college right now, I would love to have this experience. We're giving these guys a history lesson on the Internet. When I was graduating college, I didn't have someone that would explain all that stuff to me. I was prepping for a healthcare career and we had to figure all this stuff out on our own.

We're having fun with that. Social's become the next challenge. It's exciting because it's not all figured out, I feel like we're hitting the reset button. We figured out a lot of stuff during the time that I was at ValueClick, and social's become this whole new channel of opportunity, kind of like what search was originally.

Gigya is one of the hundreds, if not thousands of companies trying to create something of value within that space. And so it's terribly exciting. There's a lot of risk. Gigya raised close to $30 million as a company and there are high expectations on building that value. It's absolutely awesome not knowing what next year is going to be like. It's kind of fun to think about it that way.

CLOSING REMARKS

Dave is a leader and you know when you speak to him, he has an air that makes you want to listen to what he has to say. The key takeaway I have from his interview is the idea of patience and focus. Dave spent his career with two companies, including his most recent venture back into ValueClick. He changed roles, exceeded expectations and continued to build different businesses under the roof of these two companies, which goes to show that you can focus your attentions on one big company and still grow and develop your skills. Some people think the way to succeed is to jump around, but a lot can be said for loyalty and commitment. Dave is an example of those qualities in droves.

CHAPTER 20

SCOTT HEIFERMAN

Scott Heiferman is one of the pioneers of Internet advertising, reluctantly. He started his career at Sony, quickly recognized the opportunity that was burgeoning in the Internet and launched one of the first Internet ad agencies i-traffic. i-traffic employed and nurtured some of what would become the industry's thought leaders, and was responsible for such early breakthroughs as the Disney "101 Dalmatians" campaign, the launch of one of the first affiliate programs for CDNow, and numerous others.

The company was eventually sold to Agency.com, and Scott revisited his entrepreneurial roots by starting MeetUp, the world's largest network of local groups. MeetUp makes it easy for anyone to organize a local group or join an existing group, and meet with people interested in the same things!

Scott has always had an eye on the Internet, and has spotted trends that would affect consumer interaction far earlier than most. He is a smart guy with very little ego, and a hunger for new things. Please meet Scott Heiferman!

Scott Heiferman, CEO of MeetUp! I want to go back to the beginning. You started i-traffic in or around 1995, I arrived in 1996 and we built the company into something important. That being said, I remember an early story about how you got started. Didn't you originally bribe the tech engineers at AOL to get Sony on the front page?

That is true, although I don't know if I should publicly admit to the bribing word. It's funny you remember that because it really is kind of an interesting moment for us, part of the start of the online ad business, because at the time people didn't realize that the links would be so important and that links would be a currency.

I was basically a glorified intern at Sony. I worked on Sony's first website, and then to get Sony on AOL, which was emerging as the dominant way that Americans were getting online back in 1994, we launched, with great fanfare, via the keyword "Sony" on AOL. Which in today's terms is like "Facebook/Sony"; so keyword "Sony" on AOL was a very important thing. Basically it was one of the first companies to have a corporate presence online.

We launched this little section and it just had no traffic, because how is anyone supposed to know about it? So when I went knocking on doors around AOL, which was a relatively smallish company, a medium-sized company at the time, I realized there was no process by which they decided how anything would get promoted.

Now when I say things get promoted, I don't mean companies get promoted, I mean the internal content. It was clear that the most important spot on AOL was the welcome screen. It's pretty old school stuff, but you'd logon and get this welcome screen. I started knocking around saying, how can we get this keyword 'Sony' on the welcome screen? And no one had any idea! I said, you know what, we'll write a check. They were like we don't have any means to even account for that kind of check. There was no line item in their business model for something that would resemble 'promotion' or 'advertising' or anything like that, so I realized the decision-making was being made by some guys in the back room, some developers who would just feature different things.

So I sent them care packages of Sony Walkmans, which reinforces how old-fashioned this is that a Walkman even existed, or that a Walkman would be something of value. But sure enough, Sony started appearing on that welcome screen and you could see the traffic go from nothing to a lot. It became clear that links were critical if the online world was going to explode.

So that question fascinated me; how will the link become a commodity? How can something like that become a currency? How will it be something that companies buy, trade and sell, and how will attention get handled like that? Ultimately, I wanted to focus on that question and that's why I quit my job. I was going to start an agency around links.

I set up shop for what I'd called i-traffic, which is how do you get traffic to things online? I started calling it an "online ad agency" because the links were like ads, and it was funny because no one had really been using that term or put those words together – online ad agency. So *Advertising Age*, when it was just me and a buddy of mine in our apartment in Queens, did this big feature on, oh, look at this novel idea, an online advertising agency. So that was fun. That was with my college buddy, Ryan Nelson. It wasn't until a few months later that Seth Goldstein came into the picture.

I found myself kind of homeless. After I had to leave the apartment in Queens I had very few friends and no money, and I didn't know what I was going to do. Basically Seth Goldstein let me crash on his couch on the Upper West Side. He was just renting a room from someone. He was nice enough to let me crash. Within a couple of weeks he wanted to leave his apartment, so we became roommates and rented an apartment, 31st and Broadway, which became the home of i-traffic and the company he started called Site Specific.

I was in that office, and at one point didn't we have close to thirty-five people in your apartment?

Yeah, it was insane because we were both living there. At one point it was at least thirty full-time people that were working all these crazy hours. One of the funniest little things about that is I had been introduced to a guy named Clay Shirk by Seth, and Clay was this programmer. I had this project we were doing that he wanted to be the programmer on, so we hired Clay. Clay would basically work all night. His whole thing was that he wanted to work all night, so what the hell? He did.

It's funny because now Clay is one of the most respected thinkers, thinking about the Internet. He's written two great books. People like to hear the humble beginnings stories about Clay, but yeah, it was insane. We had rats in the apartment. We would have clients there and it just smelled, although, it was cleaned up sometimes. You worked there, Cory. You know that it wasn't so bad.

It wasn't so bad. I was there when that one rat did try to eat its way out of the rattrap.

Yeah.

At that point, though, did you really understand, or had you had the foresight to think about how big that business could be?

Well, we didn't know what the hell we were doing. There was no clear vision, no great sense of things, but it was pretty clear that the Internet was going to be something great for people, and the question of how do people navigate their way around, whether it's the commercial things or non-commercial things, was going to be really important. In fact, I remember back in those early days, after I set up shop as an online ad agency, I got called by a guy named Jerry Yang who said, "I've got this little site called Yahoo, and it's basically just me and my friend David, and we're trying to think about what the ad model might be like." But you saw how Yahoo was growing and realized that there really was something significant here. I had a lifelong obsession with advertising, and to put it more specifically I had a lifelong obsession with hating advertising.

When I was in high school, I did a big independent study project trying to prove that advertising was ineffective. Then in college I did a radio show called "Advertorial Infotainment," which was basically a glorified art project making fun of advertising. My thought was that we don't want this to get into the hands of Madison Avenue, because they would screw it up and there was something really utopian and idealistic and wonderful that was emerging with the Internet. I thought, wow, this could lead to a day where advertising is actually useful and it might not get bastardized.

On the back of every i-traffic business card, soon after we started, was this mission statement, "We're helping people find what they want to find," or something along those lines. I don't have the exact words, but really the spirit of Google and the spirit of Facebook were living in a lot of the companies then, that spirit being that this was primarily about people and there's something different here. This is not going to be your father's medium.

Based on where the business has gotten to at this point, and the fact that you started out with the idea that advertising sucks and you didn't want Madison Avenue to get a hold of it, do you think they screwed it up?

Well, I think the pendulum goes all kinds of ways. It goes back and forth, and there's always the crappy advertising online and there always will be. But what's fascinating, and I don't mean to pass judgment and use these silly labels, but the good guys are winning. The fact is, is that Google is up and Yahoo is down, and which one of them would sell anything regardless of whether it's good for the user? MySpace is down and Facebook is up, and guess which one actually is thinking about advertising as something that could be a net positive for people?

The online advertising industry, for the most part, is living up to its potential as becoming more and more net positive for society, and the good guys are winning. Ultimately, what we built at i-traffic became a part of Omnicom, so you could call me this big hypocrite because we wanted to build something that Madison Avenue wouldn't screw up, and ultimately Madison Avenue owned it. But there are examples of everything kind of good and bad. In the grand scheme of things, the good stuff's winning.

I agree with that. Another thing I remember from that time was how hard we had to work on everything, and how much there was information-wise to digest. One of the things I always thought that you were really good at is identifying early trends. We would have that meeting once a month or once a quarter where you would identify something that everybody needed to talk about. We talked about MP3s before everything else started to take off and before Napster started to take off. You were really good at staying ahead of that stuff. How did you do that?

I don't know. Just keep your eyes and ears open. Listen. Whatever you pay attention to is what you're going to absorb and think about. I think if you spend all your time thinking about how can companies get more market share then you learn about it. How can brands get more market share when you're looking at the Internet? If you do that all day you don't have the attention span or time to look at the other parts, which is how are people benefiting? I've got a modern example of that that's really fascinating, which is GroupOn. You know how many startups try to crack the online local business market?

Whether it's Big Book in 1996, or Yahoo or Yelp or CitySearch, they all tried to crack the online ad market. They were all doing innovative, great, breakthrough things in their own way, but they were coming at it from a perspective of a traditional media business. Now here you have a guy named Andrew Mason, who is obsessed with collective action, and Andrew did this startup called The Point. It was about how people can act collectively that would be powerful together.

His startup was failing and he decided to pivot a little a bit and say well, okay, this thing that he thinks about and thinks about called collective action, which is really people-centric not business-centric, he nailed the concept for GroupOn. The rest is history. But the moral of the story is that ultimately the Internet is about people being powerful together. That is YouTube; people being powerful together. That is Wikipedia; people being powerful together.

He wasn't just looking at it as a traditional media business of, how can I get advertisers to advertise online or, how can I provide a directory service online for people and then advertisers would advertise? It was a whole different thing. So if you want to see what's around the corner, it's not that hard if you're intention is really just to be thinking about people first, because people are going to drive the future of the Internet, and people will drive the future of everything. We're past the 20th Century era when companies or corporations controlled the agenda.

The more people I've talked to interviewing for this book, the more one theme comes up, and you just hit on it again. It's that this whole business has a backbone based

on people. You could take all the technology away and start over tomorrow, but the people are what drive this business. They are the innovators; they create the connections, and are ultimately responsible for the growth of the business.

Absolutely.

You started MeetUp after i-traffic, around 2001, right?
2002.

So you started it after the bubble had burst and a lot of people were down on the business. What do you think you took away from that period of 2000 to 2002, as you were getting ready to start MeetUp and launch? What did you take away from that period that has helped you with your current success?

Well, something I took away from it that might actually moderate my success now, or MeetUp's success now, was that it was kind of like living through the Depression. You develop a certain frugality and a certain pragmatic realism, and take away from it that if something is too good to be true, maybe it is.

The writing was on the wall in 1999 skipping in to 2000, which is why we sold i-traffic, and that was, hey, there's some hot air here. Not that the businesses weren't right or that people never stopped using the Internet. The bubble was not people getting benefit out of the Internet, the bubbles was were the ads working and were the businesses sustainable? They had to have a solid value proposition. Certainly eBay did and Amazon did, but for the most part they didn't.

Seeing such devastation, you come out of it and you say, okay, I'm going to make sure that the business model doesn't get too convoluted. I was looking at Jeff Bezos during those days, so in awe of how he would simply say, you know what, I've got a product, people pay for it, and that's my business model. I thought to myself, whatever I do next I just want to get paid for a good service, and I don't want to get caught up in the hot air. I want to be profitable if we are delivering value, not profitable just because we could sell some hot air.

The reason I say it might actually moderate our success is that we always had a certain timidness. We went from a free service to a paid service. We went from free to fee in 2005, and lost a lot of our activity at MeetUp. We're doing absolutely kickass great right now, and everything's doing well, but you have to wonder; if you weren't so burned by the ad explosion when the .com bust happened, would you have been more open to an ad model and thus maybe MeetUp would be bigger, better, faster now?

But it is kind of like living through the Depression. You have a certain pragmatic reality that you want to be successful slowly. I love the fact that MeetUp is profitable and sustainable, and controlling our own destiny, not dependent on the whims of some media planner who might decide we're not the hot new thing anymore, that it's not about hype. It's about people paying us for our service and it works.

You've gotten to a point now where you guys kind of own the term "meet up." People talk about getting together

as a "meet up," and you guys are powering a lot of those now.

Yeah, we're in it for the long haul. This is also a Greatest Generation kind of thing, like having lived through the Depression. But you get a little burnt out from all the hoopla and hype around the startups, and you say, hey, what about building a solid business that will last for decades? Maybe you could make yourself a job that you like to do, that isn't about building things and flipping them, and it's long-term thinking. It's like fast food versus slow food. Fast companies and slow companies! We want to be a slow company.

It's refreshing to hear somebody talk about that. There is the art of just building a business and people forget about that. How do you view the overall business these days? How do you view the methods of how today's advertising shapes content and content shapes advertising?

Well, I think that content is not the future. Let me make it really simple. The media business is a tiny business compared to the telecom business. Take the year 2000, the whole entire media business, movies, TV, magazines, advertising, and all that stuff, is a tiny business compared to the telecom business. You think, well, the telecom business is so unsexy, so old and stupid; but what is a telecom business? A telecom business is people talking to each other; it's phones, wireless phones, mobile phones and it's how people talk to each other.

You might say, oh, that's old-fashioned. Phones are not just phones anymore. You watch TV on your phones. Your phone is media. Actually, no! What people are doing on their phones is they're looking at Facebook. Facebook is not content. Sure, I'm creating content in the form of a photo and stuff like that, but it's more like the old school telecom business, meaning people are in touch with each other. They're turning to each other. They're talking to each other, texting each other, picturing to each other. It's a communication thing, not a media thing.

There was all this hubbub about Facebook being valued at $50 billion. Jack Myers had this whole thing saying, oh, this valuation for Facebook is ridiculous because Facebook has no content library, there's no "there" there. Well, that's a misunderstanding.

I think of what the Internet is, that it's not about owning a content library because it's not content. It's a collaboration community communications thing. I'm not going to use the word "medium." There's a role for advertising and marketing to play in that that can be wildly effective, and of course there's going to be a future to the media business. Is content dead? No. There's still going to be content and writers and creative content and all the stuff that content is traditionally, and if you just call it user-generated content, that's trying to shove the old media context into a box. When I'm putting a picture of my baby on Facebook, it isn't content.

It's communication, I agree with that.
I know it's a lot of pontificating about what to call things, and maybe that isn't so important but I think it is.

Think about how much pontification and idealism, and all that that we expressed when we were in college, this is the perfect time to do it.
Yeah.

You started i-traffic and that was a very successful business, and you were twenty-four according to one article that I have, and now you're running MeetUp. What do you think you've learned over the years, and what would you have gone back and maybe done differently?

Oh, man, I don't know. We're all just idiots making it up as we go along. Honestly, and I really mean this from the bottom of my heart, what you think of as idealism is actually instinct and you should listen to it, because it's what is important to you.

CLOSING REMARKS

I had the pleasure of working with Scott Heiferman for four years during the early stages of my career and have maintained a relationship with him over the years. One of the key things I learned from this interview, that I had never really thought about with Scott, was the idea of focusing on the future, maintaining the course and following your instinct regardless of what others are telling you.

MeetUp was a great idea, ahead of its time, and took awhile to get to where it is today. Scott was patient and he persevered. The same went for i-traffic, a new company in a burgeoning space that many were willing to give advice about. It too found success because Scott maintained his focus. Patience is a virtue, and that coupled with focus is a formula for success!

CHAPTER 21

SETH GOLDSTEIN

Seth Goldstein is co-founder and chairman of SocialMedia.com, a platform that helps publishers socialize their ads, as well as Chairman of Turntable.fm, a trailblazing internet social media site. Seth is an active member of the advertising community and considered a thought leader on social media. He is currently the co-chairman of the Internet Advertising Bureau's Social Media Committee and a member of the IAB's Board of Directors.

Seth has helped to create and invest in a number of pioneering businesses over his career, starting in 1995 when he founded Site Specific, one of the first Internet advertising agencies. Site Specific pioneered a number of Internet marketing practices that continue today, including interactive and pay-for-performance ads. In 1998 Seth joined Flatiron Partners where he established a practice in Pervasive Computing. In 2002 he created Majestic Research which pioneered the use of primary data for Wall Street research.

As an angel investor, Seth has advised a number of successful web services including *Delicious* (Yahoo!) and *EtherPad* (Google Wave). Over his career, Seth has been featured in *The New York Times, Wall Street Journal* and *Economist,* and has spoken at leading industry events around the world.

Seth Goldstein, how did you get involved in the digital marketing business?

When I graduated college in '92, I started working on CD-ROMs and went over to Europe for about a year, so I was kind of busy doing interactive multi-media. Then I came back, I think it was the middle of 2004, and I remember being on something called Pipeline at the time. It was one of the first Internet access providers in New York. I came across a job posting for Agency.com at the end of 1994, so I went and worked at Agency.com with Clay Shirky among other people.

It was pretty clear that the web was an interesting thing I could help with, and I was doing HTML at the time. I was working on websites and I went to work with Michael Wolff, who had a company called YPN, which was a series of net guides for the Internet, kind of like the first Internet directory. It was there that I met Heiferman for the first time.

And then I went and did some work on Epicurious for Condé Nast, where I worked with Deanna Brown, who is now CEO of Federated among other people. Scott and I took a big apartment right near Macy's in Manhattan, and he started i-traffic and I started Site Specific around the same time in the middle of '95.

Even before I started Site Specific, when Scott and I were sharing an apartment, we were called by an older guy at the time named Kevin Ryan who worked at United Media, and they had a property called "Dilbert." "Dilbert" was a really popular webpage for its cartoon and they wanted to sell advertising, and no one had really done that before. I remember calling Dolan Smith White for Intel, and various other advertisers to get them to sponsor the "Dilbert" page for $10,000 to $15,000 a month.

I also remember when I was at Condé Nast doing work for *Details* magazine, which they owned as well as *HotWired,* and working with Doug Weaver and Rick Boyce and putting together an ad for *Details* magazine to promote the magazine on *HotWired.* The ad was referencing Anka Radakovich, who was a sex columnist on *Details* magazine, and there was a picture of her with red lipstick and it said something like, "Get Oral with Anka," and it had a 30 percent click-through.

Even back then Internet advertising had to do with sex. Absolutely.

What was your vision for Site Specific? Did you really see it turning into an ad agency and did you foresee ad agencies dominating the web?

Our first claim to fame at Site Specific is we managed Duracell.com. It included a number of components.

We built the website, but it was pretty clear there was a question of why would anybody go to Duracell.com.

It would be much more interesting to tell the Duracell story outside of their website, to tell it in places where people were spending their time. So we came up with what I still believe to be the greatest online advertising campaign in history, which was this idea of "Powered by Duracell."

It was like, let's go to all these different websites and instead of putting banners, when there weren't really any banners at the time, let's take a picture of their page and flip it backwards so that when you see a battery bursting through the bottom of the page, you click on it and you see the back of that page, and it says, "Powered by Duracell." The vision was *the web* is powered by Duracell, and Duracell batteries are driving all this new innovation, and that was such a great brand-appropriate concept.

That was, for me, the vision. How do you distribute brands across the web? How do you syndicate them? Not how do you build a big webpage and drive people to your page because what's someone really going to do on Duracell.com? Over time, I remember Clay doing some really interesting things for Travelocity, in terms of enabling people to check and book ticket prices within the banner. Why go to Travelocity.com if you could achieve the same functionality on other websites that you're already spending time at?

How do you think marketers use the web differently now versus then?

I think there's still a fair degree of vanity, meaning they want to put a lot of money against commercials and big websites. Then and now, just like the bread and butter of a traditional agency is a commercial, the bread and butter of a digital agency is a big website that they spend a million dollars on, that really only costs a hundred thousand dollars to create. That's where the margins are, and I think that's where a lot of marketer's heads are. What they struggle with is how do you get people in their native environments to pay attention to you? Whether that's through display advertising or fan pages or tweets or mobile apps, that's what it's become.

Do you think that statement is still valid, given the fact that the web has become such a syndicated content environment?

I don't think it was valid then and I don't think it's valid now, but I still think that's how brands understand it. I don't think they know what to do with all these social channels. They want to control them to the best of their ability, but it kind of runs counter to proper thinking. It's more of a cluster metaphor or a network metaphor, it's not a destination. At the same time, there was a Yahoo and then there was a Google, and now there's a Facebook.

There have always been these large aggregators of audiences that brands need to do business with because they realize they're not going to get traffic themselves. It's a struggle over these last seventeen years, and on top of that there's been the whole advent of performance marketing, where there's real ROI but where brand equity gets annihilated. There's been proliferation of all sorts of bells and whistles for brand advertising where there's no ROI, but it looks good at *Ad Age*.

Do you think that ties back to your vanity comment, that a lot of the web is just vanity at this point?

It's subtler than that by now. There are lots of different flavors. Again, back in the day, it was AT&T and Zima being the only advertisers online, and now everybody is advertising online and they're advertising everywhere, and they're advertising to everybody in different ways through cookies and retargeting and social advertising, and all these other new flavors. I don't know. I haven't really stopped to think about how does what we were all doing then relate to what's going on now.

The decisions that were made back in '94, '95, '96, have had a lasting effect, and are things that took, and still are taking, a significant amount of time to rectify. People are still looking at click-through rates because when the campaigns began that was the initial metric that they evaluated. It took a long time for people to define what the impression was going to be.

It took a long time for people to understand the proper way to build a website, to build navigation so that consumers would want to utilize it. Do you think there is anything remaining that needs to be addressed in how marketers use the web beyond the click-through as a primary metric? If there were something you could have gone back and changed about how the web was being developed for marketers and used by marketers, what would you have changed?

It feels like at some point the performance and the brand advertising forked. One went one way and one went the other way. It would have been nice if they didn't diverge the way they did. I'm not exactly sure how brand advertising would have achieved the same level of accountability that direct-response did, nor am I clear how direct-response advertising would have achieved the same kind of brand equity, but I do know that brand advertising online is accountable in ways it doesn't get credit for. Direct-response advertising online achieves brand objectives in ways it doesn't get credit for.

That's fair to say. It's a running theme that people have spoken about in these conversations; brand advertisers and direct-response advertisers are very separate in their approach and they don't get the credit for activity they generate on both an awareness and direct-response perspective.

The second running theme is that even though the perception of this business is that it's about technology, when you dive down into it all these companies are being run by people, and the relationships that these people have are what seem to drive the success or the failure, not necessarily the technology. Do you think that's accurate?

I think it's accurate with social. There has been a big shift in terms of making marketing departments and brands way more transparent. So ten or fifteen years ago there was this wall between the marketing strategies of a brand and the consumption habits of consumers, of users. Over the last fifteen years users have become just more social, more participatory, and brands have also started to use the same tools themselves. So instead of it being a wall, it's become a black curtain and now it's a clear shower curtain. I think that's what you're referring to. Those have been profound changes and they are making a big difference because consumers will only be adopting the brands that are authentic.

The brands that are distant and trying to do things in a black box, consumers are rejecting. The reason they like GroupOn or whatever brands it might be, is because it's accessible to them. They like Zappos because Tony Hsieh is out there and available and vulnerable. So the marketing tools that expose and express the vulnerabilities are those that are really winning.

That's interesting, because even on the agency side of the world, where the advertising has been housed, the agency world became a lot more transparent just because of the web. Everybody knows what everything else costs now. What is it that you see in the marketplace right now that's available to marketers that's exciting to you?

I think geofencing is really interesting, the combination of geofencing and social targeting through mobile. It's a mouthful, but at Stickybits we have a simple tool now that allows you to basically say, if a woman who is 35 to 45 in San Francisco gets four other friends of hers to all scan a Pepsi can in Target, then they will all get a 50% OFF discount card. Not only can you target the location and the kind of person, you can require them to engage socially with their friends, so I think those capabilities are there now. It's going to take a couple of years before they get used at scale.

Who is going to have to adopt that first? Do you think it's going to be the consumers or do you think the marketers?

I think the marketers will have to adopt it and in this case, drive unique offers. The reason why GroupOn got to scale is Gap said, okay, we're going to try this incredible offer where someone is going to get half-off. Amazon says, okay, we're going to have an offer where someone has to pay $10 and gets a $20 gift card. So it's the marketer that comes up with the unique promotion, yet it drives consumer adoption because why, as a consumer, am I going to use a new channel if I can get the same benefit from an old channel?

Do you think marketers are pretty open to the new channels if it has an immediate benefit? Do you think they are a little behind? Do you think they're waiting to see if they can get adoption on these channels first?

I think they're open, I just think they're friggin' overwhelmed by noise. Every single website, every single mobile app, every single ad network has sales reps that are invading the agencies. Look at your life. You're just besieged by, Pick me! Pick me! Pick me! It's not like the old ones go away. AOL and Yahoo are carcasses, but they're still trying to get media dollars as well as YouTube and Google, as well as Facebook, as well as Foursquare, as well as Twitter. It's nonstop. I don't think it's that marketers have their head in the sand. I just think they're like, what the hell? Who do I trust?

Yeah, there needs to be a good solution for that doesn't there?
Think of a totalitarian government that says, okay, this is the television channel. You can watch any channel you

want as long as it's channel two. We're the opposite. Actually, we would benefit from having fewer media choices, whereas places like China and people in the Middle East right now would benefit from having more choices.

CLOSING REMARKS

Seth is an innovator and his ability to foster ideas is almost unmatched in this business. Since beginning work on this book, Seth has led the launch of Stickybits and his morph into turntable.fm, which has quickly become a darling of the Internet ad business. His offices at Pier 38, which are now a piece of history having had the city of San Francisco unfairly evict all his tenants, were widely recognized as one of the earliest and most successful incubators in the business. His vision is one that has driven many an entrepreneur and spurred many entrepreneurial ideas to success. I hope that his brief, albeit impactful, interview will give some insight into the role that Seth has played in the business. Thanks, Seth!

CHAPTER 22

NICK PAHADE

Nick is currently CEO North America for Initiative, and was most recently CEO of TRAFFIQ, a web-based tool for media management that makes digital media buying more efficient for agencies and brands. Nick has more than fifteen years of leadership experience in the advertising and marketing industries and has been responsible for some of the earliest innovations in online advertising.

He was most recently responsible for the growth strategy, client relationships, and leading the team of interactive design, technology and marketing professionals at GSI Commerce's Marketing Services Division (TrueAction, Silverlign and PepperJam) prior to TRAFFIQ. Even before that, Nick was president of Denuo, Publicis Groupe's futures practice, and led global digital development for Publicis Groupe Media. In his earliest days,

Nick was president of Beyond Interactive Inc., which he co-founded and successfully sold to Grey Global Group. He was also managing director of Mediacom Digital, part of WPP's GroupM and Grey Global Group. Nick was recognized by *MEDIA* magazine as one of the Top 50 People to Know in Interactive Marketing, *Advertising Age*'s coveted 40 under 40 list, and as a *MediaPost* Online All Star. He holds dual degrees in biopsychology and marketing from the University of Michigan.

Nick Pahade, how did you get into the digital media business?

I got involved in the business back in 1995. I was actually, oddly enough, still in college at the time. I was a resident advisor at the University of Michigan and developed a few marketing concepts with some fraternity brothers of mine that started a company. We presented the ideas in a marketing class, and what ultimately started as a small project, later turned into a full-blown digital advertising agency.

And that was Beyond Interactive, right?

The original name of the company was Wolverine Web Productions. It was eventually rebranded as Beyond Interactive, which we grew into a global digital agency powerhouse. After fourteen years they ultimately decided to integrate Beyond Interactive with the parent holding company, Mediacom, which is owned by WPP. We started Beyond officially in 1996 and sold the business to Grey Advertising in 1999. After Beyond I worked at Publicis Groupe, running their marketing futures consultancy called Denuo. For a few years I also oversaw the global digital development for Publicis Groupe Media, now branded VivaKi.

I left to build out a marketing services practice at a company called **GSI Commerce**, and I rolled out a variety of digital media offerings organically and through acquisition (mobile, social, search, attribution analytics, affiliate marketing, etc.). GSI was recently acquired by eBay. Most recently I took the plunge to redefine myself and get back into the startup media services space, and came on board as CEO of TRAFFIQ.

When you got started in this business you said it was basically a class project. What was the attraction? What opportunity did you see there?

At the time I was actually headed to medical school. I had already been accepted into a few different programs but started to fall in love with the idea of being an entrepreneur. My passion for advertising came later on in my career. Right then I wanted to run a business. The beauty of it at the time when I got started was that the industry was truly in its infancy. The first concept of display banners was just emerging. At that time the industry was really nothing but search engine optimization, strategic linking and design services. There really wasn't a heavy display-advertising component.

Everyone was learning on the fly. I was able to go from being the media account coordinator to head of sales to chief operating officer to the leader of the organization. The ability to build a business from scratch in an industry that didn't really have a mold was thrilling because we were able to shape it off the cuff.

What were some of the things you were trying to do with advertising at that point?

We were still discovering what advertising was and what could be done. As display advertising started to surface, and the graphic nature of advertising was being explored online, we were tying together the specific words and phrases you saw in search. Bringing in other components that existed in other mediums was always of interest. Lastly, we were tying together sight, sound, motion (the precursor to online video) and focusing on the ability to create advertising that allows more engagement and for interactivity with the content.

Do you remember any of the campaigns you were most proud of from that period?

I remember back to 1997 when Beyond was just getting started. We were recruiting friends, family and anyone who was willing to work for us under the condition that we couldn't always necessarily guarantee a paycheck. We had a variety of tier two and tier three businesses that were certainly paying the bills, but we hadn't been able to make it into the big game yet.

We built a relationship with a gentleman who was running the advertising for a company called Ameritech. It was a large SEO project. They issued Beyond an RFP and we were competing with folks a lot larger in stature and experience than us. We won the business based on the sheer labor and effort we put into the project, and ultimately just blew away the expectations of our client. It finally gave us something that put us on the map and allowed us to have a large, recognizable client that we could leverage to help build up the business. I'm very thankful to this day for the opportunity that project gave us.

That was a launching pad client for you. And you sold the business in '99?

That's correct, we sold in 1999. Beyond was started by four partners, primarily self-funded through our own dollars and credit cards, etc.. We didn't accept any venture capital. It was really just our own sweat equity that got us off the ground. In '99 we were doing a lot of work for traditional agencies and we were looking at different options in terms of where we wanted to take the business. We looked at raising money through the VCs and we actually got quite a bit of interest, but none of us wanted to have terms dictated to us and have a defined exit strategy.

We weren't sure that was the right direction for us. We looked at different marketing arms of large companies, like Microsoft and AT&T to see if those options were better homes. Lo and behold, we hired a woman named Michelle Madansky as a consultant who introduced us to a variety of large agency holding companies, and ultimately we got a variety of offers. We really thought that was the best opportunity for us because we were still young kids at the time. We had been in business for three or four years. For some of us it was our first job after college. It was an opportunity to learn and to be compensated to a certain extent for what we were able to achieve. It was pre-bubble as well, so there were all sorts of discussions about being acquired and holding companies rolling their digital assets together for another public offering. There were multiple thoughts at the time as to where it would ultimately lead, but we made the decision to sell the company to Grey Advertising. Grey was actually the second best offer we got financially, but we went with Grey because we felt it was the best fit for us culturally. We sold in '99 and I moved from Ann Arbor to New York to open up our New York office and to lead the acquisition.

What was it like building a business when you weren't in New York or San Francisco or Chicago? How did that influence the business?

We were headquartered in Ann Arbor, Michigan. The beauty of being in Ann Arbor at that time was that it gave us access to young talent from the University. There were three original partners and we added another partner, the original four were Michigan alum. We were very heavily vested to the area. We actually opened an office organically in '98 in San Francisco to broaden our base and grow a broader client base. Having a presence in those major markets was absolutely fundamental and critical, even, though we were winning so much business through reputation and word of mouth that, in many cases, our location played to our favor given cost of living and less direct competition. We recognized the importance of it and, of course, today it's kind of hard to be a large ad agency in North America without having a presence in New York or one of the major metropolitan areas.

So at this point, the company has been acquired by Grey and you've been rolled up into a holding company envi-

ronment. What was the mood like around the time that the bubble was getting ready to pop?

The first year was very strong and we were winning lots of new business. It was just an amazing experience for me at such a young age to have access to all these seasoned business executives; not only being in the same room, but also sitting at the same table. In some cases, I was learning from them and in other cases, they were learning from me. It was amazing what the company was able to achieve and the expertise that we built in this space.

The first year the environment was really good because we were sponges. I had never lived in New York before. I certainly never experienced what it was like to work for a large agency and have the ability to receive mentorship from folks I admired in the advertising space. There was a suite of executives and industry leaders like Ed Meyer, Steven Felsher, Joe Celia, Jon Mandel, Harvey Goldhersz and many others, and to work side-by-side with them was just an amazing experience. But we, like many others, didn't necessarily see the bubble coming, or didn't want to accept the reality.

We were hiring at a very aggressive rate, bringing on ten to twenty new employees every month just to prepare for what had been happening over the past three or four years. The sheer volume of work was intense and certainly we got caught in the bubble like many others. It was a difficult time, but it also taught me a lot in terms of what it takes to run a business and knowing when to hit the gas pedal hard and knowing when it's time to slow down. The next year or so was tough and we had to do a few rounds of layoffs and restructuring. Though hard, that made it even more interesting. Doing all this in the middle of a downturn is not something I'd want to live through again, even though it certainly was an experience to learn from.

You were involved in a very early stage and you got to know a lot of the people. Was there anything that surprised you about that the first ten years of the business?

There were lots of things that surprised me the first ten years of the business, mostly around how fun things were! It was an amazing environment to learn and to grow in. It was also, in some cases, an environment that wasn't built upon a real business reality. I can't tell you how many opportunities would come our way that we would say, "What a great idea!" But that we knew were not standalone businesses. It was shocking to see how far out of bounds many ideas were during that time.

It was just a phenomenal experience in terms of being able to get involved in starting the company from scratch in an industry that was yet to be defined, and to be able to learn, grow and evolve from it. I got a nice crash course in what it took to navigate a large publicly traded company, how that environment works, and the challenges, skill sets and expertise that is required to do just that which I have been able to apply to many other opportunities post-Beyond.

What were some of the challenges you saw in 2006? You can argue that by then the big agencies have really "gotten it," that they understand it and they're taking the reins and running with it. What kind of challenges did you have during that period?

It was a wonderful experience at Grey and I had been there a long time and learned a lot. During that period of time, though, my wife and I also had two real babies (Raina and Alana) and it was time to try something new. I needed a break. We went from running businesses of our own to creating a company that was well over a thousand employees globally, billions of dollars in digital media buying across eighty-five offices in twenty-three countries. I wanted a new opportunity to build and start fresh again.

To me, Denuo was the best sabbatical a digital executive could ask for. When running large agencies you tend to focus very much on the numbers and it's easy to move away from the work. The opportunity with Denuo was to bring together a variety of experts that had built a name for themselves in the business to see if we could just focus on the work. It was a great experiment. I partnered with a brilliant gentleman named Rishad Tobaccowala to prove to the holding company that we could build a business around getting paid for great ideas. In many cases, activation/execution is the large media agencies' bread and butter. That's how they make their money. Couldn't we prove that we could generate a real business and charge for our thinking alone? We actually did and it was a wonderful experiment. Large holding companies tend to get encumbered very easily and it's difficult to stay at the cusp of innovation and navigate the vessel forward with digital at the core, not as an adjunct or a bolt-on.

It sounds like you had a lot of fun with it, too.

Oh man, it was great. To get back into an environment of getting paid for your thinking and working alongside talented guys like Scott Witt and Rishad was a lot of fun.

One of my other tasks was something Jack had asked me to do. Jack Klues is the chairman of Publicis Groupe Media/Vivaki. While I had a great year, he ultimately said, alright guys, you proved that we could build a business around thinking and we could react to things very nimbly. But we're a large company. We still need to make digital bigger. We need to bring it to the core of everything we do. We can't have you and Rishad in a company of twenty people. We need to divide and conquer.

With that, my role there eventually moved out of Denuo into a global role running digital strategy and development for Publicis Groupe Media. There I got to work with Frank Voris, David Kenny, Steve King, Laura Desmond and their respective teams amongst many others in creating the digital strategy for the media agencies within Publicis Groupe: writing the business plans, getting buy-in, coordinating what markets were of importance and developing the strategy around the service offerings to invest in or accelerate growth around. This of course was achieved in many ways: organically, in partnership (like with MediaBank), or via acquisition (Phonevalley). Jack added me to the PGM board and I started to create digital strategies and business planning for the media agencies to implement. I think in the course of one year, I racked up something like one million miles in air travel. But, again, it's something that I certainly don't regret. It was a fantastic experience.

You started a company on the small side, grew it to a big company, merged the big company into a bigger company and then helped create small companies inside

of big companies. You've had a whole gamut of experiences. What advice would you give to someone trying to get into the business now? Where should they start? Should they start in a small company? Should they start in a big company?

It's a great question and it's one that's difficult to answer because a lot depends on the individual, their appetite, their capacity to learn and, ultimately, what it is they're trying to achieve. The ability to go broader and get a taste of a variety of different things with the company is certainly a lot easier to create in a smaller company environment. But there are also people who benefit from having structure, going through a process, learning those ropes and being able to stand out amongst a crowd. I think there are great opportunities for training and learning the discipline in a large company as well.

A lot of it is based upon the appetite of the individual, what motivates them and what their aspirations are. There are some people who do very well playing by the rules and can build a great career that way. There are others who don't ever want to play by the rules and have trouble working in certain environments. In those cases, smaller companies might be a better fit. I've been fortunate to be able to do both, and again, I really enjoyed both for different reasons. For where I am in my current life trajectory, I wanted to get back to being closer to the product, the work, and build the business with scale from the ground up.

What do you think people should be planning on in the next few years?

The industry at this point is seventeen years old. It's no longer "the new thing," if you will. While it's still relatively young it's no longer a baby, and in order for the industry to continue to grow and blossom and mature it needs to begin standardizing and creating efficiencies. There are a lot of things about the industry I love and there are many I don't love. It's still hard to actually buy digital media and it's getting more and more complicated and more and more fragmented. There's a lot of legalese and a lot of terms and conditions. There are so many different ways to purchase and access media. There's even confusion over the definition of what constitutes media versus what constitutes content.

All these things are changing and I think what really needs to happen is the development of other mechanisms to allow for the facilitation of more efficient media management. In some cases that may be through automation. In other cases, it may be through better standardizations. Maybe it's through finding other ways to create operational efficiencies. At TRAFFIQ we're trying to help make the media management project simpler and more effective for all of those involved.

CLOSING REMARKS

Nick has vision, and his role in the Internet advertising business is one that cannot be overlooked. From Beyond to Denuo to TRAFFIQ, Nick has paved the way for many other companies to follow, and his dedication to the craft of media and media strategy should be applauded. Nick is a humble yet very intelligent and influential man in this business, and if you are afforded the chance to sit and chat with him I recommend you take it. His insights are valuable and will help you see the path to your own success.

CHAPTER 23

KATE EVERETT-THORP

Kate Everett-Thorp was most recently the CEO of Real Girls Media, which was acquired by Meredith Corporation in 2011. Previously Kate was President, Digital Worldwide of industry leading ad agency, AKQA. During her tenure, AKQA's client list expanded to include ESPN, The Gap, MSN and Coca-Cola's global accounts. Before joining AKQA, Kate was Chairman and CMO of Carat Interactive, the media giant that acquired Lot21, the agency she had founded with three partners. She got her start at the top tier agencies of McCann Erickson and J. Walter Thompson.

Kate's perspective comes from seeing it from all sides: as an executive, advertiser, publisher, and as a co-founder of the influential Internet Advertising Bureau (IAB). She and her companies have earned numerous accolades; Kate was named one of the top 25 Women to Watch by

Advertising Age and a 2005 OMMA Media All Star. She was also inducted into the AAF Hall of Achievement for execs under 40. And under her command, both Lot21 and AKQA have been named Agency of the Year.

Kate Thorp, formerly founder and CEO of Real Girl's Media, what's going on with you these days?

We sold Real Girl's Media to Meredith Corporation and I left around the end of January and beginning of February. I handed the transition over to them and now they are all set free. I took two months off, and now I will set out again to something new.

Do you know what you're going to go do yet?

I do not. I promised myself I wouldn't even update my bio until this week. After thirteen years in the CEO spot I figured I can just let my brain sit for a minute.

The first time that I had interactions with you is when you were the CEO for Lot21. Lot21 was one of the first strong digital ad agencies. How did you get started with that?

Well, I was at CNET at the time working with a number of fine people, including Mike Tatum, Eric Wheeler, Louise Kong, and Andrew O'Dell. Andrew was not at CNET, the other three were, and we were at a place where I helped start the IAB, and we held the first meeting, and I then served on the board for three years. We got to this place of evangelizing advertising where everybody was in, but there was no traditional structure of agencies. In the digital world, we had many consultancies. As an example, everybody wanted to build a bank, but there was nobody setting out to advertise the bank.

Our world was filled with traditional advertising firms, but they were looking to production shops to help them handle the advertising. So basically, at a time when Agency.com and Organic were doing fine work on developing websites, and wanting to be valued on the consultancy side, we saw an opportunity. You could work hard on the technical side, and then do ten banks versus the traditional agency side where you were retained, and you worked on one bank. So we set out to say there is a need in the marketplace to have a more traditional agency structure, to buy media on behalf of the clients, and still appreciate the funkiness that digital created.

We left CNET as a group, launched Lot21 in January 1998, and we were in San Francisco and New York with 140 employees, and reached about $150 million in billings. We created a development lab as well in our New York office. The work that we sought to do there was full-service agency work from creative to strategy, account management, media, and in the case of digital we got into quite a bit more tech.

What was it like trying to sell this kind of work through to your clients at the time? Were they eager, did they anticipate this side of the business or was it an uphill sell?

We did a couple of things. One, we raised money versus setting out with a client. Most agencies are born out of one or two managers in an existing agency leaving with a client. They either duplicate the services, or they take that client to do new services, which would have been the case in digital. For us, we decided we believed there needed to be a set of services put together that we could then come to them, and say this is what you need. That worked out well. Again, the timing in the marketplace was such that we were also able to partner very strongly with the shops that were developing websites. They would develop the software behind the sites. They were building the bank and we were setting out to advertise the bank.

What was it like trying to raise money at that time for an agency with a services model?

Actually it was a dream. We raised our first round in three weeks. It unfortunately gave those who may have been on their first round an untrue view of the investment market. But our mission was clear and many in the media space, including Walden and Steve Eskinozi, who was really the one with an eye on this marketplace, recognized the gap in the marketplace of our interests and the opportunity that we had. You didn't really have the traditional marketing services firms, and there was a clean line in coming from being the person at CNET who was evangelizing the space to them, saying, well, somebody needs to actually go do it now that we have buy-ins. We were former agency people in and of ourselves, coming from the traditional side prior to our CNET experience, so it was quite a fortuitous group to come together to launch Lot21.

What was some of the work you were doing at the time that you remember sticking out, and being really proud of?

Well, we had the good fortune, and the bad fortune of working with many of the exciting startups that were happening at the time. It was exciting in the beginning. We had the web brands and we had KB kids and the Pets. com client; that was a great beginning. Of course, having your roster disappear in a 10 to 15 day period was not as thrilling. I would say we were really proud of the stuff that one of our other founders, Sasha Pave was able to accomplish with Pets.com. It was pretty amazing.

We did a number of reels which utilized QuickTime, which was a QuickTime overlay with Flash and that kind of had not been done before. In fact, we had a utility patent on it for some time, and Apple got excited about it and posted it on their home page at Apple.com. We were also quite proud of the work we did in those days for what were the brick and mortar companies. We handled a number of clients like Nations Bank, which then became Bank of America, through acquisition.

You mentioned the unfortunate experience of having a number of clients shut their doors in a 10 to 15 day period. How did you deal with the .com bust?

Well, we acted quickly. We were a services company so we did downsize right away. We also protected the business in two ways. We did not run abroad, as many of our cohorts were doing at the time. We decided that the business was strong in the U.S., and there were many traditional, brick-and-mortar companies that were in need of work here and we could focus our talents on them The second thing that we did, besides staying within the U.S., was that we didn't allow more than 40 percent of our revenue to come from online only companies. We were protected on the downside when the bubble burst.

The traditional companies, on the flip side, once they could catch their breath as to what was happening, especially the smart ones, realized that prices are lower for media now because there are more avails. The consumer didn't leave the Internet because NASDAQ suffered in the tech side, and their audience was still there. In fact, six months later they realized they were there and more. The double hit unfortunately was what happened to us as a country with 9/11, which set off its own economic downturn.

At that point, we had met with Carat who was very interested in the digital side, and were looking to set up a number of acquisitions. They looked at us as a catalyst within that cycle, being a full-service entity they could then begin their global dominance into digital media and creative, which followed with you guys, too (Freestyle Interactive).

You had some different kinds of experiences then. You had been working in a smaller agency and watched it grow. You were involved with the Carat acquisition and then became the president for AKQA, which was a big shop. How was it different to try and sell the business services after the bubble, especially given that the business was a little tenuous at that point?

It was kind of interesting. Lot21 got up to almost 140 people and was U.S. based; then downturn, sale, and then my move to AKQA. They were in the position that this was post downturn, right before the business started to recover, so it was a good time in the marketplace for coming into the U.S.. AKQA was Citron Haligman Bedecarré, AKQA in London, Magnet Interactive and Advert, Inc. in Singapore when I walked in the door. They had one website, AKQA, but it only had the London work on it. Then the DC office, which was Magnet, had an AKQADC.com office.

People were kind of just doing their own thing, and pitching their own work, and having different levels of expertise. So when I came in it was to kind of, sit down with Tom and other leaders and identify, what were we best at? What can we lead with, and what do we want to do? Strategically put that into our brand, then bring everyone under that umbrella and execute on a global basis. I think we did a fine job with that, and we brought in help to achieve that, which was bringing in large staff to manage the New York office. We cleaned up Singapore and got our services really rounded out under these leading creatives. That truly helped cement AKQA under the creative umbrella that it was. The work was there just nobody was seeing it because of a desperate execution.

You established a strong creative foundation.
Yeah, and then we went out and told everybody about it. That landed us Coca-Cola Global, we brought in GAP and ESPN, and we brought work at the levels to match the talent that was there, and that's why it worked.

Do you think that digital has gone from being a single piece of the pie, to being far more influential and leading the pie in some cases?

Definitely for some brands. It's still brand-specific, and I think that sometimes the impact of social media may actually make that perspective a bit more convoluted.

How so?
In the same way that we had very high-level PR specialists who you would allow to handle your message on a live basis representing the brand. In advertising, we were not traditionally responsible for communications of that type. We were responsible for creating messaging that was in line with the brand and that was utilized as advertising, and now that those elements are converging the more profound leadership you are going to see is on the digital side. The campaigns that are in action in real-time will set the tone for everything else a brand does going forward.

In advertising traditionally we sat back, decided what we wanted to say to whom and when! For better or for worse, that's just the way it rolled downhill. Now things are operating in reverse, with the tail wagging the dog and consumers influencing the messaging rather than the other way around. Now we are seeing and measuring true effect of sales through conversational media, social media, people tweeting about the brand, and the real-time action of what's happening. Even more importantly, the brand's responses to conversation; I think brands can sell more product based on taking the covers off their customer service than by broadcasting a message. I've always been fascinated with the fact that this customer service has been going on the whole time, but nobody hangs up after having a good experience to walk across the street to tell their neighbor that, hey, I just had a fantastic call with Comcast. They were so nice. It's gone and out of their heads.

Now if it's a bad experience, the next time they happen to be walking down to the end of their driveway for their newspaper or whatever, they might say, oh, who do you use, I just really hate these people. So the propensity for a negative was always ten times more than the positive. Now, because everybody is in this real-time sharing mode, you don't necessarily get off the phone with anybody, you tweet them that you hate their service because they're always late and they immediately respond. Then, either through hash tag or sharing, or just now it being Googled, you get to see these more positive experiences that are centered around everybody and are looped into that outer ring. So it's no longer me telling you, everyone you know and everyone I know can see that conversation.

Originally you made the point that advertising, especially online, was a continuation of what was being done in other forms of media; identifying what message to broadcast then syndicating that message out. What you're identifying now is that the business has transformed to where it's listening, reacting, and trying to integrate that into marketing. How do you think that this affects the world of advertising and marketing going forward?
If you go back to all those ridiculous acronyms and broad statements – you know, "control the message," "the consumer is your brand," "live the brand," – it's such an egalitarian thing. It truly is what they're all striving for now because those that have consistently shown the least desire for control in their message have had the largest benefit. Now none of us are silly enough to think that there aren't a lot of people trying to shape that message

and send it in a certain direction, and that does play a significant role in the outcome.

Saying your car is a huge gas guzzler, you know that's a problem, it doesn't mean that you're not pointing out all of the other features, and turning it around to be something good, right? You just give up on the things that are known and let it roll. There is a lot of active presentation going on in the social ecosphere, but to get back to what advertising versus general communication can do, I think some of the great things that have happened in the last five to seven years is there has been far more creative license granted to advertising. Brands are giving more creative license to advertising than they did before because the consumer informs their advertising.

There was a time where IBM went through a stage where you had no idea that these people could even work in the same company. Some of the things they said publicly were so totally different, and in quality too, not just in message. When you have a big brand like that which is incredibly well respected, and you see a couple of executions like that, you realize what's going on, and for better or for worse when it is a brand of that stature it calls everyone's attention to it and you get on it. You fix it.

What we learned from Real Girls Media, and what we set out to do right, was to not be the traditional publishing company that sat back and decided what the consumer needed to hear about, or what they wanted. With UGC we came out and said we are going to lead by example. We will have a very small staff that is going to write, but we'll be outnumbered by our community by thousands, or tens of thousands, which we were. We had around six writers, and there are hundreds of thousands of members, and over a hundred thousand people who write all the time, so they're writing what they care about, and people will either consume it or not consume it based on if they share those ideals, experiences or resources. We didn't have to sit in the big boardroom and decide what everybody was going to need or want and then be right or wrong, and the success of your monthly, weekly, etc..

We believed in the flow of what was happening in the overall community as well as the individual portions of the community subset. This has got to be the next evolution of what we see in overall advertising and communication. There has to be an allowable evolution for finding out from your consumer what you want, and that doesn't mean yet another website that says you're in our special group, or you're our focus group. I think it is more of a living, breathing form of advertising and communication. You look at people's profile pages, at what they say they like, what they absorb, and they are creating messages in and of themselves. That is the early version of things. But as you look at the web and what it was doing, it would be the equivalent of the *early* ad banner. It would be the way that users are harnessing brands for themselves on their profile pages, so if those two align, where can we go from there and how far can we take it?

Do you think the model of listening to the consumer and allowing them to have a voice, and integrating that into the messaging, works for every category of advertising going forward? Or do you think there are some categories that may not be totally applicable for it?

I definitely don't think there's ever a silver bullet or the single solution for everyone. There has to be different options for different categories of marketer. I listen to the Chevron ads right now and just cringe. I find it insulting. Everything else we can agree on, so just telling me how much we don't agree, I wasn't sure we didn't agree up until they just told me that I don't. It makes me wonder, what are all the things we don't agree on? I would say that's an example of a campaign where listening to the consumer didn't translate to a strong message. I don't need to hear a radio ad about how we disagree, and sending me to a URL that makes me feel worse about the company is a bad idea, too. If that was an example of a perfect solution for somebody, it's definitely not for them. So, no, I've never really subscribed to the one and only solution

It sounds like you're talking about the balance between listening and data, art and science. How do you listen to what the consumer is saying and balance that with what you already know?

Absolutely, because at the end of the day the consumer is not wowed or swayed by how you reached them, they're still looking at the message. So a big message doesn't come up and say, "I scrubbed all of this wonderful data, I know who you are and I know you need a car, and you use pump toothpaste." That doesn't work for them. What you delivered to them once you have utilized that great technology, what do you do then?

Hopefully you tied together the message and the medium.

It's still important, and they're going to have to wear out like in anything else, so I think it becomes increasingly even more important.

So the kinds of things that you would look at, as an entrepreneur with Walden, and as you are trying to figure out where you will go next, are the kinds of things that have that balance between the message and the medium, the data and the creativity?

Some of the things I am seeing out there, yes. I'm seeing a number of your tech-interested companies trying to figure out again. Technology companies are incredibly successful at building the database and cracking the filters, codes, and the abilities to make it useful. But the next step is then, wow, there's a consumer there, and there's a whole different expertise often that is presented on that side of the business. I think that's also the conundrum for the brands themselves. Do you have two companies come pitch you for your global business because you need a technology solution, but then you need somebody to handle the message, or is there somebody who does both?

In AKQA, we were always faced with that. Half the time we had both solutions in-house. Given the strength of tech at the time in London, which they still have, but now it has expanded throughout their organizations, sometimes we would go against a creative agency. And one time, I think, a small IBM. We even had eBusiness Solutions compete against us one time with Lot21. You could tell from the brand point of view that they're not sure and they don't clearly see the strengths to provide them what they need on both ends.

There are a number of areas that are combining and smoothing out, but for the most part there's so much more to do that I don't foresee it becoming any less complicated at the moment, for a good thing frankly. Innovate, innovate, innovate.

What advice would you have for a brand at this point, as they're looking at digital advertising and digital marketing? What advice would you have for them on how they should be balancing the attention between social media and standard, broadcast models?
Personally, I feel for them. Even if you look at the communication side this is a very tough time for them. Is it a PR firm? Is it an advertising firm? Is it a digital firm? Is it in-house? Is it a combination of all the above? The things they're discussing and facing at different levels within their organizations are enviable at the moment. What I would say is, first and foremost, you have consumers, you have products, and you need to move your products. You can't lose sight of that goal deciding that you're going to experiment with the best new mobile app, or that you need an iPad this or that. Some of the solid runs that we are seeing is that they're clearly looking at their budgeting process with a stability play, and I would say a non-experimental play, but still in new devices, and in a totally experimental budget which is, we're not quantifying it when it gets to an experimental stage. We need to learn from it.

The middle is, we're moving forward and now we need to know the value of it through the organization to whether it is going to get more, and more money. Then you have your traditional, not as in print, TV, but traditional as in stable selling methods and elements that need to go forward, and continuously be measured against those that are coming up from behind because the money is going to change hands.

That's good because you're right; it's a very unenviable position to be one of those folks trying to figure this whole landscape out.

But it's terribly exciting. I mean what better position to be in as well, you have more options than ever. It will thin the crowd at the top level of the brands very quickly because it's not being able to rely on a new product to come out and increase your sales. The traditional things were new product, new packaging, new this, new ingredient, whatever. Now you're going to see where strategy and sheer media and consumer insight is going to lead that charge because you're going to have your lunch eaten. You can't get in with how profound the changes in communication are among the consumers. It won't matter if you have a new product because people might not even know you did it if you don't get in the loop.

CLOSING REMARKS

Kate Everett-Thorp has been a leader in the business for many years and has mentored many successful people. The key take away from this interview was the importance of having an idea, a point of view, and sticking to it. Kate has attacked the business of online advertising and marketing from an informed point of view, and been very successful. She doesn't sit back and wait for things to happen to her or her teams. She identifies a direction and goes for it, and this kind of commitment fuels success. Having a clear direction and finely defined point of view gives you context by which to filter all that happens, and that is a formula for success.

CHAPTER 24

· ·

DAVE MORGAN

Dave is the CEO of New York City-based Simulmedia, Inc., a marketing technology company serving the television industry, which he founded, in late 2008. A serial entrepreneur, he previously founded and ran both TACODA, Inc, an online advertising company that pioneered behavioral online marketing and was acquired by AOL in 2007 for $275 million, and Real Media, Inc, one of the world's first ad serving and online ad network companies and a predecessor to 24/7 Real Media (TFSM), which was later sold to WPP for $649 million. After the sale of TACODA, Dave served as Executive VP, Global Advertising Strategy at AOL, a Time Warner Company (TWX).

A lawyer by training, Dave served as general counsel and director of new media ventures at the Pennsylvania Newspaper Association in the early 1990 and also spent several years as an associate with the Philadelphia law firm Duane Morris. He currently serves on the executive committee and board of directors of the Interactive Advertising Bureau (IAB) and on the boards of directors of newspaper publisher, A.H. Belo Corporation (AHC), the American Press Institute (API) and Chumby Industries.

Dave holds a B.A. in Political Science from Pennsylvania State University and a J.D. from the Dickinson School of Law. He and his wife, writer Lorea Canales live in Manhattan with their two girls.

Welcome Dave Morgan, CEO of Simulmedia. You started Real Media in 1995, correct?

Yes, I had been a lawyer in the newspaper industry, and for a bunch of unusual circumstances I found myself as the new media director of a newspaper trade association trying to help newspaper companies do deals to prepare for the information superhighway that we were all told was coming in the early '90s. It was about helping newspapers create ventures for digital companies, cable companies, or telephone companies, or even venturing into online bulletin board services, to get involved in the early online services. That was probably in '92, '93, '94, and the more I got involved in that the more I realized that these traditional media folks and technology companies, or telecommunications companies, couldn't speak each other's language.

They couldn't get deals done. Not because it wasn't in their joint best collective interest, but because they misunderstood each other. So after a couple years AOL appeared, then the browser, so then we had real online communications. We had the Mosaic browser and for the first time, in my mind, we had what made sense. We could have a large-scale, widely deployed, free client application for online services. To me, that was the moment because what were then the Internet dial-up ISPs could really be full online services. They could look like CompuServe, Prodigy, or AOL but not having to pay someone's toll to get AOL, Prodigy, or the others to get on them.

That inspired me, and so by late '94 I had an idea that I might as well do my own business because I was constantly seeing these big companies not figuring out how to get out of their own way. My belief was there was an opportunity for doing direct marketing within online media. The advantage of it being that you could actually deliver more targeted advertising, but you could do it not in a direct mail, letter, or a phone call. You could do it in the context of an article and media that people would really pay attention to and had stronger credibility.

So my sense was the marketplace needed at least two kinds of services. One, it needed technology to schedule and handle the deliveries, these direct marketing messages into online clients. It also needed a sales organization, a rep firm to sell them because traditional media companies weren't very good at selling new products, or aggregate products. So I had this idea and formed it in a company called Real Media, and that was when everybody was doing .coms, so the idea was Real Media was going to work with mostly newspaper companies.

We were going to aggregate lots of local newspaper companies and provide technology to them to manage ads on what are now being called websites, and we would create a national sales organization to sell ads for them.

I figured that I'd run a business before and we could be successful. I hadn't really worked in a regular business since I had been a lawyer in a law firm for a trade association, but I figured that there was a good chance one of them might make it, so I started both and we created an ad server and created an ad network separately. It turned out that they both became complimentary and supportive of each other over the years. I had expected that one of them we would shut down within the year, and we never had to.

What was the climate like when you started that business? Did people understand what you were talking about, or did you have to do a lot of education?

It was all education. I used to have a big bulletin board in my office, and every time that there would be a URL in the newspaper, we'd cut it out and stick it up there because it was so rare at that point. I moved to New York because I was living in Pennsylvania before then, but I knew that I was going to have to be in a place where things were happening. There was a lot of confusion still, most people didn't know what the Internet was. That's why it was funny. I just saw a clip of the *Today Show* from, I think 1995. They had Bryant Gumbel and Katie Couric and it was off-air, they were sort of briefing them on what this Internet thing was. What is the Internet?

That's what the time was like. There was certainly promise at that point, but even online services were not very well penetrated. Online services were still young and new. AOL, a couple years prior, had been a nobody. At that point AOL was how most people saw the Internet, even though AOL's only connection to the Internet was they had a backdoor that you could go out onto the web. But none of their content was available on the web. It was all about education. The good thing working around traditional media was that those companies had been making investments in what they saw as future distribution platforms.

In my customer base at Real Media, there was a real sense that they had to play. It's ironic now that they are the ones who probably lost. They've been the worst at taking advantage of new media, but in the middle '90s they all had new media departments. They saw an opportunity and they were eager to try something new, but it didn't work for them. There's a reason that newspapers were the first to build radio stations, the first to build TV stations, the first to build cable companies; they were the first to build websites, news information websites. I would say in my customer base, they knew that there was stuff happening they wanted to participate in. But to the advertising and marketing community it was nowhere. There was no understanding at agencies or clients what this online service stuff could mean.

So that business started to progress; you guys were representing sites, you've got the ad server up and running, and the business is growing at that point.

Yeah, and the good thing in New York at the time, there was a bit of a boom. In New York and San Francisco we had a boom of web design firms that started building web pages starting in early '94, and certainly in '95. They were building them for businesses, so it went hand in hand that you would want to drive traffic to them. Everyone had little counters on their websites telling how many people would go there, and you had some early counting companies out there, too. While the regular ad agencies weren't participating, we had a new breed of smaller website design and media buying agencies. Not only media buying agencies but ad agencies, so there were actually people for us to talk to at that point, which was great. Some of the bigger agencies had little strategic groups, too, so by '96 there was an interesting little business emerging.

By early '96 DoubleClick was formed, so Poppe.com had merged with Kevin O'Connor's company. AOL was already a public company and Netscape was out as a public company when they started essentially auctioning off the infamous homepage buttons. When they sold their buttons for $5 million a pop on their homepage, they realized they had a really big ad business there.

That fueled everything. Microsoft was making a lot of noise, AOL, at this point was starting to really pick up speed. What was surprising for me was it went from nothing in early '95 to by late '96 there was a whirlwind. New York had its Silicon Alley, Jason Calacanis was holding parties and publishing a newsletter that then became *Silicon Alley Reporter*. The IAB had been created.

What was the mood like then?
Oh, it was fun. We were going to take over the world. If you went online you were a pioneer. There was a big difference between being on the Internet and being online, so AOL was an outlier, they were the old way of doing things already but you felt like you were a cowboy. You'd go to these conferences; we had Internet World and some others that were the big conferences then. Most

everything was between New York and San Francisco. The big question whenever you met with someone was, did they "get it." If they didn't get it, you didn't even keep talking to them because it wasn't worth it.

When you asked before if it was all about education; you couldn't afford to do too much education because if someone didn't get it, you weren't likely to have time to teach them. Everything was moving too fast.

Of the people you dealt with back then, how many are still involved in the business today?

Not a lot. I think Kevin's coming back, so I know he's got a new startup after he took a number of years off, I think, surfing in San Diego. G.M. O'Connell is building websites in Argentina. Guys like Ariel Poler, who had founded IPro, I don't know where he is these days. Some of the Netscape guys are around. Kate Thorp is still around. I'm trying to think when that was, probably '96 or maybe late '96/'97. Seth Goldstein was part of Site Specific, I think, so there's a collection of them.

There's a lot more from the '98, '99, 2000 era that are still around. I remember back in those days, in '96, '97 there already were six or eight ad serving companies. They were all publisher side. You didn't have agency side ad servers then, really, until Ray built Atlas. You had MatchLogic, which was built by GM Cyberworks.

I forgot about them.

They did that one because it would be an advertiser-based solution. And then Ogilvy built a custom Net Gravity for use for IBM alone. It was pretty crazy times.

I remember everything was about your Media Metrix number, so you look in *The Wall Street Journal*, and their Tech 50 or Tech 100, they weren't listing the public companies by revenue, they would list them on their weekly Media Metrix numbers, and so all the companies were going public based on their traffic numbers, which they were buying.

In the mid and late '90s there was this idea that anything was possible. People had more fun and crazier ideas then. One of the things I think we have missed until today, is ever since the .com bubble burst, and you only had a few companies make it out, plus Google formed, everyone's had this enormous fixation on pure technology and pure technology of defensibility. Yahoo refused to call itself a media company even though 99 percent of its revenue is from advertising; the same for Google.

That would be like a newspaper company calling itself a printing company. I obviously have a bias there, but I think they refuse to acknowledge that they're in the business like it's a dirty business, of the media and advertising world. Except for Netflix and GroupOn, we haven't seen many that just really embrace business model innovation. I think there were a lot of great ideas in '98, '99 and 2000 that got killed when the bubble burst that we're going to see back again.

It used to be if you add a ".com" to anything it could be a business. Clearly we've seen with things like Zappos and others, you actually can build great businesses. Like Netflix, using web-based services tied to physical delivery. That's what I'm most excited about; I love to see people go online. A lot of business models and business plans from the late '90s never got to see the light of day because the market collapsed on them, but they probably were some of the best ideas that were out there.

Well, you started an idea around that time with TACODA that eventually shifted the landscape of how media is bought online, but you decided to build that in a relatively dismal period of history.

I'd like to say I had control of timing, that it was entirely by choice, but I had just agreed to merge my business. I left a little bit before the merger, but to basically leave Real Media so that we could combine it with 24/7. I needed a job so the easiest thing was to start my own company again. With the first wave in the '90s we built plumbing to deliver the right ad to the right person at the right time, but we never built the system to determine the right ad. The technologies we used at TACODA, parts of them had been around for a while. There had been some companies that had looked at that area. DoubleClick had a service called Intelligent Targeting that was a version of behavioral targeting. Engage had a business called Profiles. Now, those were broader, those were more like what Audience Science does today. They were fully comprehensive audience targeting, data targeting ideas. We had one at Real Media. We had cookie specific behavioral targeting in the ad server, so my view was I still believed in online advertising and I thought it would come back. I was actually really worried that other people were going to do that business quickly, so I didn't take any time.

I went from Real Media to TACODA in the same day. I left the Real Media office and walked into some office space in an incubator that was crumbling, and had a team there. I expected that we were going to see the online ad business back in six months. I didn't think it would take two or three years to get back to our old numbers, much less healthier numbers. I was fortunate. The timing really helped the notion of behavioral targeting and audience targeting, because I did not expect the explosion of the impressions; basically, the creation of so much commoditized inventory that really demanded or required that you had targeting or it would be impossible to sell.

So you had been building that idea with the concept that the web was going to grow much slower?

Not that the web would grow slower, I didn't expect the impression count to grow as much. I still expected the web was going to be more about text on pages, video maybe but we hadn't really seen it other than search in 2001. Nobody wanted to sell ads on search pages. It was a disastrous business. We repped some search at Real Media and you couldn't give the ads on search away, and that was until you had Goto.com, which later became Overture, who came up with the business model to monetize it. They launched self-serve models, placing the ads next to the results. The things like chat and message boards, we would try to put ads on, but they never worked. No brands wanted to be associated with them, and no one clicked through.

So I did not expect that we would see the explosion of web pages, and it started with blogs. I'm not surprised by how much time people spend online. What surprised me was the unit of delivery. The page views had gone up so enormously because people consumed a lot more pages.

We didn't really know how to deal with that because our metrics then were very print centric and the early sales organizations were print folks; guys like Doug Weaver over at *HotWired,* the print people, the early Softbank marketing team was Ziff Davis folks.

Virtually all the metrics we established ourselves on were print-based, and I would say in hindsight we should have evolved off of those sooner. We should have evolved a TV metrics-based approach, which might have been healthier, but I don't know that you can control those things. Some things happen because they happen.

That's a recurring belief, if we'd based the business on television metrics rather than print metrics we would have gone down a different path very quickly.

The difference was none of the TV buyers or TV sellers were in the game there, so no one would have understood the logic. What did work well was text and still photos, so the print folks took to it; it was a sandbox for print. Google quickly made it a sandbox for directory services, Yellow Pages, and then display has now really become the sandbox for direct marketers. It has never been the sandbox for the branded folks in the magazine business; they've never come in.

Local folks that bought newspapers have found some business there and the classified businesses are there, but today it's DR. I do think that if we try to guess what the web looks like in five years, it becomes very robust, it becomes totally in-session. The notion of a standard page falls way to more active pages and more video, and then it will be TV-like metrics; Share of Voice, interruptive advertising messages and things like that.

As you were starting TACODA, is there anything you would have done differently based on understanding what the time was, what the clients were looking for, and how you thought the business was going to grow?

Oh, yeah, I would have sold Real Media twice. I would have sold it the first time in '96 or '97 when I had offers, and then started another one and sold that one in '99 or 2000 when everything was high. I don't look back on any particular decisions. What I like is that there were very few key decision moments when I didn't feel like I had the control, or the team had the control of our own destiny – in hindsight, yeah. We did some early work with Amazon back in '95, '96, I would have gone and sucked up to Jeff Bezos a lot more and controlled a lot of the distribution.

I did expect the traditional media outlets and the newspapers to make smarter decisions. I understand that much better now. Now I've had time to get to know these businesses. I've worked inside Time Warner for a little while. I served on the board of a large newspaper publisher public company, so I understand now the big companies and their challenges. I was always surprised at why the agencies didn't get around this in a bigger way. I understand their economics better now.

I don't sit back and think there's a bunch of things I should have done differently. I certainly made lots and lots of wrong decisions. I missed a lot of opportunities, but was fortunate to get in the front of the right opportunities. Certainly when DoubleClick offered $800 and some million dollars for Real Media in cash, and were willing to close in ten days in 2000, part of me wishes I had said, "Sure, I'll take that money," rather than, "Hey, we're gonna go public in two months, our S1 is already filed and Frank LeTron's our banker." But that was the decision I got to make.

It's easier because we had a good transaction at the end of TACODA so I don't have to worry that. I feel secure with my children's future, education and everything else.

What do you think are good characteristics for people to be successful in this business?

Well, I think they have to be driven, optimistic, creative, resilient, friendly, in such a collegial industry. We have our share of jerks, and certainly some jerks have made their share of money along the way. They haven't been the ones that have gotten a lot of help from others. This is an industry that you can help each other, but you want to help ones that you want to hang out with, or be willing to have a beer or a drink with. One of the things I learned was the best business we ever won was usually because someone liked us, not just because they thought we had the best product. It was that they thought they could trust us, and that's something I didn't understand.

I learned a lot about being upfront, telling people when you've got a problem before they figure it out; telling them all the things that are going to go wrong or could go wrong. Confessing when something doesn't work, even if they were never going to find out, because the business is about repeat business, renewals and growths. I like the fact that in the more traditional media advertising world, they are not necessarily a monopoly, but they are dominant players, oligopolies. You don't have any choice but to work with the people you work with. You don't have a choice. You might be able to pick between Door A, Door B, and Door C but not in the online world.

You can run big national campaigns and never put an ad on AOL, Yahoo or MSN. That was even true ten years ago, so you can work with the people you want to work with, and that's one of the great characteristics of this industry. I think that we like each other, we have fun and that's one of the reasons that the industry bounced back. I remember going to an Ad Crafter's event in Detroit in October of 2000. By then the industry had collapsed. Now, it was a big tech event and Detroit had not embraced that much tech, not in the mainstream, and Ad Crafter's hadn't as an organization. They had a hall rented out for 500 people, and forty people that were there.

They had a pretty big speaker lined up, and they had it all set up with green rooms and things like that, and the organizers were like, look, we're gonna really thank you all for coming here because a lot of people won't come. You thought you were going to come speak to 400 or 700 people and you're only going to speak to forty, but this is Detroit and we take care of our own. There were forty speakers for an audience of forty over that day, and I remember just hanging out with that group. By then a lot of us had been really bloodied.

By that point I had laid off 350 of 600 people, with more layoffs to come, but I remember just hanging out with the group that was speaking there and we all liked each other, and then you look at some people I give credit for. If there's any one person I give a lot of credit to for the recovery of the online world its Rick Parkhill and iMedia because he went through a tough time. He created a network and gave the industry a couple hundred of us every three months, a place to go lick our wounds, talk about the future and make plans. I think from '01, '02, '03, '04, is when a lot of the ground work was laid for the online ad marketplace we know today.

I really give him a lot of credit for it because particularly the early ones, everybody was there. You had to be there. If you were Joanne Bradford you had to be there. The buyers were all there, the sellers were all there, and we sort of stopped complaining. You weren't allowed to complain there and I always look to that, and I tell Rick this, I think that he, more than anybody I know, helped bring the industry back.

I'm sure he appreciated hearing that because we all know he worked very hard during that period of time. The reason I asked that question originally, though, about the kinds of characteristics of people is that I know that I feel, and others feel that the people around during the TACODA period especially, those people have blossomed into some of the best in this business. They lead a lot of great people and they teach a lot of great people, they influence a lot of people in a really positive way, and what you described – friendly, ambitious, smart – is how I would describe all of them.

I got lucky. What I find is they attract each other, so once I had a couple of them around they did the work. I think the people that were part of that phase had to be leaders because we had come off some pretty tough years. A lot of people had had to go back, if they were in the media business, to the traditional side. Media people that were willing to take the risk again, and I do think some of the characteristics of those people like Matt Arkin or Hugh

McGoran or Chris Marrow, they're really good people. It's things like being polite, being respectful, and being a listener.

It's one of the things that's really important to me, which is everybody thinks that the Internet advertising business has been defined by technology, and I don't agree. I think it's been defined as much by leadership that hasn't always had to play corporate games to get visibility, particularly in areas with a lot of client services where you can really make a difference. I'm not saying they all couldn't be very successful in large corporate organizations, but not all corporate organizations promote those kinds of skills or reward them. A lot of times they're real jerks. We always had at TACODA a no assholes rule. We just don't want them.

I don't care what kind of numbers people can drive. I've fired a number of people because I didn't like how they fit in the culture, and they were pretty good producers. I'm not a believer in grinders and playing hardball, and I don't think it serves you well long-term, so yeah, for me, the most rewarding thing is that I've gotten to work with people like that. I'm really excited and proud about how well they've done, and how well they continue to do. In the end, they're happy, friendly people, which means when they go home they're happy and friendly and their families have to be a lot happier about that.

I do think that is something that has been a mark for a lot of folks in the online industry, is that we are a friendlier, nicer industry than probably other sectors of media.

CLOSING REMARKS

Dave speaks about personal relationships and integrity, and the benefits of being friendly, a concept worth re-addressing in summary. You have to treat the people around you with respect and in the manner you would wish to be treated. It's impossible to stay happy all the time, and no one wants you to be fake or false, but understanding that your business depends on relationships is of the utmost importance. It's something I am glad Dave brought up, and everyone who has ever worked with him or interacted with him knows that he represents himself in that way all of the time. Thanks, Dave!

CHAPTER 25

JOHN DURHAM

Among the first wave of marketers to grasp the potential of digital, John began to focus exclusively on interactivity in 1995. He never looked back from days at Coca-Cola!

Over the course of his career, he's held a number of leadership positions in the industry on both the agency and publisher side, and even served to help launch some industry associations as the Bay Area Interactive Group (sfBIG). He served as president of Winstar Interactive, president of Pericles Consulting, and EVP, Business Development for Carat Fusion. Most recently, he was president of sales and marketing for Jumpstart Automotive Media, where he successfully engineered the company's sale to Hachette Filipacci. In 2007 he and Cory Treffiletti co-founded Catalyst S+F to provide marketing services for startups and emerging companies.

Not content to lead the current generation of marketing professionals, John also stays busy preparing the next. He's taught marketing at the University of San Francisco since 1992. He molds young minds and helps to shape an entire industry every day.

John Durham, CEO of Catalyst S+F, how did you make the switch from traditional marketing and advertising to digital?

It was very easy. I got a job from a headhunter to go to this company called MapQuest. I talked to a friend of mine in Atlanta who had left the confines of security to go to join this guy named Ted Turner, with TBS, on this thing called cable, very early. I called this guy to talk with him about it, and he said he thought this Internet thing was cable on steroids. He thought Internet was television the way it really should be. I made the leap and have never looked back.

When you went to MapQuest, it wasn't from a marketing perspective, right?

It was a sales job; how to help these web engineers in Denver, Colorado figure out how to make money with maps.

So you went from selling TV and radio and dove into the web.

I left security in the TV and radio world.

You went from security to being very unstable. What worried you the most about that decision?

Could I keep up? Everything was happening so fast, hourly, and in traditional media it happens in years. You were already seeing the rapidity of how fast things were and how exciting it was.

How did you make the change over to Winstar Interactive?

MapQuest was getting sold; I got recruited to go to Winstar. I love sites. I love selling. I love digital. Winstar had some properties that really worked well for the web. They had a Microsoft property called Sidewalks, the very early Yelp and local-type businesses, and it was just so much fun and so exciting – $5 million deals done over a latte at Starbucks. No one had done $5 million deals in TV without taking them to the Olympics or the Super Bowl or spending an enormous amount of money, and you just saw a frenetic gold rush.

What was the hurdle for those early advertisers when they were considering putting money online?

Knowing what they were doing. Knowing what they were getting. There was a sense of, I've got to be here, though they were not sure what "here" was. They were thinking, but if I'm not here, I'm not going to be considered real. I think it was a perception. Once they started looking at the reality I'm not so sure that was the case. It's taken a few years for the reality to be real, but I think initially it was if you're not on AOL and you're not on Yahoo and you're not on MSN, and you're not doing *this* something is wrong with you.

What were the sizes of the deals, typically? You weren't doing a lot of $5 million deals. What were the types of sizes?

No, no, the sizes of the deals were $50,000, $250,000, faxing in orders for $75,000, $25,000, $50,000, maybe a $100,000 test.

And those were enough to keep the publishers happy and keep them in business?

They didn't know any better. Winstar primarily had magazine websites and viewed this as all upside. They didn't want to take away their magazine guys to have them going out and selling because those guys were used to selling ten, twenty, thirty, forty pages. This was just stuff they didn't understand. *Men's Health* was one of our sites. You literally could go to *Men's Health* and see on the webpage "Page 37" written on it. It was almost like they photocopied the magazine on the website. They didn't even bother having an editor.

Were the advertisers happy with the sites? Were they happy with these placements at the time?

For the most part, they liked just seeing their name up there. Then people talked about clicks and oh, my gosh, how many clicks are you getting? You felt like you were at Mass and found the Holy Grail – it was clicks. Then you had agencies that would say, I want to pay for those clicks.

And I know you're a big people person, what were the people like at that stage of the business?

They were like you. They were smart and fun and never had enough time. They wanted to know everything that they could. They played hard. They worked hard. I actually think more people worked smarter early. I don't think that they played smart, but I think they worked smart. You just felt like you were in a gold rush because everybody was getting in it, and you could tell very quickly those who were smart and asking the right questions and those who genuinely saw the excitement about this medium versus those who were just getting in it for the money.

What about on the publishers' side?

They were scared. One of the things that I thought the web did really well is it democratized control. Publishers were used to picking up a magazine, putting the stories in the magazine or on television and you passively reading, passively watching. All of a sudden, now you had the audience sitting in front of a screen and you called up the page. You were actively leading. They didn't understand that, men and women who were like wait a minute, the *customer* is in control.

But a lot of those early websites, they were –

Boring.

Well, boring because they were basically created on a magazine paradigm.

Right. And I always believed what my friend told me, that it was always as though you were looking at a TV monitor.

Well, you dealt with a lot of publishers, how come they didn't think about it that way? Were they unable to do so?

I don't think they could grasp the link. They still were caught up in the magazine world. They're still called publishers, not broadcasters. When headhunters call they're looking for a publisher. They're not looking for a broadcaster.

What are a couple of your favorite stories from back then?

Around the country there was always excitement. Being a rep firm, we always had to compete against the big boys, the Yahoos, the MSNs, who had money. They spent more in shwag than I would spend in salaries and they certainly spent more in entertainment. We always had to figure out how to be different. One of the first things I remember, and you were there, was the very first i-Media. It was the very first one in which we had forty buyers and forty sellers. We were one of the sponsors of the very first breakfast, and the question was, how could we be different?

We gave everybody a pair of Adidas shoes and said, "Walk a mile in our shoes." Understand our conversation. We try to talk about how to make the business better. How do you make smart buyers and smart sellers? In fact, that's how you and I met, on a panel. How do we engage in this business to be a legitimate business? Then you would just meet some purely fun people, or even some purely dumb people that had access to budgets, and you wondered how they were able to get up in the morning and put their pants on or their dress on, when all of a sudden they were responsible for spending $20 million.

You're hitting one of the topics that are worth talking about. How did you start to evangelize what the role of the buyer and the seller were going to be? You tried to talk about that a lot early on.

Because what I saw AOL and Yahoo and MSN do was they went direct to clients; they didn't respect the agency. In television if you went around a buyer, you wouldn't have had a job. You wouldn't have survived. Television stations existed on the agency relationships. Even at the highest level if the client was involved, it was still driven by the agency. I came in with that orientation of "respect the agencies." My competitors in the rep business always went around the agency, and I always said, when it's all said and done, my client's looking to you, Mr. Media Buyer, to make the best recommendations, to bring him or her the best intelligence and the best insights. I've got to make sure that we're doing the same to you, and I believed that if we were doing that we would always be in consideration.

One of the stories that I like to tell, which talks about why that evangelizing paid off, Winstar was part of a big parent phone company and it went bankrupt – the phone company did. But we were a part of the new media unit, and we were nine offices, sixty-five people. We got it sold. We were able to sell our business unit out. One of the reasons why is that there were ten media directors across the country that said, we will be references for you because you have always respected the business.

I always believed, and still do that agencies controlled 80 percent of the money. Go where the money is. But my competitors always went direct – "We'll make sure the agency is involved"— and I never did. Nobody who would work for me would ever do that. It was painful for me to do that. I didn't even know direct clients, wouldn't try to meet them.

Do you think that's the same today?
No, I believe that the agencies are not only disrespected, they're undervalued, underappreciated. I think they brought it on themselves. I think publishers are taking on the roles of total service agencies and they come out of the womb telling them to deal direct. I think the whole world doesn't know who does what, who's on second, where's on first, when's on third.

How did the mood change come 2001?
I remember sitting with Scot McLernon in what is now Coco500, which was then Bizou, on a Thursday. We were the only two in there for lunch for two and a half hours. You couldn't get a seat in there six months earlier if you weren't there by 11 a.m.. The bagel shops, the cottage industries, what people forget when the meltdown came, the obvious big players, those that sprung up in Chelsea, all those little cottage industries that supported them – delivery services, food services, entertainment – that stuff dried up and went away so quick.

South of Market, instead of seeing thousands of people you might have been lucky to see ten or twenty. I think that's when digital truly experienced a mind shift. Digital did a lot of powerful stuff during that time.

Do you think that the role of a salesperson changed in that time period?

Yes, there's sales pre-'01, and then there's sales post-'01. We got rid of all the people who shouldn't have been breathing when the meltdown happened, the people who bastardized and hurt the business. The ones that would drive you and other serious players crazy because they had no respect. What happened was a real shocker to a lot of people. A lot of people lost their fortunes, their means to get out there going. The reason to come to San Francisco or Los Angeles or Seattle and chase this gold dream was evaporating. They realized this is a business. I've got to bring a better sense of thought, a better sense of maturity and a better approach. I saw and still know the pre- and post-, and I think the people that survived in the post, it gave them a greater sense of perspective.

From a business perspective and a sales perspective, do you think that sales people in 1999 have the same, better or worse sales and business etiquette than those in 2011?

I think digital has destroyed etiquette. The twenty-five-year-old today who's out there selling doesn't understand grace and manners, or politeness They make little symbols on their phone or on their computer to imply visual. Actually, I think there's less etiquette today than there was ten years ago.

Do you think that hurts the ability for the business to grow, or that the business grows in spite of it?

I think it unfortunately grows in spite of it. That being said, I don't think you keep your business long. You will only succeed when you start learning to become better and you can retain business. I've seen people that I thought wouldn't rise to the occasion rise because they realized if they want to grow in this business, they've got to learn the human side of how to interact with people.

What about the balance of the art and the science in the business, what do you think it's weighted towards now?

It's weighted towards the science, but when it's all said and done every scientist is a frustrated artist, and I think art will get more into that test tube again. Right now people want to feel safe about making decisions. They want that safety and security. At the bottom of the Maslow hierarchy, safety and security is still there, and it's important. People have got to feel secure right now. The art still creeps up but it's definitely in favor of science.

If you could go back any time in the last seventeen years – because I keep telling people the business is seventeen years old now – who would you want to have a conversation with and why?

The two guys who founded Yahoo, and ask why they screwed it up.

Jerry Yang and company?

He'd be one of the four or five people that I think screwed up one of the truly great digital brands. Because it's a brand that is just such a part of my life, and it became such a part of my life so quickly. Why weren't you thinking about the customer? If you thought about the customer and stayed focused on the customer, the money would have continued rolling in.

Do you think that you could have helped them? Are there things you saw that you could have done differently?

Oh, yeah, I think a blind man could have helped them with the kind of egregious, stupid decisions that they were making. That just comes first because, as you know, Yahoo is a part of my life. I built this incredible page and they missed great opportunities to message to me and to market to me because of stupid things. It's amazing how dumb they were, and dumb drives me nuts.

What campaigns over the last seventeen years stood out to you as groundbreaking or just good examples of online advertising?

I thought the E*TRADE Baby, a digital brand that was able to bring video to life by using the most sacred thing in the world, and that's a baby. That campaign has legs.

It can't walk on them, but it's got legs.

It can't walk on them, but I've always liked the fact that if you've got nothing to say put babies and dogs in it. But they've made it so effective, and it just keeps getting fresh I always thought Volkswagen has done a really good job on air and on digital. I thought something stupid was Pets.com. It's just a sad way to spend a bunch of money. GoDaddy, if you believe in target marketing, in the idea of 'get attention.' Don't worry what you say. Don't worry what it is, just get attention. That probably is there. Is it effective advertising? We're all talking about it. I know many people use it, so it's probably effective. I always liked Yahoo!; "Do you Yahoo?" That crazy yodeler, I always thought it was great because it reminded me of why I liked the brand. Those are the ones that initially stand out to me.

The fact that they were integrated probably is what helps them to stand out.

But this is where I think digital probably can win; digital thinks it can stand alone. TV thinks it stands alone. Print thinks it stands alone. Customer thinks integrated is his or her part of their life every day. Customers have been ahead of marketers. We integrate everything that we do.

And the marketing has to reflect that.

And it doesn't. We as marketers, we're customers. We're users. I've always believed that a good campaign comes at you from a lot of different spaces. I think digital, fortunately, is the driver.

You've brought a lot of people into this business. What do you look for as the deciding characteristics as to whether or not they're going to be successful?

I don't do a lot of things well, but I've been pretty lucky in hiring and finding great talent. It's just that sense, you know, the questions they ask, the excitement that they bring, the drive. I've been wrong, but more often than not I have been right. They've been the people like your wife, and the people like some of the people that work for us and some of the people that now run publishing companies. They just have that body glow. That fever like, I want to succeed, I want to make a difference. You feel it in an interview.

You sense it when you talk to somebody where they want to be. Also, you see them in class, you get how they write, how they have really good interpersonal skills. That in itself is such an art because a lot of people don't have that. The people that I've been impressed with and have hired have really good personal skills and can communicate, and that sets them apart.

What excites you about where the business is headed?

Every day is an unknown. We've gone from big screens to fifteen-inch laptops and now to tablets and phones. What's next? We have sixty-inch televisions and yet we watch a lot of video on an iPhone 4. The magic of what we're in constantly amazes me. From a business perspective, I think we're going to get smart. I think the smart will survive. I think marketers will want people working for them, either in their organization or as outside vendors, who can help them make a difference and bring intelligence. They want answers. They want insights. Where they get it today, they're not married to the old way.

If you were going to start a content site now, or a publisher on the Internet, would your primary revenue be driven through advertising?

My inclination is to say, yes, because that's what I'm comfortable with. The question I would have to think a lot about it what would that content be, and does advertising make sense. Just because you have a website, advertising doesn't make sense for everything. The propensity has been advertisers will pay for it. We'll put clicks on there. That's the default, but sometimes it doesn't have to be that way. There are some sites that I would pay a subscription for because I just want the content. I want it. You may surround me with something. You may do it different. I may pay you not to have advertising as part of it.

If you could go back and talk to yourself twelve years ago, in 1998, what would you tell yourself now? What advice would you give yourself?

Try to stay focused. It's the first thing that comes to mind. I think about the job offers, the advice, the things that come to mind at that time frame were job offers. If I'd have taken this job, what would that have done? I stayed focused on where I wanted to go, and if I'd stayed focused like that, I guess that would probably be the best. My initial thing is, god, did I make the right job offer? Did I take the right job offer? I always believed that it's about focus. At times that's very hard for me to stay that way, but I have to constantly come back to that.

Focus is difficult.

With digital every day is exciting in our business, and just when you think you've seen it all somebody else reinvents it.

CLOSING REMARKS

John is a friend, a mentor, a business partner and many other things. He has been responsible for more careers, marriages and anniversaries in this business than anyone, and every day that one gets the chance to spend with him is a better day than the next. His role is that of mentor, and sometimes godfather, for the business. His point of view is always genuine, never candy-coated, and valuable. Thanks, John!

CHAPTER 26

GAYLE MEYERS

Gayle Meyers has built her career around delivering value to organizations, from her early role in the family business to her long media sales and strategy career. Gayle has a proven ability to create shared value through her deep professional network and personal relationships with digital industry leaders.

She is currently president of her own consulting firm, Meyers Consulting, which provides strategic sales, marketing and business development services to the digital media industry. Some of her consulting clients include; Advertiser Perceptions, Evidon, Aperture Audience, Operative Media, EachScape and Maxifier.

Gayle began her advertising career as an account executive for Microsoft Sidewalk in 1996. Then, as a strategic sales executive at AOL, she was responsible for creating the Digital Cities, Computer Channel and managed relationships with Dell Computers, Egghead. com and others. In January, 1998 she became a senior account executive at 24/7 Real Media, where she went on to be the top producing salesperson companywide in 1999, based mainly on her strategic sales efforts and the relationships she managed with AT&T, Travelocity and Earthlink, to name a few.

In 2000 Gayle relocated to New York to expand her career in digital media. She became director of East Coast sales for ValueClick Media in 2005. She was promoted several times at ValueClick, managing regional sales organizations in the Midwest, Northeast and Mid-Atlantic regions before eventually becoming VP of agency relations and strategic partnerships.

Gayle Meyers, strategic consultant in the online marketing business. So you've been in this business since about '95, how did you get into it?

I was working with a company by the name of Cendant, and Cendant was obviously a very big player in the earlier years, in the '90s, and they had multiple business lines. One of their business lines was The Entertainment Book. It's actually funny because The Entertainment Book really aligns with what GroupOn is today. Entertainment Book was a tool that allowed local business to drive people into their stores without utilizing advertising. They were hired by Microsoft because they had local sales people in San Francisco to sell Sidewalk.

So I brought Sidewalk, which was Microsoft's first product, to local businesses. The way that we did it was actually selling the Internet, or pages, from a flip book on what the Internet looks like and the pages that these local businesses would own. By doing that, they were creating what are storefronts online for small businesses. That's how I started my career. After being with Cendant for some time, launching Sidewalk, I was then poached from Microsoft by AOL. Back then I didn't really know what I was getting into.

I didn't know who Microsoft was. I was pretty young, and from that experience I just found it to be amazing that somebody was coming in and asking me for a job. I had no concept of who AOL was at the time either. I started to learn. I went over to AOL and started with Digital Cities, their local content guide, and that was a subsidiary of AOL Proper. I started creating opportunities with larger businesses within the San Francisco area.

What was it like trying to sell and be involved in local on the Internet that far ahead of the curve? Local on the Internet really wasn't the push at the time, but it was certainly going to become an area of interest.

Yeah, it's not easy selling into local business. They don't have tremendous money when it comes to spending, so for them it's all about efficiency in driving people into the store. Back then it was small businesses trying to understand what the Internet was. This was the early days of dial-up. There was no broadband to be heard of. San Francisco was the capital of technology and where people believe the Internet came from, hence the reason why Sidewalk was launched in San Francisco. But it was tough; it was a lot of education. There was value in that education, so people would definitely meet with you.

People knew Microsoft's name but I wouldn't say it was something they were tremendously aware of. The costs were very low. They were trying to get people signed up to it. Ultimately what they were doing is building their network. Citysearch was around during that time, I believe. AOL had local content that they were trying to develop at the same time. I loved the strategy because, ultimately, they were trying to build from the local aspect and then grow it from there. Because of the small business budgets, really their marketing dollars were just tiny, the adoption was taking a long time and there were also competitors in this space.

So it was challenging. It was a lot of education, creating sponsorships, creating merchant profiles. Merchants wanted to get online but they just didn't know what it was.

How savvy did the merchants get, versus some of the larger clients who you worked with during your career? Did they really understand it at first, or did it take a while?

It took a while. It was constantly going in and educating them on the value of it. I think they knew they had to do something, but it was just so premature. I don't think they realized the scale, and in my perspective it wasn't driving people in their stores at the same volume as The Entertainment Book was. I think people were trying to figure out what the ROI was on that.

So continuing from AOL, what else were you getting into? Did you start to broaden out beyond the local initiatives, or did you continue to go down that path?

Well, at AOL when I came on board there were at least fifteen sales people. They were all focused on this content channel, this specific area for Digital Cities, and I was representing the San Francisco headquarters. What I realized is there's no way I was going to be able to win in this environment. There were fifteen sales people, so I decided to think creatively in how do you create value for advertisers? When I was looking at the content channels that they had, they didn't have a computers channel, which is amazing. Just think about it. They had real estate, they had entertainment.

The hottest conversation was the computers, or content around understanding what's happening in that space, so I raised my hand and said I would love to create a content channel specifically around computers, educate consumers and educate the market. Also, drive in revenue through companies like Egghead, who was around at that time, companies like Dell, and really just create something more than what was there. So I did a partnership with Computer Currents to supply us the content, and I had a small team that was helping me develop this channel. Then one day we got pulled into a conference room and, in classic AOL style, they said in two weeks we're going to be letting go about 80 percent of this workforce, so just want to give you a heads-up before that happens.

I've never been laid off from any of my companies, but two weeks go by, everyone's searching in the market to see what's going on. Where are we going with this? What happens when you get laid off? Nobody had a clue. One day forty-five people piled into a conference room, five of us were put in a separate room – I was one of those five – and forty-five people were let go in one day and walked out with security guards. That was when the turn really started to happen, and you could see that you were just puppets in this overall scheme of what was happening.

AOL, I think, was a phenomenal company during that time but it got hit badly. They were doing the big $23 million preview travel deals. They were doing all of these exclusive, big partnership deals that ultimately just weren't turning revenue. It was all the content relationships that were the core of the business at that time, and I watched as all of this was going on and was so empowered by looking at the size of these deals; $23 million to own the travel section of AOL.

During that time what was so amazing was our perception of scale. I have a plaque that says nine million people were part of AOL at that time. If you remember, AOL had closed doors. They didn't open it up to the masses. You had to be on their dial-up service to access the content, so we're talking about the early days of closed walls, closed content, strategic placements and partnerships, and in my perspective I think that's coming back today. I think content will be back within the next year to year and a half, and I think everyone's hedging their bets on that.

You think people are going to be paying for content?

We can start to see this. We're starting to see the full circle happen again.

Can you do that though? Once the cat is out of the bag, can you put it back in?

Well, I think AOL tried that a couple of times, but ultimately AOL never truly, in my perspective, understood their value. They went through so many changes. I think people are testing out the closed wall to the open wall. You look at the *The Daily*, which is News Corps' product; they're only an application, so they're a closed-wall application today where you have to pay to access the content. People are testing out the different models. Over time I think consumers will have to pay for content again.

That's one of the decisions that were made early on. You pointed out that a lot of decisions that were made early on may or may not stand the test of time; one of those being in regard to content, that it had to be made free and advertising supported.

I think if they show value, whoever that publisher is, to the consumer, and that their conversation is different from other conversations that are out there then, yes, I do think consumers are willing to pay for the right kinds of content. Think about it from this perspective; consumers today, they're paying for all of these iPhone apps because they're customized to the consumer to a certain extent. They're willing to pay for these applications because it's something that interests them, there's a value exchange. There has to be that value exchange for consumers to feel they're getting something out of it, and that publisher has to create the value and customize it to consumers.

It's about customization, it's about allowing something to be special to that person and I do think the world of applications is going to grow our industry. Apps are going to be the future.

Let's assume that you're correct and that we're going to move towards a future that's application based and you're paying for content. Do you think advertising is still going to be integrated into that model, or do you think part of the value that a consumer wants is access to content without the advertising?

I think content and advertising are going to combine a bit more. It could be both. I think that there's a value, and I always go back to the core of what a consumer wants. Consumers don't necessarily want to see banners running everywhere. Some might not mind but if it's relevant, contextually relevant, and relevant to my interests, I would have no problems with that. We might see more integration of partnerships rather than it just being blatant advertising, and that really does circle back to the earlier days.

For instance, when you would go to AOL's content channel for travel, you didn't really know that you were looking at Preview Travel's content, and you didn't really get that whenever you would pull down a fare sale or book a travel that that was actually the backend technology that was provided by Preview Travel. When I moved over to 24/7 Media, I took a lot of my learnings and I applied them. When I went to 24/7 I was still just a junior account executive, but I wasn't calling on the agencies. I had to think of creative ways of selling deals. I sold AT&T their exclusive travel provider deal for roughly $1.2 million.

It was the first big deal I had ever done, but I really took that methodology of what AOL was doing in content ownership and integrating Travelscape at the time, and brought that into AT&T's backend. The AT&T travel channel was delivered by Travelscape. So back then it was a lot of that ownership of placement that everybody was just trying to get a land grab. It's different today, but I think what today's market looks like from a content perspective, is people are trying to get those consumers interested in their content to keep coming back, drive up page views and eCPMs on the site. Does that make sense?

If the model does shift to one where we're paying for content, do you think that the privacy issues the Internet advertising space currently has will diminish? Because if I'm paying for that content and they know more about me, and I'm only advertising in that location, it doesn't seem like they need to worry about privacy because they're not going to be selling the data, hopefully.

Exactly. I don't know if all companies won't sell the data. I think they'll collect the data and maybe use it as first-party. If you look at what Yahoo's done, and a lot of their behaviors, Yahoo leverages a lot of behaviors as first-party data to be able to better inform the content that I'm presented with and the messaging, as well as the different ads. I think there will be a reduction in privacy concerns for sure, but challenges that we've had from what's happening in privacy stems from consumers and consumers concerned with knowing that they're being tracked.

I think when a consumer walks into a paid environment, someone they've already built that brand relationship with, they trust that relationship. Let's pretend It's *Wired*; *Wired* is going to deliver insightful ads that are relevant to me, so I would want that level of partnership with the brand. There's already that brand's trust and the communication has already been clear there. Because if I'm paying two dollars a month to access *Wired*'s data, *Wired*'s information and their articles, I have no problem with *Wired* sending me relevant messaging based on who I am. I'm a female, married with two kids, interested in entrepreneurial business, interested in buying a car within five to six months.

I would, if anything, update my preferences so I get better, more relevant information. I think what's happened to consumers, in my perspective, is consumers are spoiled by their experience with Google. I'm a consumer, I've got limited time in my life as a busy mom and an entrepreneur, I'm always looking for the most efficient way to get what I need. Efficiency is key to my life, so if every time I went onto Google and I didn't get exactly what I wanted, I wouldn't go back there, right? If I look at the way Google paved the way for most consumers, they're spoiled by the efficiency of Google.

That's why Google has won, in my eyes, because of their search results. Because every time I put something in I get something very close to what I'm looking for, and that's created a positive user experience. If we could have that same user experience across Display, we'd win. Display wouldn't have as many challenges. I think that's the core of privacy; understanding what's important to the consumer, giving them a rich, relevant experience will build trust in our industry.

You have a good perspective of the business by being at AOL and at MSN early on, and you mentioned what kind of success they all had. We all know what kind of success they had by doing a lot of those larger all-in deals, with

Pepsi and other brands. Why do you think those deals didn't succeed? Why didn't that work?

You know, honestly, I don't think I have the answer for that. I think that would be the key to everyone's issues and challenges. Part of what we've done to our industry is creating the CPC, cost per click model, the acquisition model, models that really weren't based on brand reach and frequency. We make ourselves too responsible in this industry, and I think what happened is when we did those big deals in the earlier days, we overshot ourselves because the audience wasn't there yet. So when I was at AOL they didn't even have a technology platform to be able to measure certain aspects of what we were selling.

It was pretty much a joke if you want to know the truth. There was no technology platform serving the ads that was consistent, or that could feed us back the kind of insights we needed. There wasn't a solution for years at AOL until they bought Advertising.com. I think once we started to attach ourselves to metrics that were so granular we really shot ourselves in the foot. We were trying to be so different, to build a business that was different, but we never attached it to the way that we look at TV buying and/or radio buys and/or magazines. We made ourselves too attached to a model that was about efficiency. Efficiency made me a lot of money, so I can't complain, but unfortunately it's hindered our ability to see the bigger picture.

That's what I see as the future in our industry. I'm working with a company that I believe has a tool that could do that, but I think we need to step back and find a tool that can help our industry be able to compare ourselves to a GRP model.

That's a good question to evaluate, the comparison of online to offline media. Early on this business did not want anything to do with that comparison and we fought the GRP all day long. Now I think everybody's of the same mindset that there is a comparison which needs to be made, and that you don't plan one form of media in a vacuum you have to plan them together. Why do you think we haven't figured out this GRP model yet, because in basic math it's not that difficult? What do you think is holding us back?

I don't know why we haven't figured it out. I don't think anybody really has the answer of why we haven't figured it out, but what we have been doing is going down a channel that's very focused around data and efficiencies, and maximizing the most out of a dollar CPM. We kind of have to because there's so many players that are involved in that dollar CPM, and where the revenue gets attached to that we haven't taken a moment to step back, breathe and figure out how we can look at it from a bigger perspective. We also are limited. We're building our business off of a cookie-based model, and that doesn't solve the challenge or the issues that we have.

We need to find a way to separate ourselves from the cookie-based model and deliver a measurement tool that reaches past that. Again, everyone's trying to figure it out, and whoever does figure that out, they're going to have a phenomenal model to be able to take to the market and the agencies. In many ways the agencies are limited with the tools that they have available to them, but they're overwhelmed with so many different solutions coming in the door.

There's no one tool that gives you a holistic view of the whole campaign, no definitive attribution modeling.

Not taking it simply from attribution, but modeling of the total research and insights that they could find on the consumers who it's reaching. comScore has some of that information, but it's not dynamic, it's not something that you can leverage during the campaign to optimize the campaign at placement level. So it's that tool that ultimately delivers three things that are the most important to agencies, which is research, research, research.

The reasons why research is important is 1) It makes them look smart to their clients, 2) It makes them give the insight on who they're trying to reach, and what is that reach and frequency across all of their media. Are they hitting that consumer? How many times? It also gives them insight into which partners are actually delivering against that metric. So finding the tools that can help deliver that measurement and that research is key to the success of our industry.

I think we're getting pretty close to it.

I feel so lucky to be close to a couple of companies that can possibly do that; companies like Evidon who are changing the face of our industry. It's been an incredible experience.

If you were talking to somebody who wanted to get into this business right now, what would you look for in that person to help determine if they would be successful?

Depending on what role I was hiring them for I would bring it down to a couple of things. One is creativity; creative in the sense of understanding there's really no limits to what we're doing. There's no limit to what you can create and deliver upon. I think also education, understanding the landscape and studying it. I think most successful people in this industry are people that want to know every aspect of this industry. For me, I've studied it. I studied business models, I studied revenue models, I studied what companies do, what their offerings are compared to their competitors, and somebody that has that level of interest will succeed.

I look for people willing to listen, educate themselves, and who want to learn. And then, I guess the third aspect is it takes an entrepreneurial-type nature to succeed in this business. You need somebody that can be dynamic because if you're with a company for five years, like I was with ValueClick, every other month, to every six months to a year we were constantly changing our roles. New products were coming in and out and constantly updating, and you had to stay on top of it. Also, keep the value proposition that you bring to agencies and to marketers rich and real. Somebody that is dynamic can keep moving and going with the flow as long as they don't mind change, because change happens almost every other day in this industry.

If they have a hard time with change, then ultimately they're going to have a hard time with this space. Those are the core things I look for, and I'm always looking to bring people in this industry. I think people that are in our industry can be really jaded. When I look at what I've been part of for the last seventeen years, I'm so proud to say that I do what I do, and the main reason is three things: we changed the way that people communicate on line, the way they interact via email, the way that they're doing business. And I feel like I've sponsored that experience.

I've helped brands pay for that experience for consumers, so I've changed the way that people are educating themselves, communicating, interacting on a daily basis, dating, and by doing that I feel like I've changed the way that people live today. To me, it's an honor to be part of this industry for the last seventeen years.

CLOSING REMARKS

Gayle is an incredibly energetic woman and has made her personal mark on the industry. She has been part of a number of strong brands and her passion for it shows. What I take away most from her interview, and what she summarized so well, is that creativity is a part of the equation. Its about creating solutions to problems using technology and the relationships you have around you. That is how things get done, and that is how you can be successful in this business!

CHAPTER 27

GREG STERN

A founding partner of Butler, Shine, Stern & Partners (BSSP), Greg offers over twenty-seven years of advertising and marketing experience, both domestically and internationally. Upon graduation from Brown University, Greg began his career at Ogilvy & Mather, New York, where his assignments included American Express and Seagram. He moved with O&M, first to Hong Kong and later to Indonesia, where as Managing Director he grew that office substantially, and established divisions in direct marketing, public relations and promotions for clients, including Unilever, Nestle, Toyota and Pepsi. Greg returned to the U.S. with Goodby, Silverstein & Partners, where he ran the Sega business among others.

In 1993 he joined partners John Butler and Mike Shine to start Butler, Shine, Stern & Partners. Since then, BSSP has grown from a startup of four to over 160 people, working with clients including MINI Cooper, RadioShack, Columbia Sportswear and Priceline. One of the largest independent agencies on the West Coast, BSSP provides highly creative, strategic and accountable solutions for its clients with services including advertising, media strategy and buying, online marketing and web development, brand identity and design and strategic consulting.

Welcome Greg Stern, CEO and owner of Butler, Shine, Stern & Partners. Let's start with the fact that you began your career at Ogilvy.

Yes, I started, recruited straight out of college in 1982 by Ogilvy, and I spent ten years with Ogilvy in New York, Hong Kong and Indonesia.

You did a stint with Goodby and then started Butler, Shine, I believe around '93. Right around that time Internet marketing was beginning. You were going online through AOL, Prodigy and CompuServe, and eventually the online ad banner started showing up. At what point did you start paying attention to digital as a potential medium for advertising?

I would say that came later, more like in '96 or '97. Our own awareness of email came as early as '93 or '94, in particular through AOL, and then beyond. But we, as a small creative boutique starting up with three people in '93, '94, were more focused on television and print advertising almost by definition. That was when we knew what our clients would turn to us for. Starting around '96 we got the assignment of creating launch advertising for Charles Schwab's online trading service, and although we were not doing digital advertising for that per se, it began to open up the world that here is a service from a major advertiser that is taking place 100% online. What are the marketing and digital opportunities to actually drive traffic?

From the experiences I've had with you talking about the business, you always looked at digital advertising as an integrated component of the overall mix. Did your clients always think about it that way, or did you try to teach them that point of view?

I think it has been more, particularly in the beginning, us trying to provide them with that perspective and tell them it's really just another communication channel and shouldn't be considered independent. It is just another arm of what is happening. Sometimes it's the hub, sometimes it's just another spoke. It really depends on the effort. Things have evolved now that clients are very well aware of the concept of integration, but initially I would say we were pushing them to look at digital not as a separate communication channel, but one that is related to everything else they're doing in marketing.

Did you ever have to deal with the clients who really looked at Internet as if it was the shiniest object in the room, and it garnered all of their attention?

No, because we were never a digital agency per se. A digital agency probably had to deal with that more frequently because they would have been hired just because of the shiny object status of what they did, whereas for us, it was just another channel. Again, it might have been the center of the efforts, or it might have been just an extension of what was going on.

For the same client we have treated digital in different ways, depending on what the particular effort called for. It could be where all of the advertising existed. For instance, a campaign that we did for MINI called Hammer and Coop, which was basically a web series. There was no television. There was print driving people to the web, there was digital driving people to the web and that was where the story about the new vehicle they were introducing unfolded. But there have been just as many MINI campaigns that have been driven primarily by broadcast, by print, even through collateral and showroom materials, so it really depends on what the objectives are and the best way to reach the target.

What other things have you guys done in the digital space that you've been really proud of?

One of the most unheralded efforts we were involved in was something that SF Interactive brought to the party when we acquired them. We completed that acquisition in '03, and they had created something called the Ad Cube, and this was before broadband was fairly ubiquitous so it was a bit of a bandwidth suck. I think that was one of the hindrances, but this was essentially a three-dimensional online display banner unit. Within the banner itself you could feed livestock reports or news items about that particular advertiser. You could provide the opportunity to download a white paper directly from the banner or you could capture data, people could raise their hands and say, send me more information. For 2002, 2003 that was very innovative for a standard display unit.

Advertisers weren't quite ready for it, both in terms of the cost of production and, as I said, the bandwidth issue. But that was one of the more innovative things that had been done particularly early, and unfortunately didn't really catch on.

We've had great success with contextual advertising, and by contextual I mean where we might be talking about Columbia Sportswear – winter gear, coats, boots, etc. – and sponsor a Pandora player that really is only dealing with songs about winter. One of the early efforts that we did for MINI, again with Pandora, had to do with downloading songs on the road – road songs, road trip songs – and looking at contextual advertising in that way. The other thing that I found interesting, and this goes back probably four or five years, is video banners. Not really pre-roll, but video banners – some of them were pre-roll, but not necessarily – before Hulu existed. Not looking at taking a broadcast model and putting it on the web, but in addition to a display-advertising context, running video with extraordinary click-through rates due to the compelling nature of the creative. We would go from sub-one percent with a standard banner to 10 percent plus in click-through because of the video content in the banner, I found that absolutely fascinating.

The other thing is utility. One of the things that we did that was quite interesting for MINI was the Carfun Footprint. You would go in and enter your car based on two separate data feeds; one from the EPA that looked at emissions and environmental responsibility, and environmental indices of a car versus fun to drive, which was based on acceleration, cornering, handling, etc., and you would come up with your Carfun Footprint. Not surprisingly MINI ended up at the top each time. That was both an online application as well as delivered in the banner.

With the clients that you work on, you get to use digital in a lot of different manners. What do you think digital is really good at doing?

Engagement, primarily, it can inform, entertain, but whether it is informing, entertaining or providing utility, ultimately it's about engagement. If you think about television, about print, if somebody reads a long copy print ad they certainly are engaged, but it doesn't necessarily give them the opportunity to take action right there seamlessly. If you can engage somebody and cause action, again with MINI; if you can go from the Carfun Footprint or from the Hammer and Coop web series to a configuration, then you've got a tremendously higher rate of success or chance of selling a car. MINI was one of the first to have the online configurator where you're choosing colors, options and so forth for your car. They've got a tremendous close rate among people who send that configured vehicle to a dealer at something like 30 percent. Thirty percent actually end up buying the car, so if you can engage through entertainment, utility, information, you've got a much higher chance of actually closing the sale even on a high ticket item like a car.

It sounds like you've gone down that path for your clients and either have proven, or at least found, the correlation between engagement and actual revenue. Is that right?

Yes. Another one we found that with was Radio Shack where we were creating decision trees. Within a banner, a decision tree to figure out what kind of camera that you needed. We gave you info on a new digital camera, and you could choose your price range. You could choose features. You could narrow done the variables until it made a specific recommendation and then click through to purchase right there. We did the same thing with Epson. A decision tree model, whether it's adjusted by sliders or some other appropriate interface, ultimately leading to a purchase opportunity.

You got to watch this whole industry begin and grow. You watched it have a bit of a retrench for a while because of the bubble. What have you learned about how this industry has grown, and how to apply digital images to the overall mix? What takeaways have you learned?

If you give it larger context, the advertising industry has been around for however long, 100 plus years if you go way back. In its modern form, let's call it sixty years, it didn't really change that much. There was the advent of TV, and that didn't replace radio but added to it. Then suddenly advertising creative got more conceptual. But if you look at the last fifteen or, as you put it, seventeen years, the rate of change has accelerated exponentially. You talk about the retransfer, the reset as a result of the bubble bursting, I would talk about the more recent recession as accelerating the pace of change even more because of the need for accountability, the need for results, the fact that everything is being measured now. I think that the pace of change has simply accelerated.

Whether it will continue or not is a pretty good question. There are certainly great leaps forward, and then smaller incremental leaps forward in terms of technology, whether it applies to marketing or just the technology we use in our everyday lives; the way the consumers are consuming media entertainment, information, etc.. I think the truism is that it will constantly evolve. The pace of that evolution will change depending on technology innovations, the economy, consumer adoption of change, etc..

Is it safe to think that the rate of change is going to slow down because the fact is the technology we've been developing over the last ten or fifteen years, consumers are adopting now? I think we were planning for when they were going to adopt it, but now that they've adopted it there is almost a level of stabilization that has to happen.

I think it will slow down. It is definitely stabilizing, but I do believe that certain macro influences, not necessarily technological influences, accelerate the change at different times. If you look at our industry, not necessarily consumers, the industry had to change more quickly over the last two to three years to adopt analytics and align measurements because of the demands of clients, and because of the economy. That had less to do with technology. That had nothing to do with rate of adoption. It just had to do with a macro influence affecting our business. From a technology point of view there will be stabilization, which is a little surprising when you consider it has only been a year and a half since the iPad came out. That feels like monumental change, but it really isn't. It's been building.

It does feel like a larger scale change.
And that was a sea-change in terms of new advertising platforms, new publishing platforms, huge new revenue opportunities for consumer electronics manufacturers, primarily Apple. I won't say it came out of nowhere, but it did surprise a lot of people. At least the rate of adoption surprised them and that was only a year plus ago. What would lead us to believe that things will now slow down? I personally think you're right, that they will slow down particularly as it relates to technology, because as you said, adoption is there now and you reach a period of stabilization.

That doesn't mean the industry won't change. I think that the industry will continue to change rather quickly because it's so fragmented right now. You've got the multinationals trying to find their purpose and reason for being. Within the multinationals you have a disaggregated collection of businesses that represent redundancy and overhead for clients. What you're going to see there is the parts that make up the whole are going to begin to buy themselves back because there is now money available for them to do that. You're going to have more interesting, mid-sized, perhaps specialty, perhaps not, shops that are competing, and that is going to leave the multinationals in yet another quandary as to how they compete and differentiate themselves.

It seems to be a cycle in the advertising business, where clients and agencies agree on the ideas of bundling and unbundling. Either they will go to a holistic partner who has everything under one roof, or they will select multiple partners who are all specialized. I haven't been able to figure out where the business is headed. I definitely felt that we were moving back towards a bundling stage, and you've pointed out that there are a lot of different startups offering services now on top of technology.

Personally, I think there will be more bundling, and it begs the question of what will happen with digital specialty shops? Again it's a bit of an identity crisis, and many of them are deciding now, not part of the multinationals, but more the independent ones, are they production companies? They certainly don't want to be production companies, because that is commoditized.

So then they're saying, we want to be upstream and we want to have the ideas as well. So the "big spaceships" of the world (very talented shops), don't want to necessarily just be hired by agencies to execute what the agency has hired them to produce. And rightly so, they've got a lot of good ideas. But then it's difficult for them because they're not necessarily seen by the client as the keeper of the big idea. They're not the agency of the record. They're not buying the media.

Talk about bundling and unbundling, Martin Sorrel says as far as the unbundling of media that toothpaste has already been out of the tube and you can't get it back in. We're seeing over 20 percent to 30 percent of our pitches involve media again, and for a mid-size agency we've got a burgeoning media department. So I'm not really sure where that's going to go, but it seems like there's more desire for integration than there is desire to manage multiple shops. Having said that, Dell, I don't know if they've announced yet but they will shortly in their recent review, hired four to six different agencies to execute. I think they are dividing that more along business lines than around specialties, rather than marketing disciplines. So they'll have an SMB, they'll have a consumer and they'll have an enterprise shop.

If I said that I really don't believe that digital agencies or the standalone have much of a future, would you agree?

I would say it's tenuous. There is a lot of talent out there. I think they'll find a way to survive but it will be on their own. So, yes, I would agree but they won't survive on their own.

There seems to be a growing frustration with the fact that there are now not just digital agencies, but social media agencies, mobile agencies and continued growth with search agencies. Those folks are obviously going to have to be consolidated at some point right?

To be determined, I don't know. Social media has been a land grab, and everybody is out there. I just had lunch with a former CMO of a very significant client and we were talking about this. She was saying that a lot of the social media management is really being done in-house now by clients because they see it as an extension of their PR role, and I think that is true. It really depends on where you want to play. We've defined our role within social media as pretty much everything outside of digital PR and information seeding, so it's conceptual and idea development application development, creative concept development, monitoring, analysis, analytics related to that. When it comes to reaching thousands, if not tens of thousands of bloggers that are influential, I don't want that job. I'm not a PR agency, that's PR. We'll turn to a partner to do that. So in that sense the standalone social media companies can provide that service in the same way that a standalone PR company will continue to exist. I think they will survive. What I found interesting is that Edelman early on embraced social media, expanded their PR set of skills and what they offer, and they're one of the leading social media practitioners right now, which is really smart and showed a lot of foresight on their part.

As far as search, I don't know. Search is interesting. Search is enough of a specialty and niche area that it might make sense for it to survive. A year-and-a-half ago we eliminated a digital department. The reason is because if our strategists, creative people, media people and account people don't have digital chops and skills then they don't belong here. If they can do a TV commercial, they have to be able to do a banner, website or an application, or manage that process through. Having said that, we have a digital production department in the same way that we have print production and broadcast production; to have a parallel structure of account people, media people, creative people who are only doing digital made no sense to me, and certainly my clients wouldn't want to pay double just because it was a digital execution.

Makes sense, and I agree with that completely. Do you think that is going to be the trend? Do you think that most of the larger shops are going to start to go toward that model?

Ultimately they'll have to, but if you think of a big multinational agency where they have these parallel structures going on, I mean look at DDB. Tribal DDB is a great shop. They've always been ahead of the game, but if you're a global DDB client, why are you going to pay for a digital account director and a general account director? It makes no sense. I've been out of the big agencies long enough, but maybe they're already consolidating that, and I just don't know how they're doing it. I'm sure that a Tribal or a Neo@Ogilvy has a separate bottom line, is measured separately and has a separate staffing structure as well.

What role do you think social itself is going to play for the next five years or so?

I think it will play an important role of connecting people, and the whole notion of trusted friend's recommendations. Learning about products, and learning about things through friends is absolutely critical. I think searching through friends and your social network has Google most worried, what they are probably scrambling to try to fix and close the gaps. If you want to do a search for a doctor or a gardener or a yoga class, and you've got critical mass within your social network, are you going to search that or are you going to search Google? You're going to take advice from the people that you trust. I think that it is here to stay, and will only take an increasing role in marketing.

The question is less what role will social media have, than what role will agencies have in managing that social media process? I truly don't know the answer to that. There are ways that we can provide utility, inform, educate, engage, etc. through social media as we have been doing, and that will continue to evolve. But a lot of it can probably be done without agencies just as well, particularly if you look at the search function through social networks.

I believe brands are the ones that should be the keepers of their social presence, and the ones that should be doing the management of the community. I think you're right, from a creative perspective and from an ideation perspective the agencies have a role, but I don't think that they should be managing externally.

I agree, and if you look at Twitter in particular, as how brands manifest themselves online in social media through Twitter, it is primarily a customer service role. That's what it should be, that's what it is. It's customer retention, answering complaints, or seeing opportunities to engage a customer in that way. Given that, a lot of customer service is already being done internally and clients are much more comfortable maintaining that internal focus.

Yesterday I was talking with David Verklin over at Canoe Ventures. He is trying to spearhead the ways that television can take what we've gotten to a positive perspective, without digital, and apply it to the world of TV. How do you think TV is going to enter into the digital age over the next five years?

Well, I think there are a number of ways. At its most simple you are dealing with, for many, a multi-screen audience; a concurrently or simultaneously multi-screen audience. You've got your iPad open or your laptop open, and you're on your social network while you are watching TV. Fundamentally that is bringing television into an interactive and digital, if not seamless, at least synchronous experience. Now you've also got Internet enabled televisions, which allow you to access the web, so you can access Facebook, YouTube or whatever you might want online, and then take that a step further and there's the opportunity for truly interactive TV. You might say I like the coat that that guy is wearing on *American Idol*. I want to purchase it. So you hit a button and you can do that. Take that a step further, and based on your preferences or your profile or maybe your friends, your social network, which is also stored in there, it actually gives you suggestions and pushes things out based on what you're watching. I think that the future is ripe for it.

Adoption will be slow initially. I think it will start and kind of stay at that synchronous area I was talking about, where you are using two different devices to establish that interactivity within television. It will take a while to get to where it's a seamless, single device, interactive experience that embraces television programming through a single set.

Do you think TV is going to be able to achieve the addressability and accountability that digital seems to be creating a legacy with?

Not to the same level but it will get close. It will get there for sure. I think that's the Holy Grail, and it's a ways away still.

When talking to David, he gets very excited and seems pretty much set on the idea that within the next three years TV is going to have that accountability.

How widespread? Will that just be among early adopters? Will that just be among special Internet-enabled television set users? Will that be among Canoe subscriber users? It's hard to say. One would think, given the ubiquity of DVRs for close to ten years now that we would be closer to it and we're not. In the same way that every year starts off with an analyst saying this is the year of mobile advertising, and actually I think this probably *is* the year. But how many years have they been saying that? I think that the accountability related to broadcast television, it's more like five years, but I don't have a crystal ball. It will happen but it will take a while.

CLOSING REMARKS

Greg and his partners have built an incredibly creative business on the waters of Sausalito, California. His interview reminds me of the virtues of patience and focus, and doing the simple things better than everyone else. Greg was never distracted by the shiny object, he was focused on doing great creative work for great brands and that has paid off. The work they do with brands like MINI have lasted the longest and been the most effective. In the world of online advertising and marketing, Greg Stern is someone to emulate and look up to. Kudos to Greg and his partners!

CHAPTER 28

DAVID VERKLIN

David Verklin was most recently CEO at Canoe
Ventures, a company that was blazing the trail for new
forms of digitally-based advertising in television. David
has been a driver of the ad business for many years from
his role at Hal Riney, his pioneering role as CEO of Carat
North America, and now with Canoe. He led the roll-up of
some of the most well-known interactive agencies globally
with Carat Interactive and Isobar, with Sarah Fay and
Nigel Morris. His impact can be felt through the business
as many executives of his team, people he has mentored and
led over the years are now leading companies of their own
and making their own impact on the business.

Welcome, David Verklin.

Glad to do it, Cory. A) I'm doing it because of the
friendship we've had for so many years and the work we

did together, and B) It's a great chance to sit back and reflect a little bit.

Well, thank you. So let's just begin at the beginning. You were running Hal Riney back in '87 to about '98 or so, before you ended up with Carat. You were at Riney when the Internet started to become a viable medium for consumers as well as marketers. What was the attraction?

The date we'll go back to is 1994. I'll just tell you a quick story to show how I got fascinated with it. In the early '90s, in '92 and '93, I had started as Riney's media director. I was always on the media side of the business. When we formed Hal Riney & Partners in 1987 I was the company's first media director. Over time I went from media director to director of new business, and then in 1993 I went from director of new business development to the managing director of the agency.

So it was interesting having a media guy run a pretty well known creative agency in 1993 and 1994. I was running the shop and I always had a soft spot for new ideas and new technology. We had a group of folks in our business that were working on the biggest account we had, which was Saturn at the time. We were really rocking it with Saturn, if you can think back in 1993 and the commercials we were doing with Saturn. We were breaking the mold in car advertising.

We had a division of the company at Riney that created brochures, and they would do the Saturn brochure, which we called the Full Line Brochure, and they would do the owner's manual, and a bunch of the other collateral material that was used to support the Saturn car line. A couple of them were really interested in this new thing called the web. We started this group after work to discuss it, which just shows what a bunch of geeks we were that we would get together after work.

For us, my first involvement with the Internet came through our design group. We would get together after work and create these static screens that you could put on the web, and we did it because we all thought it was kind of fun and it was an interesting new delivery system for material.

Of course, the web back then was very static, and more importantly, we were fascinated with the idea of creating collateral material where you didn't have to pay for printing. That's how it started for us. Could we create a brochure, which is a static delivery system? Could we do it and save money on paper? And that's how it all began for me.

I haven't heard anybody come at it from quite that exact angle yet, it's a very unique way to approach the business.
We had a design firm called Bradford Huber. Linda Bradford and Paul Huber were the guys that ran our design capability. They were the ones who introduced me to it, and we came at the Internet the first time because the three of us were really fascinated with the Internet as a delivery system. It's interesting that our creative guys who were into it, were not the leading edge; they were interested in making TV commercials. Hal was always so TV focused but our media department was interested in online, although it was still early days for them.

Do you remember anything specific that brought the Internet from an after-work activity into the day-to-day client activity?

It was so much fun to be in San Francisco running a well-known national creative agency in 1994. I was lucky enough so that when guys like you are asking me my opinion about where I was when the revolution started, I can honestly say I was right in the middle of it. It's hard for me to remember a seminal event. I can only remember certain things, but a couple of things come to mind. One was the role that *Wired Magazine* played in the revolution.

You have to remember that seventeen years ago, or sixteen or fifteen years ago, when we're talking about the early days of the Internet, the Internet was a pretty static medium. We were all using AOL to get on the web. It was a dial-up service, the interface was really clunky and it was static. I find it fascinating what we're talking about today, but I remember talking to guys like you about whether we were ever going to get motion on the Internet. It was a totally static delivery system. It was a system for a printed page. The big break-through moments were when we got to animation, and when we got live, full-motion animation. I'm not talking about video – we dreamed of getting video on the Internet – I'm just talking about adding motion to the delivery system.

I would read articles about what the Internet would be and then I'd look at the screen as to what it was, but I must say that I didn't have the imagination to think about what it could be. But *Wired* opened my mind to it. A second firm that I think deserves a lot of credit was Organic. We reached out to Organic in '94, '95 on

Saturn because we began to see what the Internet could do, and frankly, we were looking at Organic as a specialty company that could help create the online content. So to me, Organic was actually an important company. I think they deserve some credit for at least one big ad agency and one big car account and helping us mainstream the idea of the Internet as a medium for commercial persuasion.

The third seminal event back then was looking at AOL and the delivery of all those diskettes. You remember the CD-ROMs that AOL would send out? We used to get them in the mail. I remember getting them in these tin boxes. They were beautiful, but AOL would send out CD-ROMs that would allow you to sign up for the AOL service. I want to say in their peak year, they mailed out 300 million of them. I remember a statistic from when we formed Carat in 1998 and one of the first companies we bought was a company called Freeman & Associates, which actually managed the AOL acquisition campaign. I believe the statistic was AOL mailed out in 1998 enough of those to have every household in the United States receive five. Every household on a per capita basis would have received five AOL sign in diskettes.

Those are the three seminal things that helped me think about the possibilities of the Internet: *Wired Magazine*, an agency called Organic and the almost omnipresence of the AOL sign-up CD-ROMs.

A couple of people have brought up the AOL diskettes as really evangelizing the Internet, and it's true because they were everywhere. I knew people that were doing art installations with those discs because there were so many of them.

Yeah, they were beautifully packaged, you'd get them in your mailbox, and it certainly got me on AOL. I remember when I got my Mac computer and I signed up to the AOL service, and I used to stay up late checking it out. If you remember, AOL was an entry ramp onto the Internet. It had its own content, and then there was a button that said, "Connect to the Internet." It was really slow and it was not a wonderful experience, but Jesus, that's the only way to get on the Internet, right? It was dial-up, and you'd dial into your phone line, you heard that little modem sound as the thing clicked on and that was your gateway to the web.

I will say one other thing that, at least in my life, helped me and that was the rise of video gaming. You would go out and buy a submarine game or a flight simulator and stick it in your Mac, and with your mouse you'd do what we would consider to be unbelievably rudimentary gaming versus what we see today. Don't underestimate the role that gaming played in getting all of us to both buy computers, as well as to begin to think about, gee, there could be some graphics on this thing. The Internet was this static delivery system and mainly text-based, but then when you turn off the Internet and pop in a game you would have some heightened graphics and you'd start saying, there's a whole lot more that can be done with the Internet part of my computer.

That's a good point and not a lot of people have correlated those two things, so it's nice to hear someone actually talk about it that way.

They showed you the possibility. If you were a gamer and you were fooling around with the Internet, the user experiences were quite different. The gaming experience was rudimentary by today's standards, but it was graphic. It was a graphic interface. You used your mouse to play a flight simulator or a torpedo game. I remember I played PT109. My wife got it for me for my birthday or something on a Mac. It was a torpedo game and it had some graphic capabilities. The Internet experience was all text and all static, but you began to see how the two worlds could collide.

You launched Carat Interactive during a period where the economy took one heck of a beating, but you continued to build a business when a lot of other people didn't believe in it. What was it that got you to say, we're going to put some money into this because we know there's an area of growth here.

Let's fast forward. We've talked about from '93 to '98 when I was running Hal Riney & Partners, the Internet was beginning to grow, we were beginning to see the growth of the Internet from 1994 to 1998. When did AOL and Time Warner merge? What year would that have been?

I think that was '98 or '99.

So roughly at this time period you're talking about AOL at its peak, market capital $170 billion, and a subscriber base that, my guess, was twenty-five million plus. That's kind of where we were when we started Carat in the United States in 1998. Now Carat was the largest buyer of advertising time and space in Europe by a mile, still is. So Carat was a media services company and the European model of advertising had broken a decade prior in the

'70s. Really, creative and media had broken apart in Europe and there were separate firms that made ads and separate firms, like Carat, that bought time and space that were both planning and buying media campaigns, the media side of media campaigns.

So I was asked in late 1997 to launch Carat and to bring the European model for Carat to the United States; to do that I moved from San Francisco to New York. That strategy that we opted to use was a fairly classic business school strategy, although one that's difficult to do, which is called a roll-up. So fundamentally, the idea was to buy companies. We bought a media buying service in New York called MBS and we bought a media buying service in Los Angeles that was named ICG, and we merged those two companies into one company called Carat. That was the beginning of Carat. We bought a marketing analytics company called MMA in Wilton, Connecticut, and so we began using acquisition as a way to build the business.

There are a couple of stories at this juncture that you may find interesting. One was we bought this company up in Boston called Freeman & Associates, and we mainly bought them because they were the AOL diskette guys. Freeman & Associates did not have an Internet division at the time. Freeman & Associates was really the leading buyer of high technology media, so you have to go back to 1998; those are the days of a magazine called *PC Week* or *PC Magazine*.

I remember I met Michael Dell right after he came out of the University of Austin. For those of us who are really old, many people don't know that the original name Michael Dell started the company, PCs Unlimited, and it was a four-page insert that would be stuck in the back of *PC Magazine*, and an eight-page magazine in the back of other high technology mags like *PC Week*. It was an eight-page insert of product, feature, and price that Michael would put in there, and it was Riney that made the conversion from calling the company PCs Unlimited to Dell.

So there was an agency called Freeman & Associates, and that was what they did. They were a media planning and buying company with a specialty in high technology companies, so they worked for AOL and did their diskette work. They worked for Citrix, they worked for a bunch of high technology companies, and they would buy advertising, manage advertising buys mainly in the specialty of high technology print, which is really how you advertised high technology companies at the time. We bought that company, and that was our foray into high technology or into technology media at the time.

The Internet was starting to take off, and for those of us that remember 1998/1999, those were the glory days. These were the days when you were seeing companies come and get multiples that were at eight times fourth-quarter revenue, or projected revenue, right? Those were *crazy* days when almost all of us in the traditional business world were looking at these companies and thinking, all you have to do is start a company, get a couple million dollars of revenue, and you can sell these companies for tens and twenties of millions of dollars. So as I was building this company in the United States, I was under real pressure from our owners, Aegis, the owner of Carat. They were a publicly traded company in the London Stock Exchange. We were doing a roll-up and I started catching grief from our board of directors and our group CEO in London who said, "What's your Internet strategy, David? What is our plan to get into the Internet?" They wanted me to buy companies. They wanted me to buy some Internet ad agencies like yours, like Freestyle Interactive.

I looked at a bunch of companies. At the time, there weren't that many to buy that were left standing. San Francisco was where a bunch of them were. I flew to see a company called i-traffic. I don't know if you remember i-traffic.

I was one of the early team at i-traffic.
I remember i-traffic was run by a guy who I knew from J. Walter Thompson. I don't think he ran it but he was adult supervision. I think his name was –

Ron Kovas.
Ron Kovas, you remember him?

We hired him to run us and get us to sell. He really helped us get over the hump, so to speak.
Yes, that's right, and the guy that started i-traffic, Scott Heiferman. I went to see Scott Heiferman. Now remember, I knew Ron Kovas because he was from J. Walter Thompson, San Francisco. So there weren't that many companies out there to buy, so I went, I sat down with Ron, I sat down with Scott, and we talked about how I was interested in the business. That company was booming. I remember walking into that New York office and you had desks that were like old wooden doors thrown up on filing cabinets, and there were eighty people in

there running campaigns, and the company was growing like a weed.

I can't remember the numbers, but Ron was very bullish on the company, Scott was unbelievably bullish on the company, and these were the guys that taught me the early Internet agency business. I looked at buying all these companies and I met Scott. I want to say Scott and Ron were prepared to sell the company for $100 million, right? Now meanwhile, this is a $100 million for a company that was maybe doing revenues of $8 million. So as a traditional businessman I just couldn't do it, I just couldn't pull the trigger on that.

So then I went to see Lot21, I came to see you at Freestyle Interactive, and there were six other companies out there and I met all of you. The multiples were just crazy. I think the seminal event came in about 2001 when I really started to take a liking to a company called Lot21. It was run by a lady called Kate-Everett Thorp, and COO was Eric Wheeler.

The funny story was I was under real pressure to buy an Internet agency. I had a big publicly traded company behind me. I had bought a couple media buying service companies and merged them into Carat. I bought two companies in Canada. I bought Freeman, and I was under real pressure to get us an online or Internet agency. Kate was prepared to sell.

We got pretty far, we were simpatico, I liked them, and so long story short I got approval to buy Lot21. I got approval to buy Lot21, so I flew out to San Francisco and had a meeting with Eric and Kate, and they had their financial advisors there; it was a company called Lazard Frères. The story that I'll tell is that I was authorization to buy Lot 21 up to a price of $40 million. I sat down and we began the negotiations face-to-face; Kate and Eric on their side of the desk with Lazard Frères, and I with my CFO and a couple of people.

We began the discussions and I said to them, I'm prepared to buy the company and I'd like to make you an offer. I flew all the way here from New York; I'm ready to make a deal. They said, okay, let's do it. So I said, I'll offer you $25 million for the company right now. We can talk about an earn-out, and you can make some more on top of that, but I'll offer you $25 million.

At the time, Lot 21 maybe was doing $4 to $5 million of revenue, and I'm not sure it was very firm revenue at that. They said, thank you very much, it's a good offer. Would you mind going into the front lobby and waiting there? We'd like to talk a little bit about it and come back and give you our reaction. I waited in the lobby maybe twenty-five minutes with my team. They asked me back in and said we'd like to make you a counteroffer. Our counteroffer is $80 million.

Meanwhile, I knew that all I had was $40 million, so I knew that even if we split the difference we weren't going to get the $40 million. So I said you know what, we're just too far apart and I don't see how we're going to bridge the gap. Thank you very much I'm heading back to New York. They were very confident, you know Kate and you know Eric.

I left for New York and I called London when I got to New York and said, I've got to fly out. I flew to London and I met with the group CEO and said, look, this is insane. I told him the story I just told you, and said for $25 million I can build an Internet company. Instead of paying $80 million for this company let's take the $25 million that we would have spent and let's start building our own company. This can't be that hard. And that's how we did it at Aegis. We took Freeman & Associates and a lady named Sarah Fay, who was the No. 2 person at Freeman; I said, I'll give you $6 million and I want you to build me an online agency.

We incubated it out of our high technology print agency and we built an Internet agency together. I'll make some other acquisitions and let's build it. I made that decision in October 2000. When did the Internet crash happen? April of 2001 is my recollection. So I made the decision not to buy, and in October 2000 I made the decision to start building my own interactive agency's capability, and by April the market fell to hell in a hand basket.

I went from being a goat, catching unbelievable grief from my board about why I had no Internet strategy and why I didn't make an acquisition in July of 2000, by April of 2001 people were calling me a frigging genius. All of a sudden my board turns to me and says, David, you are prescient. You are a visionary. I can't believe you saw this coming, David.

The only reason I hadn't done it was I just couldn't rationalize the price and we decided to build our own, then by April of 2001, when the crash happened, all of a sudden I looked like a genius. At that point I was committed to the strategy. We were starting to build our own business, Carat Interactive we called it at the time. Sarah Fay was leading it. We were starting to get some traction.

We invested $6 million in the business, hired people and went out and started pitching accounts. The funny thing that people still laugh at is then, in 2001/2002 as the business started to move, the market, as you may remember, crashed in terms of Internet agencies. I can remember at that point all we had was the static banner and this is before full-motion video. We said, is this the Internet? This is it; this silly little banner that's this big and doesn't move? This is the revolution, what we've all been waiting for, two inches big on the screen?

If you remember, all of a sudden the companies that I had been visiting went from enormous evaluations to barely hanging on. I did a roll-up of that, too. We ended up buying Lot21 for $3 million. I still tease Eric and Kate. I said, you know, I had $40 million. Had you guys countered $25 million at $35 million, you'd have $35 million in your pocket right now. I went and bought a bunch of agencies, including yours. I bought a company called Vizium, which was in the email marketing space, and Freestyle Interactive and a bunch of other interactive shops, and we used the strategy of a combined roll-up and organic growth to build the Internet business.

That's when I went back to London and met with a guy named Nigel Morris, and the two of us said we really should think about this digital space and now is the time to be buying up these agencies internationally. We made the decision to form Isobar, Nigel's name for the company, and we began to do a global roll-up. Nigel had seen what we had done in the U.S. with the creation of Carat Interactive and the roll-up of Vizium, Lot21, Freestyle and iProspect. We said, gee, if we can do that in the United States let's start doing it around the world.

Of course, that turned out to be a pretty prescient strategy because Aegis was the only company really buying these agencies from 2001 until 2004 when the market picked back up. I must tell you, we really got the pick of the litter! I remember Nigel and I talked about getting into search engine marketing, which was pretty early, and we bought a wonderful web development and integration company called Molecular, and then we started buying AgenciaClick down in Brazil, and of course, this is all a big progression, but you know the strategy when you and I worked together.

Isobar was really the first global network. I want to say we bought almost sixty companies in the course of what Isobar is today. So that's really how it happened.

After ten or eleven years you left Carat and went to build out Canoe Ventures. My understanding of what you're doing right now is trying to figure out how digital integrates into the world of television. Where do you think that side of the business is headed?

Let me just give you some basic background on Canoe. I wrote a book in 2007, a fairly simple book about the media business that guys like you and guys like me could give to our moms and dads because our moms and dads have never understood. My dad's a dentist and he still doesn't know what the hell I do. So I wrote a book to try to demystify the American media business from an advertising perspective, and in it I wrote about the opportunity if the U.S. cable TV MSOs, if the big cable companies could ever get their footprints to be interoperable and interconnected that we could create an interconnected digital platform for television.

The Internet is a ubiquitous platform, but television has been very balkanized. Comcast has a footprint, Time

Warner has a footprint, Cox, Cablevision, and those foot-prints have been built by acquisition and are very hetero-geneous. So the vision I talked about in the book was, what if we could get the six big U.S. cable TV companies to create some software and put it in set-top boxes to make it interoperable? We could turn TV into an inter-operable digital platform and begin to bring some of the functionality from the Internet on to the television.

In 2008 a guy named Steve Burke, who's the COO of Comcast showed up in my office and said, "I read your book." He said, "Let's do it. Let's do what you said to do in the book. Let's create an interoperable, interconnected cable platform by combining the six big U.S. cable TV companies. I love that idea and I'd like you to lead it. I'll give you the money, and we'll create a joint venture and do it."

I found that to be pretty interesting, and that's what I've been doing. So two and a half years ago we were able to get the six big U.S. cable TV companies to form a joint venture called Canoe. We call it Canoe because when we gave the initial speech we talked about how all six companies needed to get into a boat together; we all needed to get into the same boat. I liked the visual of a canoe. It's a wonderful way to travel but very tippy, and only if we stay together can we create a coast-to-coast, national, interoperable, interconnected footprint for tel-evision. And that's what we've been doing.

So Canoe, what we've done is created software that we've dropped in America's set-top boxes – that little device below your television set – and we've created kind of an MS Dos or Windows for a set-top box. We've cre-ated software that we can download into your set-top box overnight. You're sleeping while we update your program guide, and it's some common operating software that makes all of the American set-top box infrastructure interconnected and interoperable and allows us to create a single application, and in this case, the first product coming to America's television sets is interactive television; something we've been talking about since 1977, and son-of-a-gun if we haven't done it. We have almost 20 million households on an interconnected, interoperable, multi MSO platform that is allowing interactivity to come to your television set.

So soon, the first products you're going to see are really the interactive television coming to your television set. Imagine watching an Orbit's Gum ad, a thirty-second ad just like you see today, but what you're going to see is a little pop-up, we call it an overlay, come up on the bottom of the TV screen in the commercial and it's going to say, would you like to get a free sample of the new Orbit's Menthol Gum? – Click 'yes.' You'll use your up/down select button on your remote control, click that button, and five days later there's going to be a pack of gum in your mailbox.

That's interactive TV, and that's coming to American television sets. So what we've tried to do with Canoe is look at how can we make TV even better, how can we study what the Internet does, and where the online environment has done well from both a consumer experience and an advertising opportunity, and see if we can bring the best of the online, the best of the Internet to television. You'll use your existing remote control to click on a TV commercial and get a product sample or a brochure.

Six months from now you're going to be able to click on a TV commercial and have a coupon sent to your email address. Within a year you're going to be able to watch a cooking show and click to have the recipe emailed to your email address with coupons for the ingredients. You're going to start seeing polls come on your television set, just like you see now. Right now there are lots of polls on TV, but the way you interact with them is with SMS; you use your text message. Think about ESPN, they're doing a poll on almost every sport center but the current way you enter the poll is you text. Within eighteen months you're going to do that with your remote control.

Soon you're going to be able to vote for player of the game. You'll be watching a sports event, the Super Bowl, and you decide who the player of the game is. You'll use your remote control to vote. You're going to see trivia games come to your television set. So imagine you're watching a movie channel and all of a sudden, you've seen the movie nineteen times before and the slate pops up in the movie and says, "Would you like to play a trivia game along with today's movie?"; maybe just once an hour, or twice. You're watching *The Godfather* and the slate pops up and it says, "Who was offered the part of Michael Corleone before Al Pacino?" There will be four guesses. If you click 'yes' you'll get 10 points, if you get 100 points you'll get a free video-on-demand rental.

We're moving ourselves towards t-commerce, where you're watching that infomercial for a Snuggie, or a Sham-Wow, or a Slap Chop, or one of those CD collections and with two clicks of your remote control and a PIN code, you can buy the product. I don't know about you, but I see a lot of products on TV I'd like to buy, but

I typically don't get off the sofa and go to the Internet or take down an 800 number and call. But t-commerce is coming to your TV set within probably eighteen months of us speaking here today if you're a cable TV subscriber.

And then finally, deterministic voting, so instead of using your phone to vote for *American Idol* or to vote for *Survivor,* you're going to be able to do deterministic voting with your remote control. Imagine watching the news and being able to participate in a poll about the labor unrest or the legislation in Wisconsin that so many people are upset about. Imagine, instead of 500 people or 1,000 people being polled, 5 million people could express their opinion. That's coming to television. We think that that's the best of Internet functionality.

You're also going to see what we call "addressability" come to TV, which is the ability to put dog food commercials only in houses that own dogs, and cat food commercials only in houses that own cats. On the Internet we call that behavioral targeting. But remember, with TV as a cable company we know your name and address. We know who you are, so you're not a cookie. You're not an ISP address. In our case, you're a customer. We know exactly who you are and we could target your advertising load to your interests or your zip code. That's called Addressable Advertising. That's probably two years away. We already have it deployed in all of New York on Cablevision.

And then the third thing you're going to see come to television is really a much better video-on-demand experience. If you think about what Hulu is, or if you think about what YouTube is, they're video-on-demand. They're video-on-demand delivery systems; YouTube mainly for user- generated content, and Hulu really is just a superior video-on-demand player using the online delivery system. Add supported video-on-demand, being able to look at if you're a *Man vs. Wild* fan, which is one of my favorite shows, right now you can't really order those up on video-on-demand because we haven't figured out a way to do what's called dynamic ad insertion, which is to put an ad in pre-roll in that library on your TV set. That also is coming to your television set. That's probably about two years away. You'll be able to order up a library of TV content and we'll be able to dynamically put an ad in. So you could get a different ad than your next door neighbor. So your TV is about to get some of the best of the Internet functionality. The targeting capability of the Internet, the interactivity capability of the Internet, the on-demand playability of the Internet, and then using set-top box data we'll be able to give the metrics of the Internet. So TV is about to get back in the game, my friend.

I'm still a firm believer in television, so I'm looking forward to all this stuff coming out. I'm definitely excited about it.

You should be. It's neat stuff.

CLOSING REMARKS

David Verklin was an amazing leader to work under. He has a fervor and passion for the business that is infectious. Just re-reading this interview now reminds me of the excitement he is able to inject into you as you sit on the other side of the table. There are many ways to lead a company, and David was fond of the analogy that we were pirates raiding the seas of Internet marketing. He is a visionary, both in his view of the agency world as well as in his view of the world of marketing in general.

LARRY KRAMER

L arry Kramer is President and Publisher of USA Today
and was one of the guys that truly shaped the way ads
are shown on the Internet. Larry came into the business
by way of the world of newspapers, and along the way
he founded *CBS Marketwatch* back in February of 1994.
CBS Marketwatch became one of the original "big boys"
leading the way and blazing a path for Internet-based
content and integrated marketing opportunities. *CBS
Marketwatch* was one of the premier brands online and
pioneered the use of larger, integrated, rich media units
including full-page takeovers and synchronized units
with brands like Budweiser. Without Larry's vision
leading the way, the industry could have been overrun
by pop-ups and the 468x60 could still have been the way
things were done.

In addition, Larry has worked in the VC arena and chaired a number of companies, and most recently he authored a book called, *C-Scape: Conquer the Forces Changing Business Today.* He is a Syracuse University alumni and a mentor to a number of wonderful people in this business.

Larry Kramer, what is your title now? What do you go by?

Oh, boy, I don't know that I have a title. I am somewhere between a media consultant and an author. I currently serve on several boards and am also a director in seven companies. In addition, I teach. I'm an adjunct professor at Syracuse. I am involved in a little bit of everything but I have been spending a great portion of my time speaking lately because my book has just been published. The book release provides me with an opportunity to speak to numerous groups using it as a hook.

How did you get started in media?

I got started in media when I was about ten or eleven. I was a newspaper boy at the *Bergen Record* in New Jersey at the time and we used to have split session in junior high, which simply meant I was done with school by noon. I would spend my remaining time downtown in Hackensack where I used to walk over to the newspaper office since my side job was to deliver papers. I would then wait for the papers to be printed at around 1:00 or 1:30 and hitch a ride on the truck home so I didn't have to spend money on taking the bus.

During the hour and a half that I spent in the news-room, waiting for the papers to be printed, I fell in love with the place and became the new pet for the newsroom. As soon as I could I got a job there. I started working in the circulation department and then moved on to journalism, covering mostly junior high and high school activities. When I became the editor of the school paper, I knew from that moment on that my career goal was to edit a big city newspaper.

I attended Newhouse School at Syracuse University after I graduated from high school in New Jersey and when I completed my degree at Newhouse in '72, I went to Harvard Business School with the hopes of becoming an investigative reporter in the world of business. If you recall, all this took place during the Watergate era when journalists began to use the phrase, "Follow the money." Most of my friends in journalism school and I decided to pursue journalism because we felt it was a way for us to change the world. It wasn't about the money, it wasn't about anything else; it was simply something we felt very passionate about.

My first job out of Harvard Business School was reporting for the *San Francisco Examiner*. After spending three or four years there I was hired by *The Washington Post*, which was the very heart and soul of investigative reporting. I spent the next ten years at *The Post* with the first three or four year as a reporter. They then asked me to take an editor position up at *The Trenton Times* in New Jersey, which they owned. So I was around thirty years old when I first became a newspaper editor. *The Trenton Times* was a mess when I got there but we were able to turn it around, even make it profitable, and then the post decided to sell it.

After the sale I returned to *The Washington Post* as an assistant managing editor where I ran the local news there. I probably could have stayed there forever except I received a call from William Hearst III, who had been a reporter with me at *The Examiner* and also a friend of mine, informing me that he was going to go back to be publisher at his family-owned paper and wondered if I would like to be editor there? This was my dream job, to be editor-in-chief of a major metropolitan daily, and it was in a great city.

I was thirty-five when I took that opportunity, had a wonderful five years, and then we hit a recession in '90. It was unfortunate because we had just accomplished so much. We had opened bureaus and had dramatically improved the paper. We even won the Pulitzer! But then I had to deal with a recession and lay off numerous employees. We also had to close down the new bureaus. Realistically, I burned out after five years into my dream job and I was clueless about my future. I had spent almost a whole year just handling retrenchment. The Hearst people were great when it came to my turn. I told them, look, I'm going to negotiate my own exit. And they responded, we'll buy you a year. They basically gave me a year's worth of severance and told me if I really wanted to return after that they might be able find something for me somewhere else in the company. But they knew I wouldn't be back. They handled the situation very well.

I needed time to process what had occurred during my time off and by the time I started searching for jobs again, all of the real media jobs were no longer in San Francisco. Due to the recession, there weren't many jobs anywhere. I did have some opportunities in New York and Atlanta. It just so happened that a friend of mine wanted to start a company in Silicon Valley where he was already part of a company that transmitted real-time stock quotes over the air into a portable device called Quotrek. It was the only portable device carrying real-time stock prices. They used FM sideband to broadcast the information at a time when there was no Internet, virtually no wireless, none of that stuff.

My friend wished to create a sports version of Quotrek. They had initially built this network to transmit financial data. Financial data traffic was busy 9 a.m. to 5 p.m., Monday through Friday, which meant that this network wasn't being utilized during weeknights as well as weekends. My friend then suggested, why not broadcast sports information over the network during that down time because that's when sports are taking place? My main concern at the time was just going through the process of starting a business, which I had never done. It took me awhile to warm up to the idea. I would be transitioning my career path into becoming an entrepreneur after spending most of my time working at two big media companies, Hearst and *The Washington Post*. Even though I earned a degree from Harvard Business School, I only went there because I wanted to cover investigative business not to be an entrepreneur. However, the idea became more interesting to me, especially after going through the process of downsizing a company firsthand. That process truly inspires you to want to be in control of your business because you just think you can do it better.

This new sense of direction was really important to me because it gave me the chance to see if I could do better when in control. As for the rest of the jobs I found, they were all located in great places but, again, they would be line jobs as an editor or running a portion of a newsroom for CNN or a section of *The New York Times*. While these jobs were all interesting, I wasn't going to own anything or be in control so I decided to take a leap of faith. It would have been even more difficult for me if I hadn't had that year where I was being cushioned because I had a family of two children and a big house in Tiburon, so my decision certainly was a risk at the time.

Sometimes you have to look down the valley and say to yourself; okay, if this doesn't play out then I only have six months to turn my life around. Now my family never believed in this notion. The only thought they had regarding this change was, no problem. In fact, I remember that right before I made the decision I was talking to wife and two kids out on our deck in Tiburon, who I think were nine and five at the time, and I said, here are the choices guys, either I go to New York or I go to Atlanta or I take a chance and become an entrepreneur, which has a lot of risk, but we'll be here. They then asked me to leave the deck because they wanted to "caucus." After about five minutes, they called me back and said, okay, we think you should take the job that you want to do. Whatever you really want to do, and if it's New York or Atlanta, we'll see you on weekends.

Basically I had a lot of incentive to try and become an entrepreneur but not before I warned my wife, you know, 95 percent of entrepreneurs fail, the other 5 percent live in Tiburon. She thought everybody was a successful entrepreneur. Since many of our friends in Tiburon were entrepreneurs, why couldn't I be one? But they were very supportive and said they understood.

So I entered into that business and we started raising money from our friends and family. Once we started our business the company that created the financial device where my friend came from actually invested in us, and housed us because we used their network. We were essentially using their device, but were just creating a different look for a sports version of it. Additionally, we changed the software to produce a sports appeal and to have it take in sports information.

As we were in the midst of creating this sports product, I actually learned a lot about the difference between customer-paid content and free content; without advertising on this new platform, our business was all paid content. You couldn't really put ads on it, so in a way it was like the old digital. Think of it as an old digital watch or something like that.

Like a beeper.

Exactly, just like a large beeper. I learned a couple of things during this process. First, I learned that everyone who purchased a Quotrek, the real-time stock market transmission, absolutely loved it, but the cost was $200 per month. So in the end the only people who would pay for this service were people that were heavily involved in the stock market. They understood that it made them money.

Well, it turned out to be a very similar situation in the world of sports, except we only charged $40 or $50 a month. Now everybody wanted the information, because there was no ESPN back then there was no way of finding out of town scores. Furthermore, the absence of the Internet at the time made it tough for the displaced fan. For example, if you cared for Syracuse and lived in San Francisco, you really couldn't find out the final score until maybe the next day at the fastest. The only other alternative was to call these 900 numbers and get charged a lot of money to finally get a score of a game.

It was this aspect of the business that I found interesting. It turned out that everybody who got our service on a free trial loved it, but the only people who would ultimately pay for it were those who were heavily involved in sports betting. And of course the last thing I put on the device before we launched was real-time odds from Vegas, and the combination of the odds and the real-time scores were enough to get every heavy hitter interested because if the person could see how the movement of the line before his bookie, he would instantly know if it was a good idea or not to bet. This lesson didn't hit me until later on. Anyway, our business did well enough for the stock market transmission company to exercise an option to acquire us in '93, they also asked me to stay and continue running the business.

They told me, we want you to run the sports business but we're worried about the financial business. They owned the market for day traders, plus their product was significantly cheaper than the next product up that could give you real-time data. It was either Bloomberg or Reuter's Terminal or something like that at the time. This was the beginning of the Internet trading boom and it was becoming increasingly popular that people traded stocks at home. For that community, this was the only practical way to get real-time data.

My response to them was, look, if all you're going to give people is real-time quotes, which is a commodity itself, it's ultimately going to be about who charges less, that's it. But if you want to keep your customer base the best thing to do is the only thing I know how to do, which is to add news. Add something unique. I'll build a newsroom, a small newsroom, and we'll start to cover news about stocks. We'll do whatever it takes to give traders added value. Then they may not want to switch their subscription to somebody else who is just offering them prices.

They were happy about this suggestion, so I started building that newsroom in '93 and called it DBC Online. Once the web started to take off we were able to play with it and put up more news and delayed stock prices on the web. And I started to add more and more content to the web because there was only so much room available on the device and this allowed us to give our customers even more. The concept was to guide the people who bought the device onto the web as the web was being built. I then went to my old newspaper buddies and said, why don't we do your stock pages online? Because they were all thinking about online businesses now.

This led the way to a deal with *USA Today*. It was the first big deal we signed and we basically created the *USA Today* financial pages online. It was a way for them to have a current financial web business online without putting anything into it because they had to do something.

Sure, just to make any of the content.
Yes, as a matter of fact, we actually housed it. The only catch was we just made our pages look like theirs when it was really on our own URLs. People weren't even reading URLs then. Nobody even knew what syndication was. This was when I told myself, there's a business here. This is going to be a good business. News will be distributed

over this and financial news will be particularly important on this new platform. And I stopped to think about how the people who were spending $2,000 a month on what they were getting for their financial information; basically they had their own private Internet service.

As I'm watching this service develop, I thought; this is what every trader's going to want at home too. They want a page that's going to give them both the news and the data. This is going to be a gold mine as an Internet business. So I returned to DBC and proposed a deal. I told them I'm really getting the hunger for being an entrepreneur. This is going to be a big business. I know that news and sports information on the web are going to be big because timeliness matters. By definition, the way they get their information now is too old and if I can give anybody what looks a lot like, or better than, a Bloomberg Terminal or a Reuters Terminal for the stocks that they only care about, that could be huge. And this was an important thing for years later. I was obsessed that it would be free.

Since it's a new medium and people just don't quite understand it yet, I know that advertising will follow if I can get a big enough audience. So I approached my bosses and made them a deal; let me get a media partner – I know the media world, I know these people – let me bring them in. Let me spin this out as a separate company. You'll own 45 percent the media company will own 45 percent and 10 percent will go to me and this small staff that I put together. I'll take handshake that you'll do that, and I'll build that business. But you're going to need the media partner, so I think you should do this with me. We'll create a new company that'll have a bigger net worth than this company overnight. Even though the business will be much smaller, it'll be an Internet business. People will value it highly.

I decided to make a pitch to CBS. I first talked to CNBC about being our partner and they were interested but their response was basically, yes, this will be great. As soon as we merge it we'll take over the news operation. And I responded, you don't understand Internet news, it's different. "No, no, we know news; you just give us the technology." So I thought, oh god, they're clueless.

Now CBS, on the other hand, had an opposite reaction. They said, "This is a big story, financial news. We have one guy covering Wall Street for both CBS TV and radio"— nice man named Ray Brady who was about seventy – "and we're up against NBC," which had CNBC at the time. And they said, "We could use all the help we can get." I proceeded to show them the résumés of the people that I had hired for our newsroom, all from places like Reuters Bloomberg or AP. There were no Internet kids in that group, everyone was a professional. CBS responded, "That's what we need."

So it was a real testimony to partnerships, in fact, it was the perfect partnership. What they got was credibility in the financial space and better coverage without having to pay for it. I even offered to hire people who would go on TV for them, but I'd let them approve it before I hired them because it was their TV I had to put them on.

So I began bringing in people as the proposed television people, and I would also use them for a weekend show that I was creating. CBS could use them for free when big stories were breaking. I did everything I could to be a good partner with them and it paid off in the end. I took no cash from them in the beginning when we did the deal on CBS. As things progressed, I took $50 million worth of marketing and branding. We had a contract that stated I would pay CBS a percentage of my revenue for the use of the Eye as well as the name CBS, but only if they agree to market us on the CBS network to the tune of $50 million over the next few years.

As for DBC, it contributed to the ongoing business. The company only had about twenty people at the time with about a few million in revenue. We pretty much had no profits and were break even. We did have $5 million in cash from CBS. Despite its slow progress, DBC was an ongoing business that helped us build what *Barron's* identified as the best financial site on the web that year. By the time we made an announcement of the new separate company's launch, we received great coverage from *New York Times* on the front page of the business section.

Was it '94?

It was '97 when that happened. With $7 million in revenue the next logical step for us was to go public, which is exactly what we did fifteen months later. I did the road show offering the stock at $10 to $12 a share. In the first week of the road show, every account we had ordered the maximum number of shares they could get, which ended up totaling to around 50 million shares. The only problem was that we were only selling 2.7 million shares. So when we met with our banker, he told us, "This is ridiculous. This is unbelievable." I then said, "Well, we should raise the prices." He responded, "Let's try $12 to $14."

All of the people who ordered shares from the first week were informed that the price is going to be $12 to $14. Shockingly, everyone stayed in. By the time that the second week came around we got the same results as the first week, not one person bailed. So now we had institutional orders for over 100 million shares when we were only selling 2.7 million shares.

It is my belief that the people who wanted this the most were the ones who actually used the site, day traders. I was asked to conduct the third week on the road in Europe, which is the customary way you hit accounts and obtain funds. My immediate response was I'm not doing it. It's ridiculous we have too much demand already. At the height of its insanity in January, 1999, we were at the DLJ Internet Conference in San Francisco where we conducted our last road show presentation in front of 300 people. That occasion was the closest I have ever felt to being a rock star because people were just so hungry for this. We were the first IPO of '99.

After the presentation I met with the two big owners from CBS and Data Broadcasting in the room along with several other bankers. I told them we should raise the price to $35 because everybody wants a piece of it. And they said, no, you can't do that. You have to be able to defend the price as realistic and you have to have these sets of metrics in all the things you do.

Now this was all new to me back then but I understand it now. It turned out the highest they were willing to go was $17. Then they carved up the 2.7 million into small, bite-sized pieces for all these small cap funds that were investing for the IPO.

When I went into the office the next morning, I checked our time-in sales on our computers and it didn't open. I then watched a few hours go by with no trades at all. I then decided to call NASDAQ to ask them about the situation. NASDAQ told me, we have a very drastic order imbalance. We have massive buy orders and we don't have massive sell orders. And I said, well, that sounds pretty good. They said, yes, but it's too much. We're afraid of what's going to happen if we open the thing, but we'll open it before the day is over.

At 3:30 Eastern time they opened it, just half hour before the market closed. The first trade that went across was $65. It went to $130 after ten minutes. It eventually settled at $97, which meant that we had a market cap of $1 billion. Not bad for a company with $7 million in sales and no profits.

So all of the funds that came in from investing in us were out because they were all small cap funds and they got triggered out $1 billion. For a little while we were at midcap but it dropped down. And the volume of trading during that half hour was 12 million shares, which meant every share traded for five or six times in that time span. I called a meeting between our staff members, which then consisted of about thirty-five people all together in our one big office. My CFO and I told everyone, look, we don't want to hear that any of you have borrowed against these options. We couldn't sell our options because we were tied up for six months, one of the terms of an IPI. Out of the thirty-seven people, at least twenty were millionaires on paper simply based on what had just happened. I said, "This isn't real. It can't last and if you borrow against us I'll fire you. If I hear you've borrowed against these options to buy things I'll fire you." They're like, you can't fire us. I said, "Sure I can, there are no Unions I can do whatever I want. I can fire you for stupidity, which is what this would be."

Everyone was shocked by my statement but, thank god, nobody traded or borrowed. Six months passed and we were still pretty high up in the $80 range. So eventually some people did get to sell their shares and buy some luxury items such as houses, cars and whatever they desired. What happened in the next six months after that was surprising because the world collapsed. Despite the bubble burst, the company never missed a quarter. We built this company in a way that we were never losing really big money. We were only losing money on paper because as we used the CBS in-kind, it would go against our bottom line even though it wasn't a cash expenditure. We would actually be profitable cash flow-wise, but we weren't profitable on a global scale because it was as if we spent $10 million in advertising when in fact we'd spent nothing. But that's how CBS was burning down their ownership.

When the crash occurred in 2000, the stock was trading with a basket of Internet stocks. It never traded on our performance because even when we hit every quarter, never moved the stock either way. Suddenly Internet stocks started crashing and consequently we crashed. Yahoo went down to $3. We dropped down to $1.50. It was breathtaking how quickly everything happened. Thank goodness I had already done a secondary and it was able to help raise a bit more money, so I had money in the bank. There was huge pressure at that time to shift to a pay model because it sounded very familiar to what I'm hearing today in the industry because advertising was falling apart. Advertising revenues had dropped 50 percent.

In reality, if you stopped and examined everything, it was because idiot advertisers from the web, who had doomed startups that were never going to make it on the web, were burning venture money on advertising on the web in a very big way. And I said, this is just bad advertising that's stopped happening. Real advertising is going to keep growing. And I really believed in this point, as I had several debates at the time with Jim Cramer. We used to be called Kramer vs. Cramer. There was a big magazine piece about the two of us traveling together to have these debates in front of people during all of the Internet conventions. In the end, I stayed the course on free and he went to a pay model.

I suppose you can wait long enough for anything to look right, but it looked like we had made the right decision by the following year. Our valuation started to soar and the stocks started to rise. We were profitable, we were advertising-based, we had a good size audience and more importantly, we were growing. The stock went from $1 to $3 to $5 to $7 to $9 over the next four years, which was the way it was supposed to be. As a matter of fact, we had gone to the SCC right after the crash and said, look, we've got a lot of useless options. Everybody we hired since we went public, which was almost all of the staff, 300 out of 350 who had options in the 80's, or no lower than the 50's or 60's. He said those are just useless. It's a big chunk of overhang for the company, how can we legally reissue options? And they said, here's the way you can do it. They helped us with a plan that called for us to surrender them now, or pick a date when they would surrender them, and after six months you can reissue those options and start the clock on vesting again.

So it's a big loss. You can't predict what will happen during the six months before you're reissuing them again. Now they know they're going to get them in six months, but it's six months.

Plus they have to restart the investment.
Not only that but then they've got to stay. So when we decided to do it I called the staff together and they got their reissued options. I then said, now this is the way it's supposed to be. This company is doing well – we were at $3 at that point– I said, we're going to get better every quarter and it's because our performance is terrific. Sure enough, the results over the next five years made me an honest man. We kept going up in the company. By the time Dow Jones swooped in we were up to $80 million in revenue and had maybe $10 million of that in EBIDTA. It was good. It was a good business. And we didn't have to sell, we had $50 million in the bank.

For me it just validated my peers. Furthermore, everybody I talked to in the newspaper business was becoming very nervous about their lives at that point. It was a weird time because I started late as an entrepreneur, everybody I met was younger than I was. My wife and I laughed about this.

We used to attend these Internet conferences where I would be asked to speak in a bank event in Aspen. They would fly you there in a private plane and there would be four other couples that were all around twenty to twenty-five years old. I remember one couple that just bought a

$16 million house in Ross, and leveled it to build a new house. It's like, who are these people? Most of them had never lived through a downturn or got eaten alive when the downturn happened. Anyways, the basic lessons were pretty clear; I learned that advertising worked in mass-market media, and the free price was important but not the end of the world. I also learned that multiple revenue streams were good because I built the other half of the *MarketWatch* off of revenue sharing. We had built a licensing business and a number of our best clients, for obvious reasons, were brokerage firms because the call to action to trade a stock is in the news site.

It was great if you had an account at Schwab, but it didn't mean anything to them unless you traded because they made money on the trades. So they wanted people on our website because it inspired them to see what we were going to do and how to do it. But then they resented the fact that their competitors were all advertising on our site. They would approach us and say, "Can we put your content up on our site to keep our own people in our site?" And I said, sure, but you're going to have to pay us what we would have gotten for advertising. Then we would make sure we calculated the appropriate amount we would have received from advertisers, based on the number of pages that we estimated would shift to the broker's site and therefore wouldn't carry advertising any more.

The best part was we could increase our fees when the reported more page views. So we started selling to them. The way we put it to them was, fine, we don't care if it's advertising or cash payments, but we know our content's worth something and we'll get it either way. In addition, we built charts, too. We had a great charting company and we would license websites to use our charts and data on their sites. As for that business, the year our advertising went from $33 million to $16 million, our licensing business actually went from $10 million to $25 million. It proved to be a steady business that didn't drop overnight because it was based on two-year contracts. So even if things got worse, you wouldn't feel its impact until much later. Due to the contract, they would still owe that amount of money even if they discontinued our services, whereas advertising can drop overnight.

So during that whole disaster year of 2000, everybody showed huge drops. But we only appeared to be a flat company even though there had been a drop in advertising. The growth in our licensing business kept our revenues flat.

You had a safety net in place.

We did have a safety net in place. This was another lesson that I learned in the early days of entrepreneurship. Hedge your bets! I learned a lot from all the entrepreneurs that I talked to before I took the dive and I asked them, what is it? What's the secret sauce here? And they responded, there's no secret sauce. You're smart enough, you'll do great in it. You know it cold. You have the kind of background that's perfect for being an entrepreneur. The biggest issue you have to deal with about being an entrepreneur is your stomach. You have to really be prepared and willing to live a rollercoaster lifestyle, where every deal you're trying to do is drop-down-dead not going to happen half a dozen times before you finally get it done. You also have to pick yourself up every time you fall, be optimistic and believe in yourself so much that you just know you're going to make that deal happen, because anything less will drive you crazy. You'll get sick, you'll hate everything.

Okay, I think I understand that, I thought to myself. I had to do some deep thinking about this for a while. I didn't know if my risk profile would be enough.

Now you have the wisdom having gone through that, would you have handled any of those decisions differently?
There was a frustration about borrowing money from friends as well as family the first time, and that experience helped me to decide to finance the next business from Data Broadcasting. But I had to take investments from friends and family when I started my first company and it took five years before I was able to pay them back. The upside was that they got a lot of money in return, in the end, because the new company was successful and the IPO was actually what got them the original money back. The downside was they had to wait five years, and a lot of them had written their money off because they didn't know how long the process was going to take. Most people had a great attitude about this issue, but I did have a mixture of close family members, friends along with some sophisticated, big-time investors who had each put in $25,000 to $50,000. And everyone treats money differently.

As for these big time investors, a couple of them were billionaires and I am not sure they even noticed what happened along the way. They only did it as a favor to me and for that I wanted this to be a success for them as much as I did for the family.

When Data Broadcasting bought that company and I had converted their ownership to DBC Warrants, I gave up all my ownership and spread it out among these investors to increase their chances of getting a slice of the pie. I was so obsessed about it that it became a distraction. In the end, if I had any money at all, I would have put it into the DBC venture but I didn't.

After launching *MarketWatch,* I worked hard to become CBS' best partner. I even did things for them they didn't ask me to do. And there were times when my staff or managers were not happy about doing unnecessary things for CBS. My own lawyer even said once that could be trouble, because I was setting precedents. But I was also building a relationship that had foundations in trust. It takes time to do it, and sometimes it takes being more generous on one side of that discussion because the other side isn't used to it. But in the end it paid off. CBS was inclined to help us while at the same time their relationship with other web partners was much more businesslike and not all that cooperative.

In the end, being a good partner was the difference between me being able to sell the company for half a billion dollars rather than other digital partners, who effectively had to give their company to CBS. Those companies had negotiated hard over every detail of their relationship often forcing CBS to take certain tough stands. When things got tough, CBS wouldn't go an extra mile to help out because they had to work so hard for every other concession.

What's funny is you bring up one of the things I've seen as a theme throughout these interviews, which is to the

outside world this business is about technology. You built a technology business, or a journalist/technology business, yet what you're describing to me is a business based on business relationships. And that's one of the things that I think is great about this business.

It sure is. And let's not forget about technology. Even though you can look at technology as the foundation responsible for a lot of the changes right now, it only works when it's doing something that people want done. You and I could get to your hotel or my apartment faster when we leave this building on our Segways, but neither one of us has one. Segway was an interesting invention that solved the problem few people really had. For example, if I'm a mall cop I may want a Segway, but I really have no other reason to want one, right?

The difference between Facebook's success and the 499 other companies that had exactly the same software at the time, was that Facebook was a response to an existing consumer need – every college Freshman's desire to hook up – while the other guys were trying to build a market for their technology by asking you to sign up and meet new people. Turns out most people weren't looking to meet new people. You remember Friendster or Tribe? These sites were all going to help you make new friends by introducing you to a bunch of new people and most people initially didn't want to join at all because they were busy.

Facebook approached it the opposite way. Every college kid wanted to hook up the minute they got to college, right? So they're all going to bars and doing the things you have to do to meet people; this technology facilitated that process. The minute you met somebody you could now find out everything you needed to know about them. Additionally, it was safe with Facebook because at the time you could only sign up if you had the right email address and were a student in the school, the idea was brilliant. So technology frequently shouldn't be the driver, the driver should be – "There's something I want to do and the first guy who gives me the technology that lets me do that is gold."

Point in fact, the user interface elements of this are so important. If you look at Apple, which is one of the most successful companies in the world right now, they didn't invent a single product; the Apple computer wasn't the first PC by a long shot. The first PCs that came out were really good but impossible to use, not to mention took four days to set up. They didn't even think about things like color-coding the wires for the first twenty years. You had to plug in thirty wires on five different pieces and nobody could figure out how to make it work, it was a nightmare. DOS was not intuitive. Apple gave you a computer in a box, you pull out the computer and it's in one piece. All that was left was for you to plug in the keyboard and mouse and you were good to go. You didn't have to learn any programming either.

Apple also wasn't the first to invent a visual user interface, they simply put it together with the computer and made it easier to use. Moreover, the first iPod wasn't the first MP3 player by a long shot, but it was a lot easier to use. Next came the iPhone and exactly how many cellular phones did we have before that? If you ask some-body before the iPhone, would you watch video on your cellular phone? You'd only get a 7 percent to 8 percent response because people just couldn't see it. But when the iPhone came out half the population of phone users was consuming video on their phone.

But it is important to realize that they only changed consumer behavior because they took it into consideration when they designed their phone. The rest of the competition was more focused on the amount of money to be made. A more recent example of Apple's ability to see the consumer better is the iPad; it's not the first tablet by a long shot. What made these products successful was that Apple was able to identify a consumer need, which was the need for portability and fewer hassles. But at the time this need was growing faster than the ability of the mobile industry to provide that service to the consumers because phones had limitations. So it really came down to, okay, if we design a phone or device that also could do all that, this could be very cool.

Time and time again that's what Apple did; they think totally about the customer and their wants. And in any entrepreneurial business that's the most important thing. I was a strong believer in the creation of *MarketWatch* because I believed people wanted real-time market information when they were sitting at home trading. A lot of people didn't trust their brokers so they stopped using brokers, and the only other people trading are professionals who were using what looked like the Internet. A service like that for somebody at home is very intuitive. People also needed more context than the professional terminals give them. Bloomberg and Reuters, for example, brings you every headline one after the other, latest on top, because the people reading Bloomberg Terminal knows the meaning behind these headlines and don't need context. The general public does.

For example, when they saw that somebody has got two cents in earnings per share, professionals immediately knew if that price was higher or lower than their expectations and could then act upon it. We needed to build a system that not only informed the general public as quickly as something was happening, but also the importance behind this occurrence and whether it is good or bad. I also knew we had this wonderful window of opportunity when all the other competitors, such as Dow Jones, Reuters, Thompson, Bloomberg couldn't really give their best news away for free on the Internet because they were posting them on those $2,000 per month terminals. These other big companies simply couldn't handle their customers saying, "Excuse me, I'm paying you $2,000 and you're giving this stuff away for free?" So I had a period of time where I had room to build something.

You wouldn't believe we could have achieved the level of success we did with the number of working staffers we had. Our audience didn't care about derivatives they cared about the top 200 stocks they were investing in. We could give them enough information on those stocks now, and grow our coverage as our readership grew. It's all about knowing your customers, knowing potential partners and knowing your competition. All of those things are really something you've got to focus on if you're going to start a business.

CLOSING REMARKS

Larry speaks of passion and commitment to an idea. His passion was media, specifically newspapers, but he recognized an opportunity and his passions grew to meet them. As the Internet grew his vision expanded to include a world where content was being distributed digitally, and without that vision things could be radically different today!

C H A P T E R   3 0

RICH LEFURGY

Rich LeFurgy has been a board member, advisor or investor in over fifty-five online advertising companies. Drawing from a seventeen-year ad agency career in New York, he was head of sales at Starwave and the Walt Disney Internet Group (ESPN.com, NFL.com, NBA.com and ABCnews.com) and a venture capitalist in San Francisco, prior to starting advisory firm, Archer, a multifaceted advisory services company assisting early stage online media companies, in 2004.

Rich has served on company boards as a director (Blue Lithium and Associated Content, both sold to Yahoo), provided advisory services to large and small online advertising companies (Google, AOL, Blue Lithium, Glam and Placecast) and personally invested in promising online advertising startups (Ad Relevance, sold to Nielsen NetRatings, Grouper/Crackle, sold to Sony and Blue Lithium). He has long been a supporter and evangelist to help grow the industry and was the founding chairman of the IAB, the Future of Advertising Stakeholders (FAST) and the Bay Area Interactive Group (sfBIG), and has served on the board of the Advertising Research Foundation (ARF), the Advertising Education Foundation (AEF) and the advisory board of ad:tech. He remains on the IAB board today.

Additionally, Rich has received ad:tech's Industry Achievement Award, the IAB's Lifetime Achievement Award, was inducted into *Advertising Age*'s Interactive Hall of Fame and was recognized by *USA Today* as the "Johnny Appleseed of online advertising."

Rich LeFurgy, you are partner or founder of Archer Advisors?

General Partner and founder, Archer Advisors.

We've known each other for a long time. How did you get into this business?

Well, it's interesting you bring this up because I was reminded of my beginnings today when I reconnected with someone on LinkedIn. I started my career in the ad agency business in New York at NW Ayer on Madison Avenue and stayed there for seventeen years, which was quite unusual in the agency business. One of the hottest topics in marketing between 1993 and 1994 was the Information Superhighway, and coincidentally, one of my biggest clients was AT&T, which was a big participant in the discussion. I was the person in agency meetings who started lighting up when the concept of the Information Superhighway was brought up. At the same time, everybody's eyes would kind of glaze over and roll back in their heads because I did this so often. Then during fall of 1994 the AT&T corporate group starting running the first banner campaign on the web on Wired. com, the "You Will" campaign, and this was the first time I had truly seen the Internet, online advertising and the browser. I was instantly hooked. I told myself, this is it! This puts marketing all together. I am leaving the ad agency business.

In retrospect, I did this for a couple of reasons. First, the working environment in the agency was somewhat dismissive of online advertising during the mid 1990s. Television ruled the day and is still one of the heavy hitters in the industry, but nobody really wanted to challenge TV since it was Madison Avenue's cash cow. I ended up leaving New York and joined Starwave in Seattle. The biggest name in New York was Pathfinder at Time Warner, but I didn't see my transition from the ad agency to Pathfinder to be an easy one, so I found something else. Second, I was excited by the web like I was years ago by advertising in college.

And at the time Starwave had packaged together ESPN and a couple other properties right?

Right, ESPNetsportszone.com, later to be known simply as ESPN.com and OutsideOnline.com. Now for a fairly unknown but interesting fact, Starwave was actually a content company owned by Microsoft co-founder Paul Allen that licensed the ESPN name from ESPN and got a ton of online promotion in the deal to build awareness. We had editors, photo editors, writers, marketing and ad sales all built upon a fairly sophisticated content management technology platform, as well as e-commerce platform. We powered ESPN.com, and together with ESPN we eventually conducted content and ad sales deals with NFL.com, NBA.com, NASCARonline and ABCNews.com. Eventually our company was bought out by Disney, who in turn is a parent company of ESPN and ABC during the time when we essentially had editorial control over ESPN.com. I think the folks at Disney had a cow when they found out that Starwave had editorial control over ESPN.com, but at the time ESPN licensed their brand to a number of new technology platforms to generate revenue.

It's also interesting how I got started in online ad sales. In the ad agency world I was in the account management (strategy and client servicing) at Ayer and had worked with AT&T, Ralston, Purina, Proctor & Gamble, DuPont, Marriot, Burger King, Avon, along with a whole bunch of blue chip advertisers. I came across an *Advertising Age* article while I was on a plane to a new business pitch for the Gillette interactive AOR (Agency of Record) account when I saw a story about ESPNetsportszone.com. I knew that at Ayer we didn't have a tremendous amount of sophistication about online advertising internally, it was still early. When I got off the plane and went into the lobby of the John Hancock Towers building where the Gillette client was, I stayed downstairs and called up one of the names in the article, thus beginning my transition from leaving the agency business to joining Starwave.

And how was it trying to sell digital media and Internet to brands back then?

The whole process was challenging. There were pockets of folks in various agencies such as MCVBS that were interested in what we were doing, but paying for advertising online was still a new concept. Most potential clients wanted to put our content on their site to generate traffic rather than buying banner ads, so I spent a good three months pitching banner and sponsorship programs with very little success. Maybe it had something to do with the fact that the *Advertising Age* article that I had read stated that ESPN was planning on selling online ad campaigns for $1 million.

After a while the insertion orders finally started to come in as the Internet was growing within the agency world by midsummer of 1995, the time at which ESPN. com was one of the biggest destination sites on the web. That was also about the time when Yahoo! jumped on the scene and started to grab their share of the pie. There was no such thing as CPMs or guarantees back then. A lot of the stuff that people take for granted now, we were the ones to develop it over time and I credit InfoSeek with establishing CPMs, more specifically Molly Ford, who I think eventually went on to AOL with Richard Ward. The takeaway here is that we were living in a time where online ad sales was the Wild West.

You mentioned that at Starwave you were having difficulties in selling the banner campaigns, but eventually some of the brands turned around. But then you also mentioned an epiphany when Yahoo came in the marketplace and started doing well. Were they able to help the brands and the agencies understand the possibilities that were in the space?

I think Yahoo helped in the fashion that they were a reach story. Throughout history reach has been an incredible component of the media business, so it's safe to say that Yahoo really helped catapult the industry forward. Moreover, Yahoo was just an incredibly engaging site because that was when the term "surfing" was first coined. One of the counter-intuitive things we learned then was people love to look at multiple sources of information on the web rather than just going to one source. We initially thought that people would simply visit ESPN.com, bookmark it and never go anywhere else because we were the sports authority offline. But with the introduction of Sportsline.com and companies such as Yahoo, and Google later on, it was easy for people to obtain as much diverse information as possible. People now had access to numerous sources on any kind of topic that they wanted.

Do you think that the increasing clutter of competition, as well as the general desire for reach, was the biggest challenges facing web advertising at that stage, or were other things influencing it?

I think the biggest challenge with web advertising back in the mid 1990s was that the concept was just too fresh for anybody to piece everything together correctly. It certainly can be described as a tale of two cities. There was a media story occurring simultaneously with a technology story, which created some real tension within the industry. On one hand, there were great media and advertising programs that online publishers could come up with. On the other hand, technologists who lacked media background sold the accountability of the web based on click-throughs because this was a metric that could be accounted for. This was the original sin of online advertising, which was focusing on the click-through and trying to make it the coin of the realm. In hindsight, this was one of the biggest problems and persists at some level today.

One of the other issues that I tackled after founding the IAB, along with a dozen other people, was dealing with the problem of banner standards; everybody sold differently because everybody had different ad units. Some people had CPMs, others sold on CPC while the rest sold units based on hardwiring ads into the site, which was pretty prevalent in the early days. There were so many different approaches that it became a fulltime job for media buyers and planners just to keep up. As a matter of fact, this practice began to hinder the process of generating more revenue and scaling because there wasn't a set of standards for online ad sales.

Logically, one of the first things we decided to tackle was banner sizes because this was way more complicated in the online industry as compared to other media businesses. For example, in the world of newspapers, you can resize the ads in accordance to the Standard Advertising Units that the industry was familiar with. However, in the online world if a banner's size was off by one tiny pixel, it would become a visible little white dot that consumers could see; the bigger the size disparity between banners for different sites, the bigger the white space. We realized that having non-standard ad sizes was really getting in the way of scaling business across multiple sites, so we surveyed the industry and identified the most common sizes of the banners. Then we standardized everything down to just seven specific sizes that agencies and clients could develop to.

We were working with the Association of National Advertisers (ANA) and the American Association of Advertising Agencies (4A's) at that time through their combined digital initiative, which were aligned under something called CASIE (the Collation for Ad Supported Interactive Entertainment). We worked with those two trade associations to develop the first guidelines and standards. Now rather than trying to stifle innovation, we treated these standards as a jumping off point where people can use them as a stable kind of platform for further innovation. In order to get everybody on the same page we focused more on the physical side of things, therefore, we didn't deal with some of the other issues in terms of how people sold, CPM, CPC. Instead we let the market deal with the commerce side of the house.

An interesting part of the whole process was as we formed the IAB, I received a call from CASIE and they said, we want you guys to join CASIE, and you guys can be under the CASIE umbrella. My response to them was we were flattered but we thought there was more to be gained by having an independent IAB rather than by being underneath this sort of coalition. The other fun fact from those early days was when we told CASIE about what we were doing for the banner guidelines, they said, no, we have the answer, standard ad units just like the newspapers so guys can have a grid layout for your websites and you can have ads here, here and here. We then told them that's just not going to work. This is a different business from newspapers and magazine. These are startups. To change all these websites is going to cost us millions and millions of dollars. We can change the ad sizes, but we can't change the editorial format for every single site, and frankly, we don't want to necessarily have every website looking the same, we want them all to be different. So this is just one of the many examples in those early moments of figuring everything out.

It's interesting to think what the web would have looked like if it was built on a magazine/newspaper platform with set lines for the structure of the pages.

It would have been a completely different animal. Kind of boring at first, but then I think creativity would have bloomed and you would have seen a lot of different approaches.

The IAB turned into the standard bearer for the overall industry. Were there any other key achievements from those days of the IAB, beyond ad sizes, that you are really proud of?

Yeah, two achievements come to mind. The first is the IAB Price-Waterhouse Coopers revenue report that reported on quarterly revenue. We put that in place because there was the perception that many sites were just all paying each other funny money. The thought was that this money was never really changing hands but trading banners to generate traffic. So the IAB wanted to benchmark the actual ad dollars being generated to show everyone that that the revenue was not only real but that it was also growing. This was a really important foundation that is still being used today. At that time, we had a really interesting industry story to tell in that this was a real and growing industry. Later, as we know, the IAB PWC revenue report was used to document the decline and the rebound of the online ad market, as well as the strong shift to search, rich media and video.

The other achievement was the Terms and Conditions. Although they weren't perfect in the early years, the Terms and Conditions at least served as a starting point for publishers and agencies to meet together on how an insertion order in a campaign was going to run; this was a really critical piece.

A final important element of the IAB can be seen as a therapeutic organization in the early days because we were inventing and pioneering so much stuff. Whenever we got together it was like a gathering of a bunch of kindred souls. It's just great to see other people doing the same sort of thing.

Another thing was evangelizing the business to the brands, and giving them rationale to why they should be paying attention, and in general, providing a sense of maturity to an industry that was not yet mature.

Absolutely, that was a big part of the role of the IAB at the time; evangelism about the benefits of using online advertising, along with best practices of how things were supposed to be used and what was working best.

One of the biggest challenges we faced during this whole click-through focus in the early years was making sure that advertisers and agencies saw online advertising as a branding vehicle and not just as a direct marketing medium. It wasn't until fifteen to sixteen years later that we have proven that online is a branding vehicle and that the click-through is the wrong metric, even for

DR campaigns, but these issues still persist in some people's minds. When we trotted out a survey by the well-respected Rex Briggs that proved that online was a branding medium in 1997, no one listened. It's taken years for the message to sink in as the medium has matured.

Where do you think the industry has settled at this point? Do you think it's a little bit of both, or do you think it skews one way or the other?

I have always been interested to hear what people are thinking and it kills me that so many still think that it's really a direct marketing medium with very little brand advertising impact. This is just plain not true. I think of the medium as a combination of both direct marketing and brand building in what's called brand-response advertising, where you want to elicit some sort of engagement, response, conversation, click-through or most importantly a conversion. Tracking conversions, whether they are sales, registration or to get a brochure is an additional dimension online where you can take the next step that you don't necessarily have with television or print.

But similar to television and print, there's brand advertising and direct advertising. Both of these methods exist within the same television network as well as within magazines. The brand advertising runs during primetime or is in the front of the magazine, while the direct-response ads run during late night television or are in the back of the book. So the real question is not whether online advertising is best for branding or for direct-response, it's rather; what is the objective? Is it a brand campaign? Is it a direct campaign?

Now one of the things that have run full circle back in the mid '90s is using brands as destination sites. For example, Pepsi would create a huge *Battlestar Galactica* site in the middle of cyberspace and then expect everybody to visit. Many people did when sites were a novelty, but not every brand generates traffic like that because not every brand could promote it on their package or store. Using brands as a destination site went out of favor, and it started becoming more advertising oriented, where you would distribute the message out to where the consumers are. Now suddenly, brands want to have their own relationship with consumers. They want to own the audiences instead of rent them, similar to what they did in the traditional advertising paradigm. They also wanted to be able to have conversations and that part is achieved now through social networks instead websites. This is an evolution, not a revolution. This is not the only thing that's happening out there, it's just how things are developing.

What do you think is the longer impact of social on the overall efforts of brand marketers?

I think brand marketers are looking to own the relationships with consumers, which is what they should be doing. Social media can aid in the whole range of product development, research, news, crisis control, brand building and local promotion. And more importantly digital's future really comes down to the intersection between social and local; that is where the future of this whole medium lies. Whether you're a national brand or local brand or distributing all over the world, it's that intersection of social and local that is really where things are heading. Similar to the web itself, it is simply not going away. It's an evolution.

Alternatively, I do think it challenges the competencies of brands and advertisers regarding their level of preparation to deal with that proximity of establishing relationships with consumers. Advertisers will need to be staffed to have close relationships with consumers; which brands are going to embrace it versus the ones that are going to reject it? If you were to examine the top ten brands across a dozen categories, what is the list of those top ten brands going to look like in, by category, ten or twenty years from now? One of the fun things that I did in the early days of online was to look over fifty years ago in *Ad Age* when television first started. The only ones you can recognize today are the ones that embraced television with production capabilities. The ones that specialized in farm magazines or radio don't exist anymore. So it will be really interesting to see what brands emerge in ten, twenty or even fifty years, based on the actions that they've taken today.

What's the role of agencies going forward?

The role of agencies is the same as it ever was, coming up with consumer insights and great creative ideas. Unfortunately a lot of agencies have lost their way as the business has become less and less profitable. Great insights and ideas also applies to both the creative and media agencies, and I would personally love to see those two parts of the agency business come back together so that it's all under one roof. As media gets more commoditized with robot media plans, using DSPs and DMPs, along with all the different permutations where advertisers want to control their own social media presence, it is going to require agencies to raise the stakes and go back to their knitting; finding out consumer insights, ways to build the brand and deliver ideas to the consumer on both media and creative sides. That is the real role of agencies.

What about those ad networks and the ad exchanges? Do you think they're going to continue to have a strong role going forward as to how media is purchased?

I think they are going to have a place in the industry similar to how there is a place for the back-of-the-book, direct mail sort of ads. There's always going to be some undifferentiated inventory that publishers are willing to put into an exchange. The question is, can you get really good inventory and will those prices increase as a result of being on the exchange? What is going to occur is that marketers, brands and advertisers are going to take control of their own data as well as audiences. Having said that, I think this is going to put agencies in a really tough spot because publishers will even more want direct relationships with brands that know their own audiences. It's going to make things really challenging for agencies.

The other fundamental, beyond the underlying click-through foundation in the industry, is the glut of inventory within the industry. There's always somebody that's willing to sell at a cheaper price than what a publisher might think it's worth, and it used to be that the content as well as the context were the key differentiator. Now people are striving towards an audience view, and I think as advertisers begin to move more towards their customer view, it's going to really challenge some agencies and some publishers going forward.

That's probably a very valid statement. Trying to figure out how to balance all that and put it into action is also really important. There is a lot of information out there that you don't necessarily know how to put into action.

That's where the agency comes in. The agency can be the aggregator and analyst for all this data. What does it mean, what's the insight that you get out of it? And what should we do with it?

In direct marketing there's that old saying that if you give a consumer too many choices they'll choose not to choose one. It almost feels like marketers are in that state right now. They have so much data that they're paralyzed in many cases. They do not know what to do with all of it.

I think that's right. It's the tyranny of choice.

You've been influential for a lot of people, and you've been able to help figure out how to get certain kinds of companies to grow, and you've consulted or advised a lot of companies in your current capacity. How do you pick and choose the kinds of companies that you're going to work with? What kind of characteristics do you look for?

First of all I look into the future and determine whether the idea is an interesting one at a macro level. I have been able to see that take place over time, and my pattern of recognition is pretty good regarding the level of potential for different businesses. When I used to be a venture capitalist, the old story was investing in teams, markets and then ideas. While teams are incredibly important, ironically, I have made my business by bridging that gap between Madison Avenue and Silicon Valley. I'm helping to translate, package and position the benefit orientation in terms of what this technology does. I've been able to see the real benefits of potential products, which I attribute to my agency background. I always ask; what problem does this solve? And is it a real problem, and is it a painkiller or a vitamin?

We're still in the early stages of the whole interactive advertising space and there's a lot more to be done. I'm constantly surprised by the introduction of new companies just when you thought the industry has reached a peak. For example, you saw the big winners like Yahoo and AOL, and these guys were just gigantic. But then Google came out of nowhere and took over the world. MySpace was another example in that it was the biggest thing taking place, and then Facebook comes out of nowhere, then Google. So we're in this constant dynamic market, which makes it so exciting, and I think this next phase is the intersection between local and social in this world of portable devices. It doesn't matter whether it's a tablet or a phone; this is going to be the exciting piece, assuming of course we can navigate through all the privacy and personalization issues.

CLOSING REMARKS

Rich has been a silent mentor for me. His approach to the business, and even his career path, are ones that I have emulated. He approaches his business with a sense of calm that I have never been able to achieve, shows you how to get things done and how to do them well. His path from the agency to sales to the entrepreneurial side of things is the same path that I have tried to follow. He has taken some risks, but has been smart about the steps he's taken and never says no to a request for a meeting or some advice. His openness and willingness to listen and help have been very influential, and I want to just say thank you!

CHAPTER 31

BOB HEYMAN

Bob Heyman has been a pioneer in the world of digital media marketing since 1994, and was the man, along with Leland Harden, to coin the term "search engine optimization." In 1995 Bob launched Cybernautics as a means of realizing his vision for how to use the web, websites and marketing to generate interest and traffic for brands. That vision was initially spurred when he was engaged to create the first website for Jefferson Starship, one of the Bay Area's biggest bands. Bob recognized the direction of things immediately and launched full steam ahead into the web. Bob has been a trail blazer in search with such companies as Cybereps, eMarketing Partners and MediaSmith where he served as chief search officer for a number of years. Bob has also co-authored a number of books on digital marketing, most recently, *Digital Engagement,* which discusses how search and social work together to create engagement between brands and consumers. Bob is also founder and CEO of Kidzter, an online musical theme park for kids.

Bob Heyman, what was it that got you into this business?
The attractiveness of the business itself actually played a minor role in my initial involvement. It was more due to the fact that I was practicing music and entertainment law around that time, and it just so happened that my client, Jefferson Starship, wanted a website back in '94.

Coincidently, the first of our two clients back then was one of those requisite web kids that you needed to have under your arm. Around that same time one of the earliest game networks contacted me in search of basic PR help that could assist them in creating an online marketing plan. We initially presented our idea of online as setting up a tent with Internet connectivity at rock concerts, which they thought was a great idea! While this company eventually decided to go with another PR firm, they told me, boy, you should do something with this Internet idea you have. The Internet might just become a big thing. This occurrence was contemporaneous with Jefferson Starship wanting to start a website. And as luck would have it, our other client was one of Leland's old associates, who was not only the editor of a magazine called, *Income Opportunities Magazine* but was also a part of *Essence Publishing,* a downscale version of *Entrepreneur.* So that was the beginning of our clientele base for Cybernautics, which stood for the art and science of navigating cyber space.

When they asked about that initial website, do you know what their goal was? What did they hope to get out of that?

I think they had discovered that fans were putting up fan websites, and the establishment of an official Jefferson Starship website can serve as an outreach to fans. Now in regards to the magazine, I think they were one of the very first magazines to set up a website. It became pretty obvious in '94 and '95 that every magazine needed an online version.

So you were pulled into this business. But when you got into it you started to see the efficacy of it, correct?

I saw both the efficacy of it and that it was a lot more fun than practicing law.

There are a lot of things more fun than practicing law.

Almost anything.

So how did Cybernautics grow?

I was blessed with partners that were great sales guys, and Leland had helped to found a company called MediaLink. He had a video news release service in New York and had come out to San Francisco and done a video conferencing company that was too early, but he was a great sales guy. And along with a third partner named Lee Burkowitz who was a web designer, we were early into the web design business just as it exploded. I suppose we were among the earliest web design shops, but we were certainly the first ones to figure out to say to our clients that if they can call us when you need another website, we would say,

"Would you like us now to build traffic to it?" Back at that point, it began to be clear that if you had enough eyeballs you could go public.

Our client list grew quickly, and we also attracted a guy, an angel investor who brought onto our board a guy named Keith Schaefer, who had been the group VP for games at Paramount before the Viacom buyout, and who was also a phenomenal sales guy. He had brought the American division of NEC, and he had a magic Rolodex. So I'm a great believer in having great sales guys as partners.

Where did that business take you?
Initially we saw the business as an opportunity to grow into something that we could eventually sell off to one of the ad holding companies. First, we were able to attract an investment banker, Broadview, who then served as our conduit to Omnicom and Interpublic. In the case of Interpublic group, we were developing this concept called audience development, which was the process of building traffic to a website. In conjunction with this idea, we not only were the first people to coin the term "search engine optimization" but were probably also the first agency to practice it. In addition, we were early into the "word of web," better known now as social media. With Schaefer's help, our agency had numerous gaming companies as clients, which made Cybernautics extremely attractive to the holding firms. However, we were acquired by the investment bankers who founded U.S. Web just before they went public, so essentially Cybernautics became a part of U.S. Web when it was still considered a good thing.

U.S. Web had grown and turned into CKS, correct?

U.S. Web started with the intention of becoming the primary graphics solution of the web. Once they discovered that this plan was quickly deteriorating, they reinvested their money into purchasing the leading web design shops located in all major cities. U.S. Web's acquisition of Cybernautics was unusual because we didn't fit the profile of "local web designer." Instead, I believe they purchased Cybernautics for both the audience development practice as well as our client base with notable companies such as Intel, SGI, Avon, Bristol Meyers, U.S. West, AOL, Time Warner, REI, Harley Davidson, Sotheby's, etc.. Basically when U.S. Web went public a month and a half later, approximately two-thirds of the clients they listed on the prospectus were our clients who were essentially five-thousand-dollars-per-month audience development clients.

What was the environment like at that point?

Oddly enough, Interpublic owned a stake in CKS at that point and wanted CKS to buy us out. Although the initial deal didn't materialize, a second purchase attempt was made by their Western Media division. Ironically U.S. Web not only ended up acquiring Cybernautics, but also managed to acquire CKS soon after. The situation was eventually branded as marchFIRST which was unfortunate because it went belly up during the great Internet shakeout. Despite the debacle, Cybernautics' stock performed well enough so our shareholders could have greatly benefitted if they managed to sell the marchFIRST or U.S. Web stock before the crash. Aside from the Internet shakeup, Cybernautics became involved in various media buying and planning activities such as direct email, contesting, as well as continued web design work. Furthermore, our more notable web design work included building the first EBay interface and developing Net TV, which was the Oracle funded competitor to Web TV. Overall, we had excelled in our design shop, but the audience development was what put us on the map, more specifically the search engine optimization.

In the midst of all this, Leland and I were approached about a book deal on Cybernautics. Originally, the book was supposed to be accredited to Cybernautics when it came out. Instead the credit went to U.S. Web and the ghost writer of the book, Rick Bruner. It wasn't until U.S. Web's bankruptcy that Leland and I got our names placed on the book alongside Rick's in the following edition.

There have been a lot of changes to the business. What do you think the needs of the clients were then versus now?

The first change is the fact that the relationship between the popularity of the Internet and people who wanted a website used to be corresponding; as one grew, so did the other. Initially we didn't face any competition in regards to quality. Our main competition was the false perception of the general public, the perception that if you weren't a kid you couldn't do websites. I remember competing for a bike company that ended up having its paperboy do their website. Another change that took place is the price of building websites. It used to be extremely expensive to build websites, especially those of big corporations, when the Internet was taking off. However, the price the people expect to spend on a website has dropped significantly, and the mystery behind the process of building websites no longer exists, therefore, people don't have to go to a big time agency to get a website.

What about just how they utilize the web? Back then the web was purely a small line item on the overall mix, and it was really a promotional tool.

A promotional tool and brochureware. Interestingly enough, the concept of e-commerce was not even a concept in the very beginning. It only became a big concept after a couple of years, but initially the web was just a spot to place one's collateral or brochure online, and that was what everybody wanted back in '94, '95. Next it became the number of hits you got and how to access the directory of sites such as AltaVista, Lycos as well as Yahoo. It's worth telling the story of how we got into search, or how we coined "search engine optimization."

We had just completed the website for Jefferson Starship, and the URL was jstarship.com. I received a call at around two in the morning from the manager of Starship, and he wanted to show the website to the promoter, but nobody could remember their own URL, which leads you to wonder what they were smoking. So they had been reduced to typing "Jefferson Starship" into Lycos and the search result showed up on the second page. Their reaction was, as they said, "ripshit" and immediately deputized the manager to call me to ream me a new one because we had failed our job as web designers if the Jefferson Starship only came up on page two.

I went to the designers once I got off the phone and we tried to figure out what was placed on page one. We had accidentally stumbled upon a technique that is now basically called, keyword stuffing. It was the number of times the search phrase appeared on the homepage, and there had been fan sites that had used the name Jefferson Starship in the text more often than we had since we had a fairly tasteful site. But it turned out if you put "Jefferson Starship" in tiny black print on a black background and ran it two miles down the page, the search engine saw it and counted up the times it said "Jefferson Starship." After a couple of days the search name became number one, and the manager called up saying, boy, this is great, what do you call that? We looked at each other and said, well, I guess we call it "search engine optimization." The manager then proceeded to say, boy, this is fabulous! You ought to do that for other people. So we hung out a shingle doing search engine optimization.

How easy was that service to sell at the time?
It was an easy sell back then. Basically if you told people, we can get you more hits or eyeballs, then every CEO who played golf with another CEO would come back from the golf match saying, "My golf partner said they get X many hits. How do we get more hits? And by the way, what's a 'hit'?" So if we said, well, appearing at the top of the search engine along with direct email and contests are ways to get more hits as well as views, then everybody wanted it. And the only competition we initially had was from a guy named Eric Ward who owned a company in Knoxville, but since he really didn't have the desire to expand his company at the time, we had the field to ourselves for a little while.

What happened? Everyone else figured out what you were doing and started creating other companies?

Naturally everybody got on board. I have been questioned by my own people the reasoning behind not trademarking the phrase "search engine optimization." And I basically said, well, if we did then nobody would have used it. But the field of search engine optimization developed and became competitive rather quickly. Of course we were under the impression we were practicing audience development rather than just SEO, so our response would usually be, you need to do contests, you need to do direct email, you need to do other things.

What's funny is you think about the clients now versus the clients then, those same tactics are still the core of what they do.

Precisely, back then the business was not difficult as long as there were good sales people to obtain national brands because the ad agencies these household names possessed lacked this kind of work. Accordingly, there was a wave of buying in those shops to get themselves into the game. But it was a period in which companies like U.S. Web did really well because you didn't go to Ogilvy or the usual suspects to build websites, since those companies didn't even specialize in this area.

What other key milestones or key events happened that you think effected the growth of the business?

The development of banner ads, which I think was Rick Boyce's idea at *Wired,* combined with the pressure of entering online media buying was a milestone because that was when banners became accepted and websites became more sophisticated. Furthermore, the idea of developing e-commerce and being able to sell things on the web, which of course Amazon had pioneered, took off in '97. There were so many venture dollars during the year of the Pets.com sock puppet, all you had to do was hang out on Sand Hill Road and you could end up with clients who were newly funded web e-commerce businesses.

What about the advent of social as well?
Social was something that we were involved in when it wasn't called social; we called it "word of web." Since a lot of our clientele were game companies, we had countless twenty-five-year-olds pretending to be fifteen-year-olds who would enter chat groups and rave about how great the latest Spectrum Holobyte Microprose game was. At the time we just thought of this occurrence as guerilla marketing and not anything black hat. However, this type of word-of-mouth, the ability to stir up any topic as long as chat groups were created for it, is really to me what created social media. Think of it this way, it's the exact same thing we did back then but now its on steroids through Facebook or Twitter. The idea of encouraging others to tell their friends about your client was something that dated back to fairly early web work. The only difference was that there was no romance; it wasn't sexy back then and neither was search engine optimization. There wasn't a whole lot of money to be made in 'search' until Google came along and made 'paid search' a business. After that you could receive an agency commission on a media spend.

Is it safe to say that the "word of web" idea took probably ten years for it to mature to a point where people could use it?

In some way people always could use it, but it didn't become a priority for everybody really until two, three years ago. It was sort of this guerilla marketing approach that I found to be interesting. For example, I remember there was a local company in Sausalito that did both 'search' and the 'word of web.' They called it "guerilla marketing" and they were acquired about four years back by Web Crossing. The main reason behind the purchase was solely for the search business, and the guerilla marketing was thrown out because nobody could see that's where the money was. However, if you fast-forward to present day the sexier part of the business would be the guerilla marketing.

You've been in the agency world now for a while, and you've been in the services side of the business. What do you think the future of that private business is looking like?

During the beginning of the SEMs when some of my former employees founded Fathom Online and the time when there was a lot of buzz surrounding search, it appeared that paid search was just another form of media. I tend to think that social media is just another form of PR, and it essentially belongs in a PR shop. So what I'm doing now is trying to combine search, social and traditional PR together, particularly around the type of clients that have enthusiasm about wanting to share. To me this means food, beverage, hobbies and lifestyles. One of the basic trends taking place is that social will become a recognized part of technologically enhanced PR, similar to the ways of how paid search is now being recognized as another form of media, and how web design is just another field that an ad agency covers. I think the idea behind special standalone agencies that specifically do this won't last, only because the big agencies or PR shops buy the boutiques anyway.

You think that consolidation is going to continue over the next couple of years?

I've been surprised that there hasn't been more consolidation and acquisition of social media companies taking place, which can be partly attributed to the effects of the recession. But it would seem that there is an obvious trend of not having standalone social media.

It's funny because I heard a couple of people say that they don't think that social is a standalone vehicle, but every day there's another company popping up to talk about how to integrate social into the overall mix.

Exactly, although there is starting to be a little bit of a bloom off the rose with social because there's such an issue surrounding the difference between the real ROI from social. Simply put, it can't just be about having fans and followers it has to somehow contribute to the bottom line.

You think that the industry is moving in a direction to be able to attribute a real value to social media?

While I think there is still a major issue regarding the measurement of social media along with determining the amount of impact it possesses, I am sure everybody wants to be able to attribute a real value. I am preparing for a keynote speech at the Marketing Sherpa's optimization event in June, and they are calling the topic, "Measuring the Immeasurable." A couple of questions still persist: How do you assign value? How do you measure the efficacy of social media? There is definitely a lot of interest in this, but the metric of measurement is so uncertain, in that it is so directional as opposed to an actual quantitative number, that it is still a work in progress.

If you could wave your wand what key metrics do you think marketers should be looking at right now, whether in social or just digital in general?

I think one needs to examine the lifetime customer value, particularly in social. People need to recognize that social is a better retention marketing medium than it is an acquisition medium. It is important to convince the clients the value the impact of retention and the value of brand evangelism. The number of fans or followers doesn't matter as much as being able to develop a program that builds loyalty and creates references. It takes an actual plan that covers both recognition and reward, even if it is something as simple as presenting people with badges or gifts. For one of our clients, who is a national brand that sells spices, the most important thing for them is to get the public to request supermarkets to stock their brand, and that is a measurable unit in which a brand evangelist can perform. But in order to do so there has to be a program established not only to reward those same people, but also to continue giving them a reason to do that. So that is part of how we're trying to fully utilize social media.

Do you believe that the brands are going to enter a stage where they understand lifetime value and those metrics, or that it's something they have to figure out, how to level up to the entire media mix?

They need to figure it out. Most companies have not figured out how to correctly measure ROI throughout the media mix. One of the segments we deal with in the new book is how to measure the efficacy of marketing across channels. There has to be an approach that compares the money spent on a social media campaign and the money spent on radio, print, live events. Even then the method may still just be directional and about using proxies, which can certainly vary between clients. But I think getting alignment on ROI goals between sales, marketing and the CFO is a big challenge still. Sometimes the assessment of lifetime customer value can't just be determined by the amount of time spent on the site; customer engagement has become a trendy but very vague metric.

People define engagement in many different ways.
Exactly, and clearly engagement is a good thing, but if it doesn't move the needle on sales or leads then it is somewhat meaningless.

We talked about global, social, and we talked about search. What about mobile and video? Do you think those two avenues are going to continue to be broken

out as second tier, or do you see them also just falling under the general media model?

I think video in particular, especially user-generated video, is an essential part of the social media mix. When people think of 'social' they think of Twitter and Facebook, but not YouTube along with all of its other imitators. The desire to have a video go viral is essentially a social media goal. Unfortunately, it is also similar to having a hit record in the same way that you can't make a decision that this is going to be my viral video. As in the record business in the old days, you may have to release six or seven hit singles before one takes off. Mobile is increasingly becoming the new channel of how people are consuming the Internet. Obviously you can distinguish it from the rest of the web but I don't think it is really all that different, it is just the new device. But I do think it somewhat possesses the same marketing challenge.

If you were to give advice to somebody who was going to get into the advertising business now, what skills would you have them focus on?

Analytics; the advertising business has been increasingly quantitative, where measurement and optimization has become the main focus. Not to invoke the *biggest* cliché in advertising, but the old idea of not knowing which half of your advertising doesn't work doesn't apply today. These days, people pretty much know what works and what doesn't. It shouldn't be a mystery. People tend to overlook the quantitative part of the business because people who enter this industry generally aren't people who excelled at math. However, math is vital because you have to understand analytics to be able to optimize, and if you don't optimize then campaigns are less so about good, creative execution, but more so about learning and optimizing.

If you were to fast forward ten years, do you think that the majority of people in advertising will have PhDs in Analytics?

No, I'm not even sure you need a PhD, but I did find that the best people to hire that were really good at search mostly came from the insurance business background where they were basically just crunching numbers. I am sure there's still a place for the madmen type creative part, but what's important is the stuff that makes a lot of creative people's eyes glaze over.

Maybe that's a good thing.

Maybe so, but certainly not as much fun as it used to be. I remember when Jerry Della Famina wrote his first book and claimed that advertising was the most fun you could have with your clothes on. I'm not sure that is still the future.

CLOSING REMARKS

Bob talks about the role of analytics, and his background as what can be described as "the godfather of search" is proof that analytics are an underpinning of the business. No matter what happens, and where the business goes, data will be important. And proving the impact that the Internet has on marketing and sales is the most important job we face on a day-to-day basis.

13916728R00309